Progressions with Readings

PARAGRAPH TO ESSAY

Seventh Edition

BARBARA FINE CLOUSE

PEARSON
Longman

New York San Francisco Boston
London Toronto Sydney Tokyo Singapore Madrid
Mexico City Munich Paris Cape Town Hong Kong Montreal

For Betty Fine Shepherd, Lee Fine,
and Collette Khoury Fine

Acquisitions Editor: Melanie Craig
Marketing Manager: Thomas DeMarco
Senior Supplements Editor: Donna Campion
Production Manager: Eric Jorgensen
Project Coordination, Text Design, and Electronic Page Makeup: Electronic Publishing Services Inc., NYC
Cover Designer/Manager: John Callahan
Cover Image: Courtesy of Getty Images
Photo Researcher: Clare Maxwell
Manufacturing Buyer: Roy L. Pickering, Jr.
Printer and Binder: Von Hoffmann Owensville
Cover Printer: Coral Graphics Services

For permission to use copyrighted material, grateful acknowledgment is made to the copyright holders on page 551 and listed throughout this book, which are hereby made part of this copyright page.

Library of Congress Cataloging-in-Publication Data
Clouse, Barbara Fine.
    Progressions with readings : paragraph to essay / Barbara Fine Clouse.—7th ed.
      p. cm.
    Includes bibliographical references and index.
    ISBN 0-321-43316-5 (alk. paper)
    1. English language-—Rhetoric. 2. English language—Grammar—Problems, exercises, etc.
    3. College readers. 4. Report writing.   I. Title.
    PE1408.C5355 2007
808'.042—dc22

                                2006019248

Please visit us at www.ablongman.com

ISBN 0-321-43316-5

1 2 3 4 5 6 7 8 9 10—VHO—09 08 07 06

Contents

Checklists, Writing Process Tips, Editing Strategies, Strategies for Succeeding in College

Checklists

Writing Process Tips

Editing Strategies

Strategies for Succeeding in College

Preface

Through six editions, *Progressions with Readings* has helped students develop effective and efficient writing processes, write clear and error-free sentences, and craft strong paragraphs and essays. In this new edition, a unique academic success component shows students how to use what they learn in *Progressions* across the curriculum, and it explains strategies that will help them achieve their goals in their other classes.

To support students as they work to become better writers and more successful students, *Progressions with Readings* includes the following features:

COMPREHENSIVE COVERAGE OF THE WRITING PROCESS

- A thorough discussion of the writing process offers students a range of strategies for planning, drafting, revising, and editing. They are invited to sample these strategies to discover the ones that work well for them.
- The new Chapter 2 focuses on revising and editing to expand and emphasize the discussion of rewriting.
- Writing at the Computer features describe strategies for students who prefer to compose at the computer.
- A student work in progress illustrates the composing process with extensive annotations.
- Writing process tips help students complete assignments successfully.

COMPLETE COVERAGE OF THE PARAGRAPH AND ESSAY

- In-depth coverage of writing paragraphs and essays is anchored by instruction in the patterns of development.
- A generous number of writing prompts, including topics that call for combining patterns and ones that call for responding to images, give students a variety of writing opportunities.
- Student models both illustrate the points discussed and stand as realistic goals.
- Checklists and writing process tips support students and help them write strong paragraphs and essays.

- Material on combining patterns of development helps students appreciate the versatility of the patterns.
- Marginal notes highlight the main points and answer questions students frequently ask.

AN EMPHASIS ON SENTENCE SKILLS AND EDITING

- Explanations of grammar and usage are clear, concise, and accessible.
- Students learn specific editing strategies for finding and eliminating errors with sentence fragments, run-on sentences and comma splices, subject-verb agreement, tense, pronoun-antecedent agreement, modifiers, punctuation, and capitalization.
- A generous number and variety of exercises, including collaborative activities, offer students many opportunities to hone editing skills. Many of the exercises are high-interest, whole and continuous discourse pieces.
- Students can use pretests, post tests, and diagnostic self-assessment tests to determine their levels of achievement and measure their progress.
- Two full chapters of sentence skills workshops offer students supplemental exercises. One chapter calls for editing to find and correct a single error, and one chapter requires editing paragraphs to find and eliminate more than one kind of error.

AN EMPHASIS ON READING AND OTHER SKILLS REQUIRED FOR ACADEMIC SUCCESS

- Two chapters provide important instruction in reading, and writing in response to reading.
- Detailed coverage of the active reading process helps students in their writing classes and across the curriculum.
- Professional essays—almost half of which are new—appear with study questions and writing topics.
- Instruction in writing summaries and essay examination answers helps students learn important academic survival skills.
- Succeeding in College sections in every chapter help students apply their learning beyond the writing classroom and help them learn strategies for success in all their classes.

NEW TO THE SEVENTH EDITION

- A chapter has been added to Part One to expand the discussion of the writing process.

- Expanded discussions of paragraph closings, the thesis, and transitions enhance the material on paragraph and essay structure.
- The discussion of argument has been strengthened.
- Expanded discussions of coordination, subordination, parallelism, and sentence variety improve the coverage of sentence effectiveness.
- Writing Process Tips offer improved support for completing assigned writings.
- Pretests and Diagnostic Self-Assessment tests have been improved so they better assess the skills under consideration.
- Almost half of the readings are new.
- New questions after the readings and new writing topics emphasize how to combine patterns.
- Succeeding in College sections at the ends of chapters teach important study skills and show students how to apply what they are learning in other classes.
- An improved design makes *Progressions* even more student-friendly by highlighting important material and making instruction more accessible.
- Better graphics help students grasp the structure of paragraphs and essays.

TEXT-SPECIFIC SUPPLEMENTS

A complete Instructor's Manual with Answer Key (0-321-46296-3) is available to accompany *Progressions,* Seventh Edition.

THE LONGMAN DEVELOPMENTAL ENGLISH PACKAGE

Longman is pleased to offer a variety of support materials to help make teaching developmental English easier for teachers and to help students excel in their course work. Visit www.ablongman.com or contact your local Longman sales representative for a detailed listing of our supplements package or for more information on pricing and how to create a package.

ACKNOWLEDGMENTS

I am fortunate, indeed to be part of a talented team. At Longman, my thanks go to Melanie Craig for overseeing this new edition and for her continued faith in the book. I also thank Lindsey Allen for her ongoing, cheerful help, particularly with securing permissions. Once again, Ann Grogg worked her editorial magic and improved the manuscript in many substantive ways. With Ann's guidance, all things are possible. At EPS, Scott

Hitchcock guided the manuscript through production with his usual skill and good humor.

For their help revising the sixth edition, I gratefully acknowledge the following reviewers, who gave me the gift of their expertise and their time: Martha Funderburk, University of Arkansas Community College at Hope Alex;Wang, Normandale Community College; Sandra Barker, Kalamazoo Valley Community College; Donna Eisenstat, West Virginia University Institute of Technology; Wendy Ullman, Bucks County Community College; Melanie Lemaster, Edison Community College; and Samantha Fey, Cape Fear Community College.

Finally, I am profoundly grateful to my husband, Denny, for his unstinting support and understanding.

BARBARA FINE CLOUSE

CHAPTER 1

Planning and Writing

What do successful writers do? Let me tell you first what they *don't* do: They don't work fast or produce a finished piece in one sitting. Instead, they work in stages. Stage one is **planning,** when writers decide what they want to say and the best order for their ideas. Stage two is **writing,** when writers put their ideas down in a preliminary form called a **first draft.** Stage three is **rewriting,** when writers improve their draft so it is final and ready for a reader.

The stages of writing are
1. planning
2. writing
3. rewriting

The Writing Process

Stage 1: Planning
Decide what you want to say and the best order for saying it.

Stage 2: Writing
Write your first draft.

Stage 3: Rewriting
Make improvements until your draft is final.

To be a successful writer, you, too, should work in stages. Do not expect your writing to roll off your pen or pop off the keyboard in perfect form. Instead, expect to work and rework a piece, gradually shaping it into a satisfying finished product.

You should also realize that different people favor different writing processes. Some people need to plan more extensively than others. Some writers like to get feedback, but others prefer to work alone. Some writers outline extensively, and some outline informally. In truth, it would be more accurate to call Part One of the book "Writing Processes" rather than "The Writing Process."

This chapter discusses the planning and writing stages, and the next explains rewriting. In this chapter, you will learn techniques for

- coming up with writing ideas

- arranging your ideas in a suitable order

- writing a first draft

PLANNING YOUR WRITING: GENERATING IDEAS

At first, you may have only a broad **writing subject** in mind—something like *education* or *television.* However, subjects like these take in so much territory that you need to write a book to cover them. Therefore, your first task may be to find some aspect of your writing subject that you can handle in a reasonable (or the required) length—something like *final examinations* or *reality TV.* That manageable aspect of your writing subject is your **writing topic.**

Sometimes a writer gets lucky and a good writing topic leaps to mind, and all the right ideas spill onto the page in a burst of inspiration. However, such luck is extremely rare, so do not spend too much time staring at a blank page or computer screen. Do not wait for inspiration. Instead, go after the ideas you need with the techniques explained next. Try each one to learn which works the best for you. Or use more than one technique. Sometimes combining techniques yields more ideas than using one strategy by itself. Know, however, that at this stage, ideas may be rough. Accept those rough ideas because you will have time along the way to polish them up.

In addition to using the techniques explained next, keep your writing in mind as you go about your routine activities. Ideas can occur to you while you are walking across campus, washing the car, eating lunch, or taking a shower. Most important, no matter which strategy or strategies you use, give yourself enough time. If you wait until the last minute, you will not have time for ideas to surface.

Listing

When listing, do not evaluate how good your ideas are; write everything that occurs to you.

Listing can supply both writing topics and ideas to develop those topics. To list, spill out every idea that occurs to you without evaluating how good the ideas are. Just record everything you think of. One idea will lead to another until you have columns of useful and not-so-useful thoughts.

Here is a list developed by a student who wanted to write about athletics:

football	*player salaries*
baseball	*player strikes*
basketball	*what sports mean to boys*

coaching	betting
training	athletic scholarships
college	opportunities for women
professional	recruiting violations
when I was cut from the basketball team	preventing injuries
great athletes (Michael Jordan, etc.)	Little League

When you run out of ideas, review your list and decide what you want to write about. That's your **writing topic.** The student who wrote the above list decided to write about the time he was cut from the basketball team.

Next, list again—this time to discover ideas you can include what you write about your topic. Here is the student's second list. Notice that he crossed out the ideas he decided not to include, probably because they were not closely enough related to his topic.

Study your list to find a writing topic.

went to every practice—played well

really wanted it bad

was sure I made the team

~~my father wanted it bad too~~

after school, checked list—didn't see my name

~~it was like the time I struck out in Little League~~

cried all the way home

was embarrassed—all my friends made the team

Luis didn't talk to me anymore

~~Jerrold also didn't make the team~~

felt like a failure

lost friends because they were always at practice, etc.

felt sorry for myself and stupid

After crossing out ideas, some writers determine a suitable order for their ideas and number them to reflect this order. The result is a **scratch outline,** a guide that tells the writer what ideas will appear in the first draft and what order they will appear in. Here is the student writer's list turned into a scratch outline.

You can turn a list of ideas into a scratch outline.

② went to every practice—played well

① really wanted it bad

③ was sure I made the team

~~my father wanted it bad too~~

④ after school, checked list—didn't see my name

~~it was like the time I struck out in Little League~~

(continued)

⑤ cried all the way home

⑧ was embarrassed—all my friends made the team

⑩ Luis didn't talk to me anymore

~~Jerrold also didn't make the team~~

⑥ felt like a failure

⑨ lost friends because they were always at practice, etc.

⑦ felt sorry for myself and stupid

PRACTICE 1.1

Assume you will write about a person you admire. The subject can be a famous person, a friend, a relative, a teacher, a coach, or anyone you regard highly. To decide whom you will write about, use the space below to list five people you admire for any reason at all.

1. _____

2. _____

3. _____

4. _____

5. _____

Study your list and select the person you wish to write about. Using a separate sheet of paper, spend about ten minutes listing to discover the reasons you admire this person. Write three of these reasons in the spaces provided.

1. _____

2. _____

3. _____

Brainstorming

To brainstorm, ask questions.

Brainstorming is asking questions. The answers can help you find a specific writing topic, and they can supply ideas to include in your writing.

Some of the following questions will be helpful and some of them will not. Each time you brainstorm, select the appropriate questions and disregard the rest.

Questions for Brainstorming

- Who was involved?
- What happened?
- When did it happen?
- Why did it happen?
- How did it happen?
- How is it done?
- Why is it important?
- What can be learned?
- What is it like? (or different from?)
- What does it mean?

- What is (was) the cause?
- What is (was) the effect?
- How is it made?
- What are the physical characteristics?
- Who cares about it?
- How can it be explained?
- What controversies surround it?
- What opinion was challenged or changed?

Here are the answers to some brainstorming questions a student wrote about learning that her brother was ill. Notice that the writer used some of the questions but not others.

- **What happened?**

  My brother was diagnosed with bipolar disorder.

- **When did it happen?**

  last year

- **What is it like?**

  It's serious and scary. When he is down, he can be suicidal. When he is up, he can be reckless and out of control with money, but he can also be lots of fun and very creative.

- **What does it mean?**

  He has to take medication and stay in therapy. The family has to watch him for mood swings and intervene if we see them.

- **What is the cause?**

  It's probably genetic and the result of a problem with his body chemistry.

- **What opinion was challenged or changed?**

  I have more understanding of mental illness and more compassion for what the mentally ill and their families go through. I used to think my brother was irresponsible, but now I know he can't help how he acts.

When the writer studied her brainstorming material, she decided to write about what it's like to have a mentally ill family member, using her own experience as an example. Select your topic on the basis of which answers interest you or on the basis of what you have the most information on.

Study your brainstorming to find a writing topic.

PRACTICE 1.2

Assume you will write about a difficult decision you made. If you cannot think of a decision you want to write about, try listing on another sheet of paper. After settling on the decision, brainstorm on a separate page for about fifteen minutes to uncover ideas that might appear in the writing. When your brainstorming is complete, study your answers and decide on a specific writing topic. Write it here:

_____

Now, in the spaces provided, record five ideas that could appear in your writing about a difficult decision.

1. _____

2. _____

3. _____

4. _____

5. _____

Clustering

Clustering helps you see how your ideas relate to each other.

Clustering can help you discover a writing topic and see how ideas to develop that topic connect to each other. To cluster, write one idea down in the center of a sheet of paper and circle it:

television

Around the circled general idea, write related ideas and connect them to the central circle.

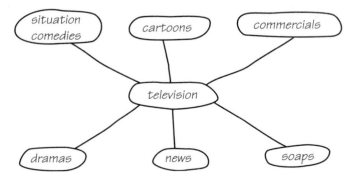

As you think of more ideas, write them down, circle them, and connect them to the ideas they are the most closely related to:

Continue writing, circling, and connecting ideas until you can think of nothing more. Do not censor yourself or evaluate your ideas—just write everything you think of.

Sometimes one clustering gives you enough to get under way. If not, study what you have and settle on a topic for your writing. For example, the writer of the preceding clustering decided to write about television commercials. Once you have settled on a topic, do a second clustering with your topic circled in the middle.

Write a second clustering to discover ideas for developing a topic.

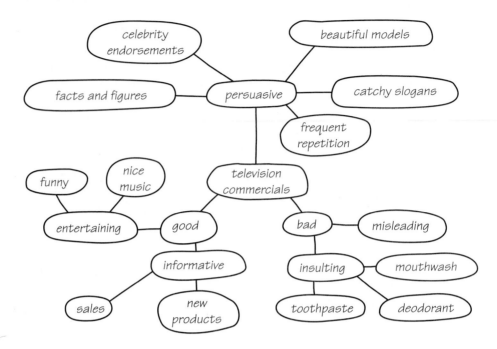

The writer of this second clustering decided to write about the techniques used in television commercials to persuade people to buy products. She used the ideas clustering around the "persuasive" circle in her writing.

PRACTICE 1.3

Assume you have been asked to write about education reform. On a separate sheet, develop a clustering with "education reform" circled in the center. When you discover a topic, write that topic here.

_____

On a separate sheet, write a second clustering. Place your topic in the center. When you can think of nothing more to add to the clustering, record four of the ideas you thought of here.

1. _____

2. _____

3. _____

4. _____

Freewriting

Freewriting is nonstop writing that works like this: for ten to fifteen minutes, write anything and everything that comes to mind. Do not decide whether your ideas are good or bad. Just record everything, even the silly ideas. Also, do not worry about grammar, spelling, or neatness. If you cannot think of anything to write, then write anything, even "I don't know what to write," the alphabet, the names of your family members, or your feelings at the moment. Eventually, more ideas will occur to you and you can record them. Continue this way, without lifting your pen from the page or your fingers from the keyboard.

When time is up, read your freewriting. Most likely you will have one or more good ideas. These ideas will require shaping, but they can get you started.

The following freewriting was done on the writing subject, "a campus issue."

> I'm suppose to write about a campus issue which shouldn't be to hard b/c there's enough of them. Parking, the cost of books, drinking, tuition ect. Which one? Parking Isn't such a serious issue. It doesn't seem worth writing about. Who cares? Drinking is serious. Parents would never believe how much their kids are drinking. Its pretty dangerous actually. Kids passing out, driving, hung over in class, generally trashed. I don't drink so I'm left out a lot. I think banning alcohol on campus is a good idea but most kids would freak out. They'd even transfer. I could also write about the insane cost of books but that's soooooooo boring. I could interview the book store manager and get good ideas though. I don't really care that much b/c I have a scholarship. I really want to write about alcohol I think. It's a big problem, a big issue, even a matter of life and death. There's lots of reasons to ban it. It kills students who binge drink and kids are so trashed half the time they can't really study. Let's see what else? I gotta think of more stuff. She said I could research so I could look up newspaper articles about students who died from drinking. Oh, I know, I could write about how colleges that don't ban drinking are responsible for the deaths.

Notice that the writer recorded a free flow of thought without worrying about grammar, spelling, abbreviations, or any other matter of refinement. Also notice that the writer discovered a topic (banning alcohol on campus) and ideas for developing that topic (students pass out, drive drunk, attend class hung over, can't study, and even die; colleges are responsible for the deaths).

Many times, one freewriting will get you started with a topic and a few good ideas. Other times, you will need to do a second freewriting to discover ideas for developing your topic. Your second freewriting will focus on the topic you discovered in your first freewriting. Do not expect polished ideas in your second freewriting. Just look for raw material to shape. If your second freewriting does not unearth enough ideas to get you started, try brainstorming, clustering, or listing. Idea-generation techniques can be combined.

When freewriting, do not stop, do not censor yourself, and do not worry about grammar, spelling, or neatness.

You can write a second freewriting focusing on a topic you discovered in the first freewriting.

PRACTICE 1.4

Assume you plan to write about ways you have changed in the past three to five years. On a separate paper, freewrite for ten or fifteen minutes to discover four ideas for this writing. Remember, do not stop writing for any reason, do not reject any ideas, and do not worry about grammar, spelling, or neatness. Record your ideas below.

1. _____

   _____

2. _____

   _____

3. _____

   _____

4. _____

   _____

Journaling

In your journal, explore how you think and feel. You can also develop a storehouse of ideas for your writing.

A journal is not a diary for recording what happened during the day. In a journal, you explore ideas and feelings. Journal writing helps you solve problems, get in touch with feelings, vent anger, consider the significance of events, and discover what you think about issues. A journal can be an excellent source of ideas for writing.

To keep a journal, buy a notebook or start a computer file and write entries at the same time every, day if you can manage it. Date each entry before you write and then take off—write anything that you are moved to write. Do not get hung up on spelling, handwriting, or grammar. This writing is for you.

Journal entries can be about anything, but here are some possibilities:

1. Write about something that happened during the day that angered you, surprised you, cheered you, or moved your emotions in some way.

2. Write about a person you admire, love, hate, respect, or do not understand.

3. Write about how school or work is going.

4. Write about your goals.

5. Write about your family relationships.

6. Write about possible solutions to a problem you are having.

7. Write about changes you would like to make.

8. Write about your childhood.

9. Write about something you observed or experienced recently.

10. Freewrite about the first thing that comes to your mind.

11. Write about something you recently read or watched on TV.

12. Describe what you would like your life to be like in five years.

13. Write about what makes you happy or sad.

14. Write about how you feel about your writing.

15. Write about what is important to you.

Make regular entries in your journal and you will soon have a considerable body of material. When you need ideas for writing, paging through your journal may turn up what you need to get started or keep going. The following sample journal entry shows how keeping a journal can help you think things through and discover topics.

October 4, 2005 I heard a very disturbing news report today. A high school teacher in New York was tortured and killed by a former student who was after the man's PIN number so he could withdraw money from his ATM account. It is not unusual to hear about murder and robbery, but this report has me very upset. The teacher was hugely popular at a tough inner city school. He was known as a kind man who really cared about kids. I heard some of his students interviewed. One student said that every student in the school was robbed as a result of this. Then I watched a film clip of the teacher dancing at the June prom with one of his students.

I've never believed in the death penalty, and I guess I still don't, but my belief is much less strong. The nineteen-year-old who has been arrested is legally an adult. If he is found guilty, I don't think I'd be upset if he were put to death. Loss of this caring teacher, who worked in a school many others wouldn't go near, is terribly sad. Loss of the murderer and torturer and robber doesn't strike me as so bad.

It's scary to find my views shaken like this. I used to know how I felt about capital punishment. Now I'm not so sure. The truth is, I want vengeance, and I don't even know the teacher who was killed. Is vengeance justice?

FAQ

Q: What if I don't like the ideas I come up with?

A: Try changing your writing topic. If that is not possible, do the best you can with what you have. During writing and rewriting, you may discover an approach that makes your ideas more interesting.

Working Together: Generating Ideas

Working with others can be as simple as asking people what they think about a particular subject or topic. Just say, "I have to write a paper on _____; do you have any ideas?" The response may get you started. Working together can also involve sitting down with one or more people and listing, brainstorming, and clustering.

To list with a group, assign a person to write down what everyone says. Then group members begin saying any and all ideas that occur to them while

Other people can help you when you need ideas.

the recorder gets them down in list form. Listing with others is helpful because one person usually says something that prompts someone else to get an idea.

Brainstorming can also be done with others. Take turns asking questions while the person who needs the ideas answers the questions and records those answers.

To use clustering in a group, assign one group member to do the writing. All group members speak their ideas as they occur to them, and the group decides where on the clustering to connect each idea. Clustering in a group has the same advantage as listing in a group: One person's ideas stimulate the thinking of other people.

PLANNING YOUR WRITING: ESTABLISHING YOUR AUDIENCE AND PURPOSE

Your **purpose** is your reason for writing. Typically, you will write for one or more of these purposes:

to share feelings or experiences with the reader

to inform the reader of something

to entertain the reader

to persuade the reader to think or act a particular way

Say you are writing about Thanksgiving. If you tell about family celebrations at your grandparents' house, your purpose might be to *share* your experiences with your reader. If you compare modern Thanksgiving celebrations with those of the nineteenth century, your purpose is to *inform*. If you argue that Thanksgiving should be a day of mourning because of our treatment of Native Americans, your purpose is to *persuade*. If you tell an amusing story about the time you made a fool of yourself carving the turkey, your purpose may be both to *share* and to *entertain*. From these examples, you can see that your purpose will influence the nature of your writing. Thus, an essay about Thanksgiving at your grandparents' house will be very different from one comparing Thanksgiving today and in the nineteenth century.

Like purpose, your **audience** (your reader) will affect the nature of your writing. Characteristics of your audience such as age, gender, race, socioeconomic standing, political views, religion, and family background can influence the detail you include. In addition, how much your reader knows about your topic and how much your reader cares about your topic will affect what you do. Say, for example, that you are writing to convince your reader to pass a school levy. If your audience has children, you can discuss improving education. However, if your readers have no children, you may want to mention the improved property values that result from better schools.

To appreciate how audience and purpose affect writing, consider the options for writing about DVD players. Possibilities include:

FAQ

Q: Why do I have to identify a reader? Isn't my audience my writing teacher?

A: Sometimes your writing teacher will assign an audience, and sometimes you will have to identify an audience on your own. Either way, your instructor can assume the identity of different readers to prepare you for writing outside the classroom.

1. explaining how to program a DVD player (a manufacturer might write this in the owner's manual for the purchaser)

2. convincing someone to purchase a particular brand of DVD player (a store owner might write this in an advertising brochure for a potential customer)

3. writing an entertaining article on the problems of owning a DVD player (a newspaper columnist might write this for the readers of a daily newspaper)

4. explaining how the DVD player has affected family life (a psychologist might write this for the readers of *Family Circle* magazine)

5. explaining how the DVD player affects the movie industry (a studio executive might write this for the readers of an industry trade magazine)

Each of these pieces will be different because the audience and purpose are different. The differences will be in the kinds of details, the vocabulary, and the approach. Let's look at each of these elements.

Kinds of Details   Purpose affects the details a writer uses. The piece about how to program a DVD player will include all the steps, but the piece convincing a reader to buy a particular brand will only mention that programming is uncomplicated. Similarly, audience affects the details chosen. If the reader of the piece about how to program the DVD player is knowledgeable about electronics, then it may not be necessary to explain where buttons are located, but this information would be needed for a reader who knows nothing about the equipment.

Your audience and purpose affect the kinds of details, the vocabulary, and the approach.

Vocabulary   Your audience will determine the level of vocabulary. For example, say that you are writing about the effects of the DVD player on family life. For an audience of psychologists you can use the term *projection,* but for the average parent you may need to say "attributing your own faults to someone else."

Approach   Audience and purpose also affect the approach you take. For example, humor would be appropriate in the piece on the problems of using a DVD player that is meant to entertain the readers of a newspaper. However, humor would be misplaced in the owner's manual that explains how to program the device. This writing needs a serious approach. It might even include illustrations, but the entertaining essay would not.

As you plan your writing, you can establish your audience and purpose by asking the questions in this chart:

Questions for Establishing Audience and Purpose

1. Do I want to entertain my reader?
2. Do I want to inform my reader? If so, of what?
3. Do I want to persuade my reader to think or act in a certain way? If so in what way?
4. Do I want to share feelings or an experience with my reader? If so what do I want to share?
5. Who will my reader be?
6. What does my reader already know about my topic?
7. What strong feelings does my reader hold about my topic?
8. How interested will my reader be?
9. Will my reader's age, gender, race, socioeconomic level, political beliefs, or religion influence the response to my topic?

PRACTICE 1.5: WORKING TOGETHER

Each group member should find a different piece of writing: a newspaper article, a recipe, a magazine article, a business letter, an advertisement, an editorial, an owner's manual, a book or movie review, a textbook chapter, and so on. As a group, analyze each piece and determine the intended audience and purpose and the effect of these factors on the kind of detail, the amount of detail, the vocabulary, and the approach.

PLANNING YOUR WRITING: ORDERING YOUR IDEAS

An important part of planning is arranging your ideas in an easy-to-follow order, so your reader understands the logical progression of your thoughts. There are many ways to order ideas. Three common ones are **chronological order** (time order), **spatial order** (space order), and **emphatic order** (order of importance). You will often use these ordering patterns, but you may also use any order that works well for a particular piece of writing.

Chronological Order

For chronological order, arrange events in the order they occurred.

Chronological order is time order. Events are arranged in the order they occurred. Chronological order is used most frequently in story-telling when the writer arranges details according to what happened first, second, and so forth. It is also used to explain how to do something, when steps are given in the order they are performed. In the paragraph that follows, details are arranged chronologically:

> The seven ten-year-olds arrived within minutes of each other. I explained that Gregory would be back in a half hour, so they all raced through the downstairs looking for the best hiding places. Julio and Emil hid behind the couch, while Heath and Tod crouched between the end table and wall. Jordan crawled under the dining room table, and Josh scrambled in behind him. Jeffrey found a perfect spot behind the front door. Soon we heard the slam of a car door, and we knew Greg was home. After he walked in the front door, the boys jumped out from their hiding places and yelled, "Surprise!"

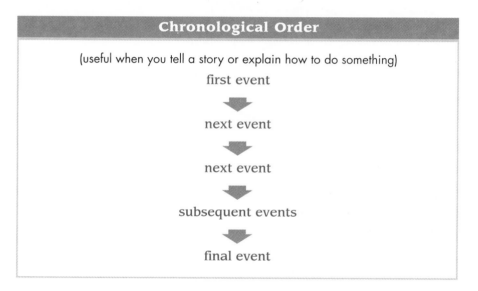

Chronological Order

(useful when you tell a story or explain how to do something)

first event

next event

next event

subsequent events

final event

Spatial Order

With a **spatial order,** details are arranged according to their location in a particular area. Spatial order is especially useful when you are describing a place and move through space in some sequence: top to bottom, front to back, near to far, left to right, and so forth. Details in this paragraph are arranged in a spatial order:

For a spatial order, arrange details according to their location.

> When I entered the living room, I was appalled by what I saw. Empty potato chip and pretzel bags littered the coffee table and couch; their contents formed a layer of crumbs on the carpet. The antique crystal lamp on the table next to the couch was resting on its side, and the table itself held at least ten beer cans, all of them squashed in the middle. Beneath the table, the once-beige carpet was stained with a dark splotch that I knew

would be permanent. Worst of all was the sight of my teenage son, who had been left in charge. There he was, sprawled across the couch asleep or unconscious—I wasn't sure which.

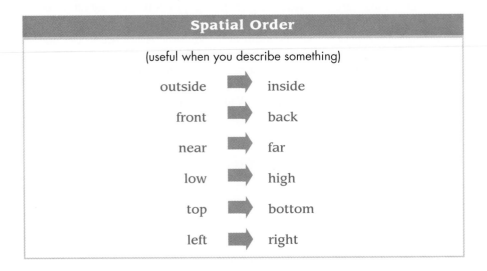

Emphatic Order

For an emphatic order, begin with your least important point and move to your most important. Also, you can begin with your second most important point and end with your most important.

With **emphatic order,** begin with the least important detail and move to the most important detail. Think of emphatic order as saving the best for last to provide a big finish.

A variation on emphatic order is to begin with the second most important point and end with your most important, sandwiching other points in between. This arrangement gives the strongest possible opening and closing. Emphatic order is useful when you want to convince your reader of something because the most compelling reasons come at the end for a persuasive final impression. The following paragraph arranges details in an emphatic order:

For several reasons, voters should pass the school levy when it is placed on the ballot during the August special election. First, the additional funds will allow the senior class to take a trip to Washington. More important, passage of the levy means the elementary schools can add computer instruction to the curriculum. Without this instruction, our students will lag behind others in the country. Finally, if the levy passes, our school system can pay its debts and avoid a state loan that will jeopardize its financial well-being for years to come.

Emphatic Order

(useful when you want to convince your reader of something)

least important detail

next more important detail

next more important detail

next more important detail

most important detail

Or

second most important detail

least important detail

next more important detail

next more important detail

most important detail

Combining Orders

You can use any combination of chronological, spatial, and emphatic orders in the same piece of writing. For example, look back at the paragraph that illustrates chronological order on page 15. Notice that, for the most part, the ideas are arranged according to what happened first, second, third, and so forth. However, notice that a spatial order is also used when the paragraph explains where the children hid (between the end table and the wall, behind the front door, and so forth).

Now look again at the paragraph illustrating spatial order on pages 15–16. For the most part, ideas are arranged according to their location, but some emphatic order is also apparent. You can tell this because the second to the last

You can use any combination of chronological, spatial, and emphatic orders.

sentence begins, "Worst of all." This phrase suggests that the most important detail is at the end.

Making a Scratch Outline

FAQ:

Q: How do I know what order to use?

A: Your writing topic will often suggest the order of your details. For example, if you are telling a story, you will use chronological order. When you are unsure of the best order, try writing scratch outlines with different arrangements. Then use the one that works the best.

Once you have generated enough ideas to get you started and you have decided on a chronological, spatial, emphatic, or other suitable order, you can make a **scratch outline,** which is a list of the ideas you will include in your draft, numbered in the order you will write them. A scratch outline is helpful because it guides your draft.

To write a scratch outline, list the ideas you generated that you plan to include in your draft. Then number these ideas in the order you will write them up. Here is an example of a scratch outline, using the ideas from the idea generation list on pages 3-4.

(2) *went to every practice—played well*
(1) *really wanted it bad*
(3) *was sure I made the team*
(4) *after school, checked list—didn't see my name*
(5) *cried all the way home*
(8) *was embarrassed—all my friends made the team*
(10) *Luis didn't talk to me anymore*
(6) *felt like a failure*
(9) *lost friends because they were always at practice, etc.*
(7) *felt sorry for myself and stupid*

PRACTICE 1.6

1. For each of the following paragraphs, indicate whether the order of ideas is chronological, spatial, or emphatic. One paragraph has a combination of orders.

   a. The exasperated mother explained to her son for the fourth time why he could not get a puppy. First, she said, paper training the animal would be too much trouble, especially since no one was home during the day. Then there was the fact that puppies are expensive and their budget was too tight to allow for dog food purchases and veterinarian bills. Most important, she said that they live in an apartment and their lease expressly prohibits all pets except birds.

   The ideas are arranged in _____ order.

   b. Paper recycling is an interesting process. First, the paper is put into a vat of water with chemicals that remove the ink and turn the paper into soft pulp. This vat is called a *pulper.* From the pulper, the pulp goes to a machine that removes staples, clips, and anything else that is not paper. Next, the pulp is cleaned and mixed with water to form a thick paste that is spread on a metal sheet where it is heated, dried, and smoothed. When the paste dries, it is crisp, new paper.

The ideas are arranged in _____ order.

   c. When I walked into the sixty-dollar-a-night hotel room, I was outraged by what I saw. Directly in front of me was an unmade bed, its sheets a dingy gray. The wall behind the bed was stained with a brown splotch that looked alarmingly like dried blood. There were no drapes on the window; instead, a tattered blind partially blocked the sun. I turned to check the bathroom to my right. There the situation was just as bad: dirty towels were on the floor; the sink was rust-stained, and the mirror above it was opaque with dust and lint. Furious, I stormed out of the room to find the manager and get a full refund.

The ideas are arranged in _____ order.

2. Assume that each of the following sentences is the first sentence of a paragraph, the sentence that presents the writer's central idea. In the space provided, indicate whether the order of ideas is likely to be spatial, chronological, emphatic, or some combination of these.

   a. It would be a serious mistake to zone Fifth Avenue to allow the construction of a shopping plaza.

The order of ideas is likely to be _____.

   b. The kitchen of the model home is the most efficient one I have seen.

The order of ideas is likely to be _____.

   c. The military should not be responsible for the development of experimental spacecraft.

The order of ideas is likely to be _____.

   d. My first day of college did not go well.

The order of ideas is likely to be _____.

   e. Anyone can learn to change the oil in a car.

The order of ideas is likely to be _____.

3. For each of the following writing topics, use the idea-generation technique of your choice to develop at least four ideas. Do this on a separate sheet.

Then, in the space provided, write the ideas in the order they are likely to appear in the writing.

a. Topic: Changes I'd Most Like to Make in Myself

First idea ___*hair*___

Second idea ___*brain*___

Third idea ___*driving*___

Fourth idea ___*tennis skills*___

The order of my ideas is _____.

The idea-generation technique I used is ___*Brainstorming*___.

b. Topic: A Time When Something Did Not Go as Expected

First idea ___*first date*___

Second idea ___*prom day*___

Third idea ___*wedding day*___

Fourth idea _____

The order of my ideas is _____.

The idea-generation technique I used is _____.

c. Topic: Why the Internet Should (or Should Not) Be Censored

First idea ___*under age starting*___

Second idea ___*Pedofiles trying to contact*___

Third idea _____

Fourth idea _____

The order of my ideas is _____

The idea-generation technique I used is _____

A first draft is your first version of a piece of writing. It is also known as a *rough draft* because it is likely to have problems you will solve later.

WRITING YOUR FIRST DRAFT

After generating ideas and deciding on a suitable order, writers can consider most of their planning complete. Now they can put their plan into action by writing a **first draft,** which is the earliest version of a piece of writing.

You should understand what a first draft is and what it is not. A first draft is not a finished piece of writing; it is not something you can copy over or type and hand to a reader. Instead, it is a first effort, an early attempt to get your ideas down on the page. As an early attempt, it will have problems, perhaps with both content and grammar. For this reason, a first draft is often called a **rough draft.** So forget perfection. No matter how rough your draft is, you should feel encouraged because now you have material you can work with.

Because the first draft is supposed to be rough, you can write it from beginning to end in one sitting. Keep your plan in mind by referring often to your list of generated ideas or your scratch outline. Keep pushing forward. If you have trouble starting at the beginning, start in the middle instead. If you still have trouble starting, try writing as if you were speaking to a close friend or writing a letter to a friend. If you get stuck, skip the troublesome part and push on. You can come back to the problems and solve them later. Finally, do not spend much time making changes as you go. You can make changes later, when you revise.

FAQ:

Q: What if I can't write my first draft, even though I have generated ideas and decided on an order for them?

A: Try speaking your draft into a recording device. Then transcribe with a pen or at the keyboard.

PRACTICE 1.7

When you completed number 3a for Practice 1.6, you generated and ordered ideas for a composition about things you would like to change about yourself. Using those ordered ideas as a guide, write a first draft for a paragraph. The first sentence of your draft should be one of these:

The change I'd most like to make in myself is _____.
(You fill in the blank.)

or

The changes I'd most like to make in myself are _____

and _____. (You fill in the blanks.)

Develop your paragraph by explaining why you want to make the change or changes. Remember that the draft is supposed to be rough. (Save your draft, because you will use it in a later activity.)

WRITING AT THE COMPUTER

The computer can help you plan your writing. To generate ideas, turn the brightness all the way down on your monitor and try freewriting with the screen dark. You will make more keystroke errors that way, but you will be less likely to censor yourself because you cannot see your work. To discuss your writing subject or topic with others, you can use e-mail to find out what other people think. Finally, you can use the copy and move commands to arrange an idea-generation list into a scratch outline.

OBSERVING A STUDENT WRITER AT WORK

In this chapter and the next, you will follow the work of Will, who wrote about the effects of moving frequently when he was a child. First in this chapter, you will observe Will's writing process as he generates ideas, establishes his audience and purpose, orders ideas, and writes a first draft. In the next chapter, you will see how Will rewrites his draft to improve it.

Planning: Generating Ideas

You have learned that writers cannot sit around waiting for inspiration. They must go after the ideas they need by using one or more idea-generation techniques.

Here is the clustering and brainstorming Will did when he worked to generate ideas. When Will was asked to write about an event or a circumstance that had a significant impact on him, he decided to write about being the son of a career soldier in the army, about being what he calls an "army brat." To come up with a more specific topic, Will wrote the following clustering:

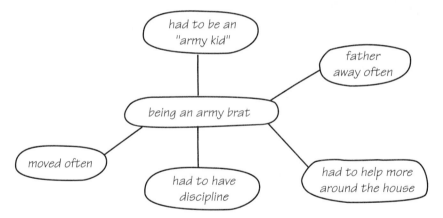

After considering his clustering, Will decided to write about the effects of moving frequently when he was a child. To come up with ideas to develop his topic, he wrote the following brainstorming list.

changed schools a lot

always behind or ahead in class

became self-reliant

lost friends

never felt I belonged

saw a lot of the country

learned to love change (?)

~~started to hate my father but outgrow it~~

Notice that when he reviewed his list, Will crossed out the last item because he decided he did not want to discuss it. Remember, during idea generation, you can add and delete ideas at any point. Also notice that Will placed a question mark next to a point he was not sure he wanted to discuss.

Planning: Establishing Audience and Purpose

To establish the audience and purpose for his writing, Will answered many of the questions on page 14. He decided that his audience would be his best friend, Tony. He characterized Tony as someone who knew that Will's father was in the army, but he did not realize how seriously Will was affected by the frequent moving around. He considered Tony to be a reader who would be interested in what he had to say. Answering the questions on page 14 also helped Will establish his purpose as informing Tony about an important part of his life so that his friend would understand him better.

Planning: Ordering Ideas

To develop a scratch outline that would guide his drafting, Will numbered the ideas in his brainstorming list in the order he would write them up. Notice that in the process of doing this, he thought of another idea, which he added to the list (tell about Mike).

1. changed schools a lot
2. always behind or ahead in class
5. became self-reliant
4. lost friends (tell about Mike)
3. never felt I belonged
7. saw a lot of the country
6. learned to love change (?)

Writing the First Draft

You learned that a first draft is usually rough and has grammatical errors because it is a first effort. The following is Will's first, rough draft. Notice that, to some extent, Will departed from his idea-generation material and scratch outline. Writers often go in new directions as ideas surface during the writing process.

One fact of my life rises above all others. My father is in the army. I spent my childhood moving from place to place. I lived from one end of the country to the other. I lived in New England, Alaska, and about seven states in between. This lifestyle has had a definite impact on me.

While traveling all over the country might sound exciting to you, it does have drawbacks. For one thing, I had to change schools every couple of years, which was really hard for me because I never knew how I would compare to the rest of the students academically. I also worried about fitting in and whether I would be treated like an outsider.

While the first few weeks in a new place were hard, the last ones were even worse because I had to say goodbye to friends who I know I would probably never see them again. This was the case when I had to leave my best friend, Mike. I met him my very first day of school in a brand new town. Mike was the only one who instantly made contact with me. We became inseperable from that moment on. Mike was like a brother to me, leaving him left a hole that no one has been able to fill. I'm not really sure why Mike and I somehow lost touch with each other, but I sure wish I knew where he was now because I would write him and try to renew our friendship.

Although there have been these disadvantages, my life as an Army brat has had its good points too. I know much more about the United States and its people than the average person, I have seen more different kinds of people than anyone else I know except my father. I have become more self-reliant, I also learned how to cope with the loss of friends and how to make new friends fast. You can't move as many times as I have and be shy.

Long ago I decided I would never force my kids to move as often as I did, however, I notice that if I live in a place more than a few years I get restless. There is so much out there to see, I feel like I have only just begun to see it.

WRITING ASSIGNMENT

Like the character in the comic strip, all of us, at some time, have gotten stuck trying to come up with an idea. Your subject for this writing assignment is one of those times. You need not limit yourself to a writing idea. If you prefer, you can discuss trouble coming up with an idea for something else, such as a suitable gift for friend or relative, a way to repair a relationship, or a method for living within your budget. In this chapter, you are being asked to generate ideas, identify your audience and purpose, order ideas, and write the first draft. In the next chapter, you will rewrite the draft to improve it.

Copyright © Cassett & Brooks/Tribune Media Services.

Writing Process Tips for Planning and Writing Your Paragraph

These tips are suggestions that may help you plan and write your paragraph.

PLANNING: MOVING FROM SUBJECT TO TOPIC

• Use any one or more idea-generation techniques explained in this chapter to move from the subject to a more specific topic. When you have decided on your specific writing topic, write it here:

_____

_____

PLANNING: GENERATING IDEAS

• When you generated ideas to discover a topic, you may also have uncovered ideas to develop that topic. If so, do you have enough? If you need additional ideas, freewrite, list, cluster, and talk to others until you have enough ideas to get underway. List the ideas you generated here:

PLANNING: ESTABLISHING AUDIENCE AND PURPOSE

• Use the "Questions for Establishing Audience and Purpose" on page 14 to establish your audience and purpose. Then review the ideas you generated to be sure they suit the audience and purpose you identified.

PLANNING: ORDERING IDEAS

• Develop a scratch outline by numbering the ideas in your list in the order you will write them in your first draft. Remember, you can add and delete ideas as your thinking evolves.

WRITING

• Using your scratch outline as a guide, write through your draft in one sitting, skipping troublesome parts, if necessary. Allow this draft to be rough.

Use Idea-Generation Techniques as Learning Strategies

Much of what you learn in this book can help you succeed in your other classes. For example, the strategies for generating ideas are also excellent learning strategies that you can use in many of your other courses.

- *Listing* can help you learn lecture and textbook material. After studying a portion of your lecture notes or textbook, stop, look away from the material, and list all the important points that you can think of. Then look back at the material to determine whether you omitted anything. If so, add it to the list in a contrasting color and study the list. Writing this way helps set the learning.

- *Brainstorming* is an excellent way to prepare for a test with a study partner. Each of you should draft questions about the material. Then trade questions and answer them. Discuss your answers and pay special attention to areas of sketchy or incorrect information.

- *Clustering* can also help you learn material and see the relationships among ideas. Write and circle a major point you are studying and then add all the points you can think of that are related to the circled point. Check your text and lecture notes for omissions and add them in a contrasting color.

- *Journaling* improves comprehension and retention. Keep a separate notebook for each subject and in each one record your reactions to reading assignments and lectures. Note how you can use the material, how it relates to your experience and learning in other classes, whether you agree or disagree with it, and any questions you have.

Write about It

Like writing, studying is a process. How do you currently study textbook material and lecture notes? Explain the process you follow, whether or not you are satisfied with the results of that process, and why. In the future, will you include listing, brainstorming, clustering, or journaling into your study process? Why or why not?

CHAPTER 2
Rewriting

Successful writers understand that a first draft is often called a *rough draft* for good reason: It has many problems and requires considerable improvement before it is ready for a reader. Rewriting a first draft to improve it involves *revising, editing,* and *proofreading.* During **revising,** writers improve the content, organization, and wording of their drafts. During **editing,** writers correct grammar and usage mistakes. Finally, during **proofreading,** writers make a final check to correct mistakes after copying or typing their writing into its final form.

Rewriting
Step 1: Revising Improve content, organization, and wording.
Step 2: Editing Correct grammar and usage mistakes.
Step 3: Proofreading Correct copying or typing mistakes.

REWRITING: REVISING YOUR FIRST DRAFT

Revising is the most important aspect of any writing process, and for that reason, it is the most time-consuming part. Revising demands a concentrated effort to see the draft from the reader's viewpoint and make substantial changes to improve content, organization, and wording. During revising, you do not attend to grammar and usage errors, such as misspellings, misplaced commas, and subject-verb agreement. Does that surprise you? Many writers mistakenly think that revising is merely a matter of reading over the draft and

When you revise, make changes in your draft to improve it. This revision process is important and often time-consuming.

During revision, consider content, organization, and wording—not grammar and usage.

fixing a few spellings and commas. However, mistakes in grammar, spelling, punctuation, and usage are attended to after revising, during editing.

When you revise, try to think like your reader. Ask yourself the questions in the chart that follows because the answers help determine what changes you should make in the content, organization, and wording of your draft. Those changes can be made directly on the draft, and they can involve scratching out, drawing arrows, and writing in margins. Revision is a messy process.

Questions for Revising

To consider content
1. Do I need to add details to explain or prove a point?
2. Do I need to delete details that are not related to my topic?
3. Is there anything my reader might not understand?
4. Are my details well-suited to my audience and purpose?

To consider organization
1. Are all my details arranged in a logical order?
2. Will my reader understand how my ideas relate to each other?

To consider wording
1. Do I need to improve any word choice?
2. Do I need to improve the flow of my sentences?

The next chapters in this book will explain what characteristics the content, organization, and wording should have. The next sections of this chapter will describe revising procedures you can follow.

Get a Different Perspective

You know what you meant to say. *You* agree with the points you are making. *You* understand how your ideas relate to each other. But the question is, will your reader understand these things? To assess that, you need to read your draft the way your reader will, and that means you need to view your draft from a different perspective. These strategies can help:

FAQ:

Q: What if I don't know what revisions to make?

A: Think like your reader. View your draft from your reader's perspective and look for places where the reader might lose interest, fail to understand a point, or need more information.

- Take a break for a day. This time-out helps restore your objectivity so you can view your draft like your reader and see its problems.

- If you wrote your draft by hand, type it before revising. You will get a new perspective because your work will resemble printed matter. You will be amazed at the number of problems you notice when your work is no longer in your own handwriting.

- Evaluate your draft from the perspective of a different sense, and read your draft out loud—or have someone read it to you. You may hear problems that you overlooked in writing.

Work in Stages

Because considering all aspects of content, organization, and wording is a time-consuming process that requires considerable concentration, you may find it best to work in stages. For example, the first time through your draft, answer the content questions in the Questions for Revising chart and revise accordingly; the second time through, answer the organization questions and revise accordingly; and the third time through, answer the wording questions and revise accordingly. Or if you prefer, make your easier changes first and then move on to your harder ones. This way, you can build momentum that will propel you forward. No matter how you work in stages, periodically, take breaks to refresh yourself.

To work in stages and attend to all the revision issues, you must have plenty of time. Never try to revise everything the night before the deadline. Instead, allow yourself several days to revise thoroughly.

Get Reader Response

Letting others read your work in progress can give you information about its strengths and weakness which you can factor in to your revision decisions. Give each of your readers a copy of your draft, along with a copy of the Reader Response Sheet on page 30. Before doing so, however, review the following suggestions.

FAQ:

Q: How do I find a good reader?

A: Use readers who know the qualities of effective writing. Good choices include writing center tutors, classmates, and students who have already taken writing courses. Avoid friends and relatives who will not be honest because they fear hurting your feelings.

Suggestions for Reader Response

If You Are the Writer Seeking Information
1. Give your readers a legible draft; recopy, retype, or reprint it if necessary.
2. If you want information not covered by the questions on the response sheet, write out additional questions.
3. Get the opinions of at least two readers. (Make copies of your draft so each reader is evaluating an unmarked writing.)
4. Do not automatically accept the responses. Instead, weigh them carefully and make thoughtful decisions about which responses to accept and which to reject.
5. If your readers disagree or if you are unsure if a response is reliable, ask your instructor for advice.

If You Are the Reader Evaluating a Draft
1. Read the entire draft before writing any comments.
2. Explain why you react as you do. Rather than say, "Sentence 4 is unclear," say, "Sentence 4 is unclear because I don't understand why you believe more men should become elementary education majors."
3. Give specific suggestions for revision. Rather than say, "Add more detail," say, "Add more detail about why you were so angry when you did not make the team so I understand what caused the emotion." In other words, suggest a revision strategy.

READER RESPONSE SHEET

Writer's Name _____

Reader's Name _____

1. What do you like best about the draft? Be specific.

2. Do all the details clearly relate to the writing topic? Place parentheses around unrelated details.

3. Underline any unclear points. What can be done to clarify?

4. Place brackets around any points that need more explanation. What detail should be added?

5. Are ideas arranged in an easy-to-follow order? If not, what changes should be made?

6. Place an ! next to any particularly effective word choice; circle any ineffective word choice.

7. Does the draft hold your interest? Explain why or why not.

You can also visit your campus writing center to find sensitive readers who will read and react to your draft. Writing center tutors will not "fix" your draft for you, but they will give you the benefit of reader reaction.

Trust Your Instincts

If you sense a problem with your draft, assume there is one—even if you can't figure out what the problem is or how to solve it. Visit your campus writing center or speak to your instructor for help if necessary.

PRACTICE 2.1

Reread the Questions for Revising on page 28 and then proceed with this practice exercise.

1. Reread the draft you wrote for Practice 1.7. As you do, place a check mark beside anything you wish to revise. (Remember, do not be concerned with grammar and usage at this point.)

   a. Did you notice problems with the draft you did not notice when you wrote it?

   _____

   If you did, you have seen how setting your work aside can help you become more objective.

   b. How many check marks did you place? _____

2. Take a few moments to type and print your draft; then reread it. On the typed copy, place a square beside anything you would like to change. (Do not be concerned with grammar and usage at this point.)

   a. Did you notice problems on the typed copy you did not notice before?

   _____

   If you did, you have seen how typing and printing a draft can help a writer.

   b. How many squares did you place? _____

3. Read your draft out loud very slowly. Each time you hear a problem you did not notice before, place an *X* by the problem.

   a. Did you hear any problems you did not notice before?

   _____

   If you did, you have seen how reading a draft aloud can help a writer.

   b. Did reading your draft out loud give you a fresh slant on your work?

   _____

4. Go over your draft again and answer these questions:

a. Do you need to eliminate points that are not related to your topic?

_____

b. Do you need to add details so a point is well explained or proven?

_____

c. Do you need to make changes to make a point clear?

_____

d. Do you need to make changes to improve word choice?

_____

e. Do you need to improve the flow of your writing because it sounds choppy?

_____

(Save your draft because you will need it for a later activity.)

PRACTICE 2.2: WORKING TOGETHER

Photocopy the Reader Response Sheet on page 30 and trade drafts with a classmate. Each of you should fill out a response sheet and then answer the following question:

What did you learn about your draft as a result of getting reader response?

_____

_____

REWRITING: EDITING YOUR DRAFT

Edit to find and correct errors in grammar and usage that detract from the effectiveness of your writing.

During revising, you may write several drafts before you are satisfied with your content, organization, and wording. Then, you can turn your attention to editing—finding and correcting any mistakes in grammar, punctuation, capitalization, and spelling. Careful editing is important because mistakes can distract a reader and create confusion.

When you edit, ask the questions in the chart that follows. The chapter numbers in parentheses direct you to the relevant sections of this book.

> ## Questions for Editing
>
> 1. Have I written any sentence fragments? (Chapter 16)
> 2. Have I written any run-on sentences or commas splices? (Chapter 17)
> 3. Have I made any errors with verb forms? (Chapter 20)
> 4. Have I made any inappropriate tense shifts? (Chapter 20)
> 5. Do all my subjects and verbs agree? (Chapter 20)
> 6. Do all my pronouns and antecedents agree? (Chapter 21)
> 7. Do I have any faulty pronoun reference? (Chapter 21)
> 8. Have I avoided person shifts? (Chapter 21)
> 9. Have I avoided dangling and misplaced modifiers? (Chapter 22)
> 10. Have I used comparative and superlative forms correctly? (Chapter 22)
> 11. Have I capitalized correctly? (Chapter 23)
> 12. Have I punctuated correctly? (Chapter 23)
> 13. Do I have any spelling errors? (Chapter 24)

Parts four and five of this book will explain the various editing issues. The next sections of this chapter will describe editing procedures you can follow.

Get a Fresh Perspective

Has a teacher ever marked an error in your writing that you cannot believe you did not catch and correct yourself? You probably overlooked the mistake because by the time you were ready to edit, you had spent a considerable amount of time planning, writing, and revising your draft. As a result, you were very close to your work—so close that you had trouble seeing your errors. You saw what you *meant* to write rather than what you actually *did* write. The following strategies can help you look at your draft with fresh eyes, so you are less likely to overlook mistakes.

- Take a break for a day to refresh yourself. This time-out will help you see your writing more clearly so you are more likely to notice mistakes.

- Read your draft out loud—or have someone read it to you—to take advantage of a different sense. You may hear problems that you overlooked visually. Be sure that you read exactly what is on the page, not what you meant to write.

- Read backward, from the last sentence to the first. Reading from the end to the beginning will help you see your work from a different vantage point, making it easier to spot errors.

Work Slowly

Careful editing simply cannot be done quickly. The faster you go, the more likely it is that you will overlook some mistakes. One way to keep your speed in check is to place a ruler under the line you are editing. Do not move the ruler to the next line until you have studied everything in that line. Another strategy is to use a pen or pencil to point to each word and punctuation mark. Linger for a few seconds studying whatever you are pointing to.

Work in Stages

You may have more success finding your errors if you edit more than once. The first time, look for one kind of mistake you are in the habit of making. The second time through, look for another kind of mistake you often make. Continue this way and then edit one last time for all other errors.

Learn the Rules

Learn the grammar rules in this book because you cannot edit with confidence if you do not know them. Pay particular attention to the errors your instructor marks on your papers, so you can make a special effort to learn the rules for correcting those mistakes. (The Personal Editing Profile on the inside back cover can help you keep track of your pattern of errors.) If you need help learning and applying the rules, visit your campus writing center.

Trust Your Instinct

If you have a nagging feeling that a grammar problem exists in a particular sentence, the chances are good that there really is a problem—even if you cannot figure out what the problem is or how to solve it. Visit your campus writing center, check the appropriate sections of this book, or speak to your instructor for help.

FAQ:

Q: Can a writing center tutor help me edit?

A: Writing center tutors will happily respond to specific questions. They will also explain grammar and usage points, such as how to find and correct fragments and when to use commas. They will *not* read over your writing to find and correct your errors—that is *your* job.

PRACTICE 2.3

1. Review the Questions for Editing on page 33. Which of these concerns have you had trouble with in the past? _____

2. Look again at the list of questions. Is there anything in that list you have never heard of before? Is there anything that you do not know the meaning of? If so, what? _____

3. What chapters of this text cover the concerns you noted in your answer to

   number 1? _____

   _____

4. When you completed Practice 2.1, exercise 2, you typed a copy of a draft. Using a pen to point to each word and punctuation mark in that draft, edit very slowly, looking for errors in grammar and usage. Be sure to read what you actually wrote—not what you *meant* to write. Make corrections directly on the page; referring to Parts 4 and 5 of this book as necessary.

   How many errors did you find? _____

   _____

5. Check the draft one separate time for each kind of mistake you have a habit of making. Place a ruler under each line as you go. If you are unsure how to correct any errors that you find, consult Parts 4 and 5.

   How many errors did you find? _____

   _____

6. What pages of Parts 4 and 5 do you think you should study first?

   _____ What pages do you think you should study second?

   _____

REWRITING: PROOFREADING YOUR FINAL COPY

After careful editing, copy or type your composition into its final form. Before submitting your work to your reader, however, run a final check for copying or typing errors. This final check is **proofreading.**

Before you proofread, leave your writing for a few hours to refresh yourself and increase your chances of noticing mistakes. Then proofread very slowly, pointing to each word and punctuation mark. If you move too quickly, you will overlook errors. If you do find mistakes, ink in minor corrections neatly, if your instructor permits. (Of course, if you are using a computer, you can easily type corrections and print out a fresh page.) A page with many corrections should be recopied in the interest of neatness.

Proofread your final copy to check for careless errors made while recopying or typing.

WRITING AT THE COMPUTER

The computer can help you revise and edit your writing. When you revise, you can use your Select and Move functions to rearrange text, and you can use e-mail to exchange drafts with classmates to secure reader responses.

When you edit, you can use the spelling and grammar checkers that are part of your word processing program, but do not rely too heavily on these tools because they are neither foolproof nor complete. For example, grammar checkers make many errors, and spell checkers cannot tell when "soundalikes," such as *hear* and *here,* are used incorrectly. You must still edit carefully on your own.

When you revise and edit, do so both on the screen and on print copy because each view gives you a different perspective. Finally, do not be fooled by appearance. Computer-generated material looks very good, so you may think a draft is in better shape than it really is. No matter how you produce your draft, you should revise and edit carefully.

OBSERVING A STUDENT WRITER AT WORK

In Chapter 1, you followed the planning and drafting done by Will, who wrote about the effects of moving frequently as a child. (To review that material, turn to page 22.) In this chapter, you will follow Will's rewriting processes.

Rewriting: Considering Reader Response

Will's teacher read his first draft and gave him the following written response to consider when he revised. First, reread Will's draft on page 23. Then read his teacher's response and consider whether you reacted similarly to the draft.

Will,

Your topic interests me because I have always wondered how people are affected by frequent moves in childhood. However, I need some more details to better understand the impact on you. In paragraph 2, tell me more about fitting in academically and socially. I would also like to know more about your friendship with Mike. I can tell he was important to you. Perhaps you could say more about how you met and the nature of your friendship. This information could replace the detail about losing touch with Mike, since that strays a bit from your focus. I like that you give the advantages as well as the disadvantages of moving often, but I could use more detail to better appreciate the positive aspects. Your last paragraph makes an excellent conclusion. It really helps me appreciate the restlessness you feel.

1. Are any of the instructor's reactions to Will's draft the same as your reactions? Which ones?

   _____

   _____

   _____

2. Do you disagree with any of the instructor's reactions? Which ones? Why do you disagree?

   _____

   _____

   _____

3. Do you have any reactions to Will's draft that are not noted in the instructor's comments? What are they?

   _____

   _____

   _____

Rewriting: Revising the First Draft

Using his teacher's responses and his own ideas as a guide, Will revised to produce the following second draft. The changes are noted in the margin. Notice that Will focused on details rather than grammar when he revised this time.

One fact of my life rises above all others. My father is in the army. I spent my childhood moving from place to place. I lived from one end of the country to the other, I lived in New England, Alaska, and about seven states in between. This lifestyle has had a definite impact on me.

While traveling all over the country might sound exciting to you, it does have drawbacks. For one thing, I had to change schools every couple of years, which was really hard for me because I never knew how I would compare to the rest of the students academically.(A) Sometimes I was ahead of the class and sometimes I needed tutoring to catch up. I also worried about fitting in and whether I would be treated like an outsider(B) because my clothes were not right or I had an accent or I did not know the local slang.

(A) Sentence added to explain not fitting in academically.

(B) Words added to explain not fitting in socially.

© Detail added on relationship with Mike.

While the first few weeks in a new place were hard, the last ones were even worse because I had to say goodbye to friends who I know I would probably never see them again. This was the case when I had to leave my best friend, Mike. I met him my very first day of school in a brand new town. © I walked into biology class in front of twenty-five strangers, feeling that familiar fear and awkwardness as I made my way over to my new lab partner. Mike looked up from his frog and immediately made a wisecrack that made me laugh. As soon as school was over, we would meet in the woods behind his house and go exploring. We spent Saturdays biking around town, then we spent evenings at each other's houses. Mike was like a brother to me, leaving him left a hole that no one has been able to fill. ©

© Irrelevant material omitted.

© Sentences added to tell about people he met.

Although there have been disadvantages, my life as an Army brat has its good points too. I know much more about the United States and its people than the average person, I have seen more different kinds of people than anyone else I know except my father. © I have fished alongside New England fishermen, and watched loggers in Washington and shrimpers in South Carolina. I have lived in an old farmhouse in the Midwest and in an old mill town in Ohio. I have played with kids whos houses line the shore of the Mississippi and kids who live in high rise apartments. © Most importantly, I have become more self-reliant, I also learned to cope with the loss of friends and how to make new friends fast. You can't move as many times as I have and be shy.

© Transition added.

© Explanatory words added.

Long ago I decided I would never force my kids to move as often as I did, © however, I notice that if I live in a place more than a few years I get restless, almost as if I am ready to move on. There is so much out there to see, I feel like I have only just begun to see it.

To understand better the kinds of changes made during revision, answer these questions.

1. What do you think of the details Will added?

_____

_____

2. Do you think Will needs to add any additional details? Explain.

_____

_____

_____

3. What does revision G contribute to the essay?

_____

_____

4. Did Will solve the problem of irrelevant detail? Explain.

_____

_____

_____

5. Did Will make any ineffective revisions? Explain.

_____

_____

_____

Here is the teacher's response to Will's second draft.

Will,

You did an excellent job of adding explanatory detail; your new material about meeting different people is particularly helpful and well written. I would still like to know more about your relationship with Mike and your efforts to fit in socially. Those points seem important. When you revise, read your first paragraph out loud to hear the choppiness. You should be able to smooth that out. When you edit, look for comma splices.

Revising and Editing the Draft

On the basis of his instructor's reactions to his second draft, Will did additional revising. Then he edited to eliminate errors in grammar and usage. The result was Will's final draft, which appears here.

On the Move(A)

(B) Because my father is in the army, I have spent most of my life moving from place to place. I have lived from one end of the country to the other, from New England to Alaska and about seven states in between. This lifestyle has had a definite impact on me.

(C) While traveling all over the country might sound exciting to you, it does have drawbacks. For one thing, I had to change schools every couple of years, which was really hard for me because I never knew how I would compare to the rest of the students academically. Sometimes I

(A) Title added.

(B) Introduction revised to eliminate choppiness.

(C) Spelling corrected.

was ahead of the class and sometimes I needed tutoring to catch up. I also worried about fitting in and whether I would be treated like an outsider because my clothes were not right or I had an accent or I did not know the local slang. If I spoke too much, I could unintentionally say the wrong thing because I did not know the local customs. If I said too little for fear of offending, I was considered shy or conceited. As a result, I could never relax and feel like one of the gang.

D Detail added to further explain problems fitting in.

While the first few weeks in a new place were hard, the last ones were even worse because I had to say goodbye to friends I knew I would never see again. This was the case when I had to leave my best friend, Mike. I met him my very first day of school in a brand new town. I walked into biology class in front of twenty-five strangers, feeling that familiar fear and awkwardness as I made my way over to my new lab partner. Mike looked up from the frog he was dissecting and in a corny accent said, "Velcome, Igor—care for some lunch?" as he dangled the mutilated frog in front of my face. We were inseparable from that moment on. As soon as school was over, we would meet in the woods behind his house and go exploring. We spent Saturdays biking around town. Then we spent evenings at each other's houses. Mike was like a brother to me, and leaving him left a hole that no one has been able to fill.

E Sentence structure revised and tense corrected.

F Mike's wisecrack given.

G Comma splice eliminated.

H Comma splice eliminated.

Although there were these disadvantages, my life as an army brat had its good points too. I know much more about the United States and its people than the average person. I have seen more different kinds of people than anyone else I know except my father. I have fished alongside New England fishermen, and watched loggers in Washington and shrimpers in South Carolina. I have lived in an old farmhouse in the Midwest and in an old mill town in Ohio. I have played with kids whose houses line the shore of the Mississippi and kids who live in high rise apartments. Most importantly, I have become more self-reliant. I also learned to cope with the loss of friends and how to make new friends fast. You can't move as many times as I have and be shy.

I Tenses corrected.

J Comma splice eliminated.

K Spelling corrected.

Long ago I decided I would never force my kids to move as often as I did. However, I notice that if I live in a place more than a few years I get restless, almost as if I am ready to move on. There is so much out there to see, and I feel that I have only just begun to see it.

L Comma splice eliminated.

M–N Comma splice eliminated.

WRITING ASSIGNMENT

In Chapter 1, you planned a paragraph about a good or bad idea you had. In this chapter, you will rewrite that paragraph to get it ready for your reader.

" No, not criticisms — just think of them as 50 simple things you can do to save your manuscript. "

Copyright © Mort Gerberg.

Writing Process Tips for Rewriting Your Paragraph

These tips are suggestions that may help you revise, edit, and proofread your paragraph.

REWRITING: REVISING

- Use the Questions for Revising on page 28 to evaluate your draft and decide what changes to make. Then make those changes. Be sure to work in stages.
- Exchange drafts with a classmate, and use the Reader Response Sheet on page 30 to give each other helpful feedback. To avoid the unrelenting negativity depicted in the above cartoon, do not focus solely on criticisms. Be sure you answer question 1 and explain what you like about the draft.
- Follow any additional procedures explained in this chapter that will help you revise.

REWRITING: EDITING

- Before editing, take a break to refresh yourself.

Tips for Rewriting Your Paragraph (continued)

- What kinds of grammar mistakes do you tend to make? Working slowly, edit one separate time for each kind of error. Take a break and edit for all other errors.

- Follow any additional procedures explained in this chapter that will help you edit.

REWRITING: PROOFREADING

- Take a break if you need one.

- After copying or typing your paragraph into its final form, proofread very slowly—pointing to each word and punctuation mark—to look for typing or copying mistakes.

- Correct any errors you find.

- Recopy or type and print new pages if necessary.

SUCCEEDING IN COLLEGE

Achieve your Academic Goals

Just as following specific procedures can help you write paragraphs and essays, following specific procedures can help you achieve your goals in college, no matter what they are.

Some of your goals will be **short-term goals** because you want to achieve them in the coming days. Examples of short-term goals are

- Learn to use the library online catalog.

- Make an appointment with my academic advisor.

- Finish my biology lab report by the end of the week.

Some of your goals will be **long-term goals** because you expect to achieve them further into the future, in the coming weeks, months, and years. Examples of long-term goals are

- Raise my overall grade average one full point.

- Decide on my major by the end of the school year.

- Complete my history paper in three weeks.

List Your Goals

Writing a list of your short-term and long-term goals helps you identify your goals, make them specific, and commit to them. Posting your list of goals in a conspicuous place will also help you. It is easy to become caught up in the routine events and inevitable distractions of the day and lose sight of your goals if you do not have a written reminder of them. Furthermore, if you are inclined to procrastinate, a written list may help keep you moving forward.

Develop a Plan

Write a specific plan for achieving each goal. For example, if your goal is to decide on a major by the end of the school year, you might develop this plan:

- Go through the catalog and check mark every major that interests me.

- Read the requirements for each major I have marked.

- Read the course descriptions for classes in each major.

- Talk to a faculty member about each major and learn about job opportunities.

- Talk to students in each major to learn what they think.

Identify Helpful Campus Resources

Your school has many support services to help students, such as a writing center, a study skills center, a reading lab, a math lab, a financial aid office, a counseling center, and an international student center. Use your college catalog to identify these resources and then visit the offices that can help you achieve your goals.

Write about It

Like writing, identifying and achieving your academic goals is a process. What are your academic goals? List three short-term and three long-term goals. Then write out a plan for achieving each of these goals. Do you think your written plan will help you succeed in college? Explain.

CHAPTER 3

Paragraph Basics

A **paragraph** is a group of sentences developing one central point. Most paragraphs have two parts: the sentence that presents the central point (the **topic sentence**) and the sentences that explain or prove that central point (the **supporting details**). In addition, some paragraphs have a **closing,** a sentence or two to tie things off in a satisfying way. This chapter will help you learn how to write an effective paragraph.

> The two main parts of a paragraph are the topic sentence and the supporting details. A closing may also appear.

A SAMPLE PARAGRAPH

As you read the following sample paragraph, decide which sentence presents the central point. That is the **topic sentence.** Also decide which sentences explain or prove the central point. They are the **supporting details.**

A Lounge for Women over Thirty

[1]Because so many women in their thirties, forties, and fifties are returning to school, our university should set up a special lounge area for these students. [2]Women in this age group are often uncomfortable in the student union because they are surrounded by students no older than twenty-two or so. [3]They are not interested in the upcoming rock concert or fraternity party, so often they find they have little to discuss with their younger counterparts. [4]A special lounge would provide a meeting place for the older women. [5]It would be a place they could go knowing they would find others who share the same interests and concerns. [6]Also, this lounge would be a place these students could come together to help each other with their unique problems, the ones they face as a result of returning to school after a long absence. [7]It would also provide a place for group study. [8]Finally, because many returning to school after an absence need some

> The topic sentence presents the central point of the paragraph, and the supporting details develop the central point.

brushing up, the lounge could be a place for tutoring activities. [9]If the university provided this facility, this important group of students would feel more comfortable as they pursued their degrees.

1. Which sentence presents the central point of the paragraph? That is, which sentence is the topic sentence?

   _____

2. Most of the sentences after the topic sentence are the

   _____

3. The last sentence is the _____

If you identified the first sentence of the paragraph as the topic sentence, you were correct. This sentence provides the central point of the paragraph (the university should provide a lounge for female students over thirty). The remaining sentences (except the last) are the supporting details (they develop the central point). The last sentence is the closing (it ties the paragraph off in a satisfying way).

The Structure of a Paragraph

Topic Sentence gives the central point

Supporting Details explain or prove the central point

Closing finishes the paragraph in a satisfying way

PRACTICE 3.1

Each group of sentences could be part of a paragraph. One sentence could be a topic sentence, and the others could be part of the supporting details. Write *TS* if the sentence could be a topic sentence and *SD* if it could be part of the supporting details.

Example:

   _SD_ He humiliates players by yelling at them in front of fans.

<u>TS</u> My nephew's baseball coach should be fired.

<u>SD</u> The coach allows pitchers to give up too many runs before he pulls them out.

1. ____ Long lines at check-in counters, security scanners, and gates are common.

____ Passengers are uncertain about what they can put in their carry-on luggage.

<u>TS</u> New security measures at airports have changed the nature of air travel.

____ More people are having their luggage opened and searched.

2. ____ Giant toads may weigh three pounds and grow to twelve inches.

____ Giant toads have glands that secrete a poison strong enough to kill a dog.

____ The number of giant toads in Florida is increasing.

<u>TS</u> If you go to Florida, watch out for the giant toads.

3. <u>TS</u> People can learn to manage their stress.

____ Regular exercise helps control stress.

____ Focusing on successes rather than defeats keeps stress in check.

____ Talking things out with a sympathetic friend relieves stressful feelings.

4. ____ The eleven-month school year saves school districts money.

<u>TS</u> More school systems should adopt the eleven-month school year.

____ The eleven-month school year keeps students from forgetting important concepts over a long summer recess.

____ The eleven-month school year makes efficient use of staff and facilities.

5. ____ Saline is injected into the blood vessel.

____ The procedure is quick, taking only a few moments.

____ If you have spider veins in the legs, sclerotherapy can help you.

____ Sclerotherapy involves only minor discomfort in most cases.

THE TOPIC SENTENCE

You should usually begin your paragraphs with a **topic sentence,** which presents the central point of your paragraph. Once readers see that topic sentence, they do not have to wonder; they *know* what the paragraph is about. Here, for example, is the first sentence of "A Lounge for Women over Thirty," which appears on page 45.

Because so many women in their thirties, forties, and fifties are returning to school, our university should set up a special lounge area for these
students.

Notice that as soon as you read this opening sentence, you understand exactly
what the paragraph will be about. That is, you know the paragraph's central point.

A topic sentence usually has two parts: one part gives your topic, and one
part gives your assertion about the topic.

> your topic + your assertion about the topic = your topic sentence

Here are some examples. The topic is underlined once, and the assertion about
the topic is underlined twice.

1. <u>Property taxes</u> are <u><u>an ineffective way to finance public education</u></u>.

2. <u>Many people</u> <u><u>do not know how to relax</u></u>.

3. <u><u>I greatly admire</u></u> my <u>Aunt Hattie</u>.

4. <u>Changing my major from engineering to computer science</u> <u><u>proved to be a
smart move</u></u>.

5. <u>Warrick Inn's</u> <u><u>best feature is its country charm</u></u>.

PRACTICE 3.2

For each topic sentence, underline once the words that present the topic
and underline twice the words that present the assertion about the topic.

Example:

> <u>If you plan to purchase a new car</u>, proceed cautiously.

1. Considering its size and location, the house is overpriced.

2. The aging shopping mall is exceptionally dreary.

3. The new state law requiring high school proficiency testing was not carefully thought out.

4. A stress management course should be taught on all college campuses.

5. If you ask me, nurses are the most underappreciated healthcare providers.

6. The auto workers' strike will have serious consequences throughout the
economy.

7. Psychologists understand that birth order significantly affects personality.

8. Carlos Morales is the most qualified candidate for student government.

9. After the party, the living room looked like a war zone.

10. The effects of depression can be devastating.

Writing Effective Topic Sentences

You have learned that your topic sentences should include both a topic and your assertion about that topic. In addition, there are other points to remember.

1. **Avoid statements of fact.** A topic sentence that states a fact leaves you with nothing to say in the supporting detail. Consider these factual statements:

   > I wake up every morning at 6:30.
   >
   > Education is very important.
   >
   > Soap operas are on in the daytime.

   These statements of fact offer no room for the writer's assertion. What can you say after noting that you wake up at 6:30? Who does not agree that education is important? How can you develop a whole paragraph about the fact that daytime TV includes soap operas?

   Statements of fact can be rewritten to be more effective by including the writer's assertion:

   > I highly recommend waking up early each day.
   >
   > To attract better teachers, we must pay higher salaries.
   >
   > The number of daytime soap operas should be reduced.

2. **Avoid very broad topic sentences.** They are impossible to treat adequately in a single paragraph. Consider these statements:

   > The terrorist attacks of September 11, 2001, affected our country profoundly.
   >
   > Our educational system must be revamped.

   These topic sentences cannot be managed in one paragraph. They require treatment in essays made up of several paragraphs.

3. **Avoid vague words.** Words such as *nice, interesting, great, good,* and *bad* do not give your reader a clear sense of your assertion.

vague:	Being a camp counselor last summer was great.
clearer:	Being a camp counselor last summer helped me decide to become a teacher.
vague:	Playing in piano recitals was awful.
clearer:	Playing in piano recitals made me feel self-conscious.

Avoid topic sentences that are statements of fact or too broad. Also, avoid the formal announcement, vague language, and reference to the title.

4. **Avoid formal announcements.** Topic sentences like these are generally considered poor style:

> This paragraph will discuss how to interview for a job.

> I plan to explain why this university should offer a major in hotel management.

> The following sentences will describe my first day of college.

Topic sentences like these are far more appealing:

> Remember two points when you interview for a job.

> A major in hotel management is needed at this university.

> My first day of college was hectic.

5. **Avoid using a pronoun to refer to something in the title.** If your title is "The Need for Campaign Finance Reform," avoid a topic sentence like this: "It is needed for a variety of reasons." Instead, write this: "Campaign finance reform is needed for a variety of reasons."

6. **Place the topic sentence first.** The topic sentence can actually appear anywhere in the paragraph. However, placing it first is convenient. You can try other placements as you become a more experienced writer.

PRACTICE 3.3

If the topic sentence is acceptable, write *OK* on the blank; if it is too broad, write *broad* on the blank; if it is a statement of fact, write *fact* on the blank; if the language is vague, write *vague* on the blank; if the sentence is a formal announcement, write *announcement* on the blank.

Example:

__*announcement*__   The following paragraph will explain how to use the principles of feng shui to improve the quality of your life.

1. _____   The time I spent working as a hospital orderly was great.

2. _____   Computers are a fact of life.

3. _____   Living in a dorm is miserable.

4. _____   The most pressing problems facing us today are world hunger and overpopulation.

5. _____   I will explain here why I believe grading on the curve is unfair.

6. _____ Children need lots of attention.

7. _____ Professor Wu's group dynamics class is interesting.

8. _____ My paragraph will describe the campus commons at sundown.

9. _____ Two tricks will help a dieter maintain willpower.

10. _____ The Cameron triplets are very different: Jud is an optimist; Jake is a pessimist; Judy is apathetic.

PRACTICE 3.4 WORKING TOGETHER

With the members of a group, pick three of the unacceptable topic sentences from Practice 3.3 and rewrite them to make them acceptable. Use a separate sheet.

PRACTICE 3.5

If the statement includes both the topic and assertion, write *OK* on the blank; if the topic is missing, write *topic;* if the assertion is missing, write *assertion.*

Example:

____topic____ It was so unexpected I was not sure what to do.

1. _____ In my senior year, a championship basketball game taught me the true meaning of sportsmanship.
2. _____ Job-sharing has benefits for an employer.
3. _____ I began my student teaching in a seventh-grade study hall.
4. _____ It was very depressing to be there.
5. _____ The governor's tax bill will be voted on in November.

PRACTICE 3.6 WORKING TOGETHER

With the members of a group, select two of the unacceptable topic sentences in Practice 3.5 and rewrite them on a separate sheet to make them acceptable.

PRACTICE 3.7

For each subject given, write an acceptable topic sentence. Remember to include both a topic and your assertion. Also, avoid broad topic sentences, statements of fact, vague language, and formal announcements. The first one is done as an example. (If you are stuck for ideas, try listing, brainstorming, clustering, or freewriting.)

Example:

pets   *My calico cat, Cali, has an annoying habit.*

1. your favorite holiday _____

2. a childhood memory _____

3. a favorite teacher _____

4. your first day of college _____

5. television   I love spending my evenings in front of the TV with good movie and popcorn

PRACTICE 3.8

For each list of supporting details, write an acceptable topic sentence. Avoid broad topic sentences, statements of fact, vague language, and formal announcements.

1. topic sentence _____

_____

   a. Check local fashions and be sure your child dresses to conform to them.

   b. Ask the new teacher to assign a friendly classmate as a lunch or gym partner.

   c. Instruct your child to strike up conversations and not just wait for others to introduce themselves first.

   d. After a week, have your child invite one of his or her new classmates over after school.

2. topic sentence _____

_____

   a. I wanted to study criminal justice.

   b. I was offered a scholarship to play football.

   c. I wanted to move away from home.

   d. My girlfriend was attending college.

3. topic sentence _____

_____

    a. The walls were covered with grease stains.

    b. Pieces of cereal, cat food, and dried food covered the floor.

    c. Dried jelly and other, unidentified matter were caked on the refrigerator door.

    d. The smell of rotting garbage filled the air.

4. topic sentence _____

_____

    a. Running improves cardiovascular fitness.

    b. It helps manage stress.

    c. It helps maintain desired weight.

    d. It can be competitive or noncompetitive, as the runner prefers.

5. topic sentence _____

_____

    a. Professor Rios involves students in class discussions.

    b. She gives extra help to those who need it.

    c. She never criticizes anyone who makes an error.

    d. She gives fascinating lectures.

Considering Your Writing Process: Planning, Writing, and Rewriting Your Topic Sentence

You can decide on the topic and your assertion for your topic sentence when you plan your writing; you can write an early version of your topic sentence when you write your first draft; and you can make sure your topic sentence is effective when your revise your draft.

Say, for example, that during planning, you came up with this list of ideas for a paragraph about modern communication.

    Cell phones are everywhere.

    They are annoying in restaurants and other public places.

    They can be lifesavers in emergencies.

They help people stay in touch.

They can play music.

They can take pictures.

They can save money on long distance calls.

They can be easily damaged.

They are not always reliable.

Computers help people connect with e-mail.

Instant messaging is more common than telephoning for teenagers.

Sometimes e-mail creates misunderstandings.

It can get lost in cyberspace.

Now say that studying the list reveals that your topic can be either cell phones or computers. You must decide which topic to use. Say you decide on cell phones. The list shows that one possible assertion about the topic is that cell phones can be a positive thing, and another possible assertion is that they can be a problem. To plan a topic sentence, you must decide which assertion to use. Say that you decide to write about cell phones as a positive thing.

topic: cell phones

assertion: they are a positive thing

When you write your first draft, your topic sentence should include both the topic and the assertion about your topic that you settled on during planning. For example, you might include this topic sentence in your first draft about cell phones:

Cell phones are a good thing.

When you revise your draft, you can rework your topic sentence to make sure it has all the qualities of an effective topic sentence. Thus, when you revise "Cell phones are a good thing," you may end up with this topic sentence:

Although people complain about cell phones, they are a convenience we would not want to live without.

Supporting details develop the topic sentence by explaining why you have your assertion about the topic. Supporting details should be adequate, specific, and relevant. They should also have coherence.

THE SUPPORTING DETAILS

You cannot expect your reader to believe what you say in your topic sentence just because you write it in a paragraph. You must *demonstrate* that your topic sentence is true, and that is where your *supporting details* come in. **Supporting details** explain or prove the topic sentence. They are all the facts and opinions you present to show why you have your particular assertion about your topic. Turn back to page 45 and reread "A Lounge for Women over Thirty." Notice that the first sentence presents the writer's topic and assertion. The university should set up a lounge for female students over thirty. Thoughtful readers will not believe that the university should set up the lounge just because the writer says it should—thoughtful readers require evidence. That evidence comes in the supporting details after the topic sentence, supporting details which explain why the university should set up the lounge.

To explain or prove the topic sentence, supporting details must be *adequate, specific,* and *relevant.* They must also have *coherence.* These characteristics are explained next.

Adequate Supporting Detail

When a paragraph has **adequate supporting detail,** it has enough facts and opinions to explain or prove the topic sentence.

Read and think about this paragraph:

> My high school biology teacher changed my life. He saw I was heading for trouble and straightened me out. He also helped me improve my grades so I could play basketball. In fact, he even helped me get into college. I will always be grateful to Mr. Friedman for being there when I needed help the most.

The paragraph begins with a fine topic sentence that includes both topic and assertion. The topic is the biology teacher, and the assertion is that he changed the writer's life. However, the supporting details are not adequate. Too few points are made to demonstrate that the topic sentence idea is true. The reader still needs information. How did the teacher straighten the writer out? How did he help the writer improve his grades? How did he help the writer get into college?

Now read and think about this revised paragraph:

> My high school biology teacher changed my life. He saw I was heading for trouble and called me in after school one day. He explained that he cared what happened to me and wanted to help if he could. When I told him how depressed I was, he arranged counseling at the local mental health center. He also helped me improve my grades by showing me how to take notes and study efficiently. As a result, I regained my basketball eligibility. In fact, Mr. Friedman even helped me get into college by talking to admissions counselors on my behalf. I will always be grateful to Mr. Friedman for being there when I needed help the most.

You probably feel more satisfied after reading the revised version because necessary details have been added. The supporting details in the paragraph are now *adequate.*

Supporting details must be adequate; the writer must supply enough information so that the reader understands why the writer has his or her assertion.

FAQ:

Q: Where do my supporting details come from?

A: As you generate ideas for supporting details, consider what you have experienced, observed, learned in the classroom, read in the newspapers, and heard on the television and radio.

PRACTICE 3.9

One of the following paragraphs has adequate detail. The others lack necessary information, so the reader will likely feel unsatisfied at the end. If the paragraph has adequate detail, write *OK* on the blank; if it does not have adequate detail, write *X* on the blank.

Darlene, the Practical Joker

_____ 1.   My sister, Darlene, is a practical joker. She drives everybody crazy with her jokes. Once she played this amazing joke on my father. She spent months planning it so everything would work just right. Even though the joke only lasted a moment, Darlene felt it was worth the effort. However, I'm not sure Dad saw it that way. Another time Darlene almost lost her best friend because of a joke she played on her. The problem was that she embarrassed her friend in the school cafeteria. Last April Fool's Day Darlene hired a male stripper to crash my grandmother's seventy-fifth birthday party. What a scene that was! I sure wish someone would play a practical joke on Darlene so she could get a taste of her own medicine.

What a Bargain!

_____ 2.   When I bought the '75 Mustang for $1800 I was sure I got a bargain until everything started going wrong. First, I had to pay a lot of money to have the engine repaired, and then I noticed how much body work was needed. Last week the suspension system was diagnosed as terminal, so there's more money I'll have to fork over for this four-wheeled "bargain." I'll never buy another used car again.

Adjusting to College

_____ 3.   A new college student can expect to make several adjustments before the first year is over. First, the student must learn to cope with more freedom. Mom and Dad are not around to set a curfew or limit activities. This means the student has only a conscience to guide behavior. With this freedom comes more responsibility to adjust to. Mom and Dad may not be limiting activities, but they are also not around to wash clothes, remind the student of appointments, and force the student to study. This means the student better learn to take care of things or things just won't be taken care of. Finally, the student must learn to adjust to pressure. Exams, crazy roommates, registration hassles, and book lines are just some of what can cause tension. The student must learn to take the pressure of college life or forget that degree. Fortunately, most students make the necessary adjustments before the sophomore year begins.

PRACTICE 3.10: WORKING TOGETHER

Paragraphs 1 and 2 in Practice 3.9 lack adequate detail. With some classmates, list details that could be added to help make the supporting details adequate.

1. Darlene, the Practical Joker

_____

_____

_____

_____

_____

2. What a Bargain!

_____

_____

_____

_____

_____

Specific Supporting Detail

Specific detail helps a reader form a clear, detailed understanding of the writer's meaning. The opposite of specific detail is **general statement,** which gives the reader only a vague sense of the writer's meaning. The following examples show the difference between general and specific.

> Specific details help ensure adequate detail.

general statement:	The car went down the street.
specific detail:	The 1962 Impala sedan rattled down Oak Street, dragging its tailpipe.

You probably formed a clearer picture in your mind when you read the sentence with specific detail. Also, you probably found the specific detail more satisfying than the general statement. Because specific detail is more satisfying and helps the reader form a clearer mental picture, strive for specific supporting details.

Use specific words to help your supporting details be specific enough.

Use Specific Words   One way to provide specific detail is to use specific words. **Specific words** are more exact than general words, so they help the reader form a clear mental picture. Study the following lists of specific and general words to appreciate the difference between the two.

General Words	Specific Words
dog	collie
song	"Home on the Range"
book	*The DaVinci Code*
music	jazz
run	sprint
said	shouted
take	grab

Now consider these two sentences to appreciate the difference specific words can make.

a. The young child was on the floor.

b. Ten-year-old Miro was sprawled across the living room floor.

Sentence B is more interesting because it gives the reader a clearer mental picture. This clearer mental picture comes from replacing the general words *young, child,* and *was on* with the more specific *ten-year-old, Miro,* and *sprawled across.* Also, the words *living room* are added to identify where Miro was.

To be sure your words are specific, choose specific nouns and verbs; also, use modifiers.

Specific Nouns:	Nouns are words for people, places, ideas, emotions, and items. Instead of general nouns like *movie, car,* and *restaurant,* choose specific nouns like *The Sixth Sense, Camaro,* and *IHOP.*
Specific Verbs:	Verbs are words that show action. Instead of general verbs like *went, spoke,* and *looked,* choose specific verbs like *raced, shouted,* and *glanced.*
Specific Modifiers:	Modifiers are words that describe nouns and verbs. Often you can use modifiers to make your detail more specific. Add the modifier *pounding* to describe the noun *rain,* and you get the specific *pounding rain.* Add the modifier *carefully* to the verb *stepped,* and you get the specific *stepped carefully.* When you use modifiers, be sure they are specific ones. Rather than the general "sang *badly,*" choose the more specific "sang *off-key*"; rather than the general "*nice* house," choose the more specific "*roomy* house."

FAQ:

Q: What if I have trouble thinking of specific words?

A: Use a dictionary or thesaurus, but use words from these sources appropriately. *Gnaw* is more specific than *chew,* but it also means something a bit different.

PRACTICE 3.11

Next to each general noun or verb, write a more specific alternative.

Examples:

shoes *penny loafers* _____   walk *stroll* _____

1. drink _____   5. house _____

2. hit _____   6. said _____

3. college course _____   7. flower _____

4. looking _____   8. took _____

PRACTICE 3.12

Use one or more specific modifiers with each noun and verb.

Examples:

the sweater *the pink angora sweater* _____

study *study diligently* _____

1. the commercial _____

2. drive _____

3. the rose _____

4. barking _____

5. the kitten _____

6. sang _____

7. the apartment _____

8. sleep _____

PRACTICE 3.13

Rewrite each sentence by using a more specific alternative for each underlined word and by following the directions in parentheses.

Example:

The <u>dog went</u> down <u>the street</u>. (Add a specific modifier after the substitute for *went*.) *The German shepherd dashed excitedly down Laurel Avenue.*

1. <u>The man</u> left <u>his tools</u> on the floor. (Add a specific modifier before *floor.*)

   _____

   _____

   _____

2. <u>Several items of clothing</u> were scattered across the floor in Ralph's bed-room. (Add a specific modifier before *bedroom.*)

   _____

   _____

3. <u>A number of things</u> were good bargains at the garage sale. (Add a specific modifier before *garage sale.*) _____

   _____

   _____

4. Jan decided to buy <u>the car</u> that Stavros was selling, even though it <u>had so much wrong with it</u>. (Add a specific modifier either before or after *decided.*) _____

   _____

   _____

5. The scouts <u>went away</u> from the campsite because it smelled <u>bad</u>. (Add a specific modifier before *scouts.*) _____

   _____

   _____

PRACTICE 3.14

Rewrite the sentences to make them more specific. Change general nouns, verbs, and modifiers to specific ones, and add specific modifiers where you wish.

Example:

A variety of people were at the convention.   *Executives, laborers, students,*

and parents attended the third annual ham radio convention in Morgantown.

1. Rhoda and I worked hard in the yard. _____

_____

_____

2. The dish I ordered at the restaurant tasted terrible. _____

_____

_____

3. The baby cried in the middle of the night. _____

_____

_____

4. The smell in Jim's apartment was awful. _____

_____

_____

5. The view from the window was very nice. _____

_____

_____

6. The heat made me miserable. _____

_____

_____

7. The teacher helped the girl feel good. _____

_____

_____

8. The dog made so much noise that he kept me awake all night. _____

_____

_____

FAQ:

Q: Why do I have to follow general statements with specific ones? Can't I just state a point and move on?

A: Thoughtful readers do not believe what they read without proof. Your specific statements provide that proof.

Follow General Statements with Specific Statements   Another way to make your supporting details specific is to follow general statements with specific ones. Here is a paragraph with general statements that are *not* followed by specific ones.

> Myrtle Beach, South Carolina, is the perfect summertime family vacation spot. First, there is something for everyone to do. Also, there is a range of excellent accommodations, all reasonably priced. For those who like to take side trips, there are a number of places a person can see in just a day.

The detail in this paragraph is not adequate—there is not enough of it, so you probably come away feeling unsatisfied. To make the detail adequate, follow each general statement with one or more specific ones, as in the following revision. (The specific statements are underlined to make studying the paragraph easier.)

> Myrtle Beach, South Carolina, is the perfect summertime family vacation spot. First, there is something for everyone to do. <u>In addition to miles of beautiful beach and warm ocean to swim in, over three dozen fine golf courses are available. Fishing is possible from rental boats, off piers, and from the shore. For the kids, water slides, grand prix car and boat rides, dozens of beautiful miniature golf courses, and an amusement park provide hours of fun. For the confirmed shopper, an outlet park with 98 stores three shopping malls, several plazas, and numerous specialty shops provide more than ample shopping.</u> Also, there is a range of excellent accommodations, all reasonably priced. <u>Hotel rooms are available, and so are efficiency apartments. One-, two-, and three-bedroom condominiums are plentiful. In fact, you can stay in a beautiful three-bedroom condominium right on the beach for as little as $120.00 a night.</u> For those who like to take side trips, there are a number of places a person can see in just a day. <u>Picturesque Conway, beautiful Brookgreen Gardens, quaint Pawley's Island and Murrells Inlet, and historic Georgetown all make comfortable day trips.</u>

PRACTICE 3.15

Follow each general statement with a specific statement that helps prove the general statement.

Example

Six-year-old Leo and five-year-old Juanita were not getting along.

They refused to share their toys and spent the afternoon arguing about

everything from the best cartoon show to what game to play.

1. Suddenly the weather turned threatening. _____

   _____

   _____

2. Some television commercials insult the viewer's intelligence.

   _____

   _____

3. The cost of textbooks is outrageous. _____

   _____

   _____

4. Dr. Stone is a dedicated teacher. _____

   _____

   _____

5. The service at Harry's New York Deli is excellent. _____

   _____

   _____

PRACTICE 3.16 WORKING TOGETHER

With the members of a group, write three specific points that could be made after each of the following general statements.

Example

The students in third-period history class were out of control.

The students in the back were talking loudly among themselves.

Two boys were roaming around the room.

When the teacher called for order, the students talked back to him.

1. Wanda treats people badly.

   _____

2. Driving with Chuyen is a frightening experience.

3. To succeed in college, students need effective study habits.

4. Babysitting the Carlson twins aged me ten years.

5. The gale-force winds caused extensive damage to the coastal town.

PRACTICE 3.17 WORKING TOGETHER

The following paragraphs lack specific details because general statements are not followed by specific ones. On a separate sheet, revise these paragraphs with your group by following general statements with specific ones.

1. Don't Eat at Joe's

Joe's Eatery on Third Avenue is the worst restaurant in town. When I was there last Tuesday, I was appalled by the condition of the dining room. Also, the service could not have been worse. When my food finally arrived,

I had to send it back because it was poorly prepared. Things at Joe's are so bad that I would not be surprised if the place went out of business soon.

2. How to Protect Your Health in College

College students should be conscious of how to take care of their health. First, they should choose carefully what they eat in the dining hall. Also, they should schedule a regular exercise session. Equally important is building in some recreation time because too much work will lead to stress. Finally, students should know what to do in the event they do become ill on campus.

Relevant Supporting Detail

Relevant detail means that the supporting details are directly related to the topic and assertion presented in the topic sentence. Details that stray from the topic and assertion create a **relevance problem** (sometimes called a problem with **unity**).

The following paragraph has two relevance problems. As you read it, look for the supporting details that are not directly related to the topic sentence.

Supporting details must be relevant. This means they must be clearly related to the topic and assertion presented in the topic sentence.

The Left-Handed Advantage

Left-handed people have the advantage in baseball and tennis. For one thing, left-handed batters are in a better position to run to first base. Left-handed first basemen also have an edge. At first base, players often field balls hit to the right side of the infield. Of course, left-handed basemen wear their gloves on their right hands, so they can catch balls without moving around, the way right-handed players have to. Unfortunately, the left-handed third baseman does not enjoy the same advantage. In tennis, too, a left-handed player is fortunate. A right-handed player generally has little experience playing a lefty, but a lefty has considerable experience playing a righty. Thus, right-handed players will be more confused playing left-handed players than left-handed players will be playing right-handed players. This fact alone helps explain the large number of left-handed tennis champions. Outside of sports, lefties still face problems with door handles and radio knobs meant to be used with the right hand, with right-handed scissors, and with writing from left to right. Still, in sports, the left-handed athlete has an advantage.

You probably noticed two relevance problems in the paragraph. First, the sentence that says the third baseman does not have an advantage is not relevant because it does not relate to the point presented in the topic sentence: that left-handed people *do* have an advantage. Second, the sentence that discusses the problems lefties have outside of tennis and baseball with knobs, doors, scissors, and writing is not relevant because it does not discuss the advantage in tennis and baseball.

You should eliminate supporting details that are not relevant to your topic sentence, or alter the details to make them relevant.

PRACTICE 3.18

In the following paragraphs, draw a line through the details that are not relevant.

1. Not Necessarily

People say that the squeaky wheel gets the grease, but my experience proved otherwise. I had been working at Gas City for three years. I began ten hours a week as a regular gas jockey, but soon I was working thirty hours a week. Each of those hours was at minimum wage. I liked this job much better than the one I used to have making fries at Hot Dog House. Mr. Stanko, the boss, said I was one of the best kids who has ever worked for him. He said he trusted me, and he said I was a hard worker. About six months ago, he started asking me to open and close the station on occasion. I knew this was a real vote of confidence and decided the time was right to ask for a raise. I worked up my courage and politely made my request—which was not so politely refused. Then I decided to be a squeaky wheel. I asked once a week for a fifty-cent-an-hour raise. After my fourth request, Mr. Stanko said it was obvious I was very unhappy, so he was going to let me go. I was too proud to ask him not to, so I was out of work. I was an unemployed squeaky wheel, and there was no grease in sight.

2. Hank

My friend Hank is a remarkable person. Although he was abused by his parents until he was sixteen and placed in a foster home, Hank is a kind, gentle guy. Studies show that abused children often become abusive adults, but Hank is different. He is a Big Brother to a fatherless child and treats this boy with love and compassion. He also works summers as a swim instructor at a local day camp, where he is a favorite among all the campers. He plans to major in math. Hank underwent three years of therapy to work through the problems that his parents caused. Clearly he has beaten the odds because he shows no signs of becoming abusive the way his parents were.

Transitions and Repetition for Coherence

Readers need adequate, relevant details arranged in some logical order—such as chronological, spatial, or emphatic order—to help them understand and believe the topic sentence. However, readers need something more than adequate, relevant details arranged in a logical order. They also need to understand how ideas relate to each other, and they need the connections to be smooth and graceful. When writers connect ideas smoothly and show how those ideas relate to each other, they achieve **coherence.** Two strategies help writers achieve coherence: using transitions, and repeating key words and ideas.

Transitions are words or phrases that help your reader understand the order of your ideas and their relationship to each other. In addition, transitions help your sentences flow smoothly. Here is an example:

> The health commissioner told the board of health that asbestos had to be removed from three schools. *Also,* he told the board that asbestos may be a problem in two libraries.

The transition *also* tells the reader that the idea in the second sentence functions in addition to the idea in the first sentence. The transition also helps the first sentence flow smoothly into the second. To appreciate this, read the sentences without the transition and notice the gap or abrupt shift:

> The health commissioner told the board of health that asbestos had to be removed from three schools. He told the board that asbestos may be a problem in two libraries.

Here is a chart that gives you many commonly used transitions:

Transitions

To Signal Addition also, and, and then, in addition, too, the next, furthermore, further, moreover, equally important, another, first, second, third

> If the school levy does not pass, some teachers will be laid off. *Furthermore,* band and choir will be eliminated.

To Signal Illustration for example, for instance, an illustration of this is, to illustrate

> Chuck became very irritable when he quit smoking. *For example,* when James asked to borrow his chemistry notes, Chuck yelled at him and called him irresponsible.

To Signal Emphatic Order more important, most important, most of all, best of all, of greatest importance, least of all, even better, the best (worst) case (example, instance, time)

> Mayor DeSalvo has been working hard to bring new industry to our area. *More important,* she has devised a plan to restore confidence in local government.

(continued on next page)

To Signal Spatial (Space) Order near, nearby, far, alongside, next to, in front of, to the rear, above, below, over, across, under, around, beyond, beneath, on one side, to the left

> The high school is centrally located, and *directly behind* it is the football stadium.

To Signal Cause and Effect so, therefore, since, if . . . then, thus, as a result, because, hence, consequently

> Only five hundred students bought tickets to the spring concert. *As a result,* the concert had to be canceled.

To Signal Contrast (Differences) but, yet, still, however, in contrast, on the other hand, nevertheless

> Nigel sprained his knee in practice; *however,* he plans to be in shape for Saturday's game.

To Signal Comparison (Similarities) similarly, likewise, in the same way, in like manner

> Most of today's movies are unsuitable for young viewers. *Similarly,* many television shows are not appropriate for children.

To Signal Purpose for this reason, for this purpose, in order to

> Theresa hopes to make the women's basketball team. *For this reason,* she is training very hard.

To Signal Chronological (Time) Order now, then, later, soon, suddenly, next, afterward, earlier, at the same time, meanwhile, often

> I bought a used car. *Then* I had it checked over by a reliable mechanic.

To Signal Emphasis indeed, in fact, truly, certainly, to be sure, surely, without a doubt, undoubtedly, of course

> Our basketball team has the best record in our division. *Undoubtedly,* we will win a spot in a postseason tournament.

To Signal Summary or Clarification in conclusion, in summary, to sum up, in other words, in brief, that is, all in all

> I cannot support a candidate who is opposed to women's rights. *In other words,* I will not vote for Nathaniel Q. Wisherwaite.

To Signal Conceding Point although, even though, while it is true, granted

> *Although* the temperature is rising quickly, I am still going skiing this weekend.

A second way to achieve coherence is to repeat key words or ideas. Here is an example with a key word repeated:

> The doctor put Dov on a special <u>diet. This diet</u> required him to restrict his intake of fats and proteins.

The second sentence repeats the word *diet,* which appears in the first sentence. This repetition helps the reader understand the relationship of the ideas in the two sentences, and it helps the first sentence flow smoothly into the second.

Now here is an example with a key idea repeated:

> The senior class raised five thousand dollars for homeless people. <u>Such an effort</u> should not go unnoticed.

In this example, the second sentence opens with *Such an effort.* These words repeat the key idea of the first sentence: that the class raised five thousand dollars for homeless people. Repeating the key idea shows how the ideas in the two sentences relate to each other; it also helps the first sentence flow smoothly into the second.

FAQ:

Q: How do I know when I need a coherence device?

A: When you revise, read your draft aloud. If you hear an abrupt shift or gap anywhere, you may need to use a transition or repetition at that spot.

PRACTICE 3.19

1. Read "Able-bodied but Addle-brained" on page 78. Cite two transitions that signal chronological (time) order.

_____

_____

2. Read "One Step Forward and Two Steps Back" on page 103. Cite one transition that signals illustration, one that signals cause and effect, and one that signals emphasis. Also, cite an example of repetition of a key word to achieve coherence.

_____

_____

_____

3. Read "Let's Hear It for Tradition" on page 131. Cite one transition that signals chronological (time) order, one that signals conceding a point, and one that signals contrast. Also cite an example of repetition of a key idea.

_____

_____

_____

_____

4. Read the first three paragraphs of "Making Money with a Garage Sale" on page 192. How is repetition used to achieve coherence in the first sentence of paragraph 3?

_____

_____

PRACTICE 3.20

Fill in the blanks with a transitional word or phrase from the chart beginning on page 68.

Example:

Douglas is the biggest practical joker I know. *For example,*_____ last week he glued Dana's shoes together.

1. I refuse to speak to Alonzo unless he learns to control his temper.

   _____ I refuse to be in the same room with him.

2. Diana was not expecting to be transferred to Houston.

   _____ she needs some time to adjust to the idea.

3. The novelty shop in the mall rarely advertises. _____ not many people realize what unusual items are sold there.

4. Television shapes our thinking more than we realize.

   _____ it can influence our emotions.

5. First I will make myself the most valuable employee I can be.

   _____ I will ask my boss for a raise.

PRACTICE 3.21

Fill in the blanks with suitable coherence devices. Use the words and phrases from the chart beginning on page 68 and repetition of key words and ideas.

The idea that the number 13 is unlucky is a superstition. _____1_____, it is probably the most widely held superstition there is. In one way or another, it is observed all over the world. _____2_____ hotels everywhere do not have a 13th floor. _____3_____, their rooms are not numbered with 13. Many people will not have 13 guests at the dinner table. Strangely, there is no single explanation for the superstition. _____4_____ has many different stories behind it. _____5_____, some experts say that 13 was unpopular from the time when people learned to count. By using their ten fingers and two feet as a unit, people came up with the number 12. _____6_____ 13 became unlucky because it was unknown and frightening—beyond 12. In religious circles, the 13 superstition is traced to the Last Supper. In attendance were Jesus and the twelve Disciples—13 in all. Others trace the superstition to the story of the Valhalla banquet in Norse mythology, to which twelve gods were invited. _____7_____, Loki, the Spirit of Strife and Mischief, intruded to make 13. _____8_____ Balder, the favorite of the gods, was killed. _____9_____ 13 is generally regarded as unlucky, the number was considered lucky by the ancient Chinese and Egyptians.

PRACTICE 3.22

1. Write two sentences that describe the location of some of the things in your writing classroom. Begin the second sentence with a transition that signals a spatial order.

2. Write two sentences about what you did this morning. Begin the second sentence with a transition that signals chronological order.

3. Write two sentences that tell why foreign languages should (or should not) be taught in high school. Begin the second sentence with a transition that signals emphatic order.

4. Write two sentences about the stress of being a college student. Use repetition to achieve coherence between the sentences.

Considering Your Writing Process: Planning, Writing, and Rewriting Your Supporting Details

When you plan your writing, you can use listing, clustering, brainstorming, freewriting, and journaling to come up with ideas for your supporting details. When you write your first draft, your goal is to express your ideas the best way you can, so do not worry about whether your ideas are adequate, specific, and relevant, and do not worry about coherence. Just do the best you can with whatever ideas you have at this point.

When you come to revising, however, pay careful attention to adequate detail, specific detail, relevant detail, and coherence. Check first to be sure that you have backed up all your general statements with specific ones, so your reader will believe that your topic sentence is true. If you need more ideas and they do not occur to you, return to your techniques for generating ideas. Try listing, clustering, or freewriting about one or more of the ideas that need specific backup.

When you judge your details to be adequate and specific, check them all against the topic and assertion in your topic sentence. Do you have any relevance problems? If so, deal with them now.

Finally, read your draft aloud and listen for any disturbance in the rhythm. If you hear such disturbances, you may need to revise to add transitions to achieve coherence.

THE CLOSING

The closing gives a paragraph a satisfying finish. This closing can refer to the topic or assertion presented in the topic sentence. It can also answer the question "So what?"

Many times a final sentence is needed to bring the paragraph to a satisfying finish. This sentence is the **closing.**

An appropriate closing often occurs to you. However, if you are unsure how to handle your closing, write a sentence that refers to the topic and/or assertion presented in your topic sentence. For example, look at the closing of "The Left-Handed Advantage" on page 65. Notice that this final sentence mentions the left-handed athlete, a reference to the topic noted in the topic sentence (left-handed people). Also notice that the closing mentions that left-handed people have an advantage in sports, a reference to the assertion in the topic sentence (having an advantage in baseball and tennis).

Another way to handle the closing is to answer the question "So what?" about your topic sentence. The final sentence of "A Lounge for Women over Thirty" on page 45 takes this approach.

PRACTICE 3.23 WORKING TOGETHER

The following paragraph lacks a closing. Work with some classmates to add a closing sentence that provides a satisfying finish. Use any approach you like, including the ones that have been described.

Wildlife habitat destruction occurs in many ways. First, habitats are ruined when large areas are taken over for agricultural, residential, and industrial purposes. Some animals, like the mountain lion, have had their environments destroyed with the clearing of forests. Another factor leading to habitat destruction is pollution. Chemicals are released into the air and water, spoiling streams, rivers, and land environments. Finally, habitats are destroyed when people bring non-native plants and animals into an area. The non-native plant or animal may interfere with the careful balance of the native ecosystem.

_____

_____

_____

Considering Your Writing Process: Planning, Writing, and Rewriting Your Closing

It is difficult to tell when an idea for your closing will strike. If it happens during planning, make note of it. If it happens during writing, use the idea in your first draft. If you are rewriting and still do not have a closing sentence, ask "So what?" about your topic sentence and let the answer shape your closing sentence. If that does not work, try referring to your topic or assertion.

✔ Checklist for a Paragraph

Before submitting your paragraph, be sure to work through this checklist.

- ☐ 1. I have written a topic sentence that includes my topic and my assertion about the topic.

- ☐ 2. I have included supporting details that explain or prove the topic sentence.

- ☐ 3. I have backed up my statements with specific information.

- ☐ 4. All my supporting details are relevant to the topic and assertion stated in the topic sentence.

- ☐ 5. Where needed, I have used transitions and repetition for coherence.

- ☐ 6. I have written a last sentence that ends the paragraph in a satisfying way.

- ☐ 7. I have edited the paragraph carefully to find and correct mistakes.

- ☐ 8. I have proofread the paragraph carefully after copying or typing it into its final form.

WRITING ASSIGNMENT

Write a paragraph that explains *one* influence a person has had on you. Perhaps a teacher—like the one in the above picture—helped you learn to love reading. Or perhaps a coach helped you gain self-confidence. Or maybe a neighbor taught you how to play guitar. Before you begin this assignment, read the sample student paragraph that follows, so you have an idea of what such a paragraph can be like.

Megen

Because of a nine-year-old named Megen, I decided to major in physical therapy. I met Megen last quarter, when I worked as an orderly at St. Joseph's Hospital. She was only nine, but she had experienced more pain in those nine years than most people experience in a full lifetime. Megen was paralyzed, but she never used that as an excuse to stop trying. Each day I would wheel Megen down for her grueling physical therapy sessions. I would watch and encourage her as she worked through exercises that brought beads of sweat to her forehead and upper lip. Sometimes the pain was so great she cried, but she never stopped working as long as there was the slightest chance it would help. More than anything, Megen wanted to go to school and play with the other nine-year-olds, and she was willing to work as hard as she could for her dream. But it wasn't to be, for Megen died October 19th. I will never forget Megen's courage, for it showed me what I wanted to do with the rest of my life. It showed me that I wanted to be a physical therapist and help others strive for their dreams.

Writing Process Tips for Composing Your Paragraph

These tips are suggestions that may help you plan and write your paragraph. Before submitting your paragraph, be sure you have worked through the paragraph checklist on page 73.

PLANNING: MOVING FROM SUBJECT TO TOPIC

- Think all the way back to your childhood. Freewrite about people who have affected your fears, ambitions, successes, failures, talents, or career plans. Once you have decided on the person and influence, fill in the blanks in this sentence:

    Because of _____, I _____.

    Put the person's name in the first blank and the influence in the second blank to get something like this:

    Because of Uncle Harry, I am no longer afraid of high places. This sentence will remind you of your topic and assertion.

PLANNING: GENERATING IDEAS

- Answer these questions to generate ideas.

How important was the influence?	How long-lasting was the influence? Why?
How did you know that person?	
What was the influence?	Are you happy about the influence? Why?
How did the influence occur?	
When did the influence occur?	

PLANNING: ESTABLISHING AUDIENCE AND PURPOSE

- Use the "Questions for Establishing Audience and Purpose" on page 14 to establish your audience and purpose. Then review the ideas you generated to be sure they suit the audience and purpose you identified.

PLANNING: ORDERING IDEAS

- Develop a scratch outline by numbering the ideas in your list in the order you will write them in your first draft. Remember, you can add and delete ideas as your thinking evolves.

WRITING

- Begin with a topic sentence that names the person and influence—one that is a version of the planning sentence you developed when you filled in the blanks.

(continued on next page)

Tips for Composing Your Paragraph (continued)

- Using your list of numbered ideas as a guide, write through your draft in one sitting. Do not dwell on problems; skip difficult parts and push on for now.

REWRITING: REVISING

- Take a break for a day so you can be more objective when you revise. Take additional breaks whenever you feel the need.

- Check your topic sentence to be sure it includes your topic (the person who influenced you) and your assertion (how that person influenced you).

- Check all your supporting details to be sure each is relevant to your topic and assertion.

- Give your draft to someone with good judgment about writing and ask that person to check to be sure that you backed up all your general statements with specific ones.

- Follow any additional procedures on pages 27–31 that will help you revise.

REWRITING: EDITING

- Before editing, take a break to refresh yourself.

- If you have not already done so, type your draft. Errors may be more apparent in type.

- Edit one separate time for each kind of error you make. Then check for spelling mistakes and any other errors you can find.

- Follow any additional procedures on pages 32–34 that will help you edit.

REWRITING: PROOFREADING

Take a break before copying or typing your paragraph into its final form. Then proofread very slowly to look for typing or copying mistakes.

SUCCEEDING IN COLLEGE

Write Paragraphs across the Curriculum

You will often write paragraph responses to homework assignments and to examination questions in your other classes. You may even write paragraph-length e-mails to your classroom instructors or to your advisor.

When you write these school-related paragraphs, follow the structure explained in this chapter. Begin with a topic sentence that has both a topic and assertion. For homework and examination questions, you will want that topic and assertion to reflect the question you are being asked. Follow the topic sentence with supporting details that are adequate, specific, and relevant. Be sure your details have coherence, and finish with a satisfying closing. Here, for example, is a one-paragraph response to a question on a psychology examination. The parts are labeled as a study aid.

Exam Question: Explain what *shaping* is and tell why it is important.

Shaping is a gradual teaching process that works by rewarding behavior that comes closer and closer to a desired behavior. At first, any behavior that is even remotely close to a desired behavior is rewarded. In the next step, behavior a little bit closer than the previous behavior is rewarded. As the process continues, only behavior that is increasingly closer to the desired behavior is rewarded until finally only the desired behavior is rewarded. Shaping is an important teaching tool because it helps both people and animals learn complicated behaviors that they might otherwise have trouble learning. For example, an animal trainer would use shaping to teach a dog to walk on its back legs. The trainer might first reward the dog for standing on the back legs for a second and then for successively longer periods. Next, the trainer might reward the dog for taking a single step and then reward the dog for taking increasingly more steps. A common expression that represents the principle of shaping is, "You have to crawl before you walk."

Topic sentence reflects question.

Supporting details are adequate, specific, and relevant.

Note the transitions for coherence.

When you write your paragraph responses in your other classes, you can follow the procedures you have learned so far in this book. In particular, try listing the ideas you want to include in the paragraph. Then number those ideas in the order you want to write them. Developing a scratch outline like this can be particularly helpful when you are taking an exam and must write both quickly and completely.

Write about It

Discuss the writing you do in one or more of your other classes. You might consider these questions: What kinds of writing have you been asked to do in your other classes? How much did that writing affect your final grade? Were you able to complete the writing tasks successfully? Why or why not? What have you learned so far in this book that you can apply to writing in your other classes?

CHAPTER 4
Narration

Narration is story-telling. You tell, hear, and read stories often. When you explain to your roommate what happened on your date last night, you tell a story. When your friend writes to you about the minor car accident she was in, you read a story. When you listen to a classmate tell what happened during the third quarter of the football game, you hear a story.

A SAMPLE NARRATIVE PARAGRAPH

Read the following narrative paragraph, written by a student.

Able-bodied but Addle-brained

¹I became very angry the day I saw an able-bodied woman get out of a car she had just parked in a handicapped space. ²Last Thursday I had just gotten out of my car in K-mart's parking lot when a woman in a beat-up Ford Fairlane swerved into a spot clearly marked for handicapped parking. ³She emerged with three children, all under six, and headed for the entrance. ⁴If she had a handicap, I saw no sign of it. ⁵I caught up with her and said, "Excuse me, but you parked in a handicapped spot." ⁶She just looked at me as if I had beamed down from Mars, and then she said that she was handicapped because she had three kids. ⁷That made me furious. ⁸I yelled at her that if she considered her children handicaps, she should be investigated. ⁹Then I told her that I would report her to store security and ask that her car be towed. ¹⁰When I told the security police officer what happened, he said there was nothing he could do because she had not broken a law. ¹¹I was so angry at the insensitive woman that I stormed out of the store without doing my shopping. ¹²If you ask me, any able-bodied person who parks in a handicapped space should have to spend a week in a wheelchair. ¹³I guarantee the person would be more careful about parking after that.

THE TOPIC SENTENCE

In the topic sentence for your narrative paragraph, the topic is the event to be narrated, and the assertion is how you feel about the event. Look again at the topic sentence of "Able-bodied but Addle-brained":

> I became very angry the day I saw an able-bodied woman get out of a car she had just parked in a handicapped space.

The topic (the event to be narrated) is the day the able-bodied woman parked in a handicapped space. The assertion is that it made the writer angry.

One way to express an assertion is to note why the story is important, like this:

> An apartment fire last week that caused the deaths of three children underscores the need for family fire drills.

Mention the event and how you feel about the event or why it is important in your topic sentence.

Here the topic (the event to be narrated) is an apartment fire causing the deaths of three children. The assertion is why it is important to tell the story: It shows the need for family fire drills.

PRACTICE 4.1

The sentences that follow could be topic sentences for narrative paragraphs. Underline the topic (the event to be narrated) once and the writer's assertion opinion about the topic (how the writer feels about the event or why the event is important) twice.

Example:

The day my dog was killed I learned the importance of leash laws.

1. My most frightening experience occurred on a Boy Scout hike.

2. My family witnessed a surprising act of courage when our town flooded after Hurricane Ophelia.

3. The need for gun education was made apparent by the recent accidental shooting of a three-year-old.

4. Mayor Fuentes's block watch program had an unexpected effect on one neighborhood.

5. When my little sister choked on a piece of steak, I learned the importance of mastering the Heimlich maneuver.

6. One of my happiest moments occurred when Dad taught me how to fish.

7. I felt like a hero when the Rayen Tigers won the City Series basketball championship.

8. My first day as a college student was stressful.

9. Getting my ham radio license was the high point of my year.

10. Finding five hundred dollars did not bring me good luck.

PRACTICE 4.2 WORKING TOGETHER

With a classmate, write a topic sentence for a narrative paragraph about each of the subjects given.

Example:

a first experience   *My first summer job was a nightmare.*
_____

1. a childhood memory _____

_____

2. a school experience _____

_____

3. a time spent with a friend _____

_____

4. a holiday celebration _____

_____

5. a time when you were disappointed (or pleasantly surprised)

_____

_____

SUPPORTING DETAILS

Supporting details answer most or all of the journalists' questions.

Supporting details for a narrative paragraph often answer the following questions, known as the **journalists' questions.**

The Journalists' Questions

- **Who** was involved?
- **What** happened?
- **When** did it happen?

- **Where** did it happen?
- **Why** did it happen?
- **How** did it happen?

Notice that the answers to most of these questions make up the supporting details for "Able-bodied but Addle-brained."

- **Who** was involved?
  the writer and a woman

- **What** happened?
  The writer became angry and had a confrontation with a woman who parked in a handicapped space.

- **When** did it happen?
  last Thursday

- **Where** did it happen?
  K-mart's parking lot

- **Why** did it happen?
  The woman was insensitive.

- **How** did it happen?
  This question is not answered. (A narrative paragraph sometimes answers most, but not all, of the questions.)

Order and Transitions

Supporting details in a narrative paragraph are arranged in a **chronological** (time) **order.** This means the details are arranged in the order they occurred, so what happened first is written first, what happened second is written second, and so forth. (Chronological order is also discussed on page 14.) Reread "Able-bodied but Addle-brained" and notice the chronological order.

Transitions can help your reader identify the order of your ideas. The transitions in the chart below signal chronological order. They will probably be very useful, but the other transitions in the chart on pages 67–68 may also help you achieve coherence.

Arrange the supporting details for your narrative paragraph in chronological order.

Transitions for Narration

To Signal Chronological (Time) Order now, then, later, soon, suddenly, next, afterward, earlier, at the same time, meanwhile, often

I explained to Kim why I was upset. *Afterward,* she apologized.

PRACTICE 4.3

We have all had our embarrassing moments. Pick one of yours and assume you will write a paragraph narrating what happened. To develop supporting details, on a separate sheet answer the who? what? when? where? why? and how? questions.

PRACTICE 4.4

To practice arranging details in chronological order, list on a separate sheet the first ten things you did today. Be sure to list the activities in the order they occurred.

Writing Dialogue

When words a person spoke are important to the story, you can reproduce them. For example, "Able-bodied but Addle-brained" includes this dialogue:

> I caught up with her and said, "Excuse me, but you parked in a handicapped spot."

When you reproduce exact spoken or written words, use quotation marks according to the guidelines explained on pages 420–422. When you just mention that something was said, do not use quotation marks, as this example from "Able-bodied but Addle-brained" illustrates:

> I yelled at her that if she considered her children handicaps, she should be investigated.

THE CLOSING

You can end a narrative paragraph any way that provides a satisfying finish. One useful approach is to state or restate the importance of the event or how you feel about the event. Consider again "Able-bodied but Addle-brained." The first closing given below mentions the importance of the event (an able-bodied woman parking in a handicapped space), and the second closing given below, which is the one that appears in the paragraph, mentions how the writer feels about the event.

Closing states the importance of event:

This woman's insensitive behavior shows that we must work to increase sensitivity to the needs of the disabled.

Closing restates how the
writer feels about the event:

If you ask me, any able-bodied
person who parks in a handicapped
space should have to spend a week
in a wheelchair. I guarantee the person would be more careful about
parking after that.

The Structure of a Narrative Paragraph

Topic Sentence
states the event
mentions your feeling about the event or its importance

Supporting Details
answer the journalists' questions
may include dialogue

Closing
may state or restate your feeling about the event or its importance

---

PRACTICE 4.5

Read the following narrative paragraph, written by a student, and answer
the questions after it:

A Deadly Afternoon

¹It was a rainy and miserable afternoon of my senior year in high
school, on May 19 to be exact, when a dramatic incident showed me
what I wanted to do with my life. ²I was walking to my seventh-period
class when I noticed a disturbance in the hallway. ³Tom's girlfriend
had broken up with him, and he was threatening to beat her up. ⁴He
had pinned her against the wall, causing her to tremble violently. ⁵"Let
her go!" I shouted as I grabbed for his arm. ⁶He squinted at me like he
was having trouble focusing, and then he stormed away, muttering,
"I'll make you sorry, both of you." ⁷At that point, the principal showed
up, so I walked away. ⁸Before going to class, I stepped into the bathroom. ⁹Tom was there. ¹⁰At first I was scared, but then I noticed the
blood spreading across his shirt and the knife on the floor. ¹¹At that
instant, Tom sagged to the floor. ¹²His skin had a blue cast, and the

FAQ

Q: How can I make my
story more interesting?

A: You can create interest
with description of a person
or scene and with dialogue.

blood covered his chest. [13]I ran to the door and screamed for help, but I was too late. [14]Tom didn't make it. [15]He was pronounced dead at the hospital. [16]When I learned of his death, I realized how troubled people can be. [17]I decided at that point to major in psychology and become a school counselor to help troubled kids like Tom.

1. What is the topic sentence? The writer's topic? The assertion?

2. Which of the journalists' questions are answered? What are the answers?

3. Are the supporting details adequate? Explain.

4. The writer chooses specific words. For example, instead of saying "afternoon," he says "seventh period." Cite four other examples of specific words.

5. Are all the supporting details relevant to the topic sentence? Explain.

6. Cite three examples of transitions to signal chronological order.

7. Does the author bring the paragraph to a satisfying close? What strategy does the author use for the closing sentence?

✓   Checklist for a Narrative Paragraph

Before submitting your narrative paragraph, be sure to work through this checklist.

☐ 1. I have written a topic sentence that includes the event to be narrated and my assertion about the event.

☐ 2. I have answered all the journalists' questions that need to be answered.

☐ 3. I have checked to be sure that every sentence is relevant to the topic sentence because it advances the story or explains my assertion.

☐ 4. I have used dialogue if it is important to the story and checked pages 420–422 for correct punctuation and capitalization.

☐ 5. I have arranged supporting details in chronological order.

☐ 6. Where needed, I have used transitions and repetition for coherence.

☐ 7. I have written a last sentence that ends the paragraph in a satisfying way.

☐ 8. I have edited the paragraph carefully to find and correct mistakes.

☐ 9. I have proofread the paragraph carefully after copying or typing it into its final form.

WRITING ASSIGNMENTS

For your narrative paragraph, you have a choice of assignments. The topic sentences you drafted for Practice 4.2 may be helpful.

1. Tell a story about a first experience.

2. Narrate a school experience.

3. Tell a story about time spent with a friend.

4. Narrate an account of an event that changed your thinking.

5. Tell a story about a time you were disappointed, angry, or pleasantly surprised.

6. Tell a story about a holiday celebration.

Combine Narration and Description

Narrate a childhood memory. Try to make the narration more vivid for your reader by describing a person or scene involved. For example, if your memory is about the time you took a road trip with your elderly grandfather, you might mention that "his bony fingers, joints swollen with arthritis, gripped the steering wheel." One of the topic sentences you drafted for Practice 4.2 may help you. In addition, see pages 90–92 for now to write descriptive detail.

Respond to a Photograph

In a paragraph, tell the story of what happens immediately after the man's toupee is blown off his head. As an alternative, narrate an account about an embarrassing moment you experienced. If you write about an embarrassing moment, the supporting detail you developed for Practice 4.3 may be helpful.

Writing Process Tips for Composing your Narrative Paragraph

To become a better writer, try out the techniques for planning, writing, and rewriting that you learned in Chapters 1 and 2, so you can discover which ones work best for you. As you compose your narrative paragraph, continue to sample those strategies. In addition, the following procedures may be helpful. No matter what composing strategies you use, however, be sure to work through the Checklist for a Narrative Paragraph on page 84 before submitting your paragraph.

PLANNING: GENERATING IDEAS

- To come up with ideas, try answering the who, what, when, where, why, how questions.

- If you need an early version of your topic sentence, try filling in the blanks in this sentence:

   I will never forget the time _____ because _____.

   Fill in the first blank with the event you are narrating and the second blank with why the event was memorable, how you feel about the event, or why the event is important so you get something like this:

   I will never forget the time I lost my temper with Sara because I learned that I have a problem with anger management.

PLANNING: ESTABLISHING AUDIENCE AND PURPOSE

- To establish your purpose ask yourself why your story matters.

- To establish your audience, ask yourself who would enjoy reading your story or who could learn something from your story.

PLANNING: ORDERING IDEAS

- Because you are telling a story and will arrange your details in time order, make a chronological list of everything that happened.

REWRITING: REVISING

- As you study your draft, look for opportunities to include dialogue. What did people involved in the events have to say? Decide which of those comments are particularly interesting or important to the story because they are the ones you should include as dialogue.

- Does your narration move smoothly from one event to the next? If not, add transitions that show chronological order.

REWRITING: EDITING

- If you have used dialogue, check pages 420–422 to be sure you have capitalized and punctuated correctly.

SUCCEEDING IN COLLEGE

Use Narration across the Curriculum

Narration is an important part of the writing you will do in your other classes. For example, on a history midterm, you might be asked to narrate the events that led to the Confederate defeat at Gettysburg. For a social work internship, you might be asked to write a case study that is a narrative account of the interaction you have with a client.

When you use narration in your other classes, you might also combine it with other patterns you will learn in this book. For example, in a paper for an American history class, you might narrate the events that led up to the Great Depression *and* explain the effects of the Great Depression on banks, using *cause and effect analysis,* which is explained in Chapter 10.

When you write narration in your other classes, you often will need to emphasize the significance of the story. For example, in addition to telling the events that led to the Confederate defeat at Gettysburg, you may also need to note why that battle was so important.

Learn the Conventions and Expectations for Writing in Your Other Classes

Different academic disciplines have different conventions, and different teachers may have different expectations, so learn what is expected of you when you write in your other classes. For example, some instructors may require you to format your papers a particular way. In some disciplines, you should not use *I,* but in others the word is acceptable. If your instructor has not discussed the conventions and expectations for your writing, ask what they are so you are fully informed.

Write about It

Interview three instructors from three different academic disciplines and ask them to describe the conventions and expectations for student writing in their classes. Then write up what you have learned in a paragraph to share with other students in your writing class.

CHAPTER 5
Description

A descriptive paragraph gives your reader a mental picture of a person, object, or scene.

When you write description, you choose words and details to create a mental picture for your reader of a person, object, or scene. Description is important in writing you encounter every day. For example, your biology text may describe the appearance of a cell, and a mail-order catalog may describe the features of the clothing it is selling.

A SAMPLE DESCRIPTIVE PARAGRAPH

The following descriptive paragraph was written by a student. As you read it, notice how carefully words and details were chosen to paint a clear mental picture.

The Plant

[1]The plant I work in five days of every week is extremely depressing. [2]Everywhere I look, there are strips of peeling green paint, revealing the dingy gray underneath. [3]The gloom is highlighted by bright gold sparks welders throw as they fuse cold steel. [4]To the right of my work area, three men (more like robots) hang parts like garments on moving clothesline conveyors. [5]They don't smile, and they don't talk. [6]They just work. [7]Behind the robot-men, hoses swell like arteries as they pump the foul-smelling lacquer paint to sprayers that change dingy gray metal to various colors. [8]To my left, gray metal desks roll down a conveyor toward more robot-men, who wrap them in plastic. [9]As the desks roll by, air tools scream as they drive screws to fasten parts, and giant presses pound, pound, pound as they gobble up steel to transform into useful shapes. [11]Each day I remind myself that I will one day earn my degree, so I do not have to work in this depressing factory.

THE TOPIC SENTENCE

In the topic sentence for your descriptive paragraph, your topic is what you describe; your assertion is your dominant impression of what you are describing. A **dominant impression** is a prominent reaction to what you are describing. Take another look at the topic sentence of "The Plant":

> The plant I work in five days of every week is extremely depressing.

The writer's topic (what is described) is *the plant where the writer works.* The writer's dominant impression of (main reaction to) the plant is that it is *extremely depressing.*

When you shape your topic sentence, keep your topic narrow enough for treatment in one paragraph. It would be difficult, for example, to describe your whole house in one paragraph, but you could describe your bedroom.

Also be sure to express your dominant impression in specific language. Avoid words like *nice, bad, great,* and *awful,* and use more specific alternatives like *peaceful, hectic, exciting,* and *run-down.*

Mention what you are describing and your dominant impression, in your topic sentence.

Your topic should be narrow enough to be treated in one paragraph. Your dominant impression should be expressed in specific language.

PRACTICE 5.1

Write a topic sentence for each of the subjects given. Include what you are describing and your dominant impression. Also, be sure your topic is narrow enough, and be sure your dominant impression is expressed in specific language.

Example:

a campus cafeteria at noon ___ *At noon, the cafeteria in Beeman Hall is hectic.* ___

1. your bedroom _is massy like a tornado has gone trough it_

2. a particular outdoor area on campus _____

3. a kitchen after a five-year-old has made breakfast _looks as neat and clean as a junk yard_

4. a favorite restaurant *[handwritten: my green]* *[handwritten: serves the best]* *[handwritten: toasted]* *[handwritten: smelling bread I've ever had]*

5. your writing classroom _____

_____

SUPPORTING DETAILS

Your descriptive details should be sensory details.

The supporting details for a descriptive paragraph are sensory details. **Sensory details** appeal to one of the five senses (sight, sound, smell, taste, and touch). Most of the details in "The Plant" appeal to sight, but some details appeal to sound ("air tools scream" and "presses pound"), one detail appeals to smell ("foul-smelling lacquer"), and one appeals to touch ("cold steel").

In a descriptive paragraph, use specific nouns, verbs, and modifiers.

For sensory details that create a vivid mental picture; use specific words. The writer of "The Plant" chose specific nouns, verbs, and modifiers like these:

strips of peeling green paint   air tools scream

hoses swell like arteries   gobble up steel

giant presses pound   dingy gray

Now is a good time to review the discussion of specific word choice on page 58.

PRACTICE 5.2 WORKING TOGETHER

With some classmates, write one description that could be used as supporting detail for each topic sentence. Be sure your words are specific. Also, try to appeal to a different sense in each sentence.

Example:

Dan's old car is ready for the junk yard *The tailpipe, eaten away by rust, hangs so low it almost scrapes the ground.*

1. The children's playroom is a disaster area. *[handwritten: The toys are all around the room, some in unimaginable places like the the Barbie hangin on one leg by the curtain hanger.]*

2. The mall on Christmas Eve was festive. _The decoration was marvelous._
Especialy the Christmas tree with all the sparkling
toys and colorful confeties

3. Eleni's backyard is beautifully landscaped. _On the left is a_
small lake with a sculpture of a beautifull _murmaid leaning on_
a roce. On the left is a verry unique chinise type garden

4. The atmosphere of the Paris Café is romantic. _On the walls_
are hanging black and white pictures of old _France._
The lights are red and green with a small vanilla
smell candels on the tables

5. My grandmother's attic is spooky. _____
It is very dark. The only window is dirty and
surrounded with spiders webs. The dusty woodden
floor makes squicky sound on every step I make.

Order and Transitions

A spatial arrangement often works well for descriptive details. With a spatial arrangement, you move from front to back, from top to bottom, from inside to outside, from left to right, or in some other ordered way across space. To help your reader identify the spatial arrangement, use the transitions in the following chart to signal spatial order. In addition, the other transitions in the chart on pages 67–68 can help you achieve coherence.

Use transitions that signal spatial order.

Transitions for Description

To Signal Spatial (Space) Order near, nearby, far, alongside, next to, in front of, to the rear, above, below, over, across, under, around, beyond, beneath, on one side, to the left.

Inside the train station, thousands of commuters scurried to reach their destinations. *Outside,* however, the scene was surprisingly tranquil.

The writer of "The Plant" used transitions to signal spatial order. Some of these are listed here:

<u>To the right of</u> my work area

<u>Behind</u> the robot-men

<u>To my left</u>, gray metal desks

THE CLOSING

You can end a descriptive paragraph any way that provides a satisfying finish. Mentally answering the question, "So what?" Can give you an effective closing because it allows you to state the significance of your description. The closing of "The Plant" takes this approach. After describing how depressing the plant is, the writer asks himself, "So what?" The answer is that the depressing quality of the plant helps him remember why getting his college degree matters, a point he makes in this closing:

Each day I remind myself that I will one day earn my degree, so I do not have to work in this depressing factory.

The Structure of a Descriptive Paragraph

Topic Sentence
states what you will describe
indicates your dominant impression

Supporting Details
appeal to the senses
paint a mental picture
are expressed in specific words

Closing
may state the significance of the description

PRACTICE 5.3

The following descriptive paragraph was written by a student. Notice the specific words and the details that appeal to the senses. Answer the questions after the paragraph to check your understanding.

A View of Winter

[1]The view from the window over my kitchen sink revealed the harsh winter we were enduring. [2]Acres of yellowed field grass lay matted on the frozen ground. [3]Trees that once stood majestically in the

field were now stripped of their colorful foliage. [4]Their naked limbs were straining under the pressure of the winter wind. [5]Row after row of dried corn stubs stood erect, in silent testimony to the tall, productive plants they had once been. [6]To the right, a gray, weather-beaten doghouse lay on its side, unable to protect its Irish setter any longer. [7]Behind the useless doghouse, a child's swing, tossed by the wind, creaked a lonely tune. [8]Overhead, gray, heavy clouds hovered close to the Earth like a shroud covering the lifeless scene. [9]Then suddenly, a gust of wind parted a cloud, and the sun's warmth caressed my face to remind me to take hope. [10]Spring would eventually arrive.

1. What is the topic sentence? According to the topic sentence, what will be described, and what is the dominant impression?

2. What senses are appealed to? Give an example of a description that appeals to each of these senses.

3. Give five examples of specific word choice.

4. Give three examples of transitions to signal spatial order.

5. Are all the supporting details relevant? Explain.

6. Does the paragraph have an effective closing? Explain.

✔ Checklist for a Descriptive Paragraph

Before submitting your descriptive paragraph, be sure to work through this checklist.

☐ 1. I have written a topic sentence that includes what I will describe and my dominant impression.

☐ 2. My topic is narrow enough for one paragraph.

☐ 3. My dominant impression is expressed in specific language.

☐ 4. My supporting details include sensory details and specific nouns, verbs, and modifiers.

☐ 5. I have used enough descriptions to show why I have formed my dominant impression.

☐ 6. I have arranged supporting details in spatial order and used transitions to signal that order.

☐ 7. All my details are related to my topic and dominant impression.

☐ 8. I have written a last sentence that ends the paragraph in a satisfying way.

☐ 9. I have edited the paragraph carefully to find and correct mistakes.

☐ 10. I have proofread the paragraph carefully after copying or typing it into its final form.

FAQ

Q: Can I have too much sensory detail?

A: Too much sensory detail can overwhelm your reader. Balance highly descriptive sentences with less descriptive ones.

WRITING ASSIGNMENTS

For your descriptive paragraph, you have a choice of assignments.

1. Use one of the topic sentences you wrote for Practice 5.1.

2. Describe a place you go when you want to be alone.

3. Describe your favorite nightspot.

4. Describe a place you find unpleasant.

5. Describe the place where you like to study.

6. Describe a scene at a sporting event or other public gathering.

Combine Description and Cause and Effect Analysis

Describe a place that is very important to you and explain why that place is important. When you explain why the place is important, you will be using cause-and-effect analysis, which is explained in Chapter 10.

Respond to a Photograph

Assume you work for a travel agency and are preparing a travel brochure. Write a paragraph describing the scene in the photo. Your goal is to describe the place in a way that will make the readers of the brochure want to visit it. Also, remember to include a topic sentence that conveys the dominant impression.

Writing Process Tips for Composing Your Descriptive Paragraph

   To become a better writer, try out the techniques for planning, writing, and rewriting that you learned in Chapters 1 and 2, so you can discover which ones work best for you. As you compose your descriptive paragraph, continue to sample those strategies. In addition, the following procedures may be helpful. No matter what composing strategies you use, however, be sure to work through the Checklist for a Descriptive Paragraph on page 93 before submitting your paragraph.

PLANNING: MOVING FROM SUBJECT TO TOPIC

- Describe a place that you can visit today or tomorrow. Description is easier to write if you can work from firsthand sensory impressions rather than from memory.

- Go to the place, stay there for a while, and decide how it makes you feel. That feeling can be your dominant impression.

PLANNING: GENERATING IDEAS

- At the place you are describing, make a list of specific details that relate to your dominant impression. Do not worry about getting the specific sensory language exactly right at this point. You can write "smelled bad" for now and later revise it to a more specific "smelled like a six-month accumulation of stale cigar smoke."

WRITING

- Begin with a topic sentence that mentions both the place you are describing and your dominant impression.

- As you draft, just the right sensory language may not come to you. Do not worry; get your descriptions down the best way you can, knowing you can revise later.

REWRITING: REVISING

- Circle general words and any descriptions you want to improve. Try to revise some of them to specific ones and add sensory language.

- Rewrite sensory language in stages. For example, your draft may include this sentence, "The room smelled bad." Next, you might revise it to "The room smelled like cigar smoke." Then you might rework it to get, "The room smelled like a six-month accumulation of stale cigar smoke." Finally, you might revise that sentence to "The paneled pool room smelled like a six-month accumulation of stale cigar smoke."

Use Description across the Curriculum

You may be surprised at how often you use description in your other classes. In a music appreciation class, you may be asked to describe the melodies of various musical compositions, or in an art history class, you may be asked to describe the distinguishing features of a Renaissance painting. In an advertising class, you may need to describe magazine advertisements to point out their persuasive strategies, or in a biology class, you may need to describe something you view under a microscope.

Make a Schedule

Writing tasks you have for your other classes will be more manageable if you make a schedule. Some of your writing assignments will require longer papers, and most certainly you will need to complete those assignments at the same time you complete other course requirements. A schedule will keep you organized and allow you to break large tasks down into manageable chunks. For example, if your history paper on the rise of labor unions is due in two weeks, you can schedule your work something like this:

- Monday—Review relevant chapters in textbook.
- Tuesday and Wednesday—Find and read three articles in the library.
- Thursday—Generate ideas.
- Friday and Saturday—Outline and write a rough draft.
- Sunday—Let draft cool.
- Monday—Revise draft.
- Tuesday—Ask three classmates to read and react to the revision.
- Wednesday and Thursday—Revise again.
- Friday—Let draft cool.
- Saturday—Revise and edit final draft.
- Sunday—Proofread.

Write about It

The next time you have a writing assignment, in this class or another, make a schedule for it. After you complete the writing assignment, write a paragraph that explains whether or not you found the schedule helpful and why.

CHAPTER 6

Illustration

Writers and speakers often use examples to make their points clear. Consider this conversation between Bob and Julio:

Bob: The food in this cafeteria stinks.

Julio: What do you mean?

Bob: The meat is always rubbery, the mashed potatoes are cold, and the Jell-O is warm.

To explain what he meant, Bob gave examples: rubbery meat, cold potatoes, and warm Jell-O. Another name for an example is an **illustration**. A paragraph with supporting details made up of examples is an **illustration paragraph**.

A SAMPLE ILLUSTRATION PARAGRAPH

The following illustration paragraph was written by a student.

With My Head in the Clouds

¹As someone who is 6 feet 9 inches tall, I speak with authority when I say that the world is not set up for tall people. ²For example, everything that is supposed to be high is too low. ³Not long ago I was home for dinner with my parents. ⁴As I stood up from the table to go into the kitchen, I slammed my head into the chandelier, causing the lights to sway wildly and my head to throb annoyingly for hours. ⁵Each time I enter a room, I must duck to avoid hitting my head on a door frame. ⁶Beds are also not made with the very tall in mind. ⁷I do not fit in a standard size bed, so I have to sleep diagonally across a double bed to keep my feet from dangling off the end. ⁸Cars are an even bigger problem. ⁹I have to recline my seat and push it back to keep my

head from scraping the ceiling. [10]Because this is so uncomfortable and a little bit dangerous, I often drive with the sunroof open so I can keep the seat in a proper position. [11]Of course, there is still the problem of getting into the car. [12]I will smash my head if I forget to fold myself over like an envelope. [13]Most people think that height has its advantages, but on most days, I do not see them.

THE TOPIC SENTENCE

Your topic sentence gives a general statement that will be supported with examples.

The topic sentence for your illustration paragraph is the general statement that will be explained or clarified with examples. It includes both a topic and your assertion about the topic. Consider this topic sentence from "With My Head in the Clouds":

> As someone who is 6 feet 9 inches tall, I speak with authority when I say that the world is not set up for tall people.

The writer's topic is tall people. The writer's assertion is that the world is not set up for them. The examples in the rest of the paragraph show how the world is not geared for tall people.

PRACTICE 6.1

Write a topic sentence that could be developed with examples for each of the subjects given. Be sure to include a topic and assertion.

Example:

surprise parties   *Surprise parties rarely go as planned.*

1. taking tests in school   *80% of the students hate taking tests*

2. first impressions   *is very important " says my mom*

3. waiting in a doctor's office   *can make you sick About 30% of the people get ...*

4. reality television   *in not for every one*

5. fast food restaurants _____

_____

◾

SUPPORTING DETAILS

Examples that explain or prove the topic sentence make up the supporting detail for your illustration paragraph. Look again at "With My Head in the Clouds." This topic sentence idea will be explained or proven with examples:

… the world is not set up for tall people.

The supporting details include these examples:

Everything that is supposed to be high is too low.

Beds are too small.

Cars are too small.

Notice, however, that the writer does more than *give* examples—he *explains* them.

Example	Explanation
Everything that is supposed to be high is too low.	hit head on chandelier; must duck entering a room
Beds are too small.	must sleep diagonally
Cars are an even bigger problem.	must recline and push back seat; drives with sunroof open; must fold himself to get into the car

"With My Head in the Clouds" also shows that details that explain an example can be descriptive details. The author hit the chandelier,

… causing the lights to sway wildly and my head to throb annoyingly for hours.

As the paragraph demonstrates, specific nouns, verbs, and modifiers contribute to adequate detail:

For adequate detail, use enough examples, and explain your examples.

I *slammed* my head…

I have to sleep *diagonally* across a *double bed* to keep my feet from *dangling* off the end.

I will *smash* my head if I forget to *fold myself over like an envelope.*

To have adequate detail, use enough examples to explain or prove your topic sentence. In one paragraph, three examples can be enough. If they are highly detailed, two examples may be enough.

Order and Transitions

You can arrange examples in an emphatic or chronological order.

Placing your examples in emphatic order is often effective. This way, you save your strongest example for last. (See page 16 on emphatic order.) The examples in "With My Head in the Clouds" are in emphatic order. The clue to this is that the last set of examples is introduced with the words "an even bigger problem." If your examples occurred in a particular time order, you can arrange them in chronological order (discussed on page 14).

When you write an illustration paragraph the transitions in the chart below will help you achieve coherence. In particular, three kinds of transitions may be helpful: transitions that signal illustration, transitions that signal addition, and transitions that signal emphatic order. In addition, use transitions to signal chronological order if your examples occurred in a particular time sequence.

Transitions for Illustration

To Signal Addition also, and, and then, in addition, too, the next, furthermore, further, moreover, equally important, another, first, second, third

> The children hid from the babysitter at bedtime. *Another example* of their bad behavior occurred when they hid her car keys.

To Signal Illustration for example, for instance, an illustration of this, to illustrate

> Juan's math teacher is too easy. *For instance*, she has not assigned homework for at least a month.

To Signal Emphatic Order more important, most important, most of all, best of all, of greatest importance, least of all, even better, the best (worst) case (example, instance, time)

> Louise is often thoughtless. *One of the worst cases* of her thoughtlessness occurred when she did not pick up her six-year-old sister at school because she wanted to finish watching her soap opera.

To Signal Chronological (Time) Order now, then, later, soon, suddenly, next, afterward, earlier, at the same time, meanwhile, often

> Carlo is unusually generous. *First*, he gave a large donation to the food bank. *Then*, he invited a homeless family to Thanksgiving dinner.

PRACTICE 6.2 WORKING TOGETHER

Complete this practice with some classmates. Under each topic sentence, list three examples that can be used for supporting details.

Example:

Ms. Lyons did more work than the average fifth-grade teacher.

She took her class camping to collect leaf specimens.

She visited a sick student at home to tutor her.

She skips lunch to grade papers.

1. Stress is a part of a college student's life.

   Stress aroud the midterms.

   Stress on the finals.

   Every student is stressed when is waiting for the resuers

2. Living alone can be difficult.

   Your are more vulnarable at home.

   You must pay the whole rent.

   You have to do All the housework

3. Elderly people can be dangerous drivers.

   They can't see as well.

   Their reactions are slower.

   _____

4. Parents sometimes take children where they do not belong.

   The take them to movies that are rated

   _____

   _____

5. Advertisements cause people to want products they do not need.

   A good ad can make you buy everything

   _____

   _____

PRACTICE 6.3

Reread "With My Head in the Clouds" on pages 97–98. Notice that most of the examples are introduced with a transition. On a separate sheet, list the transitions that introduce examples and tell what each signals.

THE CLOSING

Any approach that gives your illustration paragraph a satisfying finish is acceptable. One approach is to refer to the topic and assertion in your topic sentence. Another way is to mention an idea related to your topic sentence. Finally, you can close by both referring to the topic sentence and mentioning a related idea, the way the writer of "With My Head in the Clouds" does. Here are examples using the topic sentence from "With My Head in the Clouds":

topic sentence:	As someone who is 6 feet 9 inches tall, I speak with authority when I say that the world is not set up for tall people.
closing that refers to topic sentence:	Frequent problems like these demonstrate that the world is not a comfortable place for people of height.
closing that mentions a related idea:	Ironically, people think height has advantages because they do not realize the daily struggles it creates.
closing refers to the topic sentence and mentions a related idea:	Most people think that height has its advantages, but on most days I do not see them.

The Structure of an Illustration Paragraph

Topic Sentence
states what will be explained or clarified

Supporting Details
are examples
include details that explain the examples

Closing
may refer to the topic sentence
may mention a related idea

PRACTICE 6.4

The illustration paragraph that follows is a revision of a piece written by a student. Read it and answer the questions to test your understanding.

One Step Forward and Two Steps Back

[1]Americans are proud of their technological advancements, but technology often comes with a price. [2]Consider the cell phone, for example. [3]Yes, it gives us freedom to move around. [4]However, more often than not, these phones cross frequencies with other phones so that we hear other people's conversations, and they hear ours. [5]What we gain in mobility we lose in privacy. [6]We also lose clear conversations, for these phones snap, crackle, and pop more than most breakfast cereals. [7]The Internet is another example. [8]It offers computer users almost limitless access to a staggering amount of information. [9]However, users are so glued to their computer screens day and night that they no longer have a life away from their PCs. [10]Once on the information highway, people become so obsessed that they do not take the exit ramp. [11]Another example, one that I read about, concerns the computer-designed magnesium wheels General Motors put on its cars not too long ago. [12]Thanks to a computer error, the tire seals did not fit properly. [13]As a result, thousands of car owners woke up to discover that their brand new cars had flat tires. [14]Certainly, technological advances make life easier, but they are not without their problems.

1. What is the topic sentence of "One Step Forward and Two Steps Back"? What is the writer's topic and assertion?

2. How many examples does the writer use?

3. Are the supporting details adequate? Explain.

4. Are all the supporting details relevant? Explain.

5. List the transitions that introduce examples and tell what they signal.

6. Does the paragraph have a satisfying closing? Explain.

Note: The essay version of "One Step Forward and Two Steps Back" is in Chapter 13.

✓   **Checklist for an Illustration Paragraph**

Before submitting your illustration paragraph, be sure to work through this checklist.

☐ 1. I have written a topic sentence that presents a topic and assertion.

(continued on next page)

☐ 2. I have enough examples written in enough detail to explain or prove the topic sentence.

☐ 3. I have used specific nouns, verbs, and modifiers.

☐ 4. I have explained examples with specific information.

☐ 5. I have arranged supporting details in an emphatic, chronological, or other suitable order and used transitions to signal that order.

☐ 6. All my examples are related to my topic and assertion.

☐ 7. I have written a last sentence that ends the paragraph in a satisfying way.

☐ 8. I have edited the paragraph carefully to find and correct mistakes.

☐ 9. I have proofread the paragraph carefully after copying or typing it into its final form.

WRITING ASSIGNMENTS

You have a choice of assignments for an illustration paragraph.

1. Use a version of one of the topic sentences from Practice 6.1.

2. Use a version of one of the topic sentences from Practice 6.2. If you like, you can use some or all of the examples you generated for that exercise.

3. Use examples to illustrate that high school did (or did not) prepare you for college.

4. Use examples to illustrate that things are not always what they seem.

5. Use examples to show that little white lies are helpful (or harmful).

6. Use examples to show that cell phones are a nuisance (or a convenience).

Combine Illustration and Description

Use examples to illustrate one personality trait of someone you know. First, pick a person, such as a friend, a coworker, a relative, or a neighbor. Then decide on a personality trait that you can illustrate with examples, such as *greedy*, *generous*, *optimistic*, *ambitious*, *cooperative*, or *lazy*. Try to make the illustrations more vivid for your reader by including some description. For example, if you illustrate that your best friend is generous with an example of the time she lent you her heirloom earrings, you can describe what the earrings looked like or describe the friend's smile when she handed them to you.

Respond to an Advertisement

People buy cars for many reasons. Sometimes we choose cars because they help us project a particular image. For example, what kind of image do people

Land Shark.

who buy the car in this advertisement project? Use examples to illustrate the fact that certain products help us to project certain images. For ideas, browse through magazines and look at the advertisements.

Writing Process Tips for Composing Your Illustration Paragraph

To become a better writer, try out the techniques for planning, writing, and rewriting that you learned in Chapters 1 and 2, so you can discover which ones work best for you. As you compose your illustration paragraph, continue to sample those strategies. In addition, the following procedures may be helpful. No matter what composing strategies you use, however, be sure to work through the Checklist for an Illustration Paragraph on pages 103–104 before submitting your paragraph.

PLANNING: MOVING FROM SUBJECT TO TOPIC

Pick a writing topic that allows you to draw examples from your own experience or observation. You should not make up examples.

PLANNING: GENERATING IDEAS

- List all the examples that occur to you without evaluating how good those examples are.

- Take a break and return to your list. This time, cross out any examples that you do not want to include, and add any new examples that occur to you.

(continued on next page)

FAO

Q: Why can't I make up examples?

A: Real examples are easier to write about because they are authentic and specific.

- Place each example at the top of a column. Write ideas for details to develop each example in the appropriate column.

PLANNING: ORDERING IDEAS

Number the ideas in your list in the order you will write them in your first draft, so you have a scratch outline. If you are unsure what order to use, try an emphatic order.

REWRITING: REVISING

Is each example explained? If not, add that explanation now. Will adding some description improve the paragraph?

SUCCEEDING IN COLLEGE

Use Illustration across the Curriculum

Because examples are so important for clarifying points, you will use illustration often in all of your college writing. For example, in a research paper about alternative schools for an education class, you could cite examples of successful and unsuccessful charter schools. A midterm exam in a business class might ask you to explain and illustrate three kinds of management techniques, and an examination in a literature class might ask you to define and give examples of *irony*.

Notice Examples during Note-Taking and Highlighting

When your instructor says, "for example," "for instance," or "such as," you know one or more clarifying examples are being presented. If you are confident you understand the concept being illustrated, you do not need to take detailed notes on the examples; instead, jot down a key word or two that will remind you of the example when you review your notes.

If a long example is given, listen carefully and summarize that example more briefly.

If you like to highlight your textbooks as a study aid, you should also look for examples. If an example seems particularly important for some reason, or if you need the example to help you understand or remember the point being illustrated, then highlight it. Otherwise, you do not need to highlight examples. If a long example seems important, consider summarizing it in the margin rather than highlighting long paragraphs.

Keep in mind that examination questions may call upon you to give examples of important concepts, so even if you do not highlight them or include them in your lecture notes, you should be prepared to supply examples as supporting detail for answers to exam questions.

Write about It

Select a textbook chapter for another course you are taking or have taken. Read the chapter and count the number of examples. Then write a paragraph explaining how examples are used in the chapter, how important they are, whether or not they help you understand the important material in the chapter, and why.

CHAPTER 7
Process Analysis

A **process analysis** explains how something is made, how something is done, or how something works. Some process analyses explain procedures readers will never perform. For example, a biology textbook explains how plants turn carbon dioxide into oxygen, a pamphlet available to bank customers explains how mortgage loan rates are determined, and a magazine article explains how the Internet works. Other process analyses explain procedures readers can or might perform. For example, a recipe explains how to make burritos, instructions packaged with a toy tell how to assemble it, and a fitness magazine explains how to get a good workout in thirty minutes a day.

> A process analysis explains how something is made or done, or how something works.

A SAMPLE PROCESS ANALYSIS

This process analysis is a revision of a piece written by a student.

Making Money with a Garage Sale

[1]If you plan it right, you can make a great deal of money from a garage sale. [2]First, you must gather all the salable items collecting dust in your basement and attic. [3]Do not include anything badly broken, but keep everything else. [4]The items you think are the most worthless are likely to be the first to sell. [5]Toys and tools are hot sellers, but clothes (unless they are children's) probably will not sell very well. [6]Next—and this is very important—clean this junk up. [7]Dirty items will not sell, but you will be surprised at the weird stuff that goes if it is clean.

[8]Once your items are clean, it is important to display them properly, so get lots of tables, even if you have to rent them. [9]Arrange everything attractively, trying to keep housewares together, toys together, and so forth. [10]Now for the most important part, pricing. [11]I have just

three words of advice: cheap! cheap! cheap! [12]Remember, this trash has been in your basement collecting spider eggs for the past five years, so do not get greedy. [13]Price it to move because the last thing you want to do is drag this stuff back in the house because it did not sell. [14]If you really want a great sale, advertise. [15]Put signs up and place an ad in the classifieds. [16]Finally, pamper your customers by providing grocery bags for carrying those marvelous purchases home in, and by serving coffee—for twenty-five cents a cup, of course. [17]Believe me, follow this advice, and you can turn your unwanted items into extra cash.

THE TOPIC SENTENCE

Mention the process that will be explained and why the reader should understand the process in your topic sentence.

The topic sentence for a process analysis includes the topic and your assertion about the topic. The topic is the process. The assertion can explain why you think the reader should understand the process. Look again at the topic sentence of "Making Money with a Garage Sale":

> If you plan it right, you can make a great deal of money from a garage sale.

In this case, the topic (process to be explained) is having a garage sale. The assertion about the topic (why the reader should understand the process) is that, with the right planning, there is money to be made.

PRACTICE 7.1

For each topic sentence, tell the process to be explained and why the reader should understand the process.

Example:

If you want to keep your sanity, select your classes the way I do.

Process *selecting classes (selecting the way the author does)*

Reason to understand process *to keep sanity*

1. To get the best value for your money, shop carefully for a used car.

Process _____

Reason to understand process _____

2. In order to survive, every babysitter should know how to handle children who act like monsters.

Process _____

Reason to understand process _____

3. To move up the corporate ladder, you must learn how to network.

Process _____

Reason to understand process _____

4. College students must learn how to relax so the pressures of studying do not overwhelm them.

Process _____

Reason to understand process _____

5. To have a successful garden, you must plan carefully.

Process _____

Reason to understand process _____

SUPPORTING DETAILS

The supporting details for your process analysis are the steps in the process. Look back at "Making Money with a Garage Sale" to see that the supporting details are everything a person must do—all the steps a person must perform—in order to have a profitable garage sale.

If the reason for a step is not obvious, you can explain why it is performed. For example, in "Making Money with a Garage Sale," the writer explains the importance of cleaning items: "Dirty items will not sell." Explaining why a step is performed can emphasize its importance, especially if you fear your reader might skip it or perform it hastily.

If the proper way to perform a step is not clear, you should explain. Notice that in "Making Money with a Garage Sale," the writer explains how to display items properly: Use lots of tables, arrange things attractively, and keep similar things together.

Supporting details for a process analysis are the steps performed. Sometimes you must also explain what is *not* done, how to perform a step, or why to perform a step.

Order and Transitions

The supporting details are usually arranged in chronological order.

Since the steps in a process are usually given in the order they are performed, supporting details for a process analysis are most often arranged in a chronological (time) order. To signal that order, use the transitions in the following chart. In addition, the transitions on pages 67–68 may also be useful.

Transitions for Process Analysis

To Signal Chronological (Time) Order now, then, later, soon, suddenly, next, afterward, earlier, at the same time, meanwhile, often

Unpack the carton and make sure no parts are missing. *Next,* read through the directions from start to finish to be sure you understand them.

Notice that in "Making Money with a Garage Sale," the writer uses several transitions to signal chronological order.

First, you must gather …

Next—and this is very important …

Now for the most important part …

Finally, pamper your customers.

PRACTICE 7.2 WORKING TOGETHER

With some classmates, pick three of the following processes. On a separate sheet, list the steps performed in each.

1. checking a book out of your campus library

2. picking an advisor

3. registering for classes

4. buying a used car

5. planning a party

6. failing an exam (be humorous)

7. Christmas shopping at the last minute

8. editing

9. interviewing for a job

10. using a search engine

FAQ

Q: Some steps are obvious. Should I leave them out?

A: You can omit steps your reader will certainly know to perform. In a recipe, for example, you need not say to plug in the mixer.

THE CLOSING

If your topic sentence already states the reason your reader should understand the process, your closing can restate that idea, the way the writer of "Making Money with a Garage Sale" does:

topic sentence states why the reader should understand the process:	If you plan it right, you can make a great deal of money from a garage sale.
closing restates:	Believe me, follow this advice, and you can turn your unwanted items into extra cash.

The Structure of a Process Analysis Paragraph

Topic Sentence
gives the process that will be explained
may indicate why the reader should understand the process

Supporting Details
give the steps in the process
may explain how to perform the steps
may mention what *not* to do

Closing
may state or restate why the reader should understand the process

---

PRACTICE 7.3

Study the following paragraph written by a student and answer the questions.

Avoiding the "Freshman 15"

¹If you follow my advice, you can avoid gaining the dreaded "freshman 15"—the 15 pounds college students often pack on before their sophomore year. ²First, make wise food choices. ³The cafeteria is a mine field, so watch where you step. ⁴That crusty macaroni and cheese, pepperoni-packed pizza, cheesy pasta, and Belgium waffle topped with a "dollop" of whipped cream the size of Rhode Island will pack on the pounds before your first midterms. ⁵Choose, instead, a big

chef salad, chicken breast, or bowl of shredded wheat with a side of banana. ⁶If you are often in a hurry and need to grab and go, keep a supply of energy bars, wheat crackers, and apples around. ⁷No matter what, don't skip meals because you will only eat more later. ⁸If you snack when you study, skip the Doritos and try some popcorn instead. ⁹You'll save a ton of calories and avoid gaining almost as much weight. ¹⁰Second, drink wisely. ¹¹Always have a bottle of water in your backpack because drinking water will help you feel full. ¹²And watch that beer consumption. ¹³Too much drinking is never a good idea, but for an occasional brew with friends, try a light beer—you'll get used to the taste, honest. ¹⁴Soda can be a calorie nightmare, so go for the water instead. ¹⁵Finally, exercise every day. ¹⁶You have many choices on campus. ¹⁷You can walk, join an intramural sports team, work out in the student recreation center, or swim in the campus pool. ¹⁸If you lack motivation, ask, beg, or bribe a friend to join you. ¹⁹The freshman 15 may be common, but it doesn't have to be inevitable.

1. What is the topic sentence? What process will be analyzed? Why is it important to understand the process?

2. Which sentences explain how to perform a step in the process?

3. Which sentences explain why to perform a step?

4. Which sentences explain what *not* to do?

5. The details are not arranged in chronological order. Why?

6. Are the steps in the process clearly explained? How do you know?

7. Are all the supporting details relevant to the topic sentence? Explain.

8. Cite three examples of specific word choice.

9. Does the paragraph have a satisfying closing? Explain.

✔ Checklist for a Process Analysis Paragraph

Before submitting your process analysis paragraph, be sure to work through this checklist.

- ☐ 1. I have written a topic sentence that mentions the process and why the reader should understand the process.

- ☐ 2. I have included every important step in the process.

- ☐ 3. Where necessary, I have explained how or why steps are performed.

- ☐ 4. Where necessary, I have explained what *not* to do.

☐ 5. I have arranged supporting details in chronological or other suitable order.

☐ 6. Where needed, I have used transitions and repetition for coherence.

☐ 7. I have written details that are relevant to my topic and assertion.

☐ 8. I have written a closing that ends the paragraph in a satisfying way.

☐ 9. I have edited the paragraph carefully to find and correct mistakes.

☐ 10. I have proofread the paragraph carefully after copying or typing it into its final form.

WRITING ASSIGNMENTS

For your process analysis, you have a choice of assignments.

1. Use one of the processes in Practice 7.2. For three of these, you have already listed steps performed.

2. Use one of the topic sentences in Practice 7.1.

3. Pick something you do well and explain that process.

4. Explain how to relax.

5. Explain how to choose a great birthday gift.

6. Explain how to apologize.

Combine Process Analysis and Illustration

People often behave badly in movie theaters, making it difficult for others to enjoy themselves. Explain a process for dealing with such behavior. Include examples of the kinds of bad behavior you are dealing with (such as seat kicking) and show how the steps in the process can deal with the behavior, something like this:

> When you confront people behaving badly, try not to be confrontational. For example, if someone sitting behind you is kicking your seat, do not turn around and flash a dirty look. Instead, smile and say, "I'm sure you don't realize it, but you are kicking my seat."

Respond to a Photograph

To succeed in college and be happy, students must know many processes. The photograph on the next page depicts three of those processes: how to make friends, how to study, and how to interact with diverse people. In a paragraph suitable for inclusion in a student handbook, explain one of those processes, or another process that first-year college students should know.

Writing Process Tips for Composing Your Process Analysis Paragraph

FAQ

Q: How can I be sure I included all the important steps?

A: Give your process analysis to a reader you trust and ask that person to perform the process. If he or she cannot perform it successfully, revise. If the process analysis is not meant to be performed, ask whether your reader understands the process completely.

To become a better writer, try out the techniques for planning, writing, and rewriting that you learned in Chapters 1 and 2, so you can discover which ones work best for you. As you compose your process analysis, continue to sample those strategies. In addition, the following procedures may be helpful. No matter what composing strategies you use, however, be sure to work through the Checklist for a Process Analysis Paragraph on pages 112–113 before submitting your paragraph.

PLANNING: MOVING FROM SUBJECT TO TOPIC

- Pick a process that you have performed successfully, so you are sure of the steps.

PLANNING: GENERATING IDEAS

- List every step in the process.

REWRITING: REVISING

- Answering these questions can help you decide whether to add supporting details:

  Should I explain how to perform any steps?

  Should I explain why any steps should be performed?

  Is there anything I should caution my reader *not* to do?

Use Process Analysis across the Curriculum

Process analysis is important in college writing because you must often learn how something works or how something is done. For example, in a paper for an economics class, you might have to explain how a market economy works. In a homework assignment for a nursing class, you might have to explain how to take a patient's blood pressure. For a psychology exam, you might have to explain how positive and negative reinforcement work, and for a linguistics exam, you might have to explain how words change meaning.

Assess Your Learning Style

Like the writing process, the learning process varies from person to person so that individuals must discover their own best procedures. The procedures that work best for you will depend upon your learning style.

- **Visual learners** do best when they *see* what they are learning. They prefer to read information, watch videos, and see demonstrations. Thus, a visual learner would rather read a textbook than listen to a lecture.

- **Auditory learners** do best when they *hear* what they are learning. They prefer to read out loud, listen to CDs, and hear explanations. Thus, a visual learner would rather listen to a lecture than read a textbook.

- **Tactile learners** do best when they have their hands on something or when they are doing something. They prefer to work at the computer, build a model, or create a chart. Thus, a tactile learner would rather use flash cards than read or hear a lecture.

If you do not know what kind of learner you are, visit your campus learning lab or counseling center and complete a simple questionnaire to find out and to discover a learning process that works best for you.

Write about It

In a paragraph, explain what kind of learner you think you are: visual, auditory, or tactile. Also explain why you think you are that kind of learner.

CHAPTER 8
Definition

A definition explains the significance of a term, your opinion about the term, or your personal meaning of the term.

Y ou are no doubt familiar with dictionary definitions that explain the meanings of words. However, in this chapter you will learn to write a different kind of **definition**, one that goes beyond the dictionary definition to explain your opinion about the term, the significance of the term, or your personal meaning of a term. For example, you can look up *electoral college* in the dictionary and read a definition of what it is, but in a definition paragraph, you might not only tell what it is but explain how it affects the way candidates campaign. Similarly, if you wrote a paragraph definition of *stress*, you might define stress from a college student's point of view.

A SAMPLE DEFINITION PARAGRAPH

The following definition paragraph was written by a student.

The Crazed Coupon Clipper

[1]The crazed coupon clipper is a fanatic. [2]Fired up at the prospect of saving a few quarters, this species accumulates hundreds, even thousands, of cents-off coupons. [3]Strangely though, it does not even matter if the clipper can use the products the coupons are good for. [4]My father has been a crazed clipper for years. [5]His coupon envelope marked "pets" is so fat with coupons for dog biscuits, cat food, and flea collars you would think we had dozens of cats and dogs running around. [6]The funny thing is, we have not owned a dog, cat, or any other four-legged animal since I was born. [7]While the clipper may appear to be organized (having coupons arranged alphabetically in labeled envelopes), do not be fooled—every crazed clipper has grocery bags,

shoe boxes, and crates hidden at the back of the closet with unfiled, largely expired coupons jammed in. [8]The clipper is harmless for the most part; however, the species can be dangerous when turned loose in a market that offers double-coupon savings. [9]Stay out of these places, for dozens of crazed clippers will be there with glazed eyes and fistsful of coupons. [10]So ecstatic are they at the prospect of doubling their savings that they race their carts frantically about, snatching products in a savings frenzy. [11]More than once, normal shoppers have been run over by clippers crazed by the thought of saving twice as much. [12]So beware! [13]If ever you open your newspaper only to find rectangular holes where the news used to be, you no doubt have a crazed coupon clipper under your roof.

THE TOPIC SENTENCE

The topic sentence for your definition paragraph includes the term being defined (this is your topic) and a main characteristic of what is being defined (this is your assertion about the topic). Take another look at the topic sentence of "The Crazed Coupon Clipper":

> The crazed coupon clipper is a fanatic.

The writer's topic is the *coupon clipper*; this is the term to be defined. The main characteristic of the coupon clipper is that he or she is a *fanatic*; this is the writer's assertion about the topic.

> The topic sentence includes the term being defined and a main characteristic of the term in your topic sentence.

PRACTICE 8.1

Write topic sentences for paragraphs defining each of the terms given. Be sure to mention a main characteristic of what you are defining.

Example: Optimism *Optimism is the ability to think positively even when*

things look the worst.

1. the exercise fanatic _____

_____

2. exam anxiety _____

_____

3. courage _____

_____

4. a jerk _____

_____

5. a good sport _____

_____

■

SUPPORTING DETAILS

Your supporting details develop the characteristic of the term being defined.

Your supporting details explain the characteristic of the term. Description is often helpful with this explanation. Notice, for example, that "The Crazed Coupon Clipper" includes description to show what clippers are like in a store that offers double coupon savings:

> … they race their carts frantically about, snatching products in a savings frenzy.

Your supporting details may include description and examples.

Examples can also help explain the characteristic. In sentences 3–6 of "The Crazed Coupon Clipper," the writer's father illustrates the fact that the clipper clips coupons for products that are not used.

Our supporting details may mention what something is not.

If your audience has a misconception about what you are defining, you may explain what something is *not*. For example, when defining *patriotism*, you may explain that patriotism is *not* a blind love of every aspect of a country. After this explanation, you can go on to explain what patriotism *is*: loving a country while disliking its faults and trying to correct them. Look back at sentence 7 of "The Crazed Coupon Clipper," and notice that the writer explains that the clipper is not organized.

Do not write a definition that sounds like it came from a dictionary, and do not state the obvious or use a term in its own definition.

Try not to write a definition that sounds as if it really came from a dictionary. For example, if you are defining *freedom*, avoid saying "Freedom is the state of being at liberty or free of confinement." The definition should be in your personal writing style. Also, avoid stating the obvious. For example, if you are defining *situation comedy*, do not say that it is a kind of television program. Finally, do not use a term in its own definition. If you are defining a *floppy disk*, do not say. "A floppy disk is a disk that…." Instead, say, "A floppy disk is a device that…."

Order and Transitions

You can arrange your supporting details in an emphatic order by giving the characteristics of your term from the least significant to the most significant. If you use examples, these can also be arranged in an emphatic order. To achieve coherence, use the transitions in the chart on pages 67–68. In particular, you may want to use transitions to signal emphatic order. If you include examples, you can use transitions that signal illustration, and if you explain what your term is *not*, you may need a transition of contrast.

Transitions for Definiton

To Signal Emphatic Order more important, most important, most of all, best of all, of greatest importance, least of all, even better, the best (worst) case (example, instance, time)

> Fear of public speaking can affect a person's ability to perform well in school and on the job. *More important*, it can undermine a person's self-confidence.

To Signal Illustration for example, for instance, an illustration of this is, to illustrate

> A football fanatic is completely obsessed. *For example*, my brother, a classic football fanatic, was found listening to the Baltimore Colts during his wedding reception.

To Signal Contrast (Differences) but, yet, still, however, in contrast, on the other hand, nevertheless

> Some people think that depression is a mood a person can "snap out of." *However*, without medication, a person can be helpless to overcome it.

PRACTICE 8.2: WORKING TOGETHER

Complete this practice with some classmates. Assume you are writing a definition paragraph with this topic sentence:

> Writer's block is the curse of the writing student.

1. List three ideas that could be used for supporting details. (If you are stuck for ideas, try brainstorming, clustering, or freewriting.)

   _____

   _____

   _____

2. List an example that could be used to develop one of the ideas you wrote

   for number 1. _____

   _____

3. List three details that could be included in a description of a student with

   writer's block. _____

FAQ

Q: Can I include a dictionary definition?

A: Readers can go to the dictionary if they want to; you should give them something they cannot get there: your own thoughts on what the term means.

_____

_____

4. Mention something that writer's block is *not*. _____

_____

THE CLOSING

Any approach that provides a satisfying finish is appropriate. One approach is to refer to your topic sentence. Here is an example using the closing from "The Crazed Coupon Clipper":

topic sentence:

The crazed coupon clipper is a fanatic.

closing that refers to the topic sentence:

If ever you open your newspaper only to find rectangular holes where the news used to be, you no doubt have a crazed coupon clipper under your roof.

Another way is to explain the importance of the term being defined, especially if that was not done elsewhere in your paragraph. Here is an example that could close "The Crazed Coupon Clipper":

closing that explains the importance of the term:

Some may go overboard, but in today's difficult economy, coupon clippers can save a family a great deal of money.

The Structure of a Definition Paragraph

Topic Sentence
states the term
gives a main characteristic of the term

Supporting Details
explain the characteristic
may include description and examples
may state what the term is *not*

Closing
may refer to the topic sentence
may explain the importance of the term

PRACTICE 8.3

The following definition paragraph was written by a student. Read it and answer the questions that follow.

Christmas Spirit

¹Christmas spirit is a joyous feeling that results from the anticipation of a wondrous celebration. ²It is a feeling of excitement people get as they walk through the mall and realize Christmas carols are filtering through the speaker system. ³It is the tingle they get when their eyes catch the snow and tinsel shimmering in store windows draped in red and green. ⁴When they step outside and feel the brisk, cold wind brush their faces, Christmas spirit is the hope for a white December 25, the hope for the beauty of quarter-sized snowflakes floating down to blanket a frozen earth. ⁵Christmas spirit is the joy of helping people. ⁶It is Mr. Jones shoveling the walk of an elderly neighbor, or Mrs. Smith distributing loaves of her Christmas bread to shelters and halfway houses, or children collecting toys for the poor. ⁷No, Christmas spirit has not been commercialized, as some say. ⁸It is the special excitement people feel as they look forward to the one day of the year devoted exclusively to peace and love.

On a separate sheet, answer the following questions about "Christmas Spirit":

1. What is the topic sentence of "Christmas Spirit"? According to the topic sentence, what term will be defined, and what is the main characteristic of the term?

2. Which two sentences provide description?

3. Which sentence provides examples?

4. Give three examples of specific word choice.

5. Where does the writer explain what Christmas spirit is *not*?

6. Has the writer avoided a dictionary style? Has the writer avoided stating the obvious?

7. Are the supporting details adequate? Explain.

8. Are all the details relevant? Explain.

9. Does the paragraph have a satisfying closing? Explain.

✓   Checklist for a Definition Paragraph

Before submitting your definition paragraph, be sure to work through this checklist.

☐ 1. I have written a topic sentence that mentions the term to be defined and a main characteristic of the term.

(continued on next page)

☐ 2. I have included enough supporting detail to explain the characteristic.

☐ 3. I have included description and examples where these would be helpful.

☐ 4. If necessary, I have explained what the term is *not*.

☐ 5. I have avoided a dictionary style and stating the obvious.

☐ 6. Where needed, I have used transitions and repetition for coherence.

☐ 7. I have written details that are relevant to the term and the characteristic.

☐ 8. I have written a last sentence that ends the paragraph in a satisfying way.

☐ 9. I have edited the paragraph carefully to find and correct mistakes.

☐ 10. I have proofread the paragraph carefully after copying or typing it into its final form.

WRITING ASSIGNMENTS

For your definition paragraph, you have a choice of assignments.

1. Define one of the terms in Practice 8.1. If you choose one of these, you already have a draft of a topic sentence.

2. Define *writer's block*. You may be able to use some of the ideas you developed for Practice 8.2.

3. Define *college student*.

4. Define *friendship*.

5. Define *good teacher*.

6. Define *tacky*.

Combine Definition and Illustration

Define *peer pressure*. Use several examples to help your reader understand the term. For instance, if you say that peer pressure exists in the workplace, cite one or more examples to demonstrate, something like this:

> People think of peer pressure as something only young people experience, but adults in the workplace experience it as well. Any time one co-worker makes another co-worker feel forced to do something, such as contribute to the office football pool or gossip about the boss, that's peer pressure.

Respond to a Photograph

Using the photograph as a possible source of ideas, define *glamour, style,* or *wealth*.

 Writing Process Tips for Composing Your Definition Paragraph

To become a better writer, try out the techniques for planning, writing, and rewriting that you learned in Chapters 1 and 2, so you can discover which ones work best for you. As you compose your definition, continue to sample those strategies. In addition, the following procedures may be helpful. No matter what composing strategies you use, however, be sure to work through the Checklist for a Definition Paragraph on pages 121–122 before submitting your paragraph.

PLANNING: GENERATING IDEAS

• To settle on a main characteristic, think of three words that best describe your term. Choose one of those words as the characteristic that will be your assertion.

• Answering these questions can help you discover supporting details:

What can I describe?

(continued on next page)

FAQ:

Q: What if I can't think of a term to define?

A: Think about the roles you play and define one: student, daughter, father, softball coach, lifeguard, runner, and so on.

What examples can I give?

What is the term like? What is it different from?

What misconceptions exist about the term?

REWRITING: REVISING

- Look for opportunities to add specific nouns, verbs, and modifiers to give your reader a more vivid impression of what you are defining.

- Be sure you are using your own writing style rather than the style found in dictionaries.

SUCCEEDING IN COLLEGE

Use Definition across the Curriculum

Every course you take has the potential to require writing definition. In a homework assignment for a criminal justice class, you might have to define *reasonable force* or *civil disobedience*. In a literature class quiz, you might have to define *symbolism* or *stream of consciousness*. In a midterm for a labor studies class, you might have to define *mutual gains bargaining*. In a paper for a media course, you might have to define *pornography*. In a quiz for a women's studies class, you might have to define *sexual harassment*, and in a journal entry for a philosophy class, you might have to define *morality*.

Learn Specialized Definitions in Your Courses

Every subject you take will have its own specialized vocabulary, and you must learn the definitions of the important terms. Often the important terms you should learn will appear in boldface type in your textbooks. Other times, your instructor will mention and define important terms in class lectures. To learn these terms, one or more of these procedures may be helpful.

- Define terms in your own words. If you have any questions, check for a glossary in your textbook or ask a question in class.

- Make flashcards. Place the term on one side and the definition on the other. Study the cards alone and with a study partner.

- Highlight important definitions in your textbooks and review them often. Use the terms in class discussions, so you become comfortable with them.

- Learn to identify similar word parts. For example, in biology class, you might find it easier to remember that *renin* is an enzyme released by the kidneys if you know that the word *renal* refers to the kidneys.

Write about It

Select a specialized term from another course and in a paragraph, define it so that someone who is not taking that class can understand it and why it is important.

CHAPTER 9
Comparison and Contrast

Aparagraph that **compares** shows how two things are similar; a paragraph that **contrasts** shows how two things are different; a paragraph that **compares and contrasts** shows both similarities and differences. Comparison and contrast are important because they help us decide which of two people or items is better. For example, by comparing and contrasting two political candidates, we can decide whom to vote for. By comparing and contrasting two cars, we can decide which to buy. Comparison and contrast also help us better understand the items compared and contrasted. For example, by comparing and contrasting the workings of the human brain and a computer, we can better understand the operation of both.

A comparison shows similarities; a contrast shows differences; a comparison and contrast shows both similarities and differences.

SAMPLE COMPARISON AND CONTRAST PARAGRAPHS

The following paragraphs were written by students.

Contrasting Images of Television Children

[1]A glaring contrast exists between the problems children caused on the old television show, *The Brady Bunch*, and the ones they cause on the current program, *Malcolm in the Middle*. [2]The conflicts on *The Brady Bunch* involved the kids getting into minor scrapes. [3]In one episode, Jan (the middle daughter) is elected the most popular girl in her class, but she allows the victory to go to her head and does not keep her promises to her brothers and sisters or her school friends. [4]Soon, no one will talk to her. [5]However, as soon as loving mother Carol has a heart-to-heart talk with her, Jan sees the error of her ways and writes a speech to thank her family for teaching her an important lesson. [6]The children in *Malcolm in the Middle*, on the other hand, regularly get into serious

trouble. [7]In one episode, three of the oldest son's friends trash the house, and while cleaning up, Malcolm gets a serious head injury that necessitates a trip to the emergency room. [8]Another time, the children blow up the steam cleaner where Lois, the mother, works, and the youngest son steals a $150 bottle of cognac. [9]Problems like these are resolved without the parents' intervention or as a result of Lois screaming or scheming to make matters right. [10]Rarely are lessons learned, for more chaos occurs in the next episode. [11]If *The Brady Bunch* and *Malcolm in the Middle* are signs of their times, children today are getting into more serious trouble, and parents are not intervening as effectively as they once did.

Identical but Different

[1]My twin sister, Loretta, and I look very much alike, but we have very different personalities. [2]Because we look so much alike, Loretta and I are frequently mistaken for each other by teachers and those who do not know us well. [3]We both wear our curly, auburn hair to the shoulder. [4]We both are just over five feet, and weigh about the same. [5]Our facial features mimic each other, although I think Loretta is prettier, and she thinks that I am, so I guess it is a toss-up. [6]From our earliest days, we became accustomed to responding to "Hey Twin" because people cannot tell us apart. [7]On the other hand, our personalities have always been different. [8]As children, Loretta liked beautiful Barbie Dolls in sophisticated, feminine outfits, and I preferred rugged G. I. Joes in full battle gear. [9]Loretta would always want my G. I. Joes to be boyfriends for her Barbie Dolls. [10]Of course, I would never consent to such a thing. [11]Another difference was apparent in school, where Loretta was the more serious student. [12]When we had class together, she would be listening attentively to the teacher. [13]However, I was busy passing notes and planning the night to come. [14]Predictably, Loretta's grades were always excellent, and mine were rather ho-hum. [15]As an adult, my twin is quiet and conservative and always seems to do the right thing. [16]In contrast, I am outgoing and adventurous—and always in trouble. [17]Thus, while Loretta and I may look identical, inwardly we are very different people.

THE TOPIC SENTENCE

The topic sentence includes your topic (the subjects to be compared and/or contrasted) and assertion about the topic (the point of comparison and/or contrast).

The topic sentence for comparison and contrast includes your topic and your assertion about your topic. The topic is the subjects to be compared, contrasted, or both compared and contrasted. The assertion is the point of comparison and/or contrast the paragraph will make. Take another look at the topic sentence for "Contrasting Images of Television Children":

A glaring contrast exists between the problems children caused on the old television show, *The Brady Bunch*, and the ones they cause on the current program, *Malcolm in the Middle*.

The writer's topic is the televison shows, *The Brady Bunch* and *Malcolm in the Middle*. The writer's assertion (the point of difference) is that there is a difference between the problems caused by the children on each show.

Now look at the topic sentence of "Identical but Different":

> My twin sister, Loretta, and I look very much alike, but we have very different personalities.

The topic is the author and her twin sister. The writer's assertion (the point of comparison and contrast) is that they look alike but have different personalities.

Notice that both topic sentences indicate whether the paragraph will compare, contrast, or both. The first topic sentence makes clear that the writer will contrast, and the second topic sentence makes clear that the writer will both compare *and* contrast.

PRACTICE 9.1: WORKING TOGETHER

With some classmates, write a topic sentence for the following subjects. Be sure to state the subjects and the point of comparison and/or contrast.

Example: two friends   *My friend Jeremy is always optimistic, but Phyllis constantly expects the worst.*

1. two teachers _____

_____

2. two television comedies _____

_____

3. two ways of studying _____

_____

4. two birthday celebrations _____

_____

5. high school and college _____

_____

SUPPORTING DETAILS

Supporting details state and explain the points of comparison and contrast.

When you compare, your supporting details show the ways the subjects are alike; when you contrast, your supporting details show the ways the subjects are different. When you compare and contrast, your supporting details show both the similarities and differences.

Often, you will need to explain the points of comparison or contrast. Description and illustration can help you do that. In "Identical but Different," for example, this description helps explain the first similarity between the twins, that they look alike.

> We both wear our curly, auburn hair to the shoulder. We both are just over five feet, and weigh about the same.

In "Contrasting Images of Television Children," these examples help explain the first contrast, that the children on *The Brady Bunch* got in minor scrapes, but the children on *Malcolm in the Middle* get into serious trouble.

example from *The Brady Bunch:*	Jan fails to keep her promises, so people stop talking to her.
example from *Malcolm in the Middle:*	Malcolm gets a serious head injury after his brother's friends trash the house.

If you reread "Contrasting Images of Television Children" and "Identical but Different," you will notice that points of comparison and contrast are both stated and explained.

Order and Transitions

Use a subject-by-subject pattern to discuss first one subject and then the other. Discuss the same points for both subjects.

Your supporting details can be ordered two ways: *subject-by-subject* or *point-by-point*. In a **subject-by-subject pattern**, you write everything about your first subject and then go on to write everything about your second subject. "Contrasting Images of Television Children" follows this pattern. First the writer says everything about *The Brady Bunch*, and then the writer says everything about *Malcolm in the Middle*. An outline of this paragraph using a subject-by-subject pattern looks like this:

   I *The Brady Bunch*
      A. Seriousness of problems caused
      B. Role of parent in solving problems
      C. Whether lesson is learned

  II *Malcolm in the Middle*
      A. Seriousness of problems caused
      B. Role of parent in solving problems
      C. Whether lesson is learned

Notice that the writer discusses the same points (seriousness of problems caused, role of parent in solving problems, and whether lesson is learned) for both subjects. You, too, should discuss the same points for both subjects.

The ideas in the contrast part of "Identical but Different" are ordered in a **point-by-point pattern**. A point is made about one subject and then it is made about the second subject. Another point is made about the first subject and then it is made about the second, and so on. Here is an outline of the contrast portion of that paragraph:

I As children
  A. Loretta
  B. Author

II In school
  A. Loretta
  B. Author

III As adults
  A. Loretta
  B. Author

Use a point-by-point pattern to alternate between subjects. The points discussed for one subject should also be discussed for the other.

Notice that with the point-by-point pattern, too, the writer treats the same points about both subjects.

If you want to discuss both similarities and differences, you can do what the writer of "Identical but Different" does. You can briefly mention the similarities and then go on to explain the differences using a point-by-point pattern.

The following transitions can help you achieve coherence, as can the ones in the chart on pages 67–68.

To compare and contrast, first mention the similarities and then explain the differences using a point-by-point pattern.

Transitions for Comparison and Contrast

To Signal Comparison similarly, likewise, in the same way, in like manner

> A college football coach must have years of experience before he becomes a head coach. *Similarly,* a professional football coach is an assistant coach for a long time before taking on the top spot.

To Signal Contrast but, yet, still, however, in contrast, on the other hand, nevertheless

> I thought motherhood would be nothing but bliss. *However,* I soon learned it is a trying time.

THE CLOSING

You can use any approach that provides a satisfying finish for your comparison and contrast paragraph. Referring to your topic sentence is often effective. The writer of "Identical but Different" uses this approach.

topic sentence:	My twin sister, Loretta, and I look very much alike, but we have very different personalities.
closing that refers to the topic sentence:	Thus, while Loretta and I may look identical, inwardly we are very different people.

Another approach is to explain the significance of your comparison or contrast, as the writer of "Contrasting Images of Television Children" does.

topic sentence:	A glaring contrast exists between the problems children caused on the old television show, *The Brady Bunch*, and the ones they cause on the current program, *Malcolm in the Middle*.
closing that explains the significance of the contrast:	If *The Brady Bunch* and *Malcolm in the Middle* are signs of their times, children today are getting into more serious trouble, and parents are not intervening as effectively as they once did.

The Structure of a Comparison or Contrast Paragraph

Topic Sentence
gives the subjects to be compared or contrasted
states the point of comparison or contrast to be made

Supporting Details
explain the comparisons or contrasts
may include description and examples

Closing
may refer to the topic sentence
may explain the significance of the comparison or contrast

PRACTICE 9.2

There are three transitions of contrast in "Identical but Different" (page 126). On a separate sheet, write the sentences that contain these transitions; underline each transition.

PRACTICE 9.3

The following paragraphs were written by students. Read them and answer the questions.

Let's Hear It for Tradition

[1]The Christmas gatherings we used to have at my grandparents' house were much better than the celebrations I now have at my house. [2]It used to be that all the aunts, uncles, and cousins gathered for a festive reunion. [3]Now the gathering is just my husband, my children, and me. [4]In the past, every family brought a tasty dish, so no one had too much work to do. [5]Now I spend days knocking myself out making turkey with all the trimmings. [6]My aunts used to bake scrumptious cobblers and pies to go with all the traditional holiday cookies. [7]Somehow my children's iced trees and stars do not compare, although they are special in their own right. [8]At my grandparents' there was a ritual for opening gifts that took the whole afternoon. [9]Everyone took turns opening one gift at a time. [10]This stretched out the excitement and allowed everyone a chance to ooh and aah. [11]In contrast, my children rip into their gifts in record time without savoring anything. [12]There was conversation and laughter at my grandparents'. [13]Everyone tried to catch up on what had happened since the last gathering. [14]Now, however, we talk about what we talk about any other day. [15]I miss the old gatherings. [16]However, Grandma and Grandpa and most of the aunts and uncles are gone, and the rest of us are too scattered around the country to have many gatherings.

College Is Not What I Expected

[1]Now that I have been a college student for half a year, I can say that college is not what I thought it would be. [2]After being accepted at YSU, I thought about all the fun I would have living away from home. [3]I figured I would meet a lot of new people and do a lot of new things. [4]I never had much trouble with my high school classes, so I did not think college work would be too tough. [5]After being here a short time, I knew I was wrong. [6]I have not had much fun yet. [7]Most of the nightlife centers around bars, and I am not much of a drinker. [8]I have been to a few parties, but everyone seems to know everyone else, and no one knows me. [9]I usually stand around with my roommate, and usually we go home early without meeting anyone. [10]Most of the time I cannot go out anyway because I have to study so much. [11]The homework keeps me up late at night, and still it is a struggle to get Cs. [12]Everyone tells me I need more time to adjust to college life, so maybe things will look up for me soon, and college will be more like I expected it to be.

1. The supporting details for "Let's Hear It for Tradition" are arranged in a point-by-point pattern. To understand this pattern better, complete the following outline of the paragraph.

    I. Number of people
      A. In the past
      B. Now
    II. Food preparation
      A.
      B.
    III. Opening gifts
      A.
      B.
    IV.
      A.
      B.

2. The supporting details for "College Is Not What I Expected" are arranged in a subject-by-subject pattern. To understand this pattern better, complete the following outline.

    I. What college was expected to be
      A. Fun
      B. Meeting people
      C.
    II. What college really is
      A.
      B.
      C.

PRACTICE 9.4

Reread "Let's Hear It for Tradition" and "College Is Not What I Expected" in Practice 9.3, and then answer the following questions.

1. What is the topic sentence for each paragraph? What does each topic sentence mention as the topic and the assertion about the topic? Do the topic sentences indicate the writer will compare, contrast, or do both?

2. For each paragraph, indicate whether the details are arranged in a subject-by-subject pattern or point-by-point pattern.

3. In each paragraph, are the points discussed for one subject also discussed for the other?

4. For each paragraph, cite a point that is explained with examples or description.

5. In "Let's Hear It for Tradition," what transitions signal contrast?

6. Does either paragraph have a problem with adequate or relevant detail? Explain.

7. Do the paragraphs have a satisfying closing? Explain.

✔ Checklist for a Comparison and Contrast Paragraph

Before submitting your comparison and contrast paragraph, be sure to work through this checklist.

☐ 1. I have written a topic sentence that mentions the subjects to be compared and/or contrasted and the point of comparison or contrast.

☐ 2. Where necessary, I have explained points of comparison and contrast.

☐ 3. I have mentioned the same points for both subjects.

☐ 4. I have ordered details with either a subject-by-subject or point-by-point pattern.

☐ 5. I have checked to be sure that every sentence is relevant to the topic sentence.

☐ 6. Where needed, I have used transitions, especially of comparison and contrast.

☐ 7. I have written a last sentence that ends the paragraph in a satisfying way.

☐ 8. I have edited the paragraph carefully to find and correct mistakes.

☐ 9. I have proofread the paragraph carefully after copying or typing it into its final form.

WRITING ASSIGNMENTS

You have a choice of assignments for a comparison and contrast paragraph.

1. Use one of the topic sentences you wrote for Practice 9.1.

2. Contrast two of the same type of television programs, such as two situation comedies, two crime dramas, or two reality shows.

3. Compare and contrast—or just contrast—the way something is with the way you thought it would be.

4. Compare and contrast—or just contrast—the techniques of two athletes who play the same sport or two musicians who play the same instrument.

5. Contrast two print or television advertisements for the same kind of product, such as toothpaste, automobiles, life insurance, or soft drinks.

6. Compare and contrast—or just contrast—two people you admire.

Combine Comparison and Contrast and Process Analysis

Contrast two processes for doing something, such as eliminating sugar when dieting, avoiding distractions when studying, or avoiding procrastination when faced with a writing task. Use a subject-by-subject pattern of organization, so you explain one process and then explain the other process.

Respond to a Photograph

The photograph shows a family from the 1950s. Compare or contrast some aspect of the family or family life shown in this photo with that aspect of your family or family life.

Writing Process Tips for Composing Your Comparison and Contrast Paragraph

To become a better writer, try out the techniques for planning, writing, and rewriting that you learned in Chapters 1 and 2, so you can discover which ones work best for you. As you compose your comparison and contrast paragraph, continue to sample those strategies. In addition, the following procedures may be helpful. No matter what composing strategies you use, however, be sure to work through the Checklist for a Comparison and Contrast Paragraph on page 133 before submitting your paragraph.

PLANNING: GENERATING IDEAS

- List every comparison and/or contrast you can think of without evaluating the worth of your ideas. Then go back and circle the ones you want to use.

PLANNING: ESTABLISHING PURPOSE AND AUDIENCE

- You can establish your writing purpose by answering these questions:

  Do I want to show which of my subjects is better? Who do I need to convince of this?

  Do I want to increase understanding of the subjects? Who does not currently have this understanding?

PLANNING: ORDERING IDEAS

- If you are unsure how to order your ideas, try outlining with both a subject-by-subject pattern and a point-by-point pattern. Which pattern looks more manageable?

REWRITING: REVISING

- If you used a subject-by-subject pattern, check to see if you need a transition where you move from one subject to the next. If you use a point-by-point pattern, check to see if you need transitions each time you move from one point to another.

SUCCEEDING IN COLLEGE

Use Comparison and Contrast across the Curriculum

The technique of comparison and contrast is important in college writing, often because it helps students understand one subject in terms of another. For example, an exam in an art appreciation class might require you to compare and contrast the styles of two Renaissance painters, and an exam in an exercise physiology class could require you to compare and contrast two methods of strength training. A research paper in an economics class might involve comparing and contrasting socialism and capitalism, while a report in a history class might require you to compare and contrast the foreign policies of two presidents.

Make Good Decisions

As a college student, you have many important decisions to make, such as what to major in, which material to study first, whether to take a part-time job, whether to join the basketball team, whether to transfer schools, and whether to move out of the dorm and into an apartment. When those decisions are difficult to make, comparison and contrast can help. If you have only two choices—such as whether to attend school

(continued on next page)

part time or full time—try listing the advantages and disadvantages of each option so you can compare and contrast them. If that does not help you decide, give each advantage and disadvantage a point value from 1–5. Use 5 for the most compelling points and 1 for the least compelling. Then add up the values for the advantages and for the disadvantages and let the totals help you decide.

Here are some other tips for making sound decisions:

- Compare your choices to your long-term goals, and try to choose the options that help you realize those goals.

- Use your resources. Are there people on campus who can advise you, perhaps people in the counseling center, housing office, admissions office, or financial aid office? Are there any friends or relatives with good judgment who can advise you?

- Take your time, but not too much. If you wait awhile, the right decision may reveal itself. However, if a reasonable amount of time passes and you are still unsure, make the best decision you can and move on.

- Write about the decision. Freewriting or writing in your journal about your decision may help you find clarity.

WRITE ABOUT IT

Select a decision you made in the not-too-distant past. Then write a paragraph that explains what the decision was, what you did to make the decision, and what you think of the decision-making strategy you used.

CHAPTER 10
Cause-and-Effect Analysis

When you write a **cause-and-effect analysis**, you explain why something happens (the causes) or what its results are (the effects). People need to understand why events occur and what their effects are so that they can better understand their world. Thus, cause-and-effect analysis occurs frequently. For example, to analyze cause, a biology textbook can explain why leaves turn color in autumn, or a magazine article may explain why women live longer than men. To analyze effects, a newspaper editorial may predict the results of passing a tax bill, or a medical journal may explain the results of using a particular medication.

A cause-and-effect analysis explains why something happens or the results of an event.

SAMPLE CAUSE-AND-EFFECT ANALYSIS

Each of the following cause-and-effect analyses was written by a student. The first paragraph explains causes, and the second explains effects.

Fitness and the Media

[1]The media are causing people to feel dissatisfied with their bodies. [2]At any time of the day or night, a half dozen aerobics or weight training programs are on television. [3]The people on these shows do not have normal bodies—they have super bodies. [4]Normal channel-surfing folks see these people and instantly feel inadequate. [5]Commercials are no better. [6]They are loaded with beautiful bodies selling treadmills, exercise videos, and health spa memberships. [7]One look at these people and a perfectly healthy, reasonably fit person feels hopelessly out of shape. [8]Leafing through a magazine does not bring any relief, either. [9]The pages are filled with ads for Slimfast and articles about how to cut fat. [10]Of course, all are illustrated by bodies with 0% body fat, so the reader, no matter how fit and trim, feels like a

whale. ¹¹It is time the media bombardment stopped because it is causing people with perfectly fine bodies to feel dissatisfied with themselves.

What Happened When I Quit Smoking

¹When I quit smoking two years ago, I was miserable. ²First of all, I gained fifteen pounds. ³As a result, I looked terrible, and I was like a sausage in a casing when I wore my clothes. ⁴Even worse, I was so irritable no one could stand to be near me. ⁵I snapped at people and picked fights with my best friend. ⁶Once I screamed at my girlfriend and called her a nag when she reminded me to go buy my mother a birthday present. ⁷I did not mean it, but she spent the rest of the night in tears. ⁸For the first month, I was actually hallucinating. ⁹I would turn suddenly, thinking I heard a sound, or jump up startled, feeling like something clammy had touched me. ¹⁰At night I would wake up in a cold sweat after dreaming about smoking a Winston. ¹¹It has been two years since I have had a cigarette, and I am in much better shape now, but I still have some weight to lose and in social situations I still get a little jumpy.

THE TOPIC SENTENCE

The topic sentence mentions the topic and assertion. It can also suggest whether causes or effects will be explained.

The topic sentence for your cause-and-effect analysis includes your topic and your assertion about the topic. Look at this topic sentence from "What Happened When I Quit Smoking":

> When I quit smoking two years ago, I was miserable.

The topic is the time the writer quit smoking, and the assertion is that the writer was miserable.

In addition to stating your topic and assertion, the topic sentence can indicate whether you plan to explain causes or effects. Consider this topic sentence from "Fitness and the Media":

> The media are causing people to feel dissatisfied with their bodies.

The writer's topic is the media, and the assertion is that people feel dissatisfied with their bodies. The word *causing* makes clear that causes will be discussed. The reader knows the paragraph will explain *how* the media *causes* people to feel dissatisfied with their bodies.

PRACTICE 10.1

For each of the following subjects, write a topic sentence for a cause-and-effect analysis. Then indicate whether the paragraph will explain *causes* or *effects*. The first one is done as an example.

Example: computers *Rather than help students work efficiently, computers*

can cause students to procrastinate.—causes

1. losing a job _____

   _____

2. exam anxiety _____

   _____

3. moving to a new city _____

   _____

4. working while attending school _____

   _____

5. cell phones _____

   _____

SUPPORTING DETAILS

Each time you mention a cause or an effect, think of that sentence as a general statement that must be followed by one or more specific statements (see page 57 for a discussion of following general statements with specific ones). The specific statements can be explanation, illustration, description, or narration. For example, look again at "Fitness and the Media." The first cause is given in the general statement "At any time of the day or night, a half dozen aerobics or weight training programs are on television." This is followed by a specific explanation that the people on these shows have such super bodies that they make others feel inadequate.

Now look again at "What Happened When I Quit Smoking." The general statement of the first effect is gaining fifteen pounds. This is followed by the specific description of looking like a sausage in a casing. Sometimes a general statement of cause or effect is followed by a brief narration. This is the case when the writer follows the general statement of being irritable with the story of making his girlfriend cry. Examples, too, can follow a general statement of cause or effect. Notice that after the general statement of hallucinations as an effect, the writer gives a specific example of a hallucination.

Do not assume that an earlier event is the cause of a later event. For example, if a university builds new residence halls and then experiences an enrollment increase, you may be tempted to assume that the residence halls *caused*

Think of each statement of cause or effect as a general statement that should be followed by one or more specific statements. The specific statements can be explanation, examples, description, or narration.

Do not assume that an earlier event caused a later event, and remember that an event may have more than one cause or effect.

the increase. However, other factors may be the cause: a new recruitment campaign, a tuition decrease, or an increased unemployment rate.

Finally, remember that most events have more than one cause or effect. You need to consider all possibilities. The enrollment increase may actually be the result of the new residence halls, the recruitment campaign, the tuition decrease, *and* the unemployment rate.

PRACTICE 10.2: WORKING TOGETHER

Complete this practice with some classmates. After each topic sentence, write one cause or one effect (whichever is appropriate) in a general statement. Then note a specific point that could be made after the general statement.

Example: Our football team is doing poorly for three reasons.

general statement: *Many of our starters are inexperienced freshmen.*

specific point: *Nichols, the quarterback; Sanders, the end; and Zanders and Michaelson in the backfield are all first-year players.*

1. Jan is failing history, and no one is surprised.

general statement: _____

_____

specific point: _____

_____

2. Teenagers drink for a number of reasons.

general statement: _____

_____

specific point: _____

_____

3. Owning a pet can be beneficial.

general statement: _____

_____

specific point: _____

_____

4. Several benefits will come from raising teacher salaries.

   general statement: _____

   _____

   specific point: _____

   _____

5. If the school levy does not pass, the result will be disastrous.

   general statement: _____

   _____

   specific point: _____

   _____

   ■

Order and Transitions

You can arrange your detail for your cause-and-effect analysis in an emphatic order by moving from your least important causes and effects to your most important causes and effects. If your causes or effects occur in a particular time sequence, you can use a chronological order. For example, if you lost your job and as a result had to sell your home immediately and later became depressed, you can give those effects in that time order.

Use the transitions on pages 67–68 to achieve coherence. In particular, the transitions in the following chart can help you signal emphatic or chronological order. You may also find that the transitions that signal cause and effect and those that signal addition are helpful, as the examples in the chart illustrate.

Transitions for Cause-and-Effect Analysis

To Signal Emphatic Order more important, most important, most of all, best of all, of greatest importance, least of all, even better, the best (worst) case (example, instance, time)

> Because of the hurricane, tourists stayed away from the coastal town. *Of greater importance* is the fact that beach erosion is a serious threat to most of the oceanfront homes.

To Signal Chronological (Time) Order now, then, later, soon, suddenly, next, afterward, earlier, at the same time, meanwhile, often

> *At first*, regular exercise increased my energy. *Later*, it improved my self-image.

(continued on next page)

To Signal Cause and Effect so, therefore, since, if … then, thus, as a result, because, hence, consequently

> Movies are becoming increasingly violent. *As a result*, parents should pay careful attention to what their children are viewing.

To Signal Addition also, and, and then, in addition, too, the next, furthermore, further, moreover, equally important, another, first, second, third

> The tax levy failed because senior citizens, who are often on a fixed income, did not support it. *In addition*, many supporters did not go to the polls because of the snowstorm.

THE CLOSING

You can close a cause-and-effect paragraph any way that provides a satisfying finish. One approach is to refer to your topic sentence. Another is to refer to the topic sentence and also mention a related idea. Here is an example using the closing from "Fitness and the Media":

topic sentence:	The media are causing people to feel dissatisfied with their bodies.
closing that refers to the topic sentence and mentions a related idea:	It is time the media bombardment stopped because it is causing people with perfectly fine bodies to feel dissatisfied with themselves.

In this example, reference to the topic sentence is made with the restatement that the media are causing people with fine bodies to feel dissatisfied; the new, related idea is that the bombardment must stop.

The Structure of a Cause-and-Effect Paragraph

Topic Sentence
states the topic and the assertion
may indicate whether causes or effects will be explained

Supporting Details
state each cause or effect
explain each cause or effect

Closing
may refer to the topic sentence
may mention a related idea

PRACTICE 10.3

The following two cause-and-effect analyses were written by students. Read them and answer the questions that follow.

Why Children Grow Up Too Fast

[1]The reasons children become sexually active at an early age are clear. [2]For one thing, there is a great deal of peer pressure for sexual experimentation. [3]I know one fourteen-year-old who ran around with sixteen- and seventeen-year-olds. [4]The older kids made it clear that to be accepted, the fourteen-year-old would have to demonstrate her maturity by sleeping with a particular seventeen-year-old. [5]Parents are also a contributing factor. [6]Parents are now more open with their sexual displays and speech. [7]They tell dirty jokes in front of children and tease about sex in front of them. [8]Parents are also more lenient. [9]They are letting their children wear makeup, date, and wear mature fashions at a younger age, all of which lead to growing up faster. [10]Finally, the greater sexual explicitness of rock lyrics has caused children to mature faster. [11]These lyrics teach kids that sex is expected and virginity is outdated. [12]Thus, it is no surprise that today's youth are engaging in sex at an early age.

Raising the Driving Age

[1]Recently, there has been some discussion about raising the driving age from sixteen to seventeen, and perhaps even eighteen; however, I believe that raising the driving age would have negative consequences. [2]First of all, many teenagers hold jobs that require them to drive distances to get to work. [3]If sixteen-year-olds cannot drive, they cannot work, and if they cannot work, then they cannot bring extra income into the family. [4]This could create a financial hardship in some cases. [5]Furthermore, teens who do not work are more likely to get into trouble because they have too much time on their hands. [6]You might think that parents, particularly mothers, could drive their teenagers to work, but both mothers and fathers are working these days and unavailable to drive their children around. [7]Also, because both parents work, teenage drivers are a real help. [8]The working mother, in particular, appreciates having a sixteen-year-old around to help with errands. [9]Take away the sixteen-year-old's license and the already overworked working mother has an even harder time. [10]Finally, if the sixteen-year-old cannot drive, then dating becomes difficult. [11]Teenagers are supposed to date. [12]It is a part of the maturation process. [13]Yet modern dating requires a car to get to malls, theaters, restaurants, and parties. [14]Without a license, the sixteen-year-old would be denied this important part of growing up. [15]Yes, teenage drivers have accidents, but they are often because of lack of experience, not age. [16]A new seventeen-year-old driver is just as likely to have an accident as a sixteen-year-old. [17]So, let's not take away the sixteen-year-old's ability to drive. [18]Both the sixteen-year-old and the family would suffer.

FAQ

Q: What is the difference between *effect* and *affect*?

A: Affect is a verb that means "to influence," and *effect* is a noun meaning "result."

1. Which paragraph explains causes and which explains effects?

2. What is the topic sentence for each paragraph? What is the topic and what is the assertion? Which words mention whether causes or effects will be explained?

3. In "Why Children Grow Up Too Fast," which sentences are statements of cause? In "Raising the Driving Age," which sentences are statements of effect?

4. Are the general statements followed by specific ones? Explain.

5. In "Why Children Grow Up Too Fast," one general statement is followed by an example. What is that example?

6. Cite two transitions that signal effect. Cite three that signal addition.

7. Are there any problems with adequate or relevant detail? Explain.

8. Do the paragraphs have satisfying closings? Explain.

✔ Checklist for a Cause-and-Effect Analysis Paragraph

Before submitting your cause-and-effect analysis paragraph, be sure to work through this checklist.

☐ 1. I have written a topic sentence that mentions my topic, my assertion and, perhaps, whether I am explaining causes or effects.

☐ 2. My statements of cause or effect are followed by specific explanation, examples, description, or narration.

☐ 3. I have not assumed that an event was necessarily caused by an earlier event.

☐ 4. I have considered that an event likely has multiple causes or effects.

☐ 5. I have checked to be sure that every sentence is relevant to the topic sentence.

☐ 6. Where needed, I have used transitions, especially of effect and addition.

☐ 7. I have written a closing that ends the paragraph in a satisfying way.

☐ 8. I have edited the paragraph carefully to find and correct mistakes.

☐ 9. I have proofread the paragraph carefully after copying or typing it into its final form.

WRITING ASSIGNMENTS

You have a choice of assignments for your cause-and-effect analysis.

1. Use one of the topic sentences your wrote for Practice 10.1.
2. Explain what would happen if _____ (you fill in the blank). For example, you can explain what would happen if tuition were lowered, if there were no required courses, if smoking were illegal, if public schools were in session twelve months a year, and so on.
3. Explain how attending college has affected you.
4. Explain the causes of cheating among college students.
5. Explain the causes or effects of a bad habit that you have, such as smoking.
6. Explain how the way we dress affects how people perceive us.

Combine Cause-and-Effect Analysis and Description

In a few sentences, describe a situation that creates stress, such as a traffic jam, waiting in a long line, a person talking loudly on a cell phone in a public place, or oversleeping. Use specific nouns, verbs, and modifiers to create your description. Then use cause-and-effect analysis to explain one or more effects of this stress.

Respond to an Advertisement

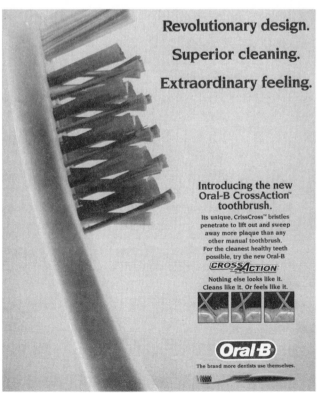

In a paragraph, explain the effect this advertisement has on you. Is the effect positive or negative? Does the ad make you want to buy this toothbrush? Why or why not?

Writing Process Tips for Composing Your Cause-and-Effect Analysis Paragraph

To become a better writer, use the techniques for planning, writing, and rewriting that you learned in Chapters 1 and 2, so you can discover which ones work best for you. As you compose your cause-and-effect analysis paragraph, continue to sample those strategies. In addition, the following procedures may be helpful. No matter what composing strategies you use, however, be sure to work through the Checklist for a Cause-and-Effect Analysis Paragraph on page 144 before submitting your paragraph.

PLANNING: GENERATING IDEAS

- List every cause or effect you can think of without evaluating the worth of your ideas. Then go back, and ask "why?" after every cause and "then what?" after every effect. The answers to these questions can help you uncover more causes and effects.

PLANNING: ORDERING IDEAS

- Make a list of the causes or effects you will discuss. For a scratch outline, number the ideas in an emphatic order.

REWRITING: REVISING

- Check every statement of cause or effect to be sure it is followed by specific information.

REWRITING: EDITING

- If *affect* or *effect* appears in your paragraph, be sure you have used these words correctly.

FAQ

Q: What if there are too many causes or effects to explain in one paragraph?

A: Limit yourself to the most important ones. You can explain that a tuition increase will cause some full-time students to drop out, others to attend part time, and a subsequent layoff of teachers. You do not have to discuss the anger students will feel.

SUCCEEDING IN COLLEGE

Use Cause-and-Effect Analysis across the Curriculum

You will use cause-and-effect analysis often in your college writing. In a history research paper, for example, you might have to explain the causes or effects of important events or developments, such as the Industrial Revolution. For an examination in a real estate class, you might need to explain the effects of the prime interest rate on the housing market. For a paper in an educational psychology class, you might have to explain the causes of violence in schools, and for a business administration homework assignment, you might need to explain the effects of the Internet on interstate commerce.

Manage Stress

For college students, the causes of stress are many, and the effects can be serious. Stress can make you feel anxious, it can interfere with your academic performance, and in the extreme, it can harm your health. Still, there are ways to manage that stress, so it does not get the best of you.

- Maintain good physical and mental health. Eat wisely, sleep well, and exercise regularly. Keep balance in your life by scheduling time with friends.

- Identify the source of your stress and deal with the cause. For example, if you have math anxiety, go to the math lab and become a better math student. If you fear taking tests, go to the study skills center and learn how to manage test taking situations. If you are you short of money, visit the financial aid office to learn about scholarships and part-time work.

- Practice relaxation techniques. Your campus may offer regular yoga or meditation classes at the recreation center. They can be very effective ways to cope with stress.

- Stay in control. People experience stress when they feel governed by circumstances they cannot influence. You can keep control by staying on top of your assignments and attending classes, so you do not fall behind. Write to-do lists (see page 42) that represent realistic goals.

- Accept what you cannot change. If you have a miserable class schedule, but it is too late to add and drop classes, then know that you can try for a better schedule next term. If your roommate makes you crazy, but you are stuck with that person for the year, then practice patience.

- See a counselor, if necessary. If you are having trouble dealing with stress, see a campus counselor and tackle the problem head on.

Write about It

In a paragraph, explain the biggest cause of stress in your life. Explain why this factor is a source of stress and mention the offices on campus with services that can help you deal with that stress. (You might also visit these offices to get some assistance.)

CHAPTER 11
Classification

A classification paragraph places items in groups according to a specific principle.

Classification places items in groups according to a specific principle. For example, medical personnel in a hospital emergency room classify patients according to how seriously ill or injured they are, so they can determine who to treat first, second, and so on. The principle of classification in this case is the degree of sickness and injury. Similarly, a human resources manager may classify job applicants according to how experienced they are in order to determine who to interview. In this case, kind and amount of experience are the principles of classification. Often, items can be classified more than one way—according to more than one principle. For example, colleges can be classified according to their size, according to their location, according to their course offerings, or according to their cost.

Classification is important because it helps us sort and group things. To appreciate its importance, think of how hard it would be to find a book in the library without a classification system.

A SAMPLE CLASSIFICATION PARAGRAPH

The following classification paragraph was written by a student.

Different Kinds of Shoppers

[1]After working at Kmart for over a year, I have come to know well the four different kinds of shoppers. [2]The first shopper is the browser. [3]Browsers have endless amounts of time to waste. [4]Nonchalantly, they wander around my department picking up every item that catches their eye. [5]Unfortunately, browsers never put things back in the right place, so I have to straighten stock when they leave. [6]The browsers are also a pain because they want to look at every item locked in the showcase. [7]Of course, after all this, the browsers leave without buying a thing.

[8]The dependent shoppers are also annoying. [9]They have to be shown where everything is, including the items in front of their noses. [10]Dependent shoppers never bother to look for anything. [11]They walk through the front door, find a clerk, and ask him or her to get a dozen items. [12]The hit-and-run shoppers are much easier to deal with. [13]They are always frantic and rushed. [14]They will buy anything, regardless of price, if they can get it fast. [15]Price does not matter. [16]One recent hit-and-runner raced in, asked breathlessly if he could pay for a stereo by check, picked out the first one he saw, and bought two of them. [17]He wrote a check for over four hundred dollars as if it were $1.98 and raced out. [18]Independent shoppers are the easiest to deal with. [19]They want no part of sales clerks except for ringing up the sales. [20]Independent shoppers find what they want on their own, put things back in the right places, and never ask questions. [21]As far as I am concerned, this world needs more independent shoppers.

THE TOPIC SENTENCE

The topic sentence for your classification paragraph presents your topic and your assertion, which is the words to let your reader know the paragraph will place items in groups. Look again at the topic sentence of "Different Kinds of Shoppers":

> After working at Kmart for over a year, I have come to know well the four different kinds of shoppers.

This topic sentence indicates that the writer's topic is shoppers. The words "the four different kinds of shoppers" indicate that the paragraph will place items into groups (classify them).

The assertion portion of the topic sentence can also state the principle of classification, like this:

> After working at Kmart for over a year, I have come to know that shoppers vary according to how much trouble they cause the sales clerk.

In addition to stating the topic (shoppers) and indicating that classification will occur (with the word *vary*), the topic sentence gives the principle of classification as how much trouble is caused for the sales clerk.

Finally, the assertion portion of the topic sentence can state the groupings you will discuss, like this:

> After working at Kmart for over a year, I realize that people who shop can be browsers, dependent shoppers, hit-and-runners, or independent shoppers.

This topic sentence gives the topic (people who shop) and the groupings (browsers, dependent shoppers, hit-and-runners, and independent shoppers).

The topic sentence mentions the topic. It can also indicate that items will be placed in groups, the principle of classification, or the groupings.

PRACTICE 11.1

The sentences below could be topic sentences for classification paragraphs. For each, do the following:

a. Underline the topic once.

b. If there are words to indicate that items will be placed in groups, underline them twice.

c. If there are words that state the principle of classification, bracket them.

d. If there are words that indicate the groupings, place them in parentheses.

Examples:
<u>Three chief types</u> of <u>babysitters</u> can be identified by most mothers of small children.

<u>Automobiles</u> can be (high-performance cars, luxury cars, or family cars).

Most <u>horror movies</u> <u>can be classified</u> according to [how they scare people].

1. An athlete soon learns of the several kinds of coaches.

2. Four categories of employers exist in the workplace.

3. Four methods of studying for an exam are practiced by college students.

4. If you have eaten in as many restaurants as I have, you know that most table servers can be classified as attentive, uninterested, or rude.

5. With so many brands and models to choose from, buying a computer can be confusing unless you look at which types give you the best value for the dollar.

SUPPORTING DETAILS

Place items in groups according to a single principle of classification.

Place items in groups according to *only one* principle. For example, you may group shoppers according to how hard they are to deal with (like the writer of "Different Kinds of Shoppers") or according to age or according to how carefully they shop. However, you cannot mix the groupings. You cannot discuss the careful shopper, the careless shopper, and the teenage shopper, for you would be using two principles of classification.

The sentence that mentions a particular group is a general statement that must be followed by specific statements that describe the group.

When you develop your supporting details, think of each sentence that presents a particular group as a general statement that must be followed by specific statements. For example, look again at "Different Kinds of Shoppers." Each of the following sentences presents a group. (The group is underlined as a study aid.)

The first shopper is the <u>browser.</u>
The <u>dependent shoppers</u> are also annoying.

The <u>hit-and-run shoppers</u> are much easier to deal with.
<u>Independent shoppers</u> are the easiest to deal with.

After each general statement that presents a group, specific statements explain what the members of the group are like. For example, the following details are given to explain what browsers are like:

- They have time to waste.

- They wander around picking up items.

- They don't put the items back.

- They want to look at every item in the showcase.

- They don't buy anything.

PRACTICE 11.2 WORKING TOGETHER

With a classmate, write a principle of classification, groups that fit the principle, and items that belong in each group.

Example: kinds of group exercise classes

principle of classification ___*degree of difficulty*___

group 1 ___*gentle*___

group 2 ___*moderate*___

group 3 ___*extreme*___

items in group 1 ___*yoga, toning classes*___

items in group 2 ___*low-impact aerobics, spinning*___

items in group 3 ___*boot camp, high-impact aerobics*___

1. kinds of teachers

   principle of classification ___homework___

   group 1 ___gentle___

   group 2 ___moderate___

   group 3 ___extreme___

   people in group 1 ___won or few___

people in group 2 _enough_

people in group 3 _lot and every class_

2. kinds of restaurants

principle of classification _type of food_

group 1 _cheap_

group 2 _moderate_

group 3 _expensive_

items in group 1 _outers fast food_

items in group 2 _family restorants_

items in group 3 _four five stars restorants]_

3. kinds of friends

principle of classification _by character closeness_

group 1 _very close_

group 2 _close_

group 3 _so far that I don't know why I call them friends_

people in group 1 _family and best_

people in group 2 _co-workers_

people in group 3 _old and forgotten_

PRACTICE 11.3

After each topic sentence, state a principle of classification and list three classification groups.

Example: I have attended three kinds of dinner parties.

principle of classification _degree of formality_

group 1 _formal_

group 2 _semiformal_

group 3 _casual_

1. Bosses fall into one of three groups.

   principle of classification ___knowledge___

   group 1 ___big – experts___

   group 2 ___moderate___

   group 3 ___dumies___

2. It is possible to identify three kinds of birthday celebrations.

   principle of classification ___age___

   group 1 ___kids___

   group 2 ___adults___

   group 3 ___seniors___

3. A sales clerk is usually one of three types.

   principle of classification ___knowlidge___

   group 1 ___know every thing___

   group 2 ___skillfule___

   group 3 ___new apprentice___

4. Radio stations can be classified according to the audiences they appeal to.

   principle of classification ___type music___

   group 1 ___altersuative___

   group 2 ___r n b___

   group 3 ___classic___

5. A person can have one of three kinds of neighbors.

   principle of classification ___presence___

   group 1 ___not there at all___

   group 2 ___there but quiet___

   group 3 ___there and loud___

Order and Transitions

Sometimes the order of your groupings does not matter. Other times, you will find it effective to arrange your groups in an emphatic order. For example, if you classify ways teachers grade, you can classify from the easiest to the hardest graders. Sometimes you can arrange your groups in a chronological order. For example, if you classify ways to discipline children, you can move from techniques for preschool children, to those for elementary school children, and on to techniques for high school children.

To help you achieve coherence, transitions that signal emphatic order, chronological order, and addition may be helpful. Consult the following chart and the one on pages 67–68.

Transitions for Classification

To Signal Emphatic Order more important, most important, most of all, best of all, of greatest importance, least of all, even better, the best (worst) case (example, instance, time)

> Students like teachers who allow them to assign their own grades. *The most popular teachers* are still those who grade on the curve.

To Signal Chronological (Time) Order now, then, later, soon, suddenly, next, afterward, earlier, at the same time, meanwhile, often, suddenly

> Isolating preschool children is an effective disciplinary technique. *As soon as* they reach elementary school, children respond better when valued possessions and privileges are withheld.

To Signal Addition also, and, and then, in addition, too, the next, furthermore, further, moreover, equally important, another, first, second, third

> Horror movies that frighten with graphic blood and gore are popular among adolescents. *Another* kind of horror movie is one that frightens with suspense rather than graphic violence.

THE CLOSING

Any approach that creates a satisfying finish makes an acceptable closing. One approach frequently used with classification is mentioning an idea closely related to your topic sentence, the way the writer of "Different Kinds of Shoppers" does:

topic sentence: After working at Kmart for over a year, I have come to know well the four different kinds of shoppers.

closing that mentions a closely
related idea:

As far as I am concerned, this world needs more independent shoppers.

Another useful approach is to explain the value of your classification, like this:

closing that mentions the value
of the classification:

Anyone who works in retail sales needs to understand the different kinds of shoppers.

The Structure of a Classification Paragraph

Topic Sentence
mentions the topic
indicates that items will be grouped
may give the principle of classification

Supporting Details
group items according to one principle of classification
explain or describe the members of each group

Closing
may mention a related idea
may mention the value of the classification

PRACTICE 11.4

Study this classification paragraph written by a student and answer the questions that follow.

Three Kinds of Students

[1]College students fall into three categories: the grinds, the goof-offs, and the well-adjusted. [2]The grinds are easily recognized. [3]They live for school, so they spend all their waking hours in pursuit of an education. [4]You know them: They answer every question, they do every assignment, and they linger after class to discuss the lecture with the teacher. [5]When not in class, they are in the library, and when not in the library, they are in the bookstore buying a 300-page book for extra-credit reading. [6]The grinds always throw off the curve because they study so hard. [7]The next group is the goof-offs. [8]They are the ones in school to party hearty. [9]You won't see them in class or in the library—they're too busy shooting pool in the student union or drinking suds in a local bar. [10]As

for the bookstore, well, the goof-offs haven't found it yet because they haven't bought their books. [11]The goof-offs are important to academic life because they help balance out the curve the grinds keep throwing off. [12]Between the grinds and the goof-offs are the well-adjusted. [13]They study and pull passing grades, but they know how to party, too. [14]They might skip a good time to cram for finals, but they are known to party instead of study for a test that only counts 25 percent. [15]The well-adjusted know life is short, so they take college seriously but know the importance of fun as well. [16]Fortunately, on our campus the well-adjusted outnumber the grinds and goof-offs.

1. What is the topic sentence? What is the topic? Which words mention that items will be placed in groups? What other information does the topic sentence give?

2. What is the principle of classification?

3. What general statements mention the groups?

4. Is there enough specific information after the general statements? Explain.

5. Does the paragraph have a satisfying closing? Explain.

✓ Checklist for a Classification Paragraph

Before submitting your classification paragraph, be sure to work through this checklist.

☐ 1. I have written a topic sentence that states my topic and mentions that items will be placed in groups, the principle of classification, or the groupings.

☐ 2. I have classified according to a single principle.

☐ 3. I have written a general statement that introduces each grouping.

☐ 4. I have followed the general statements that introduce groupings with specific statements about the groups.

☐ 5. I have checked to be sure that every sentence is relevant to the topic sentence.

☐ 6. Where needed, I have used transitions and repetition for coherence.

☐ 7. I have written a last sentence that ends the paragraph in a satisfying way.

☐ 8. I have edited the paragraph carefully to find and correct mistakes.

☐ 9. I have proofread the paragraph carefully after copying or typing it into its final form.

WRITING ASSIGNMENTS

For your classification paragraph, you have your choice of assignments.

1. Use one of the topics and principles of classification in Practice 11.2.

2. Use one of the topic sentences in Practice 11.3. You may want to use the groups and principle of classification you developed when you completed this exercise.

3. Classify types of scary movies.

4. Classify types of people in a theater audience.

5. Classify sources of frustration.

6. Classify kinds of women's or men's magazines.

Combine Classification and Cause-and-Effect Analysis

Classify the different kinds of lies according to how serious the effects of those lies are. When you give each grouping, use cause-and-effect analysis to specify the effects of the lies in the group.

Respond to a Photograph

Using the photo for inspiration if you like, classify kinds of sports fans or spectators. You may find it easier to limit yourself to fans or spectators for one sport, such as football, baseball, or little league.

Writing Process Tips for Composing Your Classification Paragraph

FAQ

Q: Should my classification have a certain number of groupings?

A: Three groupings is often a good number for a paragraph. If you have only two, you are really comparing and contrasting. If you have more than three, you may have too much to discuss in a single paragraph.

To become a better writer, try out the techniques for planning, writing, and rewriting that you learned in Chapters 1 and 2, so you can discover which ones work best for you. As you compose your classification paragraph, continue to sample those strategies. In addition, the following procedures may be helpful. No matter what composing strategies you use, however, be sure to work through the Checklist for a Classification Paragraph on page 156 before submitting your paragraph.

PLANNING: MOVING FROM SUBJECT TO TOPIC

- To decide on a principle of classification, list every applicable principle you can think of. For example, if you are classifying restaurants, you could list these:

food	atmosphere
service	price
patrons	location

Study your list and decide on the principle you will use.

PLANNING: GENERATING IDEAS

- Make columns on a sheet for each of your groups. For example, if you were classifying restaurants according to their food, you might have one column for fast food, one for homestyle cooking, and one for gourmet food. In each column, list every characteristic you can think of without pausing to decide if your ideas are good or not.

- Study your columns and cross out the ideas you do not want to include. Decide which group you want to handle first, second, and third, and number the columns accordingly.

REWRITING: REVISING

- Check to be sure you have used only one principle of classification and that you have introduced each category with a statement.

Use Classification across the Curriculum

Classification is common in college writing. In a paper for an advertising class, you might classify kinds of radio advertisements, and for a communications class exam, you might have to classify kinds of hate speech. An assignment for a sociology class might require you to classify kinds of nuclear families, and one in a political science class might require you to classify ways to organize city governments.

Overcome Procrastination

Procrastination is putting off until later tasks you should be doing now. Occasional procrastination is not a serious problem, but if you habitually wait until the last minute to begin assignments, or if you often delay studying for exams until the night before the test, then something is wrong, and you should address the issue in the following ways.

- **Understand your pattern of procrastination.** Are you avoiding some tasks but not others? Ask yourself why you are avoiding these tasks and devise a solution. If you habitually avoid studying for exams, for example, you may need more efficient study skills. Visit your campus learning center for suggestions.

- **Create a realistic, balanced schedule of tasks.** Schedule a reasonable mix of work and play for yourself. And if possible, schedule the work before the play. A Saturday filled with nothing but schoolwork will be oppressive and invite procrastination. But a Saturday that includes three hours of studying followed by intramural sports will likely work better.

- **Break tasks down into steps.** If a task is so large it intimidates you, break it down into a series of smaller tasks, and reward yourself after you complete each step. For example, if you must study a hundred pages for an exam, study ten at a time and treat yourself to a break after each ten pages.

- **Get a study partner.** If you make a commitment to work with someone at regularly scheduled times, you are less likely to procrastinate because you will be letting down another person.

Write about It

In a paragraph, tell about the last time you procrastinated. What did you put off? Why? What were the consequences? Is procrastination normally a problem for you?

CHAPTER 12
Argument

An argument paragraph aims to convince a reader to think or act a certain way.

Argument, which aims to convince a reader to think or act a particular way, is everywhere. Magazine advertisements try to convince you to buy toothpaste, cleaning products, and life insurance; newspaper editorials try to convince you that tax reform is a good idea; campaign literature tries to persuade you to vote for particular candidates; letters from credit card companies try to persuade you to use their charge cards; e-mail from a friend may try to persuade you to cut class and go to a movie. How successful these arguments are—that is, whether or not you are convinced—will largely depend on how effectively the argument is written. In this chapter, you will learn about writing effective argument paragraphs.

A SAMPLE ARGUMENT PARAGRAPH

The following argument paragraph was written by a student.

Wear a Helmet

[1]Every state should pass a law requiring motorcyclists to wear helmets. [2]First of all, helmets provide increased visibility. [3]Motorcycles are sometimes hard to see, but the glare from a helmet can help solve this problem. [4]Many times I have seen the flash of a helmet before I have seen the motorcycle itself. [5]Because automobile drivers are not conditioned to look for motorcyclists, anything that increases the cyclist's visibility will improve safety. [6]The main reason for requiring helmets is decreasing the number of deaths. [7]As proof of this, I offer a friend of mine who swerved to miss a car that pulled out in front of him. [8]As a result, my friend hit a ditch at sixty miles per hour. [9]He had several broken bones and some horrendous bruises, but because he was

wearing a helmet, he did not sustain a head injury that could have killed him. [10]Another friend of mine was married only three months when a car pulled out in front of his Harley. [11]Wearing no helmet, he hit the car at thirty miles per hour. [12]He flew off the bike and hit his head on the curb. [13]After a week in a coma, he died. [14]If he had worn a helmet, he might have lived. [15]Because helmets increase visibility and provide protection, all motorcyclists should be required by law to wear them.

THE TOPIC SENTENCE

The topic sentence for an argument paragraph includes your topic and your assertion about the topic. The topic should be an issue that people disagree about—that is, it should be something debatable. The assertion should express your position on that debatable issue. Look again at the topic sentence of "Wear a Helmet":

> Every state should pass a law requiring motorcyclists to wear helmets.

The topic is whether states should require motorcyclists to wear helmets. People disagree about whether or not motorcyclists should have to wear helmets, so the issue makes a suitable topic. The assertion portion of the topic sentence expresses the writer's position on the issue: All states should pass laws requiring motorcyclists to wear helmets.

Debatable issues—that is, issues suitable as topics for an argument paragraph—are *never* statements of fact. A **fact** is something that can be proven or that has already been proven. For example, it is a fact that many college students have credit cards. Thus, you cannot write an argument paragraph with the topic sentence "Many college students have credit cards." You can, however, use this topic sentence because the issue is debatable:

> Colleges should require all first-year students to take a course in debt management.

Suitable topics for an argument essay should not be matters of personal taste. You cannot argue that country living is better than city living, or that dogs make better pets than cats, because these issues are matters of personal preference.

Include a debatable issue and your position on the issue in your topic sentence.

Statements of fact and matters of personal taste do not make suitable topics for argument.

EXERCISE 12.1

1. On a separate sheet, write the debatable topic and the writer's position on it for each topic sentence.

example: Jan Mineo is the best candidate for governor.

debatable topic: the best candidate for governor

position: Mineo is the best candidate.

   a. The federal government should not subsidize galleries that display porno-graphic art.

   b. State property taxes are a poor way to finance public education.

   c. Students should have a say in the hiring and firing of teachers.

   d. Laws should be passed requiring the recycling of aluminum cans.

   e. Deregulation of the airline industry has caused more problems than it has solved.

2. For each of the following, write a topic sentence for an argument para-graph.

Example: placing warnings on compact discs with sexually explicit lyrics.

Putting warnings on CDs with sexually explicit lyrics is a misguided effort to

protect young people.

   a. 21 as the legal drinking age

   b. having to pass an exam to get a high school diploma

   c. mandatory drug testing for high school athletes

   d. the sale of handguns

   e. single-sex schools

SUPPORTING DETAILS

Supporting details for an argument paragraph include the reasons for your position on the debatable topic. However, since your purpose is to convince your reader to think or act a particular way, you want those reasons to be persuasive. To accomplish that goal, you must back up your reasons with specific information, called **evidence**. You can write your evidence with the patterns you have already learned—narration, description, illustration, process analysis, definition, comparison and contrast, cause-and-effect analysis, and classification.

To appreciate that reasons backed up by evidence can be convincing, here is an example from "Wear a Helmet." The writer gives this reason first:

> First of all, helmets provide increased visibility.

Then the writer backs up the reason with evidence that combines an example of increased visibility with cause-and-effect analysis to show the effect of the increased visibility:

> Many times I have seen the flash of a helmet before I have seen the motorcycle itself. Because automobile drivers are not conditioned to look for motorcyclists, anything that increases the cyclist's visibility will improve safety.

Now look at the writer's second reason:

> The main reason for requiring helmets is decreasing the number of deaths. This reason is backed up with evidence that combines example, narration, cause-and-effect analysis, and comparison-contrast.

example:	the friend who swerved to miss a car that pulled out in front of him
narration:	the story of the friend hit by the car
cause-and-effect analysis:	the first friend lived because he wore a helmet; the second friend died because he did not wear a helmet
comparison-and-contrast:	the contrast in the fates of the two friends

In addition to giving reasons and evidence, your supporting details can include cause-and-effect analysis to indicate the consequences of adopting or not adopting your position, like this:

Effect if the position is adopted:	If states require motorcyclists to wear helmets, fewer motorcyclists will die or sustain brain damage.

The supporting details are the reasons for your position and the evidence that shows the reasons are true. Evidence can be written in any of the patterns explained in this book.

You can mention reasons against your position and go on to make those reasons less compelling. You can also note what would happen if your position were or were not adopted.

Avoid name-calling and expressions like "most people believe."

Effect if position is not adopted:

Without mandatory helmet laws, we are risking the lives of motorcyclists unnecessarily.

You can also mention one or more of the most compelling reasons *against* your position and then say something to make those opposition points less powerful, like this:

Some people say that helmet laws infringe on personal freedom. In fact, they are no more a threat to freedom than seat belt laws.

Finally, there are two strategies you should avoid. The first is name-calling. Saying things like, "Only the uninformed believe" or "As any fool knows" will alienate your reader who may not "believe" or "know." You can attack ideas, but do not attack people. Second, avoid expressions like "most people believe" unless you are certain that they are true.

Order and Transitions

Details are often arranged in an emphatic order.

Very often, your supporting details will be in an emphatic order, so they gradually build up to the most convincing reason, which appears last. To signal that emphatic order, you can use the transitions in the chart below. If you mention a reason against your position and then say something to make the point less powerful, you may want to use a transition that signals conceding a point, like this:

While it is true that students in the United States are falling behind in math and science, proficiency tests will not solve that problem.

Transitions for conceding a point are also in the chart below. In addition, the transitions on pages 67–68 can help you achieve coherence.

Transitions for Argument

To Signal Emphatic Order more important, most important, most of all, best of all, of greatest importance, least of all, even better, the best (worst) case (example, instance, time)

The university should revise the core curriculum because it does not reflect twenty-first century priorities. *Even more important* is the fact many students are transferring to other schools to take a more contemporary curriculum.

To Signal Conceding a Point although, even though, while it is true, granted

Even though hybrid cars are more expensive than their gasoline-driven counterparts, the money saved on gasoline makes up for the higher sticker price.

THE CLOSING

Any approach that gives your argumentation paragraph a satisfying finish is acceptable. One approach is to restate the reasons for your position, the way the writer of "Wear a Helmet" does.

topic sentence:	Every state should pass a law requiring motorcyclists to wear helmets.
closing restates the two reasons explained in the paragraph:	Because helmets increase visibility and provide protection, all motorcyclists should be required by law to wear them.

Another approach is call your readers to action. Here is an alternate closing to "Wear a Helmet" that illustrates this approach:

closing with a call to action:	Before anyone else dies unnecessarily, write your senators and representatives and urge them to support helmet laws.

The Structure of an Argument Paragraph

Topic Sentence
mentions a debatable issue
gives your position on the issue

Supporting Details
give the reasons for your position
back up the reasons with evidence

Closing
may restate your reasons
may call readers to action

PRACTICE 12.2: WORKING TOGETHER

With some classmates, list three reasons to support each topic sentence.

Example: Little League baseball places too much pressure on young children.

a. *The pressure to win teaches the wrong values.*

b. *The pressure not to let teammates down causes stress.*

c. *The pressure not to let parents down affects self-esteem.*

1. Beer and wine commercials should (or should not) be banned.

    a. _____

    b. _____

    c. _____

2. Workplaces with more than seventy-five employees should (or should not) have a day-care center.

    a. _____

    b. _____

    c. _____

3. Parents should (or should not) help select the textbooks used in public schools.

    a. _____

    b. _____

    c. _____

4. Alcohol should (or should not) be banned on college campuses.

    a. _____

    b. _____

    c. _____

5. An eleven-month school year is (or is not) a good idea.

    a. _____

    b. _____

    c. _____

PRACTICE 12.3

1. Pick one of the following topic sentences and give one reason for the position stated in that topic sentence.

    a. Rather than require certain courses, colleges should allow students to take whatever courses they want.

    b. Requiring college students to take certain courses is an educationally sound idea.

    c. After age sixty-five, drivers should have to pass a driving test every year.

    d. After age sixty-five, drivers should not have to pass a driving test every year.

    e. Final examinations should be abolished.

    f. Final examinations should not be abolished.

    reason: _____

    _____

2. List two pieces of evidence that show the truth of the reason you wrote for number 1.

    evidence: _____

    _____

    _____

    evidence: _____

    _____

    _____

PRACTICE 12.4

Complete the following on a separate sheet:

1. Select one of the topic sentences from Practice 12.2 and write a sentence or two that mentions a reason against the position and says something to make that opposition point less powerful.

2. Select one of the topic sentences from Practice 12.2 and write a sentence or two that mentions what would happen if the position were adopted. Then write a sentence or two that mentions what would happen if the position were *not* adopted.

PRACTICE 12.5

The following argument paragraph was written by a student. Read it and answer the questions.

No Degree Required

[1]We should discontinue the requirement that people must earn teaching degrees before they can teach in public schools. [2]The requirement

that a person have a teaching degree from a four-year college means that talented, knowledgeable people, people who would be terrific teachers, cannot give what they have to offer—just because they have not taken a handful of teaching courses. [3]Consider an accountant who loves children and has a way of inspiring them. [4]He or she cannot teach arithmetic without earning a teaching degree even though that person already has the knowledge and talent to be a fine teacher. [5]Or what about a former U.S. senator who loves children and knows the government inside out? [6]That person cannot teach social studies without going back to school to earn a teaching degree. [7]In both cases and countless more like them, people who could educate and inspire young people are prevented from doing so. [8]This fact is particularly disturbing when you consider that the accountant and senator probably know more about math and government than some people with teaching degrees who are currently teaching math and social studies. [9]Of course, we can't let just anyone with knowledge of a subject into the classroom. [10]We must be sure the person has the other qualities necessary to teach. [11]We should set up training programs to teach prospective teachers about classroom management, and we should have tests to judge the knowledge and talent of people who want to teach. [12]Then we should require a year of probation to weed out those who are not suitable. [13]Beyond that, anyone with the knowledge, desire, and talent should be able to teach. [14]Deans of colleges of education all over the country are likely to cry out that only accredited schools can train teachers, but that point of view is self-serving. [15]After all, our current method of requiring teaching degrees has done little to assure quality education.

1. What is the topic sentence of "No Degree Required"? What is the writer's debatable issue? What is the writer's position on the issue?

2. Write the sentences that state the reasons for the writer's position.

3. The evidence to prove the first reason is which of the following:

   a. narration

   b. example

   c. narration and example

4. What reason against the writer's position is given? How does the writer attempt to make that reason less powerful? Does the writer succeed in making the reason less powerful? Explain.

5. Does the paragraph have a satisfying closing? Explain.

✔ Checklist for an Argument Paragraph

Before submitting your argument paragraph, be sure to work through this checklist.

☐ 1. I have written a topic sentence that states a debatable issue and mentions my position on that issue.

☐ 2. I have given reasons for my position and backed up those reasons with evidence.

☐ 3. The reasons and evidence are aimed at convincing my reader to think or act a particular way.

☐ 4. If it would help convince my reader, I have mentioned important reasons against my position and made them less compelling.

☐ 5. If it would help convince my reader, I have noted what would happen if my position were or were not adopted.

☐ 6. I have avoided name-calling and expressions like "most people believe."

☐ 7. My supporting details are arranged in an emphatic or other logical order.

☐ 8. I have used transitions and repetition for coherence.

☐ 9. I have written a closing that ends the paragraph in a satisfying way.

☐ 10. I have edited the paragraph carefully to find and correct mistakes.

☐ 11. I have proofread the paragraph carefully after copying or typing it into its final form.

WRITING ASSIGNMENTS

For your argument paragraph, you have your choice of assignments.

1. Use one of the topic sentences you wrote in response to number 2 of Practice 12.1.

2. Use one of the topic sentences from Practice 12.2. You may want to use some or all of the reasons you developed when you completed this exercise.

3. Write a paragraph to persuade someone who graduated from your high school to attend your college.

4. Write a paragraph arguing that Internet chat rooms are harmful (or helpful).

5. Write a paragraph arguing that military women should (or should not) be allowed to serve in combat.

6. Argue for or against using torture to interrogate suspected terrorists.

Combine Argument and Cause-and-Effect Analysis

Write a paragraph to convince the appropriate campus administrator that a specific change is needed at your college, such as a change in registration procedures, course requirements, parking facilities, or residence hall rules. Use cause-and-effect analysis to give the effects the change would have.

Respond to a Photograph

Currently, some states outlaw talking on a cell phone while driving a car. In a paragraph, argue for or against such laws.

Writing Process Tips for Composing Your Argument Paragraph

To become a better writer, try out the techniques for planning, writing, and rewriting that you learned in Chapters 1 and 2, so you can discover which ones work best for you. As you compose your argument paragraph, continue to sample those strategies. In addition, the following procedures may be helpful. No matter what composing strategies you use, however, be sure to work through the Checklist for an Argument Paragraph on page 169 before submitting your paragraph.

PLANNING: MOVING FROM SUBJECT TO TOPIC

- Choose a debatable issue you know something about.

PLANNING: GENERATING IDEAS

- List all the reasons you can think of for your position.

- Write notes about evidence you can use to back up each reason and add them to the list.

PLANNING: ESTABLISHING AUDIENCE

- To establish your audience, ask yourself who currently disagrees with you. Write to convince those people.

PLANNING: ORDERING IDEAS

- Review your list and cross out and add ideas, using your audience as a guide to what to add and delete.

- Number your ideas in an emphatic or other logical order.

REWRITING: REVISING

- Note one of the most compelling reasons against your position. What can you say to make that point less compelling? Should this information be in your draft?

FAQ

Q: Should I explain both sides of the issue I am arguing?

A: No. You can mention one or two reasons against your position and make them less powerful, but do not give all the reasons on both sides of an issue. Present a case for just one side.

SUCCEEDING IN COLLEGE

Use Argument across the Curriculum

Argument is an important part of college writing because it requires you to do more than recall information: It requires you to analyze, evaluate, and draw conclusions. In other words, argument is a real test of your understanding of material and how carefully you have reflected on it. Thus, in an education class, you might be asked to do more than say what proficiency exams are—you might be asked to argue for or against such exams. In a labor studies class, you may be asked to argue for or against unions for public employees. In a literature class, you might have to give and then defend your interpretation of a poem.

Learn How to Resolve Conflict

From time to time, you may experience a conflict with a classmate, roommate, or instructor. You can resolve that conflict gracefully using some of what you learned about writing argument.

- Consider what would happen if your position were not adopted. Maybe you will realize that nothing much would change, so you might as well drop the matter. If you received a B– and believe you deserve a B, the disagreement with your instructor may not be worth pursuing because your overall average is not affected.

- Identify areas of agreement. You may discover that you have common ground that you can use to forge a solution. For example, say that you and your roommate disagree about how often to clean your room, but you agree that you both need to study hard to keep your scholarships. You might discuss the fact that studying in a neat, clean room is easier than studying in a messy, dirty one.

- Try to see the other person's point of view, and you might find a good solution. For example, say that you are annoyed because a classmate is not completing her parts of a group assignment. When you look at it from her point of view, you may realize that she did not get to choose her tasks the way other group members did because she joined the group late. The solution may be to ask her if she would prefer to do a different task.

- Talk over the disagreement respectfully. Explain how you see the disagreement and offer a solution. Then let the other person talk, and listen respectfully without interruption. Above all, avoid name-calling. It will only create anger and lessen the chances of resolving the conflict.

Write about It

Write about a recent conflict you had with someone. What was the conflict about? Did you resolve it? How? If you had the chance, would you have handled the conflict differently? If so, how?

CHAPTER 13
Writing an Essay

In college, you will often write **essays**, which are compositions made of several paragraphs. Because an essay has several paragraphs, it allows you to develop a topic in more detail than you can in a single paragraph. When you write research papers, book reviews, reports, summaries, and other papers in your classes, you will use the essay form so you can treat your topic in the appropriate depth.

> An essay is a composition made of several paragraphs.

THE PARTS OF AN ESSAY

An essay has three parts:

1. the introduction

2. the supporting paragraphs

3. the conclusion

> The parts of an essay are the introduction, supporting paragraphs, and conclusion.

Each part serves an important purpose. The **introduction** presents the writer's central point and stimulates the reader's interest in that point. The **supporting paragraphs** provide details to prove or explain the central point. The **conclusion** brings the essay to a satisfying finish.

The Structure of an Essay

Introduction
states the writer's central point in a thesis
stimulates the reader's interest in that point

First Supporting Paragraph
states in a topic sentence an idea to explain or prove the thesis
gives details to develop the topic sentence

Next Supporting Paragraph
states in a topic sentence the next idea to explain or prove the thesis
gives details to develop the topic sentence

Next Supporting Paragraph
states in a topic sentence the next idea to explain or prove the thesis
gives details to develop the topic sentence

Conclusion
closes the essay in a satisfying way

You may have noticed the similarities between essay and paragraph parts. The topic sentence and the introduction both give the central point; the supporting details and supporting paragraphs both explain or prove the central point; the closing and the conclusion both finish the writing in a satisfying way. These similarities are shown in this chart:

Similarities between the Paragraph and the Essay

Paragraph Part	Function	Essay Part
topic sentence	▶ presents writer's central point	◀ introduction
supporting details	▶ explain or prove writer's central point	◀ supporting paragraphs
closing	▶ brings writing to satisfying close	◀ conclusion

A Sample Essay

The following essay is an expansion of the paragraph on page 167. It illustrates the three essay parts.

As a study aid these parts are labeled in the margin.

No Degree Required

[1]Education in the United States is in trouble. That statement won't surprise anyone because we hear it all the time. What is surprising is that we don't seem to be doing much about the problem. Well, one suggestion can improve the quality of education in the United States, and it won't even cost a lot of money. We should discontinue the requirement that people must earn teaching degrees before they can teach in public schools.

[2]The requirement that a person have a teaching degree from a four-year college means that talented, knowledgeable people, people who would be terrific teachers, cannot give what they have to offer—just because they have not taken a handful of teaching courses. Consider an accountant who loves children and has a way of inspiring them. He or she cannot teach arithmetic without earning a teaching degree, even though that person already has the knowledge and talent to be a fine teacher. Or what about a former U.S. senator who loves children and knows the government inside out? That person cannot teach social studies without going back to school to earn a teaching degree. In both cases and countless more like them, people who could educate and inspire young people are prevented from doing so. This fact is particularly disturbing when you consider that the accountant and senator probably know more about math and government than some people with teaching degrees who are currently teaching math and social studies.

[3]Of course, we can't let just anyone with knowledge of a subject into the classroom; we must be sure the person has the other qualities necessary to teach. We should set up training programs to teach prospective teachers about classroom management, and we should have tests to judge the knowledge and talent of people who want to teach. Then we should require a year of probation to weed out those who are not suitable. Beyond that, anyone with the knowledge, desire, and talent should be able to teach. Deans of colleges of education all over the country are likely to cry out that only accredited schools can train teachers, but that point of view is self-serving. After all, our current method of requiring teaching degrees has done little to assure quality education.

[4]An important benefit of this plan is that it taps an important source of potentially gifted teachers: retired people. These days, people are retiring younger, and they are looking for productive second careers. Teaching could be that career. Men and women with lifetimes of valuable experience and knowledge have much to share with young people. They should be able to teach without spending time and money to go back to school themselves to take courses that may not even make them better teachers. Furthermore, these people are, in many cases, financially secure because their children are grown and gone, their mortgages are paid off, and their expenses are fewer. Thus, they are likely to be more satisfied with the meager salaries that teachers often make. Hiring retirees to teach means we can spend less on teacher salaries, a real saving to financially troubled school districts.

PARAGRAPH 1, INTRODUCTION:

The first four sentences create interest. The last sentence gives the central point: that people should not have to earn teaching degrees to teach in public schools.

PARAGRAPH 2, SUPPORTING PARAGRAPH:

Sentence 1 presents the first idea to prove the central idea (people who would be terrific teachers cannot teach). The rest of the paragraph develops that idea.

PARAGRAPH 3, SUPPORTING PARAGRAPH:

Sentence 1 presents the second idea to prove the central idea (the person who teaches must both know the subject and possess other necessary qualities). The rest of the paragraph develops that idea.

PARAGRAPH 4, SUPPORTING PARAGRAPH:

Sentence 1 presents the third idea to prove the central idea (retired people, who can be gifted teachers, can teach). The rest of the paragraph develops that idea.

PARAGRAPH 5, CONCLUSION:

This paragraph brings the essay to a satisfying close.

[5]With American education in trouble, we need creative solutions that do not cost more than school districts can afford. Hiring talented people without teaching degrees to educate our children can be one such solution.

THE INTRODUCTION

The two parts of the introduction are the thesis and lead-in.

The introduction, which opens the essay, has two purposes:

1. The introduction mentions the central point of the essay. The statement of the central point is the **thesis**.

2. The introduction stimulates reader interest in the central point. The material that stimulates interest is the **lead-in**.

The Thesis

The thesis states the essay's central point.

The **thesis** is the sentence or two in the introduction that states the central point of the essay. Like the topic sentence of a one-paragraph composition, the thesis gives the writer's topic and the writer's assertion about the topic. Look again at the thesis of "No Degree Required" to see the parts of a thesis:

thesis:	We should discontinue the requirement that people must earn teaching degrees before they can teach in public schools.
topic:	the requirement that people must earn teaching degrees before they can teach in public schools
assertion:	We should discontinue it.

Here is another example:

thesis:	Situation comedies portray American families in a negative light.
topic:	situation comedies
assertion:	They portray American families in a negative light.

Your thesis includes your topic and assertion about the topic. It can also state the main points you will cover.

You can also write an effective thesis by stating your topic, your assertion, and the main points you will make in your supporting paragraphs. Here is an example:

thesis:	I love my brothers, but living with them is difficult because they eat all the food, they expect me to be their maid, and they treat me like a child.
topic:	living with the writer's brothers
assertion:	It is difficult.
main points to be made in supporting paragraphs:	The brothers eat all the food, they want the writer to be their maid, and they treat the writer like a child.

Here is another example:

thesis:	College students should study a foreign language because knowing a second language increases job opportunities, and it creates important cultural perspective.
topic:	studying a foreign language
assertion:	College students should do it.
main points to be made in supporting paragraphs:	It increases job opportunites; it creates important cultural perspective.

PRACTICE 13.1

For each thesis, underline once the words that state the topic, and underline twice the words that state the assertion. If the thesis also indicates the main points to be covered, place those words in brackets. The first one is done as an example.

Example: Animals should not be used to test cosmetics because [the testing is cruel to animals, and it is unnecessary.]

1. The summers I spent at Lake Erie as a child were always a time of discovery.

2. Despite what our state senator claims, tax cuts are not the best way to stimulate the economy.

3. Because it would increase the amount of instructional time, make more efficient use of resources, and keep young people out of trouble, the school year should be extended to ten months.

4. Although they are twins, Matthew and Michael have very different personalities.

5. Most magazine advertisements cause both males and females to have negative self-images.

The Qualities of an Effective Thesis

To write an effective thesis, you need to understand the following points.

1. **Avoid statements of fact.** A thesis that merely states a fact that everyone agrees about will leave you with nothing to say in your essay.

statement of fact:	Many people enjoy watching game shows.
acceptable revision:	Game shows are popular because they entertain people and make them feel smart.

The statement of fact is an unacceptable thesis because it gives the writer nothing more to say. The revision is acceptable because it allows the writer to explain two reasons that game shows are popular.

2. **Avoid very broad statements.** An essay allows you to discuss more ideas than you can discuss in a one-paragraph composition, but there are still limits to how much territory you can cover.

too broad:	Computers have changed the way we live.
acceptable revision:	Computers have changed the way students communicate.

Computers have affected so many aspects of life for so many people that to discuss them all would take a book. However, in a single essay you can reasonably limit yourself to one group of people (students) and one aspect of life (communication).

3. **Avoid expressing your assertion in vague words.** Vague words, such as *good*, *bad*, *nice*, *great*, *awesome*, and *interesting* do not give your readers a clear enough understanding of your assertion.

vague:	Google is an awesome search engine.
acceptable revision:	Google is an efficient search engine for researchers who know how to use it.

The thesis with *awesome* as an assertion merely gives the reader a vague sense that Google is good. However, the second thesis gives reader a specific understanding of the assertion: Google is efficient for researchers who know how to use it.

4. **Avoid formal announcements.** A formal announcement can seem abrupt, so many readers consider it poor style.

formal announcement:	This thesis will explain why people should buy hybrid cars.
acceptable revision:	Hybrid cars will protect our environment and reduce our dependence on foreign oil.

In many science and social science classrooms, the formal announcement is acceptable. If you are unsure whether you can use it, check with your instructor.

5. **Avoid referring to the title as if it were part of the introduction.** The title is an independent entity, not the first sentence of your introduction.

part of the introduction	[The title of the essay is "The Benefits of Yoga"] It helps manage stress and create a positive outlook.
acceptable revision:	Yoga helps manage stress and create a positive outlook.

PRACTICE 13.2

If the thesis is acceptable, write OK on the blank. If it is unacceptable, indicate the problem on the blank by writing one of the following: fact, broad, vague, announcement. On a separate sheet, rewrite the unacceptable thesis statements to make them acceptable.

broad   Example: The United States should revise its economic policy.

                revision: The United States should place tariffs on imported steel.

_____ 1. No one should drive a car when drunk.

_____ 2. Public education would improve if students were required to wear uniforms.

_____ 3. Trying juvenile offenders as adults—even for violent crimes—is a bad idea.

_____ 4. Some people oppose stem cell research on moral grounds.

_____ 5. Until we can eliminate unjust convictions, we should abolish the death penalty.

_____ 6. As the next paragraphs will illustrate, HBO's original programming includes excessive violence.

_____ 7. Modern technology has improved our lives in many ways.

PRACTICE 13.3 WORKING TOGETHER

For each topic given, work with some classmates to write a thesis for an essay. Include a topic and your assertion. Also, be sure to meet the requirements for an effective thesis.

Example: an annoying relative   *My cousin Lee is very stubborn.* _____

_____

1. the best way to relax (Mention two or three points that will be developed

   in supporting paragraphs.) _____

_____

2. the rewards of college life _____

_____

3. the frustrations of college life _____

_____

4. television advertisements _____

_____

5. writing classes _____

_____

The Lead-in

Stimulating interest in your essay is important. Remember the last time you started reading something and put it aside because the opening did not engage your interest? You do not want your reader to put your essay aside or push through it feeling bored. To stimulate interest in your essay, you can draw on a number of strategies.

1. **Give background information.** Tell your reader something he or she should know to understand the importance of your thesis or some of the detail in your essay.

> On the first day of classes, students who applied for guaranteed student loans were inconvenienced by a lack of funds. Clearly, the loans should be distributed in advance.

The writer's thesis is that guaranteed student loan funds should be distributed in advance. The first sentence is the lead-in, which provides the background fact that students did not have their loans on the first day of school.

2. **Tell a story.** A brief story can create interest in your essay and help prove the truth of the thesis.

> When I was nine, I woke up in the middle of the night to the sounds of yelling. Terrified, I went to the top of the stairs and discovered my parents were screaming at each other. I sat there, confused, shaken, and unable to move. Then the horrible thing happened. I watched my father throw a vase at my mother. It missed her and shattered against the wall. However, from that moment on, I knew that married people should not stay married "for the sake of the children."

The thesis is that people should not stay married because they think divorce will hurt the children. To create interest in this point and help prove its truth, the writer tells a story from her childhood.

3. **Ask a question that relates to your thesis.** However, ask a question that your reader will find interesting, not something like, "Don't you just hate parking decks?"

Do you change from a nice, polite, helpful, caring individual into a monster when you park in one of the campus parking decks? If so, you are not alone, because parking in these structures brings out the worst in everybody.

The question in the lead-in relates to the writer's thesis: Parking in the campus decks brings out the worst in people.

4. **Describe a person or a scene.** Be sure the description relates to your essay. Do not describe the weather, for example, if it is not important to events in your narration.

My legs were shaky and weak. My whole body trembled, and my heart pounded violently in my throat. My palms were wet. The smell of chlorine sickened my stomach as the screams of children having fun and the hum of gossiping adults surrounded me. I knew I had to jump if I was ever going to overcome my fear of water.

5. **Use a quotation.** Select something likely to interest your reader.

In "School Is Bad for Children," John Holt says that "any kid in class who, for whatever reason, would rather not be there not only doesn't learn anything himself but makes it a great deal tougher for anyone else." Because Holt is right, I believe we should abolish compulsory school attendance.

The writer's thesis is that we should abolish compulsory attendance. The quotation in the lead-in is original, not overused, such as "Don't count your chickens before they hatch."

SUPPORTING PARAGRAPHS

Supporting paragraphs explain or prove your thesis so that your reader accepts it. In "No Degree Required," for example, the supporting paragraphs (paragraphs 2, 3, and 4) prove the thesis assertion that earning a teaching degree should not be required to teach in public schools.

Supporting paragraphs have the same two parts you learned when you studied the one-paragraph composition:

1. The **topic sentence** gives the central idea of the paragraph.

2. The **supporting details** develop that central idea.

Your supporting paragraphs explain or prove your thesis.

Your supporting paragraph should have a topic sentence and supporting details.

The Topic Sentence

The topic sentence of a supporting paragraph states one idea that will help explain or prove the thesis. That idea is the central idea or the **focus** of the paragraph. Consider, again, the thesis of "No Degree Required":

We should discontinue the requirement that people must earn teaching degrees before they can teach in public schools.

Each topic sentence states an idea to explain or prove the thesis.

Study these topic sentences from the supporting paragraphs to notice that each one gives the central idea or focus of the supporting paragraph, which is an idea to help explain or prove the thesis.

topic sentence: The requirement that a person have a teaching degree from a four-year college means that talented, knowledgeable people, people who would be terrific teachers, cannot give what they have to offer—just because they have not taken a handful of teaching courses.

topic sentence: Of course, we can't let just anyone with knowledge of a subject into the classroom; we must be sure the person has the other qualities necessary to teach.

topic sentence: An important benefit of this plan is that it taps an important source of potentially gifted teachers: retired people.

In Chapter 3, you learned about connecting ideas with transitions and repetition of key words or ideas. When you write an essay, you should also use transitions and repetition in your topic sentences to achieve coherence from one paragraph to the next. To illustrate this point, look again at "No Degree Required."

end of paragraph 1: We should discontinue the requirement that people must earn teaching degrees before they can teach in public schools.

beginning of paragraph 2: The requirement that a person have a teaching degree…

coherence device: repetition of word *requirement*

end of paragraph 2: …the accountant and senator probably know more about math and government than some people with teaching degrees who are currently teaching math and social studies.

beginning of paragraph 3: Of course, we can't just let anyone with knowledge of a subject into the classroom.…

coherence device: *Of course* is a transition of emphasis.

Supporting Details

When you learned about the one-paragraph composition in Chapter 3, you learned the importance of adequate supporting detail, specific supporting detail, relevant supporting detail, and coherence. These qualities are just as important in the supporting paragraphs of an essay.

To have **adequate supporting detail**, you must have enough facts and opinions to explain or prove your topic sentence. (You can review adequate detail on page 55.) In addition, you must have enough supporting paragraphs to explain or prove your thesis. To have **specific supporting detail**, you should use specific words and follow general statements with specific statements. (You can review specific supporting detail on page 57.)

For **relevant supporting detail**, you must be sure that all the supporting details in a paragraph are directly related to the topic sentence. (You can review relevant detail on page 65.) In addition, each topic sentence must be directly related to the topic and assertion in the thesis. To have **coherence**, you must use transitions and repetition to show how the ideas within each paragraph relate to each other and how the ideas from one paragraph to the next relate to each other. (You can review coherence on page 66.)

Supporting paragraphs must have adequate, specific, relevant details and coherence.

A Supporting Paragraph to Study

The following supporting paragraph from "No Degree Required" is annotated to help you recognize and understand the important features of supporting paragraphs.

The requirement that a person have a teaching degree from a four-year college means that talented, knowledgeable people, people who would be terrific teachers, cannot give what they have to offer—just because they have not taken a handful of teaching courses. Consider an accountant who loves children and has a way of inspiring them. He or she cannot teach arithmetic without earning a teaching degree, even though that person already has the knowledge and talent to be a fine teacher. Or what about a former U.S. senator who loves children and knows the government inside out? That person cannot teach social studies without going back to school to earn a teaching degree. In both cases and countless more like them, people who could educate and inspire young people are prevented from doing so. This fact is particularly disturbing when you consider that the accountant and senator probably know more about math and government than some people with teaching degrees who are currently teaching math and social studies.

The topic sentence states an idea to help prove the thesis. In that way, it gives the central idea or focus of the paragraph: that people who would be terrific teachers cannot teach without the degree. Note that requirement *provides coherence between paragraphs.*

The supporting details are relevant to the topic sentence. Examples (the accountant and senator) help make the details adequate and specific.

PRACTICE 13.4

Pick two thesis statements you wrote when you completed Practice 13.3. For each of these thesis statements, write two topic sentences that could be in supporting paragraphs.

Example

Thesis: <u>*My cousin Lee is very stubborn.*</u>

Topic sentence: <u>*Once Lee refused to go to the prom because he wasn't*</u>

<u>*chosen for the prom committee.*</u>

Topic sentence: <u>*Lee will never apologize to anyone for anything, even when*</u>

<u>*he knows he is wrong.*</u>

1. Thesis: _____

_____

   Topic sentence: _____

_____

   Topic sentence: _____

_____

FAQ

Q: How many supporting paragraphs should an essay have?

A: The number of supporting paragraphs varies from essay to essay, depending on how many aspects of the thesis you want to discuss. However, you should discuss at least two aspects in two supporting paragraphs. If you have only one point, which is developed in one supporting paragraph, you are better off writing a one-paragraph composition.

2. Thesis: _____

_____

   Topic sentence: _____

_____

   Topic sentence: _____

_____

PRACTICE 13.5: WORKING TOGETHER

The following are thesis statements and topic sentences for three essays. With some classmates, write three supporting details on a separate sheet to develop each topic sentence. (If you need help with ideas, try the idea-generation techniques.)

Example:

Thesis: Babysitting is not an easy way to make money.

Topic sentence: The children can be difficult to care for.

Supporting detail: <u>*Marco refused to eat supper.*</u>

Supporting detail: <u>*Carlotta wasn't toilet-trained.*</u>

Supporting detail: <u>*Ed hit his brother.*</u>

Topic sentence: The parents can be just as hard to deal with.

Supporting detail: _The Calloways returned at 3 a.m._

Supporting detail: _The Chus did not pay._

Supporting detail: _The Kellys didn't tell me where they were going._

1. Thesis: People often change when they get behind the wheel of a car.
   Topic sentence: Normally calm people become enraged.
   Topic sentence: Also, normally cautious people become reckless.

2. Thesis: Two kinds of sales clerks work in the mall.
   Topic sentence: The first kind of clerk ignores me.
   Topic sentence: The second kind of clerk smothers me with attention.

3. Thesis: In my study skills class, I learned how to study.
   Topic sentence: Preparations before sitting down to study are important.
   Topic sentence: Students should follow a specific procedure once they sit down to study.

THE CONCLUSION

The **conclusion** is the paragraph that brings the essay to a satisfying finish. Some approaches to the conclusion are illustrated here.

Your conclusion brings your essay to a satisfying finish.

1. **Refer to the topic or assertion presented in the thesis.** Here is an example for an essay with this thesis: Student loans should be distributed before the term begins.

   > Students count on their loan money to pay for tuition, books, and other college-related expenses. Therefore, to avoid problems for students, the loans should be given out before classes begin.

2. **Summarize the main points of the essay.** Here is an example for an essay with this thesis: We should abolish compulsory school attendance.

   > Compulsory attendance serves no purpose because when students are required to attend against their will, they disrupt the classroom and distract the teacher's attention. Students who do not want to be in school will not learn anyway, so we should let them leave and enter the workforce or the military, where they can contribute to society and earn their way in the world.

3. **Introduce an idea closely related to the thesis or main points of the essay.** Here is an example for an essay with this thesis: I knew I had to jump in the pool if I was ever going to overcome my fear of water.

Now that I have overcome my fear of water, I feel better about myself. I realize that I can face whatever obstacles are in my path by using the same courage I used to jump in the pool.

FAQ

Q: Why don't the professional essays in the book always have the organization explained in this chapter?

A: Professional writers often follow the organization explained here, but they often depart from it as well. As you become more experienced, you, too, may want to try different strategies. If so, consult with your instructor.

4. **Combine approaches.** Here is an example for an essay with this thesis: People should not stay married "for the sake of the children." The conclusion combines a reference to the thesis and a summary of main points.

More often than not, staying married for the sake of the children is a mistake. The spouses' resentment and anger grow until the children are affected by the tension. Ultimately, the children are better off living with one parent in an atmosphere of harmony than with two parents in an atmosphere of discord.

PRACTICE 13.6

The following student essay lacks a conclusion. On a separate sheet write a suitable conclusion.

Braces at Twenty-One

[1]I was seventeen and without a care in the world when my mother woke me at 9:00 a.m. for my dental appointment. After the dentist finished checking my teeth, he informed me that I had no cavities, but I needed braces. The news came as a total shock because I thought only children got braces. I have had them for four years now, and I can truly say that having braces at the age of twenty-one creates serious problems.

[2]Because the braces make me look younger than I really am, people never believe I am twenty-one and in college. Once when I met a friend's father, he wanted to know what high school I went to. When I go to the local bars, the person carding twists my ID every possible way, sure that it is a fake and I am too young to drink. When I am out with friends, people always think I am the kid brother who is tagging along. All of this makes me feel very self-conscious.

[3]The braces also affect my social life. I am afraid girls do not want to go out with someone who wears braces, so I hesitate to ask for dates. If I do manage to get a date, I am in the embarrassing situation of excusing myself after I eat so I can go get the food out of my braces. Kissing is not the fun it should be, either, because when my lips are pressed against the metal, they get sore.

[4]Worst of all, the braces are painful. By the age of seventeen, a person has adult teeth that are pretty well set. When the dentist tightens my braces, all the teeth in my mouth hurt because they are difficult to move. I am unable to eat anything harder than Jell-O for a week. The tightening of my braces also gives me headaches from my upper jaw to the top of my skull. The insides of my lips become raw, and it is difficult to talk. It seems that as soon as the pain passes, it is time to go back to the dentist to get my braces tightened again.

PLANNING YOUR ESSAY WITH AN OUTLINE MAP

You can use the following outline map to help plan your first draft. The number of supporting paragraphs you outline can vary from essay to essay, but you should have at least two.

FAQ

Q: Where do I get the ideas for my supporting paragraphs?

A: The idea-generation techniques explained in Chapter 1 can help you discover ideas to develop and prove your thesis.

Paragraph 1: Introduction

Approach to lead-in _____

_____

Early version of thesis _____

_____

Paragraph 2: Supporting paragraph

Topic sentence idea _____

_____

Supporting details _____

_____

Paragraph 3: Supporting paragraph

Topic sentence idea _____

_____

Supporting details _____

_____

Paragraph 4: Supporting paragraph

Topic sentence idea _____

_____

Supporting details _____

_____

Paragraph 5: Conclusion

Approach to conclusion _____

_____

PRACTICE 13.7

The following essay was written by a student. Read it and answer the questions that follow.

Insecure Hospital Employment

[1]At one time, working in a hospital meant secure employment. Even when our economy was at its worst, hospital employees could count on regular paychecks. They never worried about standing in long unemployment lines. Unfortunately, this is no longer true. The effects of our declining economy have reached hospitals at last, and problems have resulted for everyone, employees and patients alike.

[2]Although it took a while, the effects of unemployment in the general workforce finally reached hospitals. Eventually unemployment benefits and union health care benefits ran out for the jobless, and suddenly many people could no longer afford even a brief hospital stay. Elective surgery was put off indefinitely, and even required procedures were neglected because of lack of money. Fewer patients are in hospitals as a result, and one must wonder about the state of our health. Obviously, with fewer patients, hospitals must cut their staffs.

[3]Another reason for hospital layoffs is the increased number of ambulatory care facilities. These units are treating patients who once were treated in hospital emergency rooms. For some, it makes sense to use an ambulatory care facility because it can be less expensive and more convenient. For others, insurance companies dictate use of ambulatory care units. Either way, the effect on hospitals is to cause more layoffs.

[4]With fewer patients being cared for by hospital personnel, the need for such personnel is decreased, and layoffs occur. This cycle has many effects, including low hospital morale. The workers who remain on the payroll feel threatened and insecure. They become worried about whether they will be the next to be axed, and this anxiety affects their performance. Certainly, worried, depressed employees do not make good employees.

[5]Another detrimental effect of layoffs is understaffing. When the number of workers on a shift is reduced, there are fewer employees to do the required work. For example, under normal working conditions a registered nurse on a general medical floor is responsible for approximately nine patients. However, once the staff is diminished, the patient load increases, and the nurse no longer has time for needed breaks. The nurse is overworked and unable to perform at peak efficiency. The morale of the overworked nurse declines even more, and more seriously, patient care suffers.

[6]Understaffing is aggravated by the high absenteeism that occurs after layoffs. Employees not laid off experience a great deal of stress

because they are overworked and worried about losing their own jobs. This stress leads to fatigue and illness, which leads to absenteeism. To make matters worse, when employees call in, they are often not replaced with substitutes. As a result, the remaining employees become more overworked and depressed.

[7]All of this has an adverse effect on patients. People who require the best that medicine can offer are treated by overworked personnel who are more likely to make mistakes. Not only is patient welfare jeopardized, but so is patient comfort. Layoffs mean poor kitchen and laundry service, irritable orderlies, and slower response to requests.

[8]Finally, the layoff of hospital personnel worsens the hospital's unemployment situation. Unemployed hospital workers have their medical benefits interrupted. Thus, if the unemployed worker should require hospital care, he or she is likely to postpone it. The postponement reduces the hospital census more and leads to additional layoffs.

[9]A vicious cycle exists. The high unemployment rate in general means fewer admissions, and the reduction creates unemployment among hospital workers. The layoff of hospital workers, in turn, leads to a higher general unemployment, causing even more hospital layoffs. And through it all, everyone, including the patient, suffers.

1. What is the thesis of "Insecure Hospital Employment"? What is the writer's topic? What is the writer's assertion about the topic?

2. What strategy is used for the lead-in?

3. What is the topic sentence of each supporting paragraph? What does each topic sentence state as the focus?

4. Is each topic sentence relevant to the thesis? Explain.

5. Are the supporting details adequate? Explain.

6. Are the supporting details relevant? Explain.

7. What transitions open paragraphs 3, 5, and 8?

8. What strategy is used for the conclusion?

STUDENT ESSAYS TO STUDY

The student essays that follow illustrate the types of writing explained in Part Two: narration, description, illustration, process analysis, definition, comparison and contrast, cause-and-effect analysis, classification, and argument.

Narration

The following narrative essay is an expansion of the paragraph on page 83. Before studying this essay, review the discussion of narration in Chapter 4.

A Deadly Afternoon

[1]Many of my friends are anxious because they have no idea what they want to do with their lives. They have tried a number of majors, but, so far, they have not discovered anything they feel passionate about, and they worry that they will never find something they can get excited about doing. I am fortunate that I do not have their concern because I discovered what I wanted to do even before I came to college. On a rainy and miserable afternoon of my senior year in high school, on May 19 to be exact, a dramatic incident showed me what I wanted to do with my life.

[2]I was walking to my seventh period class when I noticed a disturbance in the hallway. I could see that Tom had Collette pinned against the wall, causing her to tremble violently. Collette had broken up with Tom just a few days earlier, and everyone was waiting for trouble because Tom had a history of violence and most sensible people were afraid of him. If I had stopped to think, I probably would have run for help, but instead I acted reflexively. I grabbed Tom's arm and shouted, "Let her go!" He squinted at me like he was having trouble focusing, and at that moment I became afraid. Then, suddenly he stormed away muttering, "I'll make you sorry, both of you." At that point, the principal showed up, so I told her what I knew and walked away.

[3]I was shaken up, so before going to class, I stepped into the bathroom to splash water on my face. I was startled to see that Tom was there. At first I was scared. Tom had a short fuse and was likely to use his fists. I fully expected him to lash out at me for my interference in the hallway. Then I noticed the blood spreading across his shirt and the knife on the floor. At that instant, Tom sagged to the floor. His skin had a blue cast, and the blood covered his chest. I ran to the door and screamed for help. Instantly, the principal and three teachers arrived. They frantically tried to stop Tom's wound from bleeding. After what seemed like hours, the paramedics arrived. They did what they could, but Tom did not make it. He was pronounced dead at the hospital. Everyone knew Tom was violent, but no one expected him to turn that violence on himself.

[4]Eventually, it came out that Tom was an abused child who equated love and violence. His life had been an extremely difficult one of poverty and deprivation, as well as abuse. There were some pretty good reasons for his antisocial behavior, and if any of us had bothered to look more closely, we would have seen them.

[5]Tom's death made me realize how troubled people can be. I decided at that point to major in psychology and become a school counselor to help troubled kids like Tom.

Description

The next essay is a description. Before studying it, review the discussion of description in Chapter 5.

My Place of Solitude

[1]Whenever I need to be alone, I go to Cherry Flat, a little-known area in the mountains of Sequoia National Forest. It is a peaceful, isolated, rustic place.

[2]To get to Cherry Flat, I have to ascend Sugarloaf Mountain. The road resembles a snake. The turns are so sharp I cannot resist the temptation to take a quick peek back to make sure the rear end of my car made it around with me. A little-used turnoff at the summit leads down a deeply rutted, muddy lane to Cherry Flat.

[3]Cherry Flat is a primitive campground. There is only a small, unpainted, rough wood hut with a half-moon cut into the door. The only place to pitch a tent is on one of the four flat spots carved out of the sloping hillside.

[4]Any hardship I encounter because of the lack of conveniences is made up by the spectacular scenery. Majestic mountains surround the camp. Redwood Mountain stands to the north; Burnt Point is to the east, and Big Baldy, its granite dome glistening, to the west. The Kaweak River at the bottom of the gorge resembles a silvery ribbon. My eyes are slowly pulled upward following the march of tall pines to the crest of Redwood Mountain where the azure sky begins.

[5]After setting up camp, I hike down the mountain and explore along the river. The trail is a mile long and drops one thousand feet in elevation on its way to the bottom. Halfway, I stop for a sip of clear, cool spring water that is trickling down the face of a rock ledge. Down a steep section and around a bend, the path leads past Disappearing Creek. In a small pool are brilliantly colored rainbow trout. The fish, when they sense my presence, dart away to hide. Lying on a smooth, warm boulder beside the swift running river, I like to watch the billowy clouds float by. The trail ends by a small waterfall. Water spills over the edge and falls twenty feet into a deep pool below. Ripples radiate outward and lap gently on the shore.

[6]As the light grows dim and the clouds glow orange and pink, the sun inches its way behind a mountaintop. I relax and enjoy a cold drink back at camp—a fitting end to a peaceful day.

Illustration

The following illustration essay is an expansion of the paragraph on page 103. Before studying the essay, review the discussion of illustration in Chapter 6.

One Step Forward and Two Steps Back

[1]Americans love technology. Every time some new time-saving or labor-saving device hits the market, we rush out to buy it. Price is no object. If it is new and more advanced, we want it. Americans are proud of our technological advancements, but technology often comes with a price.

[2]Consider the cell phone, for example. Yes, it gives us freedom to move around. However, more often than not, these phones cross frequencies with other phones so that we hear other people's conversations, and they hear ours. What we gain in mobility, we lose in privacy. We also lose clear conversations, for these phones snap, crackle, and pop more than most breakfast cereals. If you use your phone for business, that can be a real problem. Then, there is the matter of finding the phone in the first place. Since the user tends to leave the phone wherever the last conversation ended, hunting the phone up for the next call can be a frustrating challenge. If you were the last user, chances are good that you will find it after painstakingly recalling the events of the previous five hours, but if someone else in your household has used it—forget finding the thing. It can be anywhere from the tool chest in the basement to the potted plant on the back porch. Of course, since no one recharges the phone, the chances are good that your conversation will be cut off midsentence as your batteries sputter to the end of their lives.

[3]The Internet is another example. It offers computer users almost limitless access to a staggering amount of information. However, users are so glued to their computer screens day and night that they no longer have a life away from their PCs. Almost weekly, some new service, bulletin board, or information source is added to the Internet, so users can never feel on top of things. They must spend ever-increasing amounts of time "staying informed." Thus, once on the information highway, people become so obsessed that they do not take the exit ramp.

[4]Another example that I read about concerns the computer-designed magnesium wheels General Motors put on its cars not too long ago. Thanks to a computer error, the tire seals did not fit properly. As a result, thousands of car owners woke up to discover that their brand new cars had flat tires. By the time GM figured out what went wrong, recalled the cars, and fixed them, it had lost a tremendous amount of money. The people who bought the cars were frustrated and unhappy, so it is unlikely they will buy GM products again soon.

[5]It is commonly believed that everything has its price, and technological devices are no different. They may make life easier, but they are not without their problems.

Process Analysis

The next essay, an example of process analysis, is an expansion of the paragraph on page 107. Before studying the essay, review the discussion of process analysis in Chapter 7.

Making Money with a Garage Sale

[1]Have you noticed how many garage sales there are every spring, summer, and fall? Do you assume people must be crazy to flock to these things just to buy other people's junk? Maybe they are crazy, but people do love to buy other people's used stuff, and if you plan it right, you too can make a great deal of money from a garage sale.

[2]First, you must gather all the saleable items collecting dust in your basement and attic. Do not include anything badly broken, but keep everything else. The items you think are the most worthless are likely to be the first to sell. Remember that Buddha statue with the clock in the belly that you would not be caught dead having in your living room? That will sell. So will the velvet painting of Elvis, the pink lawn flamingoes, and all those trashy trip souvenirs. Toys and tools are hot sellers, but clothes (unless they are children's) probably will not sell very well.

[3]Next—and this is very important—clean this junk up. Dirty items will not sell, but you will be surprised at the weird stuff that goes if it is clean. Two days before the sale, take an afternoon, a bottle of Fantastik spray cleaner, and some paper towels and get the years of dust and grime wiped away. Be careful, though. Once this stuff is clean, you may be tempted to keep it. This would be a big mistake. Not only will you not make a profit, but you will be stuck with your own junk again.

[4]Once your items are clean, display them properly. Get lots of tables, even if you have to rent them. Arrange everything attractively, trying to keep housewares together, toys together, and so forth. Do not crowd the items, and put large objects to the rear of the table so you do not hide the smaller things from the discriminating eyes of eager bargain hunters.

[5]The most important part is pricing. I have just three words of advice: cheap! cheap! cheap! Also, be prepared to bargain. Shoppers will often ask if you will take less than you are asking, and your answer should always be yes. Remember, this trash has been in your basement collecting spider eggs for the past five years, so do not get greedy. Price it to move because the last thing you want to do is drag this stuff back in the house because it did not sell. Also, write the price of each item on a white sticker placed on the object.

[6]If you really want a great sale, advertise. Put signs up on telephone poles and trees, directing people to the sale, and place an ad in the classifieds.

[7]Finally, pamper your customers. Provide grocery bags for carrying those marvelous purchases home in, and serve coffee—for twenty-five cents a cup, of course. If the day is hot, lemonade or iced tea at a reasonable price is always a hit.

[8]Follow these steps, and you can pocket a significant amount of money. I once made two hundred dollars with a garage sale and got my basement cleaned out for good measure.

Definition

The next essay is an example of definition. Before studying it, review the characteristics of definition in Chapter 8.

Runner's High

[1]Some people run religiously (five or six times a week); some run periodically (five or six times a month); and some run whenever they feel an urge to be physically fit (once a year). What makes these people run? What

inner drive makes them go out onto the lonely road, with their Discmans by their sides and their large sticks to beat off attacking dogs? Do they like the feel of Ben Gay rubbed all over their tired, aching bodies? No, these people run to experience that special feeling known as runner's high.

[2]Some runners feel this high when they begin running, while others feel the rush as soon as they are finished. The most common time to feel the high, though, is about halfway into the run when the adrenaline is pumping.

[3]The high is difficult to explain to nonrunners, but put simply it feels like getting an A on a final exam you were sure you failed. The high takes you by surprise. Just when you feel you are about to see your dinner come out through your nose, the high picks you up and gives you incentive to keep going. The high is similar to a painkiller in the way it suppresses the pain in your joints. It also relaxes your tense muscles. In some instances, it even replenishes your energy, which makes you go farther and faster.

[4]The high can even be the deciding factor in a race. If a runner peaks too early and experiences the high, then the runner will more than likely "hit the invisible wall" sooner and therefore lose the race.

[5]If the high lasted longer than its normal few seconds (or even minutes in distance races), then the track world would have an incredible number of outstanding runners. However, all good things end, and a runner's high disappears just as suddenly as it comes.

[6]Many people wonder why runners make themselves suffer so much just to achieve a few moments of bliss. Unfortunately, there is no way to explain this to someone who has never experienced runner's high.

Comparison and Contrast

The next essay is an example of contrast. Before studying it, review the characteristics of comparison and contrast in Chapter 9.

Identical but Different

[1]There are two kinds of twins, fraternal and identical. Fraternal, or dizygotic twins, are the product of two fertilized ova. Identical twins develop from a single fertilized ovum. I am an identical twin. My twin sister Loretta is older by six minutes. During our infancy, my twin and I were so identical that our baby bracelets were left on for quite a while after we were released from the hospital. Her bracelet identified her as Baby A; I was known as Baby B. Although physically we are still similar, my twin sister and I have very different personalities.

[2]Loretta and I still look alike, so we are frequently mistaken for each other by teachers and those who do not know us well. We both wear our curly, auburn hair to the shoulder. We both are just over five feet, and I weigh only two pounds more than my twin. Our facial features mimic each other, although I have been told there is more of a sparkle in my eyes than in Loretta's. This, of course, angers my twin. I think Loretta is prettier, but she thinks I am, so I guess it is a toss-up. From our earliest days, we

became accustomed to responding to "Hey Twin" because people cannot tell us apart.

[3]When we were young, my twin and I realized that our interests were different. We would often play dolls together. Loretta had beautiful Barbie Dolls with sophisticated, feminine outfits. I had rugged G.I. Joes in full battle gear. Loretta would always want my G.I. Joes to be boyfriends for her Barbie Dolls. Of course, I would never consent to such a thing. Once Loretta was particularly persistent; she wanted Barbie and Joe to marry. I got angry and made one of my G.I. Joes drive through the little house we had constructed from old cardboard boxes and trample over her Barbies. Then I ran outside to play in the dirt pile behind our house, leaving Loretta crying in the midst of the destruction.

[4]Another difference was apparent in school, where Loretta was the more serious student. When we had class together, she would be listening attentively to the teacher, while I was busy passing notes and planning the night to come. After dinner, Loretta would faithfully retreat to our bedroom to read and do her homework. I would race outside to throw a Frisbee, play basketball, or do anything that was not homework. Needless to say, Loretta's grades were excellent, and mine were rather ho-hum.

[5]Even now, the difference in our personalities is obvious. My twin is quiet and conservative. She always does the right thing. I'm outgoing and adventurous—and always in trouble. A good example of this difference occurred during spring break in Florida. Loretta and I met some guys on the beach, and they invited us to a party. Loretta declined and begged me not to go. She said we hardly knew them and that they were rowdy. She was afraid we would get into trouble. I went anyway. Guess which twin was arrested two hours later for disorderly conduct?

[6]Thus, Loretta and I may look identical, but inwardly we are very different people.

Cause-and-Effect Analysis

The following cause-and-effect analysis is an expansion of the paragraph on page 138. Before studying the essay, review the characteristics of cause-and-effect analysis in Chapter 10.

What Happened When I Quit Smoking

[1]People who have never smoked do not understand how difficult it is to kick the habit. They think quitting is a relatively simple matter of throwing the cigarettes away and never lighting up again. However, these people are wrong. When I quit smoking two years ago, I was miserable.

[2]First of all, I gained fifteen pounds. As a result, I looked terrible, and I was like a sausage in a casing when I wore my clothes. Every morning it was a struggle to find something to put on that did not cut off my circulation. When I looked in the mirror, I was depressed by my appearance and self-conscious about how terrible I looked. I tried not to eat, but I had to do

something if I was not going to smoke, and eating was the only alternative because it kept my hands and mouth busy.

[3]Even worse, I was so irritable no one could stand to be near me. I snapped at people and picked fights with my best friend. I knew I was being unreasonable, but I could not help myself. Once I screamed at my girlfriend and called her a nag when she reminded me to go buy my mother a birthday present. I did not mean it, but she spent the rest of the night in tears.

[4]For the first month, I was actually hallucinating. I would turn suddenly, thinking I heard a sound, or jump up startled, feeling like something clammy had touched me. Once in a movie theatre, I jumped a foot out of my seat because I thought I felt someone put a hand on my shoulder.

[5]Even in my sleep there was no relief. I would wake up in a cold sweat several times a night after dreaming about smoking a Winston. Then I would lie in bed and shake, unable to get back to sleep because the craving was so bad. I would feel depressed because the pleasure I felt from smoking in my dream was not real.

[6]It has been two years since I have had a cigarette, and I am in much better shape now, but I still have some weight to lose, and in social situations, I still get a little jumpy. Believe me, people who think it is easy to quit smoking have never been through what I have gone through.

Classification

The following classification essay is an expansion of the paragraph on pages 148–149. Before studying the essay, review the characteristics of classification in Chapter 11.

Different Kinds of Shoppers

[1]Anyone who has been a sales clerk knows that shoppers fall into different categories. After working at Kmart for over a year, I have come to know well the four kinds of shoppers.

[2]The first shopper is the browser. Browsers do not have much to do with their lives, so they have endless amounts of time to waste. Nonchalantly, they wander around my department picking up every item that catches the eye. Unfortunately, browsers never put things back in the right place, so I have to straighten stock when they leave. I guess browsers think that sales clerks have as much time on their hands as they do. The browsers are also a pain because they want to look at every item locked in the showcase. Of course, after all this, the browsers leave without buying a thing.

[3]The dependent shoppers are also annoying. They have to be shown where everything is, including the items in front of their noses. Dependent shoppers never bother to look for anything. They walk through the front door, find a clerk, and ask him or her to get a dozen items. Dependent shoppers can never make decisions for themselves. "Which color do you think is best?" they ask, and "Which watch do you think my niece will like better?" Half the time they just walk away without buying anything because they can-

not decide what to get. Of course, they never leave empty-handed unless the sales clerk has spent at least fifteen minutes with them.

[4]The hit-and-run shoppers are much easier to deal with. They are always frantic and rushed. They will buy anything, regardless of price, if they can get it fast. Price does not matter. One recent hit-and-runner raced in, asked breathlessly if he could pay for a stereo by check, picked out the first one he saw, and bought two of them. He wrote a check for over four hundred dollars as if it were $1.98 and raced out.

[5]Independent shoppers are the easiest to deal with. They want no part of sales clerks except for ringing up the sales. They have done their homework. They know what they want, the particular brand, and the amount they are willing to pay. They find what they want on their own, put things back in the right places, and never ask questions. An independent shopper can walk into a store and five minutes later walk out again with the desired item.

[6]Any sales clerk will tell you that dealing with the public is not easy. As far as I am concerned, this world needs more independent shoppers.

Argument

The following essay is an example of argument. Before studying the essay, review the characteristics of argument in Chapter 12.

Let's Pay College Athletes

[1]College athletics is big business. A great deal of money is at stake, so colleges are under pressure to recruit the best players. To do so, they offer full and partial scholarships, hoping to lure players to their schools. However, rather than offer scholarships, colleges should pay the players a salary.

[2]Athletes attending school on scholarships have a difficult time. To keep their scholarships, they must carry full-time loads. Because their sport demands so much of their time, they often find that they do not have enough time to study. As a result, their grades suffer. However, if athletes were paid, they could attend part-time and perform better academically without being stretched so thin.

[3]Some people say that without athletic scholarships many students could not afford to attend school, but this is not true. Paid athletes would simply use their salary to pay for tuition and books. Some athletes may even decide to save their salary and wait to attend school until they are finished playing ball. They could thus attend during the off-season or when their athletic careers are over, when they can really focus on their studies.

[4]Paying college athletes would also eliminate the people who are in college but who will never graduate. Some scholarship athletes were recruited to play ball, but they really are not college material. Paid athletes would not have to take classes, and we would be left with qualified students in the classroom, not athletes who are marking time for four years or trying to get a shot at the pros. Furthermore, the seats these athletes now occupy could go to academically qualified students who do want to graduate.

⁵If we paid athletes, colleges would benefit financially. Attendance would be up at games because the level of play would be high. Also, tuition could be collected from the students who take the athletes' places in classrooms.

⁶Awarding athletic scholarships is an old tradition. However, not all traditions stand the test of time. Now we should reconsider how we recruit athletes. Why not just pay them and let them decide if they want to use the money to attend college? Everyone would benefit.

✔ Checklist for an Essay

Before submitting your essay, be sure to work through this checklist.

- ☐ 1. I have written a thesis that states my topic and assertion.

- ☐ 2. My thesis is not a statement of fact, a formal announcement, or too broad. It does not refer to the title as if it were part of the introduction. My assertion is expressed in specific language.

- ☐ 3. I have written a lead-in designed to create interest in my essay.

- ☐ 4. Each supporting paragraph has a topic sentence that presents the paragraph's focus and that is relevant to the thesis.

- ☐ 5. Supporting details are adequate, specific, and relevant.

- ☐ 6. I have used transitions and repetition for coherence.

- ☐ 7. I have written a conclusion that ends the essay in a satisfying way.

- ☐ 8. I have edited carefully to find and correct mistakes.

- ☐ 9. I have proofread carefully after copying or typing my essay into its final form.

WRITING ASSIGNMENTS

For your essay, you have a choice of assignments.

1. Use one of the thesis statements you wrote for Practice 13.3. If you use one of these, check your responses to Practice 13.4 for possible topic sentences.

2. Write an essay that tells about the disadvantages of or the problems you have experienced with something.

3. Use examples to illustrate the best or worst job you have had.

4. Explain how to do or make something that can earn a person some money. As an alternative, explain how to either buy or sell something on the Web Site, eBay.

5. Write a definition of a particular emotion.

6. Write an essay that argues the assertion opposite that given in "No Degree Required" on page 175.

Combine Description and Cause-and-Effect Analysis

Describe a popular fashion or a current fad and explain why that fashion or fad is popular.

Respond to a Photograph

Think of a law you think Congress should pass, and then write an essay explaining why our country would be better with this law.

Writing Process Tips for Composing Your Essay

To become a better writer, you should try out the techniques for planning, writing, and rewriting that you learned in Chapters 1 and 2, so you can discover which ones work best for you. As you compose your essay, continue to sample those strategies. In addition, the following procedures may be helpful. No matter what composing strategies you use, however, be sure to work through the Checklist for an Essay on page 198 before submitting your work.

(continued on next page)

PLANNING: OUTLINING THE ESSAY

- Photocopy the map on page 187, and use it to outline your essay.

- If you cannot fill in some parts of the map, try freewriting or clustering to discover more ideas.

WRITING YOUR DRAFT

- Write your draft using the outline map as a guide. Do not try to revise or edit as you go; just push on, skipping troublesome spots if necessary.

REWRITING: REVISING

- Ask two people to read your introduction and tell you whether it creates interest in the essay. If it does not, rework it until your readers say that it does.

- Underline each topic sentence to be sure you have one for every supporting paragraph. Check each one against your thesis to be sure it is relevant.

- Be sure you have followed your general statements with specific ones.

- Check for transitions or repetition for coherence between paragraphs.

SUCCEEDING IN COLLEGE

Be a Successful Note-Taker

To become a better note-taker, read the assignment before the lecture, so the terminology and ideas are familiar to you. Then you can write about them without pausing to wonder what your instructor is saying. Use abbreviations to maintain speed and do not worry about neatness. However, you should rewrite your notes after class, while the lecture is fresh in your mind, while your abbreviations still make sense, and while you can still decipher your handwriting. Rewriting has the added advantage of "setting" ideas so you remember them.

When you rewrite your notes, you can use a version of the outline map, like this:

Subject of Lecture _____

Main point _____

_____

Supporting details _____

_____

Main point _____

_____

Supporting details _____

_____

If you miss something during the lecture, leave a blank area in your notebook, and after class, check with a classmate to recover what you missed. If you like, you can routinely trade notes with a reliable classmate to make sure that you wrote all the important points.

If your note-taking skills need considerable improvement, visit your campus study skills center to learn about the different kinds of note-taking techniques.

Write about It

Learn about two different strategies for taking notes by visiting your campus study skills center, checking out a study skills book from the library, or purchasing a study skills book in your campus bookstore. Explain what you learned that can help you take better notes. As an alternative, compare and contrast your current note-taking process with one you learned about.

DIAGNOSTIC SELF-ASSESSMENT

Note: To check your answers, turn to Appendix II.

■ **Identifying Subjects and Verbs** If you make errors in this section, pay particular attention to Chapter 14.

1. Write the subject and verb for each sentence.
   a. During the last week of December, many stores have excellent sales.

   subject ___sales___   verb ___have___

   b. The number of first-year students was increased by 15 percent.

   subject ___number___   verb ___was increased___

   c. Mateo will not be happy with this job.

   subject ___Mateo___   verb _____

   d. Do you know her name?

   subject ___you___   verb _____

   e. The union and management have endorsed the same candidate for governor.

   subject ___un man___   verb _____

■ **Using Coordination and Subordination** If you make errors in this section, pay particular attention to Chapter 15.

2. A **main clause** has a subject and a verb and can be a sentence; a **subordinate clause** has a subject and a verb but cannot be a sentence. **Coordination** joins two main clauses in a sentence. **Subordination** joins a main clause and a subordinate clause in a sentence. Write a C if the sentence has coordination; write an S if it has subordination.

   a. __S__ If you want to use a search engine effectively, you must learn how to use plus and minus signs to focus your search.

   b. __C__ Most high schools have computers in their classrooms, so more students are graduating with computer skills.

   c. __S__ Cable television stations are very popular; nevertheless, network channels are still the most frequently watched.

D
I
A
G
N
O
S
T
I
C

d. __C__ The voter turnout for the midterm elections was at a record low; apathy among voters is at a record high.

e. __S__ Leah, who wants to become a physical therapist, is working as a hospital volunteer.

■ **Avoiding Sentence Fragments** If you make errors in this section, pay particular attention to Chapter 16.

3. If all the word groups are sentences, write an *S* on the blank. If not, write the number of word groups that are not sentences.

a. __S__ Different kinds of mosquitoes favor different parts of their victims' bodies. Some attack shoulders and above. Others prefer the backs of ankles. Either way, they find the thinnest skin of the body.

b. __1__ Born the son of Russian-Jewish immigrants. George Gershwin created music that fused classical, jazz, blues, and ragtime elements. This fusion is particularly noticeable in his enduring compositions *Porgy and Bess* and *Rhapsody in Blue*.

c. __2__ Walt Disney holds the record for the most Academy Award nominations. Having been nominated 64 times. Although the most nominated living person is John Williams. Disney won a total of 32 Academy Awards.

d. __3__ The U.S. Navy's elite flying squadron is called the Blue Angels. The group got this name in 1946. During the original flying team's trip to New York. When one of the pilots saw the name of the city's Blue Angel Nightclub in the *New Yorker* magazine.

■ **Avoiding Run-On Sentences and Comma Splices** If you make errors in this section, pay particular attention to Chapter 17.

4. A **run-on sentence** or a **comma splice** occurs when main clauses are not correctly joined in the same sentence. (A **main clause** has a subject and a verb and can be a sentence.) If the passage is correct, write C on the blank; if it is incorrect because it has a run-on sentence or comma splice, write I on the blank.

a. __I__ The world's deadliest plant is the castor bean plant, it is 6,000 times deadlier than cyanide. The source of the plant's poison is its protein, which is called *ricin*.

b. __C__ In 1981, members of the first space shuttle crew wanted candy to be included in their food supply, so they chose M&Ms to go into space with them. Thus, M&Ms are now on permanent display at the National Air and Space Museum, located in Washington, D.C.

c. __I__ The alphabet used by the Vikings was called the *Futhark*. The letters were made of straight lines therefore they were easier to carve on wood or stone. The letters were called *runes*, the stones with writing on them were called *runestones*.

d. __I__ Linus Pauling won the Nobel Prize in chemistry in 1954, eight years later, he won the Nobel Peace Prize. He won the Peace Prize for his support of the nuclear test ban treaty.

■ **Writing Sentences with Variety and Parallelism** If you make errors in this section, pay particular attention to Chapter 18.

5. **Sentence variety** refers to varying sentence openers to create a pleasing mix of sentence structures. If the passage has sentence variety, write *yes* on the blank; if it does not, write *no*.

_____ As the storm approached, the townspeople boarded up their homes and businesses. When the mayor ordered voluntary evacuations, most people chose not to leave. After the mayor ordered mandatory evacuations, almost everyone left. When the storm veered north, everyone returned.

6. Place a checkmark next to the correct sentence in each pair.

a. _____ The instructor told the class to read Chapter 5 and that they should take careful notes.

b. _____ The instructor told the class to read Chapter 5 and to take careful notes.

c. _____ I will either get a part-time job, or I will apply for financial aid.

d. _____ Either I will get a part-time job, or I will apply for financial aid.

■ **Choosing Words Carefully** If you make errors in this section, pay particular attention to Chapter 19.

7. Fill in the blank with the better word or phrase from the pair given in parentheses.
   a. (anything/nothing) Even though the child didn't do _____, she was sent to her room.
   b. (any/no) I can't see _____ reason to leave this early.

8. Place a check next to the better sentence.

a. _____ Joanie asked Uri for the 411 on tomorrow's midterm exam.

b. _____ Joanie asked Uri what chapters she should study for tomorrow's midterm exam.

c. _____ I admire Conchetta because she can turn a negative situation into a positive one.

d. _____ I admire Conchetta because when life hands her lemons, she makes lemonade.

CHAPTER 14
Identifying Subjects and Verbs

Much of your success learning and applying grammar rules will depend upon your ability to identify subjects and verbs. If you have trouble identifying subjects and verbs, this chapter will help you. If you already identify subjects and verbs successfully, this chapter will reinforce your understanding and perhaps teach you a few new points. First, take the following pretest to assess your current level of understanding.

PRETEST

Underline each subject once and each verb twice. If you are unsure, do not guess; just move on. Check your answers in Appendix II.

1. Before work, Jeffrey's mother packed his school lunch.

2. Tuition at this school is the second lowest in the state.

3. Marcos has eaten peanut butter sandwiches for lunch every day this week.

4. Mother returned to school and studied business administration.

5. Many people in this city do not know about the proposed industrial park.

6. Joan and her brothers bought their parents a DVD player for their anniversary.

7. The carton of Grandmother's clothes is in the attic.

8. Jacques has been studying for his law school entrance examination.

9. Are the keys still in the car?

10. There will be no excuse for tardiness.

11. Please answer me.

12. At last the holidays are over, and all of us can relax and recover.

13. The students in the reference room of the library are making too much noise.

14. There can be no accidents this time.

15. At the end of the summer, my parents and I will move to Texas and buy a small horse ranch.

SUBJECTS AND VERBS

A sentence has both a subject and a verb. A **subject** is one or more words telling who or what the sentence is about. A **verb** is one or more words telling what the subject does or how the subject exists.

s.	v.
<u>Babies</u>	<u>cry.</u>

Babies: tells who the sentence is about, so this word is the subject.

cry: tells what the subject does, so this word is the verb.

IDENTIFYING VERBS

You may find the subject and verb of a sentence more easily if you first find the verb and then go on to find the subject. The verb is the word or words that change form to show present, past, and future times (known as **tenses**).

> I walk five miles every day.

In this sentence, the verb is *walk*. We know this because *walk* is the word that changes form to show present, past, and future time.

present tense:	Today I *walk*.
past tense:	Yesterday I *walked*
future tense:	Tomorrow I *will walk*

Because verbs indicate time, you can locate them with a simple test. Speak the words *today I*, *yesterday I*, and *tomorrow I* before a word or word group. If the result is sensible and if that word or word group changes form, it is a verb. Try the test with this sentence:

> The wide receiver fumbled the football.

Can we say, "Today I *the*"? "Yesterday I *the*"? "Tomorrow I *the*"? No, we cannot, so *the* is not a verb. Can we say, "Today I *wide*"? Can we say, "Today I *receiver*"? "Today I *football*"? No, of course not, so *wide*, *receiver*, and *football* are not verbs. Notice, however, what happens if we apply the test to *fumbled*:

> Today I *fumble*.
> Yesterday I *fumbled*.
> Tomorrow I *will fumble*.

Fumble changes form to indicate different tenses (times), so it is a verb.

> **NOTE:** A few verbs (like *cost*) do not change form to show time.

Action Verbs

The most common kind of verb is the **action verb**, which shows activity, movement, thought, or process. Here are some examples:

<u>Action verbs showing activity or movement</u>: hit, yell, dance, kick, walk, run, eat, play (The trees *sway* in the breeze.)

<u>Action verbs showing thought</u>: think, consider, wonder, remember, want, ponder (Pat *judges* people harshly.)

<u>Action verbs showing process</u>: learn, try, read, enjoy (I can *explain* her anger.)

Linking Verbs

Another kind of verb is the **linking verb,** which joins or links the subject to something that renames or describes that subject. Here are two examples:

Roberto *is* the best skier in the group. [The verb *is* does not show action. Instead it links the subject *Roberto* with words that describe the subject—"the best skier in the group."]

Roberto	is	the best skier in the group.
subject	linking verb	describes Roberto

Yolanda *was* my best friend. [The verb *was* does not show action. Instead it links the subject *Yolanda* with words that rename the subject—"my best friend."]

Yolanda	was	my best friend.
subject	linking verb	renames Yolanda

Review the following list of linking verbs so you will recognize them in your own sentences:

Linking Verbs

am	was	appear	taste
be	were	feel	smell
is	been	seem	look
are	being	sound	become

Helping Verbs

An action verb or linking verb can appear with another verb, called a **helping verb**. Here are some examples:

Grandma Ramirez *can speak* three languages. [The action verb is *speak*; the helping verb is *can*.]

The train *will be* late. The linking verb is *be*; the helping verb is *will*.]

Review the following list of helping verbs so you will recognize them in your own sentences:

Helping Verbs

am	been	could	have
be	being	will	has
is	may	should	had
are	must	do	shall
was	might	did	
were	can	does	

Notice that some verbs are on both the linking and helping verb lists (*am, is, are, was, were*, for example). When these verbs appear alone, they are linking verbs. When they appear with other verbs, they are helping verbs.

linking verb:	The food *is* too spicy.
helping verb:	The tree *is* dropping its leaves.

Be aware that a sentence can have more than one helping verb.

two helping verbs:	The plane *has been* delayed.
three helping verbs:	I *will have been* gone by then.

Finally, know that *have*, *has*, *had* are usually helping verbs, but the following examples show two times when they are action verbs:

A cat *has* kittens. (*Has* means "gives birth to.")

We *have* lunch at noon. (*Have* means "eat.")

KINDS OF VERBS

Kind	Function	Examples
action verbs	show activity, movement, thought, or process	The bride and groom *dance* beautifully.
		Everybody *hopes* for the best.
		I *try* hard every day.
linking verbs	join the subject to something that renames or describes the subject	Our teacher *is* also a captain in the National Guard.
		The piano *sounds* out of tune.
helping verbs	appear with an action or linking verb	The play *will* not begin on time.

PRACTICE 14.1

Identify each underlined verb as an action verb (av), helping verb (hv), or linking verb (lv). The first two are done as examples.

[1]More than 260,000 people <u>are</u> (hv) <u>buried</u> (av) at Arlington National Cemetery, which <u>conducts</u> approximately 5,400 burials each year. [2]The average number of funerals held there <u>is</u> 20 a day. [3]Of all the national cemeteries in the United States, Arlington <u>has</u> the second-largest number of people buried there. [4]Calverton National Cemetery on Long Island <u>holds</u> the distinction of being the largest. [5]At the cemetery, there <u>can be</u> as many as 7,000 burials a year.

[6]The first graves in Arlington National Cemetery <u>were dug</u> by James Parks. [7]Parks <u>was</u> a former Arlington Estate slave. [8]He <u>was born</u> on the property and <u>can claim</u> to be the only person buried in the cemetery who <u>came</u> into this world on the property. [9]He <u>is interred</u> in Section 15.

PRACTICE 14.2

Underline every verb in the following paragraph.

¹Almost everyone can recognize the opening of Ludwig van Beethoven's *Fifth Symphony*. ²The composer may have expected its popularity. ³However, he would have been surprised about one particular use of his composition. ⁴During World War II, the first four notes became a rallying cry for the Allies. ⁵The first three short notes and the one longer note sounded like the Morse code for the letter *V*—three dots and a dash. ⁶The Allies had adopted the *V* as the symbol for victory. ⁷Beethoven's first four notes from the *Fifth Symphony* were played every night between programs of the British Broadcasting Corporation and extensively in the United States as well. ⁸Clearly, the music had a stirring effect.

Sentences with More Than One Verb

In a sentence, the action verb or the linking verb is called the **main verb**. If the main verb (the action or linking verb) appears with a helping verb, the verbs together are called the **complete verb**.

sentence:	The candidates will debate the issues next Tuesday.
main verb (an action verb):	debate
helping verb:	will
complete verb:	will debate
sentence:	The children do seem cranky.
main verb (a linking verb):	seem
helping verb:	do
complete verb:	do seem

A single sentence can have more than one complete verb. In the following examples, each complete verb is italicized, each main verb is underlined, and each verb is labeled as an action verb, linking verb, or helping verb.

Paul *sat* ^{av} at the window and *waited* ^{av} for Maria.

My sister *had arrived* ^{hv av} by noon, but I *was* ^{lv} too sick to see her.

As the storm *pounded* ^{av} the coastal town, volunteers *evacuated* ^{av} residents who *had ignored* ^{hv av} earlier warnings that winds *could damage* ^{hv ... av} property and life.

NOTE: Be careful of descriptive words such as *not, just, never, only, already,* and *always.* These words are not verbs, although they often appear with verbs.

Earl will not agree to such a scheme. (The verb is *will agree.*)

NOTE: A verb that follows *to* is known as an **infinitive.** The infinitive form will never be part of the complete verb functioning with the subject.

I hesitated to answer the question. (The complete verb is *hesitated,* not *answer,* which follows *to.*)

PRACTICE 14.3

Underline each complete verb. Remember, a verb that follows *to* is not part of the complete verb, and descriptive words are not part of the verb.

Example: The tornado <u>had struck</u> before the warning siren <u>sounded</u>.

1. The class asked the instructor when the final examination would be given.

2. The fire alarm sounded, but many people ignored it because there had been so many false alarms in the past.

3. If I were you, I would take Professor Goldstein for history.

4. It will be years before we know the full effects of the new tax law.

5. If interest rates rise, many people will not purchase new homes.

PRACTICE 14.4

Underline each complete verb. Remember, a verb that follows *to* is not part of the complete verb, and descriptive words are not verbs.

Example: The versatile entertainer <u>sang</u>, <u>danced</u>, and <u>told</u> jokes.

1. Julio always asks the most perceptive questions in class.

2. Michael visited several car lots before he decided which used car to buy.

3. The community health center gives free flu shots, adminsters vaccinations to babies, and checks blood pressure.

4. In my son's third-grade math class, students will learn how to multiply.

5. Jane has already left because she wants to arrive early.

REVIEW PRACTICE 14.5

Underline each complete verb.

[1]Unlike hurricanes and winter storms, thunderstorms affect relatively small areas. [2]The typical thunderstorm spans 15 miles in diameter and lasts an average of 30 minutes. [3]Nearly 1,800 thunderstorms are occurring at any moment around the world—that is, 16 million a year. [4]Despite their small size, all thunderstorms are dangerous. [5]They can produce lightning, which kills more people each year than tornadoes. [6]Heavy rain from thunderstorms can lead to flash flooding. [7]Furthermore, strong winds, hail, and tornadoes are also associated with some thunderstorms.

IDENTIFYING SUBJECTS

The **subject** of a sentence is who or what the sentence is about. You can locate the subject by asking "who or what?" before the verb. The answer will be the subject of the sentence. Consider this sentence:

>   Ivan earned the highest grade on the history midterm.

The verb in this sentence is *earned*. To find the subject, ask, "who or what earned?" The answer is "*Ivan* earned." Therefore, *Ivan* is the subject. Now look at this sentence.

>   Before Easter my cat was ill.

The verb is *was*. Ask "who or what was?" and the answer is *cat*. *Cat*, then, is the subject of the sentence.

CAUTION: Some words can be subjects in some sentences and verbs in others. *Run* is such a word.

run as verb: I *run* five miles before breakfast every day.

run as subject: My morning *run* was refreshing.

FAQ

Q: Why should I know how to identify subjects and verbs?

A: You must be able to identify subjects and verbs in order to write effective sentences and avoid errors with pronouns, verb forms, fragments, run-ons, and comma splices.

PRACTICE 14.6

Underline the subject once and the complete verb twice. To find the verb, locate the word or words that change form to show time; to find the subject, ask "who or what?" before the verb.

Example: Every <u>child</u> <u>is</u> familiar with Cracker Jack.

1. The snack was created by F. W. Rueckheim at the Chicago World's Fair in 1893.

2. The popular snack got its name from a popular expression of the day.

3. People used to say "crackerjack" to mean "great."

4. The toy prize was added to Cracker Jack boxes in 1912.

5. Cracker Jack's popularity has not declined over the years.

PRACTICE 14.7

Underline the subject once and the complete verb twice. To find the verb, locate the word or words that change form to show time; to find the subject, ask "who or what?" before the verb.

Example: <u>Champagne</u> <u>is</u> often <u>drunk</u> at celebrations.

1. Surprisingly, this alcoholic beverage was invented by Dom Perignon, a Benedictine monk.

2. The cleric was put in charge of the vineyards at his monastery in 1668.

3. During his tenure there, Perignon developed sparkling wines.

4. These wines were named for the Champagne section of France.

5. Also, Dom Perignon has come to be the name of a very prestigious and expensive bottle of wine.

Sentences with Prepositional Phrases

A **preposition** shows how two things relate to each other in time or space.

The wallet was *behind* the couch. [*Behind* is a preposition; it shows how the wallet and couch are positioned in space: One is behind the other.]

We had dinner *before* the concert. [*Before* is a preposition; it shows how dinner and the concert are positioned in time: One was before the other.]

You can identify many (but not all) prepositions if you think of a box and a baseball. Any word that can describe the relationship of the baseball to the box is a preposition. The baseball can be *in* the box, *on* the box, *near* the box, and *under* the box; so *in*, *on*, *near*, and *under* are prepositions. Here is a list of some common prepositions:

Common Prepositions

about	before	inside	through
above	behind	into	to
across	between	like	toward
after	by	of	under
along	during	off	up
among	for	on	with
around	from	out	within
at	in	over	without

A **prepositional phrase** is a preposition and the words that work with it. Here are examples of prepositional phrases. The prepositions are underlined as a study aid.

<u>about</u> this time	<u>among</u> my best friends	<u>at</u> noon
<u>by</u> tomorrow	<u>into</u> the lake	<u>to</u> me
<u>in</u> the back	<u>over</u> the rainbow	<u>on</u> the dog

The subject of a sentence will *never* be part of a prepositional phrase. Therefore, to find the subject of a sentence, you can cross out all prepositional phrases first. The subject will be among the remaining words.

The leader ~~of the scouts~~ is a wilderness expert. (The subject is <u>leader</u>.)

A box ~~of old clothes~~ is ~~on the kitchen table~~. (The subject is <u>box</u>.)

If you do not eliminate prepositional phrases in the preceding sentences, you might be fooled into thinking the subject of the first sentence is *scouts* and that the subject of the second sentence is *clothes*.

PRACTICE 14.8

Cross out the prepositional phrases and then underline the subject.

Example: ~~In the middle of the night~~, heavy <u>winds</u> damaged the orchard.

1. The top of the dresser is covered with dust.

2. The flock of geese flew in formation across the horizon.

3. At the back of the lecture hall, one student slept with his head resting on a pile of books.

4. The last twenty minutes of the movie were fast-paced and cleverly directed.

5. With a little practice, anyone can learn word-processing skills.

PRACTICE 14.9

Cross out the prepositional phrases and then underline the subject.

Example: The <u>pile</u> ~~of leaves~~ must be raked ~~into the street~~.

1. Six of us plan to visit New York during winter break.

2. The entire defensive line of the football team earned high grades last semester.

3. Some people with allergies find it difficult to live in this part of the country.

4. This stack of old encyclopedias can be taken to the used book sale.

5. In the corner, the mother cat stretched out for her nap.

Sentences with Inverted Order

The subject usually comes before the verb, as in this example:

       s.   v.
The children romped with the playful dog.

Sometimes the subject comes *after* the verb. Then the sentence has **inverted order**. A sentence that asks a question has inverted order.

  v. s.
Is the soup hot enough?

In this sentence, the verb *is* comes first. When we ask "who or what is?" we get the answer *soup*, so *soup* is the subject. In this case, the subject comes after the verb.

A sentence that begins with *there is, there are, there was, there were, here is, here are, here was, here were* will also have inverted order.

    v.   s.
There were twenty people on a waiting list for that apartment.

The verb is *were*, and the subject is *people*. (*Were* is the verb because it changes form to indicate different tenses, and *people* is the subject because it answers the question "who or what were?")

PRACTICE 14.10

For each sentence, underline the subject once and the verb twice. Remember, find the verb first and then find the subject by asking "who or what?" before the verb.

Example Here <u>are</u> the <u>folders</u>.

1. Is the storm over yet?

2. There are twelve people in this elevator.

3. Was your week in Ft. Lauderdale relaxing?

4. In the kitchen drawer were three dirty knives.

5. Here are the missing files.

PRACTICE 14.11

For each sentence, underline the subject once and the verb twice. Remember, find the verb and then find the subject by asking "who or what?" before the verb.

Example: There <u>are</u> only three <u>people</u> here.

1. Is the exam next Tuesday or next Wednesday?

2. On the window sill sat the fat calico cat.

3. There is some confusion about the new graduation requirements.

4. Are you free for dinner Thursday night?

5. Beside the peaceful brook sat Rusty and his dog.

Sentences with More Than One Subject

A sentence can have more than one subject:

The *money* and the *credit cards* were stolen from my wallet.

The verb in this sentence is *were stolen*. When we ask "who or what were stolen?" we get the answer *money* and *credit cards*. Thus, *money* and *credit cards* are both subjects.

Now study this sentence:

Greg slid into home plate as the shortstop made a play at second base.

This sentence has two verbs: *slid* and *made*. When we ask "who or what slid?" we get *Greg* for an answer; when we ask "who or what made?" we get *shortstop* for an answer. Therefore, this sentence has two subjects: *Greg* and *shortstop*.

PRACTICE 14.12

Each sentence has more than one subject. Underline each of these subjects. Begin by finding the verb or verbs and then ask "who or what?"

Example: Both <u>Senator Polanski</u> and <u>Governor Perry</u> favor the proposed jobs bill.

1. The school board and the leaders of the teachers' union met behind closed doors for most of the afternoon.

2. Police work is rewarding, but police officers do not make much money.

3. Too many accidents have occurred at the junction of Routes 11 and 45, so a traffic light will be installed.

4. The singer and her accompanist performed an encore in response to the standing ovation.

5. The rain fell for hours, and soon the small streams began to flood low-lying areas.

PRACTICE 14.13

Each sentence has more than one subject. Underline each of these subjects.

Example: Your <u>time</u> and your <u>energy</u> are needed on this project.

1. The rabbit and her young fled in panic when the lawn mower ran over their burrow.

2. Both the manager and the assistant manager apologized for the poor service.

3. The fire alarm sounded, so the students filed out of the room in an orderly fashion.

4. I planted a garden in my backyard, but the rabbits ate most of my crops.

5. Two robins and three sparrows fed contentedly at the bird feeder outside the kitchen window.

REVIEW PRACTICE 14.14

Underline the subjects in the sentences in the following paragraph.

¹There are more than two billion quarts of ice cream eaten in the United States each year. ²With that figure, you would think ice cream originated in the United States, but the treat was first created in the Orient. ³Marco Polo encountered it there and brought the idea back to Italy. ⁴From Italy, recipes for the confection were carried to France. ⁵In France, ice cream became very popular with the nobility. ⁶An effort was made to keep the recipes for ice cream a secret from the common people. ⁷The first factory for the manufacture of ice cream was started in Baltimore in 1851, but the real development of ice cream did not occur until after 1900, with the advent of refrigeration. ⁸There is sugar in ice cream, but the treat is still a fairly nutritious food. ⁹One-third pint of vanilla ice cream has as much calcium as one-half cup of milk. ¹⁰Protein and vitamin B are also plentiful in vanilla ice cream.

POST TEST

In both A and B, underline the subjects once and the complete verbs twice. You will have to draw on everything you have learned so far about subjects and verbs.

A.

1. Six of us had decided to travel to Bowling Green for the big game.

2. For the past year, Juan, Lisa, and Maria have volunteered to work in the children's hospital for three hours every week.

3. The first American to orbit the earth was John Glenn.

4. Luis will never agree to your plan, but you may convince Margo.

5. As the price of cigarettes rises, more people will quit smoking.

6. The trees in Vermont have already changed color.

7. The quarterback faked a pass and then ran up the middle for a five-yard gain.

8. Why are you going alone on your vacation?

9. Behind the old barn there is a beautiful patch of clover in bloom.

10. You should take this book and return it to the library.

11. Here is the report, but I must have it back in a week.

12. On the top shelf of my closet are the clothes for the rummage sale.

13. More people must be told about organ donation programs, for such programs save lives.

(continued on next page)

14. Since Mario quit smoking, he has become irritable and generally unpleasant.

15. As more people become comfortable with computers, information will be processed faster than ever.

16. To me, swearing is offensive.

17. The pile of dirty clothes in the closet is beginning to smell.

18. You must add the eggs before you add the flour and salt.

19. Peter, Helen, and David decided that they would never campaign for Jeffrey in the student council election.

20. The issue of fair play must be considered in this case.

B.

[1]People have dreams every night. [2]The early dreams usually last only a few minutes, but the dream just before morning can be as long as an hour. [3]This is the dream we are most likely to remember. [4]There are conflicting explanations for dreams. [5]Freud thought that dreams hide worrisome ideas. [6]He said that troublesome thoughts would wake us if they were not disguised as something else. [7]However, many scientists and dream researchers disagree. [8]They have said that dreams are caused by the jumble of electrical impulses in the brain at night. [9]Dreams occur when the brain tries to make sense of these confusing impulses. [10]For example, if you dream that you cannot move, your brain may be trying to explain the paralysis of deep sleep.

SUCCEEDING IN COLLEGE

Learn Strategies for Reading and Studying Textbooks

When you read your textbooks, pay attention to the verbs because they can affect meaning significantly. Consider, for example how meaning is different in these sentences:

- Researchers *believe* that birth trauma can cause attention deficit disorder.

- Researchers *suspect* that birth trauma can cause attention deficit disorder.

- Researchers *doubt* that birth trauma can cause attention deficit disorder.

Textbook material can be difficult, so reading and studying it requires special strategies. Some of the following may work for you. If you need additional help, visit your campus reading lab or study skills center.

- Preview the material to get a sense of what is in store. Read chapter introductions, headings, captions, and charts. If the chapter closes with a summary, read that summary.

- Read long or difficult material in stages. Try 3-5 pages in the morning, another 3-5 in the afternoon, and so on.

- Look up words you do not understand.

- Read the material more than once. The first time through, concentrate on what you do understand and do not worry about material you do not understand. In subsequent readings, work to understand more. If there is still some material that you do not understand, ask questions in class or during your instructor's office hours.

- At the end of every section, look away from the book and review in your mind what you have read.

- Take notes on or highlight important points.

- Write to "set" the material. Summarize what you have read, outline the material, write and answer study questions, or list main points and important supporting details.

Write about It

Study five pages from a textbook from another class, using two or more of the procedures above—preferably ones that you have not tried before. Then, in a paragraph evaluate the success of the strategies you tried. Be sure to explain why you think the strategies did or did not work for you.

CHAPTER 15
Using Coordination and Subordination

If you can use coordination and subordination effectively, you can express yourself with precision and in a more pleasing style. This chapter will help you learn what you need to know, but first take the following pretest to assess your current level of understanding.

PRETEST

A **main clause** has a subject and a verb and can be a sentence; a **subordinate clause** has a subject and a verb but cannot be a sentence. **Coordination** joins two main clauses in a sentence. **Subordination** joins a main clause and a subordinate clause in a sentence. Write a C if the sentence has coordination; write an S if it has subordination. If you are unsure, do not write anything. Check your answers in Appendix II.

1. _____ William decided to become a vegetarian, even though he loved beef.

2. _____ None of the new fall television series has become a runaway hit, but I do not know why.

3. _____ After she took a nap, Louise felt ready to begin studying.

4. _____ I am moving out of the residence hall, and I am renting a house with friends.

5. _____ Before the last note sounded, the audience jumped up and applauded.

6. _____ The committee deliberated for more than an hour before it reached a decision about the new bylaws.

7. _____ Timothy sprained his ankle, but he refuses to use crutches.

8. _____ The plumber did not have the right tools on the truck to fix the problem with the pipes, so he went back to his shop.

9. _____ Marta decided that she would rather be happy than right, so she apologized to Curt.

10. _____ Surprisingly, the mayor decided not to run for reelection, but she may consider a senate bid next year.

IDENTIFYING CLAUSES

A **clause** is a group of words with both a subject and a verb (see Chapter 14 on how to identify subjects and verbs). The following word groups are clauses (the subjects are underlined once, and the verbs are underlined twice).

the snow fell softly

after the marathon runner crossed the finish line

Helen was not invited to the reception

before the storm warnings were issued

The following word groups are *not* clauses because they do not have both a subject *and* a verb. (Word groups that do not have both a subject *and* a verb are **phrases**.)

seeing the log in his path

in the pantry

behind the sofa in the den

frightened by the snarling dog

> **NOTE:** Look again at the lists of clauses and phrases and notice that length has nothing to do with whether a word group is a clause or a phrase.

PRACTICE 15.1

Place an *X* next to each clause. Remember, a clause has both a subject and a verb.

1. _____ before Lorenzo could finish his sentence

2. _____ around the corner from my house

3. _____ against the wishes of her parents and friends

4. _____ she means well

5. _____ wishing I could help you more

6. _____ the lead singer was the best performer in the show

7. _____ federal funds were requested to repair the dam

8. _____ not wanting to intrude on Martha's privacy

9. _____ the construction foreman took full responsibility for the damages

10. _____ a hawk soared in the distance

Two Kinds of Clauses

A clause that can be a sentence is a **main clause**; a clause that cannot be a sentence is a **subordinate clause**. The following clauses are main clauses because they can be sentences. In fact, if you add capital letters and periods, you *do* have sentences.

main clause:	the movie ended very late
sentence:	The movie ended very late.
main clause:	freedom of speech is our most valuable liberty
sentence:	Freedom of speech is our most valuable liberty.
main clause:	her advice was not very helpful
sentence:	Her advice was not very helpful.

The following are subordinate clauses. They have subjects and verbs (all clauses do), but they cannot stand alone as sentences.

subordinate clause:	because the union went on strike
subordinate clause:	the doctor examined the patient's throat
subordinate clause:	when the pitcher threw his best curveball

PRACTICE 15.2

Write *SC* next to each subordinate clause and *MC* next to each main clause.

1. _____ after Tony checked the locks on the doors

2. _____ when he tried desperately not to show fear

3. _____ we asked the committee to reconsider its report

4. _____ the board of trustees raised tuition

5. _____ when the last vote was counted

6. _____ because the summer drought created a food shortage

7. _____ I left for the appointment ten minutes late

8. _____ before the movers lifted the chest of drawers in the attic

9. _____ the consumer price index points to a recession

10. _____ since Jan was awarded two scholarships

COORDINATION

Coordination is the proper joining of two main clauses in one sentence. (Remember, main clauses can stand as sentences.)

Joining Main Clauses with Coordinating Conjunctions

You can join main clauses in one sentence with a comma and one of the following **coordinating conjunctions**:

FAQ

Q: Is there an easy way to remember the coordinating conjunctions?

A: Think of "fanboys." Each letter stands for one of the coordinating conjunctions: *for, and, nor, but, or, yet, so.*

Coordinating Conjunctions

and	or	so
but	for	yet
		nor

Here are two main clauses:

> The traffic light at Fifth and Elm is not working.
>
> No major accidents have been reported.

Here are the main clauses properly joined in one sentence with a comma and the coordinating conjunction *but*:

> *main clause* ↓
> The traffic light at Fifth and Elm is not working, but no major
> *main clause* ↓
> accidents have been reported.

Here are two other main clauses:

> Jake's frustration was building quickly.
>
> He decided to get away for the weekend and relax.

These main clauses can be properly joined with a comma and coordinating conjunction *so*:

> *main clause* ↓
> Jake's frustration was building quickly, so he decided to
> *main clause* ↓
> get away for the weekend and relax.

With a comma and coordinating conjunction, you can do more than join main clauses. As the following chart explains and illustrates, you can show the relationship between the clauses.

Relationships Shown with Coordinating Conjunctions

1. and (shows addition)

   Three of us wanted to visit the museum, and two of us wanted to see a play.

2. but (shows contrast)
   yet (shows contrast)

   Your plan is a good one, but we do not have the money to implement it.

   Your plan is a good one, yet we do not have the money to implement it.

3. or (shows an alternative or choice)

   Professor Jennings explained that we could write a ten-page research paper, or we could take a final examination.

4. for (means "because")

   The linoleum floor in the basement was buckling, for water had seeped in during the spring rains.

5. so (means "as a result")

   The new model cars are in the showrooms, so now is the time to get a good deal on last year's models.

6. nor (means "not either one")

   My keys are not on the table, nor are they in my coat.

NOTE: When main clauses are joined by *nor*, the verb comes before the subject in the second clause.

Coordination: Joining Main Clauses with a Comma and a Coordinating Conjunction

Two main clauses can be joined as a single sentence with a comma and a coordinating conjunction.

main clause	+	comma and coordinating conjunction	+	main clause

, and

, but

, or

, for

, so

, yet

, nor

PRACTICE 15.3

To join the main clauses properly in a sentence, place a comma and write an appropriate coordinating conjunction on the blank.

Example: Harry's throat was sore and raspy _____*, and*_____ his temperature was well above normal.

1. Scattered afternoon thundershowers are predicted _____ Enrico decided to begin painting the house anyway.

2. Mother enrolled in college _____ she has always regretted marrying before she earned her business degree.

3. The Cubs were behind by five runs in the fourth inning _____ the coach was forced to change pitchers.

4. Nicotine-flavored gum can help a person quit smoking _____ it is no substitute for willpower.

5. We can travel the turnpike and arrive quickly _____ we can take the back roads and enjoy the countryside.

6. In the lake behind the house, Gregory caught a three-foot catfish

   _____ Jorges caught a four-foot bass.

7. This afternoon while we are in Charleston, we can visit Ft. Sumter

   _____ we can go to an authentic plantation.

8. The highway department received a 30 percent increase in revenue

   _____ two-thirds of the roads remain in disrepair.

9. The board of education decided to cancel night football games

   _____ too much vandalism was occurring when the games were over.

10. The bride carried a bouquet of daisies _____ she wore a vintage dress.

PRACTICE 15.4

Join the main clauses into one sentence, using a comma and coordinating conjunction.

Example:

To earn tuition money, Josef dropped out of school for a semester.
He took a job as a nurse's aid.

To earn tuition money, Josef dropped out of school for a semester, and he

took a job as a nurse's aid.

1. Maria and John are poor choices to head the committee.
   They are disorganized and unreliable.

   _____

   _____

2. The plot of the movie was boring and predictable.
   The actors were fresh and engaging.

   _____

   _____

3. You can borrow my laptop to type your term paper.
   You can pay someone to do it for you.

   _____

   _____

4. The National Weather Service issued a thunderstorm warning.
   The umpire postponed the Little League championship game.

   _____

   _____

5. Michael passed the ball to Jeff.
   Jeff kicked it into the net to score the winning goal.

   _____

   _____

6. Many people thought videocassette recorders would seriously hurt the movie industry.
   The opposite proved to be true.

   _____

   _____

7. Currently, no cure exists for myasthenia gravis.
   Researchers are working hard to help those afflicted with this neurological disorder.

   _____

   _____

8. Those in need of extra help can visit the Tutoring Center.
   They can go to the Student Services Office.

   _____

   _____

9. Self-hypnosis can help people suffering from stress.
   It is an effective relaxation technique.

   _____

   _____

10. Lorenzo began a rigorous exercise program.
    He had to lose ten pounds before winter practice drills began.

    _____

    _____

11. With the new state funds, the school board hired three teachers.
    They decided to remodel the high school library.

    _____

    _____

12. Thirty students were accepted into the medical program.
    Only two-thirds of them will eventually graduate.

    _____

    _____

13. Not everyone enjoyed the theater department's production.
    Those who did raved about it.

    _____

    _____

14. Be sure to determine what you need before buying a computer.
    You could end up with a system that does not fill your needs.

    _____

    _____

15. Fifty percent of the student body was absent with the flu.
The principal still did not cancel classes.

_____

_____

PRACTICE 15.5

Create more coordination in the paragraph by combining sentences 2 and 3, sentences 4 and 5, sentences 6 and 7, sentences 8 and 9, sentences 10 and 11, and sentences 12 and 13. To combine each pair of sentences, add a comma and an appropriate coordinating conjunction. Cross out periods and capital letters as necessary.

Example:

Adolescence is a difficult time, /~~Teenagers~~ need their friends.
, so teenagers

[1]When people become teenagers, they begin to need intimacy in their friendships. [2]Adolescents are eager to share their hopes and fears. [3]They enjoy trading secrets with others they trust. [4]Furthermore, teens have a stronger need for close friends than younger people. [5]They spend more time away from their parents. [6]Some parents fear the influence friends exert on their teenagers. [7]Contrary to popular belief, peer pressure is not necessarily stronger than family ties. [8]Still, friends are very important to teens. [9]They help them make key decisions about college and careers. [10]Also, friends help them sort out right decisions from wrong ones. [11]Friends provide "reality checks" for adolescents. [12]Some teen friendships are short-lived. [13]Others last long into the teenagers' adulthood.

PRACTICE 15.6

On a separate sheet, write eight sentences. Each sentence should have two main clauses joined with a comma and a coordinating conjunction. Use each coordinating conjunction at least once.

Joining Main Clauses with Conjunctive Adverbs

You can join main clauses in one sentence with a semicolon, one of the following **conjunctive adverbs**, and a comma:

Conjunctive Adverbs.

; however,	; furthermore,	; thus,
; nevertheless,	; moreover,	; consequently,
; nonetheless,	; therefore,	

Here are two main clauses (word groups that can be sentences):

The editorial in Sunday's paper made a good point.

It will not change many people's minds.

Here are the main clauses properly joined in one sentence with a semi-colon, the word *however*, and a comma:

main clause   *main clause*

The editorial in Sunday's paper made a good point; however, it will not change many people's minds.

Here are two other main clauses:

Next fall, tuition will increase by 10 percent.

The cost of living in a dorm will rise by 5 percent.

These main clauses can be properly joined with a semicolon, the word *furthermore*, and a comma:

main clause

Next fall, tuition will increase by 10 percent; furthermore, the cost of living in a dorm will rise by 5 percent.

main clause

With a semicolon, conjunctive adverb, and comma, you can do more than join main clauses. As the following chart explains and illustrates, you can show the relationship between the clauses.

Relationships Shown with Conjunctive Adverbs

1. however, (means "but")
   nevertheless, (means "but")
   nonetheless, (means "but")

   The snow plows worked through the night to clear the roads;
   however, many streets were still impassable.

(continued on next page)

The snow plows worked through the night to clear the roads; nevertheless, many streets were still impassable.

The snow plows worked through the night to clear the roads; nonetheless, many streets were still impassable.

2. furthermore, (means "in addition")

moreover, (means "in addition")

To save money, the transit authority must raise fares; furthermore, it plans to reduce the number of buses in operation.

To save money, the transit authority must raise fares; moreover, it plans to reduce the number of buses in operation.

3. therefore, (means "as a result")

thus, (means "as a result")

consequently, (means "as a result")

I am hoping to earn a scholarship my sophomore year; therefore, I must maintain a B average.

I am hoping to earn a scholarship my sophomore year; thus, I must maintain a B average.

I am hoping to earn a scholarship my sophomore year; consequently, I must maintain a B average.

FAQ:

Q: The words in the conjunctive adverb list are also mentioned as transitions on pages 67–68. Why?

A: Conjunctive adverb is the words' part of speech. *Transition* is the words' function. Thus, these words are conjunctive adverbs that can function as transitions.

Coordination: Joining Main Clauses with a Semicolon, Conjunctive Adverb, and Comma

Two main clauses can be joined in a single sentence with a semicolon, a conjunctive adverb, and a comma.

main clause	+	semicolon and conjunctive adverb and comma	+	main clause

; however,

; nevertheless,

; nonetheless,

; furthermore,

; moreover,

; therefore,

; thus,

; consequently,

PRACTICE 15.7

Join the main clauses properly with a semicolon, an appropriate conjunctive adverb, and a comma.

Example: The temperature only went up to 65 degrees

_____*; however,*_____ most of us decided to go swimming anyway.

1. The mayor spoke to city council members for over an hour

   _____ he did not persuade them to pass the budget bill.

2. The examination has five essay questions and thirty true and false questions

   _____ I was able to complete it in less than the time allowed.

3. Julian is the top rebounder on the basketball team _____ he is a star defensive lineman on the football team.

4. Many researchers claim that children who watch violence on television

   become desensitized to violence in real life _____ too few parents control the amount of violence their children watch on the small screen.

5. Federal funding for public television has been cut _____ contributions from private businesses are being sought.

6. After the storm, power was not restored for twenty hours _____ much of the food in my refrigerator had to be thrown out.

7. Dr. Juarez explained that caffeine interferes with the body's absorption of

   iron _____ caffeine can contribute to the formation of cysts.

8. To write an effective argument essay, avoid personal attacks

   _____ acknowledge the point of view of those who disagree with you.

9. Some parents believe schools should pile on the homework

   _____ recent studies reveal that excessive amounts of homework are counterproductive.

10. The police have no suspects in custody _____ they hope to make an arrest soon.

PRACTICE ·15.8

Join the main clauses in one sentence with a semicolon, an appropriate conjunctive adverb, and a comma.

Example:

Emilio is a charming child.
He is a loyal, caring friend.

Emilio is a charming child; furthermore, he is a loyal, caring friend.

_____

1. For years there were more teachers than teaching jobs.
   Now this trend is beginning to reverse itself.

   _____

   _____

2. To locate the escaped convict, the police set up roadblocks.
   They conducted a house-to-house search.

   _____

   _____

3. New signs have been put up on campus.
   Finding most of the buildings is easier.

   _____

   _____

4. Good writing skills are important for success in college.
   They are just as important on the job.

   _____

   _____

5. The school tax levy was defeated by voters.
   No new school texts can be purchased this year.

   _____

   _____

6. The new automobile assembly plant will be open by November.
   The unemployment rate in this area should drop.

   _____

   _____

7. Carlo was accepted into graduate school to study chemistry.
   He was awarded a scholarship for academic excellence.

   _____

   _____

8. Louise has been a hospital volunteer for three years.
   Now she has decided to apply for a paid position.

   _____

   _____

9. Writers who wait for inspiration may never get much done.
   Writers who freewrite for ideas will make more progress.

   _____

   _____

10. Gary was in top condition for the marathon.
    He still did not expect to place in the top ten.

    _____

    _____

11. Susan pretended she was not bothered by losing her job.
    Those close to her knew she was depressed.

    _____

    _____

12. The assembly-line workers ended their two-week strike.
    The plant would be back in operation by mid-afternoon.

    _____

    _____

13. Ivana earned a scholarship for her high math grades.
    She won a scholarship to play on the women's basketball team.

    _____

    _____

14. Some students become overly nervous when they take exams.
    They are too tense to perform well.

    _____

    _____

15. The firefighters were granted a 5 percent pay raise.
    They still make less than they deserve.

    _____

    _____

REVIEW PRACTICE 15.9

On a separate sheet, rewrite the following paragraph by joining some sentences with coordination. Then read your revised version out loud to notice how much more smoothly it reads than the original. (More than one satisfactory revision is possible.)

[1]In 1920, Josephine Dickinson was newly married. [2]She was a willing cook. [3]She was somewhat clumsy and kept injuring herself in the kitchen. [4]Her husband, Earl, a cotton buyer for the local Johnson and Johnson plant, found himself constantly tending to Josephine's little cuts and burns. [5]One night, Earl tried to design a bandage that would stay in place. [6]He unrolled a length of sterile gauze along the middle of the tape. [7]Then he wrapped the whole assembly in crinoline. [8]As needed, Josephine could cut an appropriate length from the roll. [9]She could peel off the crinoline and apply the bandage. [10]Earl told a company manager about his invention, which soon emerged as Johnson and Johnson's Band-Aid. [11]At first, sales were slow. [12]They soon gained momentum, thanks to a campaign giving Band-Aids to the Boy Scouts and butchers.

SUBORDINATION

A **main clause** has a subject and a verb and can be a sentence. A **subordinate clause** has a subject and a verb but cannot be a sentence.

main clause: the doctor explained the symptoms

subordinate clause: when the doctor explained the symptoms

A subordinate clause is introduced by one of the **subordinating conjunctions**, words like the following:

Subordinating Conjunctions

after	before	when
although	even though	whenever
as	if	where
as if	in order to	wherever
as long as	since	whether
as soon as	so that	while
as though	unless	
because	until	

Joining a Main Clause with a Subordinate Clause

A subordinate clause and a main clause can be joined in the same sentence. This joining is called **subordination**.

subordinate clause: since the polls do not close for another hour
main clause: we do not know the election results

Now here are the subordinate clause and main clause in one sentence:

Since the polls do not close for another hour, we do not know the election results.

In the preceding example, the subordinate clause comes before the main clause. You can also place the main clause first:

We do not know the election results, since the polls do not close for another hour.

Here are another subordinate clause and main clause:

subordinate clause: when I graduated from high school
main clause: I expected to join the army.

Now here are the subordinate clause and main clause in one sentence:

When I graduated from high school, I expected to join the army.

or

I expected to join the army when I graduated from high school.

PUNCTUATION NOTE: When the subordinate clause comes before the main clause, place a comma after the subordinate clause. This rule is illustrated in the previous example sentences.

PRACTICE 15.10

Each sentence has a main clause and a subordinate clause. Underline the subordinate clause once and the main clause twice. Draw a circle around the subordinating conjunction that introduces the subordinate clause. (Notice the commas after the subordinate clauses at the beginning of sentences.)

Example: (When) Paul saw the stranded motorist, he quickly pulled to the side of the road to help.

1. If it does not rain in the next day or two, most of the corn crop will be lost.

2. Because Scarsella's serves the best food in town, the restaurant is always crowded.

3. The woman was clearly embarrassed when a cake with candles was brought to her table in the center of the crowded restaurant.

4. Lizette decided to end her relationship with Howard, since he had such a bad temper.

5. After the orchestra sounded its last note, the audience applauded.

6. Janice will leave for Florida when final exams are over.

7. Since I am working thirty hours a week in the record store, I can only attend school part-time.

8. The first-grade teacher was concerned about Tad because he seemed tired all the time.

9. While the insurance agent explained the difference between the two policies, I decided what to buy.

10. Tavi cut up his credit cards before he went too far into debt.

PRACTICE 15.11

Join the main clause and subordinate clause into a single sentence. Place the subordinate clause first or last according to the directions given. (Place a comma after a subordinate clause that comes before the main clause.)

Example:

(Place the subordinate clause first.)
while the teacher explained cell division
the class took notes furiously

While the teacher explained cell division, the class took notes furiously.

1. (Place the subordinate clause last.)
because she had a frightening dream
the child woke up crying

2. (Place the subordinate clause first.)
until you exercise regularly and quit smoking
you will be short of breath

3. (Place the subordinate clause last.)
since she was not sure what she wanted to do after high school
Tasha decided to enlist in the navy

4. (Place the subordinate clause first.)
although I loved the book
I hated the movie version of *Hitchhiker's Guide to the Galaxy*.

5. (Place the subordinate clause last.)
before he auditioned for a role in *Rent*.
Juan took six weeks of voice lessons

_____

_____

PRACTICE 15.12

Change one of the main clauses to a subordinate clause by placing an appropriate subordinating conjunction in front of it. Then join the new subordinate clause and the remaining main clause into a single sentence. Place some of the subordinate clauses first and some of them last. Also, place a comma after a subordinate clause that comes first.

Example:

Diane and Mohammed moved to Virginia.
Seth and Janet were afraid they would not see them again.

Because Diane and Mohammed moved to Virginia, Seth and Janet were afraid

they would not see them again.

1. Cass was unsure of what courses she should take next semester.
She made an appointment with her academic advisor.

_____

_____

2. Kevin apologized for being inconsiderate.
Miguel still could not forgive him.

_____

_____

3. The senator has no money to finance a reelection campaign.
He decided not to seek a second term in office.

_____

_____

4. The employer improved working conditions.
The union has vowed to remain on strike.

_____

_____

5. Many people believe anger is a destructive emotion.
   I find it to be a healthy, adaptive one.

   _____

   _____

PRACTICE 15.13

On a separate sheet, rewrite the following paragraph by joining some sentences with appropriate subordinating conjunctions to create subordination. Then read your revised version to notice how much more smoothly it reads than the original. (More than one revision is possible.)

[1]A talent scout met Margaret Mitchell, the author of *Gone with the Wind*. [2]He was in Atlanta to find new writers. [3]He had been told that Mitchell was writing a very important book. [4]However, Mitchell wrote for her own satisfaction. [5]She would not show the talent scout her book. [6]He was about to leave the city. [7]Mitchell changed her mind and called him from the lobby of his hotel. [8]He arrived downstairs to find the 4 feet 11 inch Mitchell sitting on a sofa dwarfed by two piles of manuscript stacked to her shoulders. [9]The manuscript was very large. [10]He had to buy an extra suitcase to lug it back to New York. [11]His publishing company, Macmillan, snapped up the novel. [12]*Gone with the Wind* sold 50,000 copies in one day and won the Pulitzer Prize. [13]Macmillan's decision proved to be a wise one.

PRACTICE 15.14

On a separate sheet, write five sentences that join one main clause and one subordinate clause.

Joining a Main Clause with a Relative Clause

One kind of subordinate clause begins with one of these words:

who, whose (to refer to people)

which (to refer to things and animals)

that (to refer to people or things)

These words are called **relative pronouns**, and the subordinate clauses they introduce are called **relative clauses**.

The second method of subordination involves joining a main clause and a relative clause, like this:

sentence:	The boy who won the award is my son.
main clause:	the boy is my son
relative clause:	who won the award.

Here are other examples:

sentence:	The class that I am taking is time-consuming.
main clause:	the class is time-consuming
relative clause:	that I am taking
sentence:	Jocelyn, whose art is displayed in the student gallery, will paint your portrait.
main clause:	Jocelyn will paint your portrait
relative clause:	whose art is displayed in the student gallery
sentence:	You may use my car, which needs gas.
main clause:	you may use my car
relative clause:	which needs gas

If a relative clause is needed to identify who or what is referred to, it is **restrictive**. If the relative clause is not needed to identify who or what is referred to, it is **nonrestrictive**.

restrictive: The police officer *who saved the child from drowning* is my neighbor.

"Who saved the child from drowning" is needed for identifying the police officer. Without the clause, we cannot tell which police officer is referred to.

nonrestrictive: Officer Manuel, *who saved the child from drowning*, is my neighbor.

"Who saved the child from drowning" is not needed for identifying who saved the child because the person's name is given.

PUNCTUATION NOTE: Set off nonrestrictive (not needed for identification) relative clauses with commas:

Bridgett, *who scored fifteen points*, was the most valuable player.
That man, *whose name I forget*, is suspicious looking.
That movie, *which appeals to me*, is playing at the Strand.

Do not set off restrictive clauses:

Any employee *who works for me* must have good computer skills.
The watch *that I found* looks valuable.
The child *whose balloon broke* began to cry.

PRACTICE 15.15

Combine the sentences by turning the second sentence into a relative clause that begins with *who, whose, which,* or *that*. Place the relative clause after the subject of the first sentence. Be prepared to explain your use of commas.

Examples:

The mayor does not plan to run for reelection.
The mayor does not get along with the city council.

The mayor, who does not get along with the city council, does not plan to run

for reelection.

The kitten is now a member of my family.
I found the kitten last week.

The kitten that I found last week is now a member of my family.

1. The large oak tree must be cut down.
   The tree was struck by lightning.

   _____

   _____

2. The book of Longfellow's poems is very old and valuable.
   I found the book in Grandfather's attic.

   _____

   _____

3. Frank Mussillo has decided to retire at the end of the summer.
   Frank Mussillo has been fire chief of our town for thirty years.

   _____

   _____

4. The Theatre Guild's production of *Porgy and Bess* has been held over for another week.

   The production is playing to packed houses every night.

   _____

   _____

5. The house needed more repairs than they realized.
   Pilar and David bought the house.

   _____

   _____

6. The woman offered to give me directions.
   The woman noticed my confusion.

   _____

   _____

7. Marty finally sold a short story to a literary magazine.
   Marty has been writing in his spare time for ten years.

   _____

   _____

8. Aunt Maria's arrival was a pleasant surprise to all of us.
   The arrival was unexpected.

   _____

   _____

9. The police officer questioned the witnesses.
   The police officer was off duty.

   _____

   _____

10. The man offered to draw us a map.
    The man noticed we were lost.

    _____

    _____

PRACTICE 15.16

On a separate sheet, write ten sentences of your own with relative clauses. Remember to use commas with clauses that are not needed for identification.

REVIEW PRACTICE 15.17

The following paragraph can be improved with coordination and subordination. On a separate sheet, rewrite the paragraph according to the directions given at the end.

^{1}A Florida hotel called Jules' Undersea Lodge is located under the ocean. ^{2}The hotel is the size of a small house. ^{3}The hotel can accommodate six people. ^{4}You are ready to depart for the hotel. ^{5}A guide puts your belongings in a waterproof suitcase and secures it with screws to keep out water. ^{6}Then the guide takes you by boat to a platform from which you dive into the water. ^{7}Breathing fresh air pumped through a hose held in your mouth, you swim underwater to the lodge. ^{8}A guide carries your suitcase. ^{9}The guide swims with you. ^{10}The hotel itself has two bedrooms, a kitchen, and a living room. ^{11}The kitchen has a microwave and a fully stocked refrigerator. ^{12}The living room has a VCR, stereo, and television. ^{13}You can relax in the lodge. ^{14}You can go diving outside. ^{15}You are ready to leave. ^{16}A guide swims with you back to the platform.

a. Join sentences 2 and 3 by making sentence 2 a relative clause.

b. Join sentences 4 and 5 by adding a subordinating conjunction to sentence 4 and making it a subordinate clause.

c. Join sentences 9 and 8 by making sentence 9 a relative clause.

d. Join sentences 11 and 12 by adding a comma and coordinating conjunction.

e. Join sentences 13 and 14 by adding a comma and coordinating conjunction.

f. Join sentences 15 and 16 by adding a subordinating conjunction to sentence 15 and making it a subordinate clause.

POST TEST

On a separate sheet, rewrite the next passage to include coordination and subordination. Then read both the original and revision aloud to notice how much better the coordination and subordination make the revision sound. (Many revisions are possible.)

^{1}Meredith West and Andrew King studied cowbirds for many years.^{2} West and King are scientists in North Carolina.^{3} A male cowbird

(continued on next page)

sings.[4] The female cowbird lets him know what songs she likes without making a sound.[5] She likes a song. She lifts her wing.

[6]Cowbirds in different parts of the country sing different tunes. [7]West and King put male cowbirds from North Carolina with female cowbirds from Texas.[8] The males learned to sing Texas cowbird songs.[9] The scientists were puzzled.[10] The males learned these songs.[11] The females did not make a peep.[12] They videotaped the birds.[13] They saw that the females would flash a wing when they liked a song.[14] The males would repeat the song.[15] The females liked it. [16]Now, if the birds could just learn some Billy Joel tunes.

SUCCEEDING IN COLLEGE

Know How to Talk to Instructors about Your Grades

From time to time, you will want to talk to your instructor about your grade. You may be seeking clarification so you better understand why you earned a particular grade, or you may be seeking a grade adjustment. Most instructors are receptive to conversations about your grade. However, there is an etiquette for such discussions that you should follow, most of which is based on common sense.

First, grade discussions are confidential, so meet in your instructor's office, either during office hours or at a scheduled appointment. Remember that instructors are human and unlikely to respond well to anger, accusations, or rudeness, so be respectful. If you are seeking clarification about a grade, open with something like this: "Thank you for seeing me. I want to discuss my last test because I am hoping you can help me understand why I did not get a higher grade." If you are seeking a grade adjustment, you can say something like this: "I've studied my exam and your responses, and I believe my grade should be a bit higher. Would you be willing to discuss that with me?"

If you are seeking a grade adjustment, be prepared to state your case. Explain politely why you believe you deserve a higher grade. Then listen—really listen—to your instructor's response. Your instructor could well have an excellent justification for the grade that never occurred to you. However, if you are not satisfied with your instructor's response, learn your school's procedure for resolving grade disputes and follow it exactly.

Write about It

Find out your school's procedure for resolving disputes between students and faculty. Do you think the procedure is a good one? Why or why not?

CHAPTER 16
Avoiding Sentence Fragments

Sentence fragments look like sentences because they have periods and capital letters; however, they are really not sentences, so you should avoid them. If you currently know little about avoiding fragments, this chapter will help you. If you already do a good job of avoiding fragments, this chapter will reinforce your understanding and perhaps teach you a few new points. Before getting under way, however, take the following pretest to determine your current level of understanding.

FAQ

Q: Other writers often use fragments. Why can't I?

A: Fragments often appear in certain kinds of writing, particularly advertising. However, they are rarely acceptable in college papers. Professional writers may use fragments to achieve a special effect. If you want to use a fragment for a particular effect, consult with your instructor first.

PRETEST

Write *S* on the blank if the pair of word groups includes only sentences, and write *F* if the pair includes a sentence fragment. Do not guess. If you are unsure, do not write anything. Check your answers in Appendix II.

1. __F__ I enjoy one activity more than any other. Eating Mexican food.

2. __F__ Rico's dog likes playing hide-and-seek. And playing with balls too.

3. __S__ Although many people do not appreciate Sondra's sense of humor. I think she is very funny.

4. __S__ After I took a study skills course, I learned to take better notes. Now my grades are improving steadily.

5. __S__ One thing will convince Marion to study. The threat of flunking out of school.

6. __F__ Pilar having spoken too soon. Regretted her action.

7. __F__ Apologizing for the misunderstanding. Jeffrey asked for another chance.

(continued on next page)

8. _____ Before you go on a job interview, you should learn something about the company offering the job. This information will enable you to ask intelligent questions.

9. _____ Bitten by the acting bug. My sister went to New York to try for a career on the stage.

10. _____ Some people refuse to believe the earth's resources are dwindling. Even though the evidence is all around them.

IDENTIFYING SENTENCE FRAGMENTS

To be a **sentence**, a word group must have a subject, a verb, and a sense of completeness. If any one of these elements is missing, the word group cannot be a sentence. A **sentence fragment** is a word group being passed off as a sentence because it has a capital letter and a period. However, a fragment cannot really stand as a sentence because it lacks one of the essential elements: a subject, a complete verb, or a sense of completeness.

The italicized words in the following examples are fragments.

fragment (subject missing):	The gale force wind toppled power lines. *And interrupted radio communications.*
fragment (complete verb missing):	*The mother wondering what the children could be up to.* She quietly peeked into the bedroom.
fragment (lacks sense of completeness):	*When the band played its last song.* The audience cheered wildly.

Missing Subject Fragments

To be a sentence, a word group must have its own subject. Without a subject, a word group is a fragment.

> The sales clerk told us she would be with us in a minute. *But spent ten minutes with another customer.*

The italicized words are a fragment because they contain no subject for the verb *spent*. The subject in the preceding sentence (*sales clerk*) cannot operate outside its own sentence. (If you need help finding subjects and verbs, study Chapter 14.)

Here is another example:

> Dr. Barolsky passed out the exam papers. *Then announced we would have one hour to complete the questions.*

The italicized words are a fragment because they contain no subject for the verb *announced*. The subject in the preceding sentence (*Dr. Barolsky*) cannot operate outside its own sentence.

To correct fragments that result from missing subjects, you have two options.

1. Join the fragment to the sentence before it.

   fragment: The sales clerk told us she would be with us in a minute. *But spent ten minutes with another customer.*

   sentence: The sales clerk told us she would be with us in a minute but spent ten minutes with another customer.

   Now the verb *spent* has a subject: *sales clerk*.

2. Add a subject so the fragment becomes a sentence.

   fragment: Dr. Barolsky passed out the exam papers. *Then announced we would have one hour to complete the questions.*

   sentence: Dr. Barolsky passed out the exam papers. Then he announced we would have one hour to complete the questions.

   Now the verb *announced* has a subject: *he*.

PRACTICE 16.1

Each pair of word groups has one sentence and one fragment. Underline the fragment. Then rewrite to eliminate the fragment, using the option given in parentheses. Option 1 is joining the fragment to the preceding sentence; option 2 is adding the missing subject.

Example

(option 1) Alexander enrolled in a CPR course. <u>And learned valuable life-saving techniques.</u>

Alexander enrolled in a CPR course and learned valuable lifesaving techniques.

_____

1. (option 1) I quit smoking for three months. But started again when I changed jobs.

   _____

   _____

2. (option 1) During the depression, my great-grandmother raised four daughters alone. And sold insurance to keep food on the table.

_____

_____

3. (option 2) Dr. Juarez described the requirements for the research project. Then answered questions from the class.

_____

_____

4. (option 2) The movers gently positioned the antique sofa against the wall. However, dropped the oil lamp that has been in my family for generations.

_____

_____

5. (option 1) The cruel children made fun of their new classmate. And caused her to feel like an outcast.

_____

_____

6. (option 2) The comedy special earned the highest ratings for a program in that time slot. Still, offended many people because of the profanity used by three of the comedians.

_____

_____

PRACTICE 16.2

On a separate sheet of paper, rewrite to eliminate the four fragments created by missing subjects. If you have trouble finding the fragments, try reading the paragraph slowly, from last sentence to first sentence.

[1]One modern convenience we tend to take for granted is the shopping cart. [2]This device was invented by Sylvan Goldman, who lived in Oklahoma City. [3]And ran a grocery store there. [4]Goldman felt sorry for customers. [5]He watched them struggling as they shopped and tried to hold onto their purchases. [6]He hit upon an idea to help them. [7]And built the first crude shopping cart. [8]First, he fastened two folding chairs together. [9]Then put wheels on the legs and baskets on the seats. [10]The contraption looked weird. [11]But worked. [12]From that point on, shopping became easier. [13]The next time you push a shopping cart, think of Sylvan Goldman.

Incomplete Verb Fragments

A fragment will result if you do not include a necessary helping verb. (See page 209 on helping verbs.)

fragment:	Jane going to the store.
sentence:	Jane is (or was) going to the store. [The helping verb *is* (or *was*) is added.]

In general, *-ing* verb forms and past participle verb forms (see page 317 and page 327 for an explanation of past participles) must appear with a helping verb, or the result will be a fragment.

-ing fragment:	The baby sleeping soundly in the crib.
sentence:	The baby is (or was) sleeping soundly in the crib.
past participle fragment:	The police officer angered by the driver's attitude.
sentence:	The police officer was (or is) angered by the driver's attitude.

To correct fragments that result from incomplete verbs, you have two options.

1. Add the missing helping verb. Choose from *is, are, was, were, have, has,* or *had*—whichever is appropriate.

fragment:	The sun setting in the west.
sentence formed by adding helping verb:	The sun is setting in the west.

2. Change the *-ing* or past participle form to the simple present or past tense, whichever is appropriate.

fragment:	The baby sleeping soundly in the crib.
sentence with simple present tense verb:	The baby sleeps soundly in the crib.
fragment:	The police officer angered by the driver's attitude.
sentence with simple past tense verb:	The driver's attitude angered the police officer.

PRACTICE 16.3

Change each fragment to a sentence using the method of correction given in parentheses. Option 1 is adding the missing helping verb; option 2 is changing the verb to the simple present or past tense form.

Examples:

(option 1) The university's faculty promotions committee considering the promotion requests of fifty instructors.

The university's faculty promotions committee is considering the promotion

requests of fifty instructors.

(option 2) The adolescent boys devouring everything in the refrigerator.

The adolescent boys devoured everything in the refrigerator.

1. (option 2) Before the second half began, the coach reminding the front line to avoid off-sides penalties.

2. (option 2) The president's speech was enthusiastically received. Both Democrats and Republicans vowing to help pass the legislation requested.

3. (option 1) The union leaders want to call attention to their political agenda. Therefore, they taken a hard-line stand during the negotiations.

4. (option 1) Many people believe that we are not the only life forms in the universe. They noting frequent UFO sightings and other unexplained events as proof.

5. (option 2) A female named Hatshepsut being an ancient Egyptian pharoah.

6. (option 1) The hawk riding the air currents and soaring majestically.

PRACTICE 16.4

Revise to eliminate the four fragments that result from incomplete verbs. If you have trouble finding the fragments, try reading the paragraph slowly from last sentence to first.

[1]When Allesandra makes up her mind, it is permanent. [2]Nothing proves that point more than the following story about her broken engagement. [3]Allesandra broken off her engagement with Roberto. [4]Roberto hoping to win her back, so he sent her 1,480 roses. [5]This amounted to one rose for each day of the more than four years they were engaged. [6]One day after the arrival of the roses, Allesandra dining in a restaurant with her family. [7]Roberto arrived on horseback to deliver the last rose in person. [8]He made an impassioned plea to the woman to resume the engagement. [9]Allesandra, however, not interested. [10]She said, "no thanks," and continued eating her meal.

Missing Subject and Verb Fragments

Some fragments lack both a subject and a complete verb. In the examples that follow, the fragments are italicized.

Gloomy weather always depresses me. *Also snowy weather.*

All the Smiths are very considerate. *Particularly in times of trouble.*

Unable to assemble Leo's bike. Dad was frustrated.

I walked across campus. *Reading my biology notes.*

To correct fragments that result from missing subjects and verbs, you have two options.

1. Some fragments can be corrected by joining them to sentences before or after them.

   fragment: *Unable to assemble Leo's bike.* Dad was frustrated.

   sentence: Unable to assemble Leo's bike, Dad was frustrated.

   fragment: I walked across campus. *Reading my biology notes.*

   sentence: I walked across campus reading my biology notes.

2. Some fragments can be corrected by adding the missing subject and verb.

   fragment: Gloomy weather always depresses me. *Also snowy weather.*

   sentence: Gloomy weather always depresses me. I am also depressed by snowy weather.

   fragment: All the Smiths are very considerate. *Particularly in times of trouble.*

   sentence: All the Smiths are very considerate. They are particularly considerate in times of trouble.

PRACTICE 16.5

Each set of word groups contains one fragment and one sentence. First underline the fragment. Then rewrite to eliminate the fragment, either joining the fragment to the sentence or adding the missing subject and verb.

Example: <u>Fearing she would not get a satisfactory grade in physics</u>. Joanie hired a tutor.

Fearing she would not get a satisfactory grade in physics. Joanie hired a tutor.

_____

1. Hoping to confuse the opposition. The coach switched defensive strategies.

_____

_____

2. Because of his high cholesterol level, Rudy began a low-fat diet. On the advice of his physician and at the urging of his wife.

_____

_____

3. To do well on the Law School Admissions Test. A person must have strong verbal skills.

_____

_____

4. All the starting players are sophomores. Except Morrison, who is a graduating senior.

_____

_____

5. Caffeine is found in many everyday foods. Including candy, soft drinks, and coffee.

_____

_____

6. A wide range of idea-generation techniques is available to writers. Facing writer's block and searching for ideas to write about.

_____

_____

7. Before beginning any exercise program. You should have a complete physical. With a blood pressure screening.

_____

_____

8. Surprisingly, some fruits are a prime cause of tooth decay. Raisins, for example, with their high sugar content.

_____

_____

EXERCISE 16.6

On a separate sheet of paper, revise to eliminate the five fragments that
result from missing subjects and verbs. If you have trouble finding the fragments, read the paragraph slowly from last sentence to first.

[1]There are fundamental differences between the alligator and the
crocodile. [2]The head of the alligator is shaped like a spade. [3]The crocodile has a pointy nose. [4]With protruding teeth. [5]Living in swampy
areas of the southeastern United States. [6]The alligator is particularly
numerous in Louisiana and parts of Florida. [7]The crocodile, however,
likes salt water, and in the United States is found only in south Florida.
[8]The alligator is dark brown. [9]Also yellow markings. [10]The crocodile is
olive green and black. [11]While there are differences, both animals benefit the environment. [12]Offering refuge to many species during floods.
[13]Their nests are important. [14]Also, their droppings add vital nutrients
to the water. [15]Thus, these animals, which offer little threat to humans,
should be protected. [16]To preserve the balance of nature.

Subordinate Clause Fragments

In Chapter 15, you learned that a **subordinate clause** has a subject and a
verb, but it cannot be a sentence because it is incomplete.

	s.	v.
subordinate clause fragment:	When Jorge was a child.	
sentence:	When Jorge was a child, he had sev-eral health problems.	

The following are subordinate clause fragments. Read each one aloud to
hear that it cannot stand as a sentence because it is incomplete.

After the meeting was over.

Before we can leave on our vacation.

Although Jessie admitted he made a mistake.

Since I have begun taking college courses.

Subordinate clauses begin with **subordinating conjunctions**, one of the words or short phrases in the list that follows. When you check your work for fragments, pay special attention to word groups that begin with one of these words or short phrases. Be sure the necessary completeness is there.

Subordinating Conjunctions

after	before	when
although	even though	whenever
as	if	where
as if	in order to	wherever
as long as	since	whether
as soon as	so that	while
as though	unless	
because	until	

Some subordinate clause fragments begin with *who, whose, where, which,* or *that,* so watch for word groups that begin with one of these words.

fragment:	Who lives next door to my parents.
fragment:	Where the Allegheny River meets the Monongahela.
fragment:	That I told you about.

To correct subordinate clause fragments, you can often join the fragment to a sentence that appears before or after it.

fragment:	*After the meeting was over.* We all went out for coffee.
sentence:	After the meeting was over, we all went out for coffee.
fragment:	My self-esteem has improved. *Since I have begun taking college courses.*
sentence:	My self-esteem has improved since I have begun taking college courses.
fragment:	This is the Italian restaurant. *That I told you about.*
sentence:	This is the Italian restaurant that I told you about.

EXERCISE 16.7

Each pair of word groups includes one subordinate clause fragment and one sentence. Underline the fragment and correct it by joining it to the sentence.

Example:

<u>Because Miro's grades are so good</u>. He is an excellent candidate for the humanities scholarship.

Because Miro's grades are so good, he is an excellent candidate for the

humanities scholarship.

1. If it snows another two inches. We will be able to go skiing in the morning.

   _____

   _____

2. Gail is an interesting person. Who understands how to relate to people.

   _____

   _____

3. Voter turnout is expected to reach an all-time high. Because the Senate race is so hotly contested.

   _____

   _____

4. By the time the box office opened at 6:00. A line had already formed halfway around the block.

   _____

   _____

5. If schoolchildren do not eat a nutritious lunch. Their schoolwork in the afternoon will suffer.

   _____

   _____

6. Professor Weinblatt is a talented teacher. Whose lectures hold everyone's attention.

   _____

   _____

EXERCISE 16.8

On a separate sheet of paper, revise to eliminate the six subordinate clause fragments. If you have trouble finding the fragments, try reading the paragraph slowly from last sentence to first.

[1]Motown, the most successful black-owned American record company, was founded in 1960 in Detroit by Berry Gordy Jr. [2]Who began as a song-writer in the mid-1950s. [3]Led by the writing talents of Smokey Robinson, who also sang with the Miracles. [4]Motown artists were an important presence on the record charts in the 1960s and 1970s. [5]A reference to "Motor Town" (Detroit), Motown came to signify a particular performance style. [6]A Motown song often featured elaborate structures, heavy rhythms, and background orchestras. [7]Because the company kept a tight rein on the image of its performers. [8]It often prescribed their manners and style of grooming. [9]Live performances required carefully controlled choreography and elaborate costumes. [10]Which added up to the Motown-style package. [11]Clearly, the formula was a success. [12]Because it made stars of many performers, including Diana Ross and the Supremes, Stevie Wonder, Marvin Gaye, the Jackson Five, and Lionel Richie. [13]At its best, Motown represented the best of mass-produced, black-derived pop music. [14]Although its later productions were more obviously the products of a musical assembly line. [15]Motown was largely responsible for introducing the sounds of contemporary black music to a white audience.

REVIEW PRACTICE 16.9

On a separate sheet, rewrite to eliminate the sentence fragments.

FAQ

Q: When two correction options are possible, how do I know which to use?

A: Use the method that works better with your other sentences, perhaps because it improves your sentence variety. If both methods work equally well, it does not matter which you use.

[1]All families should plan and practice how to escape from their homes in the event of a fire. [2]Especially at night. [3]Because every minute spent in a burning house means extra danger. [4]Escape routes should be planned and practiced periodically. [5]Family members should practice crawling through the house in the event rooms are filled with smoke. [6]Also learning how to move through the house in darkness. [7]In addition, family members should plan where to meet outdoors. [8]And what to do when they get there. [9]If families plan and practice their escape, a house fire does not have to mean complete tragedy. [10]To learn more about fire safety in the event of a house fire. [11]Contact your local fire department.

Finding and Eliminating Sentence Fragments in Your Writing

Finding and eliminating sentence fragments is best reserved for part of your editing process. If you check for fragments during drafting or revising, you may be checking sentences that you decide to delete.

To Find Fragments

- Read backwards, from your last sentence to your first. You may notice fragments this way because you are less likely to connect them mentally to other sentences.
- Pay special attention to word groups with *–ing* and *–ed* verb forms. Be sure each verb is complete.
- Be sure each word group beginning with a subordinating conjunction is sufficiently complete to be a sentence and is not a subordinate clause.
- Check word groups that begin with *who, whose, where, which,* or *that.* Be sure each is sufficiently complete to be a sentence and is not a subordinate clause.

To Eliminate Fragments

- Ask yourself what is missing and add it. It might be the subject, all or part of the verb, or both the subject and the verb.

  fragment: On the side of the garage hidden by trees.

  sentence: I found my wallet on the side of the garage hidden by the trees.

- Change an *–ing* or past participle verb form to the simple present or past tense.

  fragment: My family singing in the choir.

  sentence: My family sings in the choir.

- Join the fragment to a sentence next to it.

  fragment: Since the sales tax was repealed. City workers have been laid off.

  sentence: Since the sales tax was repealed, city workers have been laid off.

- If you compose at the computer, try this strategy: Press the enter key before each capital letter starting a sentence to create a list of sentences. With word groups separated this way, you may find it easier to check for fragments. Be sure to reformat your paper after checking.

POST TEST

On a separate sheet of paper, rewrite the paragraphs to eliminate the sentence fragments.

a.   [1]The California condor looks very strange. [2]When perched in a tree. [3]It has a bald head and a wrinkled neck. [4]And a large black, feathered body. [5]Near the ground, the bird is hilariously awkward. [6]It lumbers on takeoffs, and it crashes on landings. [7]In the air, however, the bird is a breathtaking sight. [8]Its wings spreading out nine feet. [9]It can soar at an amazing 80 miles an hour.

[10]At one time, one wild condor was left in California. [11]Scientists managed to capture it when it swooped down to feed on a dead goat. [12]The scientists took it to the San Diego Zoo. [13]Where it lived with thirteen other condors. [14]These condors, along with fourteen in the Los Angeles Zoo, the only remaining California condors in the world. [15]Scientists captured these birds. [16]To protect them from being shot or poisoned.

b.   [1]Learning how some familiar foods got their names can be interesting. [2]Graham crackers, for example. [3]Were named after Reverend Sylvester Graham. [4]Graham encouraged people to eat special diets. [5]In the nineteenth century. [6]Sometimes, foods are named after the people who invented them. [7]Eggs Benedict being one example. [8]The popular breakfast food was named after a New York businessman, Sam Benedict, who came up with the concoction one night at the famous Waldorf-Astoria hotel. [9]The name Sanka is derived from the French phrase *sans caffeine.* [10]Which means "without caffeine." [11]Although foods are often associated with people. [12]They are also associated with cities. [13]Lima beans, for example, named after Lima, Peru, and brussels sprouts named for Brussels, Belgium. [14]Mayonnaise got its name from Mahon, the Mediterranean city. [15]Where it was first made.

SUCCEEDING IN COLLEGE

Use Fragments and Other Short Forms in Note-taking

Avoid sentence fragments in your formal college writing. However, when you take lecture notes, speed is important, so writing fragments can be useful. For example, assume your business instructor says, "The service industry is becoming increasingly computerized and interactive." You can write this fragment in your notes:

Service industry becoming more computerized and interactive.

In the interest of speed, you can shorten further with abbreviations by writing just the first or the first two or three syllables of words, like this:

Serv. indus. becoming more comp. & interact.

Sometimes, the easiest way to abbreviate is with symbols rather than shortened words. For example, assume your business instructor says, "A databank is an electronic storage file." You can write a note with a symbol, like this:

Databank = electron. storage file.

Here is a list of some common abbreviations and symbols you can use:

abbreviation or symbol	meaning
cf.	compare
e.g.	for example
vs	versus
w/	with
w/o	without
#	number
&	and
%	percentage
>	greater than
<	less than
=	is/equals
≠	is not/does not equal

Write about It

Select a page from one of your textbooks and take notes on it using fragments and other shortened forms. Then close your book and rewrite your notes in complete sentences.

CHAPTER 17

Avoiding Run-On Sentences and Comma Splices

Run-on sentences and comma splices are a problem because they can confuse readers by blurring sentence boundaries. You may currently know very little about how to avoid sentences that are run together without punctuation (run-ons) or with just a comma (comma splices), and that is not a problem because this chapter will help you learn what you need to know. On the other hand, you may already know more than you realize, in which case this chapter will reinforce your understanding and perhaps teach you a few new points. The following pretest will help you assess your current level of understanding.

PRETEST

If the word group is a run-on because sentences are run-together without punctuation, write *RO* on the blank; if it is a comma splice because sentences are improperly linked by a comma, write *CS* on the blank; if it is correct, write *C* on the blank. Do not guess. If you are unsure, do not write anything. Check your answers in Appendix II.

1. _CS_ I heard a siren, I pulled my car to the edge of the road.
2. _RO_ The sudden spring rains caused flash flooding the townspeople moved to higher ground.
3. _RO_ Roberto's singing career is going very well he has signed a contract with an important talent agent.
4. _C_ If I had the opportunity, I would travel to Europe.
5. _RO_ The last day of the month is the best time to buy a car at that time dealers are anxious to reduce their inventory.
6. _CS_ People are changing their eating habits, more of us are restricting fat and cholesterol.
7. _C_ Because I spilled bleach on it, the shirt is ruined.

8. _C_   I do all my grocery shopping on Sunday to avoid the crowds.
9. _CS_   Martha subscribes to ten magazines she doesn't know where to put them all.
10. _C_   To be sure that your car runs well, change the oil regularly.

IDENTIFYING RUN-ON SENTENCES AND COMMA SPLICES

If two main clauses (word groups with subjects and verbs that can be sentences) are run together without any punctuation, the error is called a **run-on sentence**. If the main clauses are joined by just a comma, the error is called a **comma splice**. (You can review main clauses on page 224.)

Here are two main clauses (word groups that can be sentences):

> Randy could not wait to tell everyone his good news.
>
> He got the job he wanted so badly.

If you run the main clauses together, the result is a **run-on sentence**:

run-on:	Randy could not wait to tell everyone the good news he got the job he wanted so badly.

If you join these main clauses with just a comma, the result is a **comma splice**:

comma splice:	Randy could not wait to tell everyone the good news, he got the job he wanted so badly.

Correcting Run-ons and Comma Splices with a Period and Capital Letter

One way to eliminate a run-on sentence or comma splice is to use a period and capital letter to make each main clause a separate sentence.

run-on:	I left the party at 11:00 then I went to a movie.
sentence:	I left the party at 11:00. Then I went to a movie.
comma splice:	Darla is the perfect person for the job, she is reliable, intelligent, and efficient.
sentence:	Darla is the perfect person for the job. She is reliable, intelligent, and efficient.

PRACTICE 17.1

Eliminate each run-on or comma splice by adding a period and capital letter. Two sentences are correct.

Example: You have probably heard the expression "~~pan out," it~~ "pan out." It is used when things work out satisfactorily.

1. When a plan goes well, you can say that "everything panned out."
2. When a plan does not go well, you can say the opposite, you can say that "things did not pan out."
3. "Pan out" is a gold-mining term one method of finding gold is to take a handful of sand and place it in a little pan.
4. By sloshing the water back and forth in the pan, miners cause the lighter sand, dirt, and pebbles to slide over the edge.
5. The heavier gold stays in the pan thus it "pans out."
6. We do not often pause to think about common expressions their origins can be very interesting, however.

EXERCISE 17.2

FAQ

Q: Why do run-ons and comma splices matter?

A: When readers cannot easily tell where your sentences begin and end, they can become confused about where ideas start and stop.

Eliminate the three run-on sentences and comma splices by using periods and capital letters.

> [1]Bill Haley was the first real rock-and-roll star, his recording of "Crazy Man Crazy" was the first rock-and-roll record to make *Billboard's* pop music charts. [2]Although he started out as a country singer, Haley decided to make a bid for teen appeal in the mid-1950s. [3]When his "Rock Around the Clock" became the theme song for the movie *The Blackboard Jungle* in 1955, Haley scored big with teen audiences he was at this point a genuine rock-and-roll star. [4]For the next two years he had a dozen top-40 hits, these included "See You Later Alligator" and "Burn That Candle." [5]When Haley died in 1981, he was 55, and he had sold 60 million records.

Correcting Run-ons and Comma Splices with a Comma and Coordinating Conjunction

You can eliminate a run-on sentence or comma splice by joining the main clauses with a comma and one of the following coordinating conjunctions.

Coordinating Conjunctions

and	or	so
but	for	yet
	nor	

run-on:	The hamburger was not completely cooked I asked the waiter to take it back to the kitchen.
sentence:	The hamburger was not completely cooked, so I asked the waiter to take it back to the kitchen.
comma splice:	This compact disc player costs more than that one, it is worth the extra expense.
sentence:	This compact disc player costs more than that one, but it is worth the extra expense.

PRACTICE 17.3

Eliminate the run-ons and comma splices by adding commas and coordinating conjunctions. One sentence is correct. In some cases, more than one coordinating conjunction can be selected.

Example: One name above all is associated with the dictionary, *and* that name is "Webster"

1. Many dictionaries bear the name "Webster," Noah Webster does not have anything to do with these books.

2. Webster published the first major dictionary in the United States in the early 1800s his name is practically synonymous with "dictionary."

3. His rights to dictionaries ran out many years ago, the word "Webster's" entered the public domain.

4. Anyone can now use Webster's name in connection with a dictionary, regardless of the author or publisher.

5. Any company can call its dictionary "Webster's," many companies do.

6. We will most likely think of Noah Webster whenever we check a word in a dictionary he is the one whose name means "dictionary."

PRACTICE 17.4

Use commas and coordinating conjunctions to eliminate the four run-ons and comma splices.

¹Exercise does not have to be unpleasant. ²If you follow some simple guidelines, you can enjoy the road to fitness. ³First pick a form of exercise you like, walking, swimming, running, bicycling, or whatever. ⁴You should set goals for yourself, you should make those goals a little harder as you move along. ⁵You should swim a bit farther you should run a little longer each day. ⁶It is important to go slowly at first, you might sustain an injury. ⁷To avoid injuries, you should also do warm-up and cool-down stretching exercises. ⁸Finally, exercise with a friend you can encourage each other and enjoy the companionship.

Correcting Run-Ons and Comma Splices with a Semicolon

A second way to eliminate a run-on or comma splice is to use a semicolon to join the main clauses.

run-on:	None of us wanted to go out we were all too tired.
sentence:	None of us wanted to go out; we were all too tired.
comma splice:	Jim and Clarice bought a house that is a hundred years old, they will have to work hard to fix it up.
sentence:	Jim and Clarice bought a house that is a hundred years old; they will have to work hard to fix it up.

A run-on or comma splice can also be corrected with one of the following **conjunctive adverbs** used with a semicolon and a comma.

Conjunctive Adverbs

; however,	; furthermore,	; thus,
; nevertheless,	; moreover,	; consequently,
; nonetheless,	; therefore,	

run-on:	The examination was harder than I expected I believe I passed it.
sentence:	The examination was harder than I expected; however, I believe I passed it.

comma splice: On April Fools' Day my son put a rubber snake in my bed, he poured salt in my coffee.

sentence: On April Fools' Day my son put a rubber snake in my bed; furthermore, he poured salt in my coffee.

CAUTION: When you use a semicolon to avoid a run-on sentence or comma splice, be sure you have a main clause on *both sides* of the semicolon.

Incorrect: Carol decorated the Christmas tree; before Philippe got home from work. (A main clause does not appear after the semicolon.)

Correct: Carol decorated the Christmas tree before Philippe got home from work.

PRACTICE 17.5

Eliminate the run-ons and comma splices by adding semicolons. Three sentences are correct.

Example: Some laws currently on the books are wacky ; it is hard to understand why.

1. For example, stores in Providence, Rhode Island, are not allowed to sell toothbrushes on Sunday, however, they can still sell toothpaste.

2. In Paraguay, dueling is illegal if both parties are blood donors.

3. In Atwoodville, Connecticut, people cannot play Scrabble while waiting for a politician to speak, now that is an odd ordinance.

4. According to the Recruitment Code of the U.S. Navy, anyone "bearing an obscene and indecent" tattoo will be rejected.

5. The U.S. patent laws prohibit granting patents on useless inventions, that law is not always enforced.

6. Items in the catalogs mailed to me prove that many useless items are patented.

PRACTICE 17.6

Add semicolons to eliminate the three run-on sentences and comma splices.

¹An increasing number of employers are providing day-care centers at their places of business they have learned that employees are more productive when they do not have to worry about baby-sitting arrangements for their children. ²In addition, when child-care is on company premises, employees do not have to call off work when the babysitter fails to show up. ³Many companies are learning that on-site day-care is a valuable fringe benefit. ⁴Employees are less likely to change their places of employment when day-care is available this means companies do not have to worry about rapid employee turnover. ⁵Undoubtedly, more and more companies will be providing day-care facilities, they are a benefit to both employer and employee.

Warning Words and Phrases

Pay special attention to the following words and phrases. When you edit and come across one of these words or phrases, check to see if it is joining main clauses. If it is use a semicolon before the warning word or phrase.

as a result	furthermore	moreover	similarly
consequently	hence	nevertheless	then
finally	however	next	therefore
for example	in addition	on the contrary	thus

PRACTICE 17.7

If the word group is a run-on, write *RO* on the blank; if it is a comma splice, write *CS;* if it is a correct sentence, write *S.* Circle the warning word or phrase.

Example:

_RO_ We do not often pay attention to movie sound effects (however,) they are an important aspect of many films

1. _CS_ Henri completed the committee report for his fraternity, then he took it to the chapter president.

2. _RO_ Carla's cavity was so deep she had to have two shots of novocaine consequently she could not feel the right side of her face for three hours.

3. _C_ We waited most of the morning for Joan to arrive; finally, we just left without her.

4. _C_ Not everyone understands Dad's sarcastic sense of humor; as a result, some people feel insulted when he teases them.

5. _C_ In addition to losing my keys last week, I misplaced my good leather gloves.

6. _CS_ First you should choose an advisor in your major field of study, next you should select an advisor in your minor field of study.

7. _RO_ Dr. Schultz is sick with the flu therefore our midterm has been post-poned until next week.

8. _RO_ The football team lost three games in a row as a result of errors by the defensive squad.

REVIEW PRACTICE 17.8

Edit to eliminate the run-on sentences and comma splices, using any of the correction methods explained in this chapter.

¹Margaret Chase Smith was the first woman elected to both the United States House of Representatives and the United States Senate. ²Her husband, a Republican congressman from Maine, died in 1940, Mrs. Smith replaced him in the House of Representatives. ³She served in the House for eight years. ⁴She was elected to the Senate in 1948 she was reelected in 1954 and 1960. ⁵In 1950 she was one of the first senators to oppose Senator Joseph McCarthy. ⁶In 1965 she campaigned for the Republican presidential nomination, she was the first woman to do so. ⁷Smith was an influential legislator during her years in Congress, moreover, she was not put off by the fact that at the time, politics was largely the domain of males. ⁸In fact, Smith helped pave the way for other women to enter the political arena at the national level.

FAQ

Q: Can I find run-ons and comma splices by looking for long sentences?

A: No, run-ons and comma splices can be very short. For example, this short word group is a comma splice: Joan left, Henri did not. Also, long sentences are not necessarily run-ons or comma splices. For example, this long sentence is correct: When the tornado struck the Midwestern town, the early warning system functioned so well that all residents were able to take cover, and no loss of life was reported.

Finding and Eliminating Run-On Sentences and Comma Splices in Your Writing

Finding and eliminating run-on sentences and comma splices is best saved for editing. If you check for them during drafting or revising, you may be checking sentences that you later decide to delete. The following tips can help you find and eliminate run-ons and comma splices when you edit.

- Determine the number of main clauses in every word group you have punctuated as a sentence. If there are two or more, be sure they are joined with a comma and coordinating conjunction, or with a semicolon.

- Be on the alert when you have used commas. If there is a main clause on *both* sides of the comma, be sure to include a coordinating conjunction.

- Pay attention to warning words or phrases. If these are joining main clauses, be sure a semicolon is used before the warning word or phrase.

- If you compose at the computer, try this strategy: Use the Search or Find function to locate the warning words given on page 268. Each time your computer finds one of these, check whether they are joining main clauses. If they are, use a semicolon.

POST TEST

Edit to eliminate the run-on sentences and comma splices. You may use any or all of the correction methods explained in this chapter.

a.   [1]Many schools have alcohol-awareness programs to steer children away from drinking, however, parents need to be involved as well. [2]Parents can do a number of things, for example, they can discuss drinking scenes in programs and movies they watch with their children. [3]Parents should ask questions such as "Why do you think grown-ups drink?" and "Can grown-ups have fun without drinking?" [4]Because children may become confused seeing adults drink when they have been told to say no, parents should explain the health risks associated with alcohol and the fact that the legal drinking age is 21. [5]It is also a good idea to emphasize positive reasons for saying no: Children need to keep their heads clear for school, they also need to keep their bodies healthy for athletics. [6]Parents can also role-play with their children. [7]Give them a glass of water and have them practice saying "No thanks." [8]Parents must be actively involved, they cannot leave the full responsibility to the schools.

b.   [1]The children's song "Pop Goes the Weasel" does not mean what many people think it does. [2]In England in the seventeenth and eighteenth century, a weasel was a tool used by hat makers, they used it to apply the fabric to the outside of a hat. [3]"Pop" was a slang term it meant "to pawn something." [4]When the hatter in the song runs out of money, he pawns his hatter's tool. [5]In other words, "That's the way the money goes pop goes the weasel." [6]As you can now see, the song has nothing to do with a furry animal, nor does it relate to an animal bursting.

SUCCEEDING IN COLLEGE

Make Inferences When You Read

When writers join main clauses with a comma and coordinating conjunction, the conjunction will tell you how the clauses relate to each other. For example, in the following sentence, the coordinating conjunction *but* tells you that the idea in the second clause is in contrast to the idea in the first clause:

> The government phased out lead in gasoline and paint, but this dangerous substance still exists in other products.

When writers join main clauses by a semicolon alone, you must determine on your own how the ideas in the clauses relate to each other. You may need to reflect for a moment or even read between the lines. When you assess stated ideas to draw conclusions about what is not stated but merely suggested, you are making an **inference**.

For example, read the following sentence, and reflect for a moment to make an inference about the relationship between the ideas in the main clauses:

> Americans are weary of the preferential treatment given to special interest groups contributing large amounts of money to political campaigns; Congress will have to consider additional campaign finance reform soon.

Did you infer that the relationship between the ideas in the clauses is one of cause and effect, that the idea in the second main clause is a result of the idea in the first main clause?

When you read your textbooks and other college materials, you will often need to make inferences, and not just when semicolons separate main clauses. When you make these inferences, make reasonable ones supported by the clues in the text. Consider this passage, for example:

> Americans are becoming increasingly frustrated by the amount of violent crime in this country and the apparent failure of the judicial and penal systems to stem the violence. Uncertain what to do about the problem and seeking a quick fix, we are demanding harsher penalties, even to the extent of trying youthful offenders as adults. Despite the fact that studies confirm the utter futility of locking away our youngest criminals, we demand harsher sentences, even life imprisonment for young teens convicted of murder.

You can reasonably infer from the material that the writer believes that trying juveniles as adults is a bad idea, but you cannot infer that the writer believes we want vengeance against youthful offenders, because no evidence in the text supports that inference.

Write about It

Photocopy an article from a magazine or newspaper. Note one inference you can make from the article and explain why you can reasonably make that inference.

CHAPTER 18

Writing Sentences with Variety and Parallelism

Sentence variety and parallel structure are important to good sentence style, and this chapter will teach you what you need to know. If you already are competent in these areas, this chapter will reinforce your understanding and perhaps teach you a few new points. Before beginning, take the following pretest to assess your current level of understanding.

PRETEST

1. If the group of sentences has sentence variety (that is, has varied sentence openers), write yes on the blank. If it does not have sentence variety, write no. If you are unsure, do not guess; leave the space blank. Check your answers in Appendix II.

   a. _____ If we educate people about the importance of recycling, more people will recycle. When we increase the amount of recycling, we can live on the land more gently. Because we must take care with our resources, we must try to live more gently on the land.

   b. _____ More people will recycle if we educate them about the importance of recycling. Of course, if we increase the amount of recycling, we can live on the land more gently. Then, we will take better care of our resources.

   c. _____ Children today are at risk from inadequate health care. Unfortunately, the government is not taking the risk seriously enough, so clearly we need to lobby our legislators on the matter.

   d. _____ Sadly, children today are at risk from inadequate health care. Unfortunately, the government is not taking the risk seriously enough. Clearly, we need to lobby our legislators on the matter.

2. Place a checkmark next to the better sentence in each pair. If you are unsure, do not guess; leave both spaces blank. Check your answers in Appendix II.

a. _____ The twins are energetic, talented, and personable.

_____ The twins are energetic, talented, and they are personable.

b. _____ Cal's blood test showed that he had high cholesterol and a triglyceride level that was too high.

_____ Cal's blood test showed that both his cholesterol and triglyceride levels were high.

c. _____ The new house is not only beautiful but it is energy efficient.

_____ The new house is not only beautiful but energy efficient.

d. _____ Either Hank will spend his savings on a trip to Europe, or he will use the money to buy a car.

_____ Hank will either spend his savings on a trip to Europe, or he will use the money to buy a car.

SENTENCE VARIETY

To improve the flow of your writing and have a mature style, use a variety of sentence structures. This mix of sentence structures is known as **sentence variety**. You have already learned about subordination and coordination. When you use these, you are contributing to sentence variety. In addition, you can achieve sentence variety by using the sentence structures described on the following pages.

Begin with One or Two -*ly* Words

Words that end in -*ly* are descriptive words called **adverbs**. Adverbs describe verbs.

adv.
Mother <u>carefully</u> eased the heavy cake pans out of the oven.

Carefully describes how Mother eased the pans out of the oven. An -*ly* word can be an excellent way to open a sentence:

Carefully, Mother eased the heavy cake pans out of the oven.

Hoarsely, the cheerleaders shouted for a touchdown.

Patiently, Dr. Vardova explained differential equations.

PUNCTUATION NOTE: When you open a sentence with an -ly word (adverb), place a comma after the word. This rule is illustrated in the previous example sentences.

You can also begin a sentence with two *-ly* words:

> Slowly and steadily, the workers slid the refrigerator into the narrow space next to the stove.

> Quickly yet cautiously, Frank crossed the narrow bridge.

> Loudly but politely, she explained her complaint to the manager.

> Softly, sweetly, the nurse sang a lullaby to the infant.

As you can tell from the preceding examples, two *-ly* words can be separated with *and*, *but*, *yet*, or a comma.

PUNCTUATION NOTE: Two -ly words (adverbs) are separated with a comma when no word is between them. Also, when a pair of *-ly* words opens a sentence, place a comma after the second *-ly* word. This rule is illustrated in the previous example sentences.

PRACTICE 18.1

Open the following sentences with *-ly* words (adverbs) of your choice. At least two sentences should begin with a pair of *-ly* words.

> *Example:* The frustrated sales clerk explained for the third time why she could not give the customer a refund.
>
> *Loudly, the frustrated sales clerk explained for the third time why she could*
>
> *not give the customer a refund.*

1. Valerie arranged the roses and mums in the antique vase.

_____

_____

2. Ted maneuvered the car around the fallen rocks.

_____

_____

3. Dominic cradled his newborn daughter in his arms.

_____

_____

4. Jeffrey ran around the bases after hitting his third home run of the season.

_____

_____

5. The first-grade teacher showed the class how to write cursive letters.

_____

_____

6. Dr. Chun performed his duties as head of the art institute.

_____

_____

7. Jan entered the classroom ten minutes after the lecture had begun.

_____

_____

8. I shouted at the truck driver who changed lanes and cut me off.

_____

_____

PRACTICE 18.2

On a separate sheet, write two sentences of your own that begin with an *-ly* word (adverb) and two sentences that begin with a pair of *-ly* words. Remember to use commas correctly.

Begin with an *-ing* Verb or Phrase

The *-ing* form of a verb is the **present participle**. The present participle can be used as a descriptive word and an effective sentence opening.

> Whistling, John walked past the cemetery.

Whistling is the *-ing* form of the verb *whistle*. In the preceding sentence, it describes John. Opening some of your sentences with present participles contributes to sentence variety. Here are more examples:

> Crying, the child said that he fell off his bicycle.

Coughing, Maria left the classroom to get a drink of water.

Limping, I crossed the street.

You can also begin a sentence with an *-ing* verb phrase (**present participle phrase**). An *-ing* verb phrase is the present participle (*-ing* verb form) and one or more words that work with it. Here is a sentence that opens with a present participle phrase:

Whistling softly, John walked past the cemetery.

The present participle phrase is *whistling softly*, which describes John.

By opening some of your sentences with present participle phrases, you can achieve sentence variety. Here are more examples:

Crying pitifully, the child said that he fell off his bicycle.

Coughing into her handkerchief, Maria left the classroom to get a drink of water.

Limping more than usual, I crossed the street.

CAUTION: The *-ing* word or phrase should appear immediately before the word or phrase it describes, or the result will be rather silly, like this sentence:

Dancing in the moonlight, the band played a romantic song.

Dancing in the moonlight is a present participle phrase that is not followed by a word it can logically describe. As a result, the sentence says that the band was dancing in the moonlight. (For more on this point, see **dangling modifiers** on pages 384–385.)

PUNCTUATION NOTE: When you begin a sentence with a present participle or a present participle phrase, follow the participle or phrase with a comma. The previous example sentences illustrate this rule.

PRACTICE 18.3

Open the following sentences with the *-ing* words (present participles) of your choice. At least two sentences should begin with *-ing* verb phrases. Remember to place commas correctly.

Example: Mother prepared Thanksgiving dinner for fourteen people.

Working feverishly, Mother prepared Thanksgiving dinner for fourteen people.

1. Donna explained why tax reform would hurt the middle class.

_____

_____

2. Juanita accepted her award for scholastic achievement in mathematics.

_____

_____

3. Pete and Lorenzo tried to tell us what was so funny.

_____

_____

4. Jalil bench-pressed 250 pounds.

_____

_____

5. Diana planted tulip and daffodil bulbs in her spring garden.

_____

_____

6. The collie ran across the yard.

_____

_____

7. Dr. Dominic announced that everyone passed the exam.

_____

_____

8. The ten-year-old was bored by the pastor's sermon.

_____

_____

PRACTICE 18.4

On a separate sheet, write two sentences of your own that begin with an -ing verb (present participle) and two sentences that begin with an -ing verb

Grinding slowly, I was dancing on my favorite song.

FAQ

_Q:_ How can I tell if my writing needs sentence variety?

_A:_ Read your writing out loud, or have someone else read it to you. If it sounds choppy or sing-songy, it needs sentence variety.

phrase (present participle phrase). Be sure to follow the *-ing* verb or verb phrase with a word the participle can describe. Also, remember to use commas correctly.

Begin with an *-ed* Verb or Phrase

The *-ed* form of a verb is the **past participle**. The past participle can be used as a descriptive word and an effective sentence opening.

> Frightened, the child crawled in bed with his parents.

Frightened is the *-ed* form of the verb *frighten*. In the preceding sentence, it describes the child. By opening some of your sentences with past participles, you can contribute to sentence variety in your writing. Here are more examples:

> Tired, Dad fell asleep while watching the Raiders game.
>
> Irritated, Mandy threw her books on the floor.
>
> Excited, Leonid told his friends about his good fortune.

You can also begin a sentence with an *-ed* verb phrase (**past participle phrase**). An *-ed* verb phrase is the past participle (*-ed* verb form) and one or more words that work with it.

> Frightened by the dark, the child crawled in bed with his parents.

In this case, the past participle phrase is *frightened by the dark*, which describes the child.

Opening some of your sentences with past participle phrases will help you achieve sentence variety. Here are more examples:

> Tired after raking the leaves, Dad fell asleep watching the Raiders game.
>
> Irritated by her low exam grade, Mandy threw her books on the floor.
>
> Excited about being promoted to manager, Leonid told his friends about his good fortune.

CAUTION: The *-ed* verb or phrase should appear immediately before the verb or phrase it describes, or the result will be a silly sentence, like this:

Delighted by the victory, a celebration was in order.

Delighted by the victory is a past participle phrase that is not followed by a word it can logically describe. As a result, the sentence says that a celebration was delighted by the victory. (For more on this point, see **dangling modifiers** on pages 384–385.)

PUNCTUATION NOTE: When you begin a sentence with an *-ed* verb (past participle) or an *-ed* verb phrase (past participle phrase), follow the *-ed* verb or verb phrase with a comma. The previous example sentences illustrate this rule.

PRACTICE 18.5

Open the sentences with *-ed* verbs (past participles) of your choice. Begin at least two sentences with *-ed* verb phrases. Remember to place commas correctly.

Example: The referee threw the coach out of the game.

Angered, the referee threw the coach out of the game.

1. The kitten curled into a furry ball and fell asleep.

   _____

   _____

2. Three-year-old Bobby ran crying to his nursery school teacher.

   _____

   _____

3. Maria sprinted frantically after the man who stole her purse.

   _____

   _____

4. The tenants voiced their complaints to the apartment manager.

   _____

   _____

5. Lorenzo reached over and turned off the blaring alarm.

   _____

   _____

6. The steak was worth the twelve dollars I paid for it.

   _____

   _____

7. The police officer told Alicia she was lucky to get off with just a warning.

_____

_____

8. The cookies were too brown to sell at the charity bazaar.

_____

_____

PRACTICE 18.6

On a separate sheet, write two sentences of your own that begin with *-ed* verbs (past participles) and two sentences that begin with *-ed* verb phrases (past participle phrases). Be sure to follow the *-ed* verb or verb phrase with a word the participle can describe. Also, remember to use commas correctly.

Begin with a Prepositional Phrase

A **preposition** shows how two things relate to each other in time or space. (See page 24 for a more detailed explanation of prepositions.) Here is a list of common prepositions:

Common Prepositions

about	before	inside	through
above	behind	into	to
across	between	like	toward
after	by	of	under
along	during	off	up
among	for	on	with
around	from	out	within
at	in	over	without

A **prepositional phrase** is a preposition and the words that work with it. Here are examples of prepositional phrases. The prepositions are underlined as a study aid.

<u>in</u> May	<u>across</u> the street	<u>toward</u> the end <u>of</u> the book
<u>behind</u> me	<u>during</u> the concert	<u>inside</u> the oven
<u>on</u> top	<u>out of</u> bounds	<u>without</u> a doubt

Beginning some of your sentences with prepositional phrases will help you achieve sentence variety. Here are examples of sentences that begin with prepositional phrases:

Under the kitchen table, Rags sat contentedly chewing on his bone.

In the spring, the senior class will travel to Washington.

From now on, everyone in this state must wear a seat belt.

> **PUNCTUATION NOTE:**   A prepositional phrase that begins a sentence is usually followed by a comma.
>
> Between the oak trees, two squirrels were chasing each other.
>
> By noon, all the sale items were sold.

PRACTICE 18.7

Underline the prepositional phrases in the following sentences. (Several of the sentences contain more than one prepositional phrase.)

Example: The infant began crying in the middle of the night.

1. At ten o'clock, the church bells chimed in unison.

2. Charlie announced that there was a thief among us.

3. The truth of the matter is that no one cares.

4. With the help of everyone, the fund-raiser can be a huge success.

5. By daybreak, a foot of snow had fallen in our city.

PRACTICE 18.8

Combine the two sentences into one sentence that begins with the prepositional phrase or phrases in the second sentence. Remember to use commas correctly.

Example:

The children woke up.
They woke up in the middle of the night.

In the middle of the night, the children woke up.

1. The fire alarm sounded.
   It sounded during our history examination.

_____

_____

2. The members of the committee decided to change the bylaws.
They decided at their spring meeting.

_____

_____

3. The orchestra played a Gershwin medley.
They played the medley after a fifteen-minute intermission.

_____

_____

4. A more efficient registration process will be tested.
It will be tested at the beginning of the fall semester.

_____

_____

5. The flowering crab tree was severely damaged.
It was damaged after the unexpected spring frost.

_____

_____

PRACTICE 18.9

On a separate sheet, write four sentences that begin with prepositional phrases. Remember to place a comma after each phrase.

REVIEW PRACTICE 18.10

On a separate sheet, rewrite the paragraphs to add more sentence variety. Use a combination of the techniques you have learned: *-ly* openers, *-ing* verb openers, *-ed* verb openers, and prepositional phrase openers. You may change word order, and you may also begin some sentences with the subject.

a.   Amelia Earhart and her navigator tried to fly around the world during the summer of 1937. They were supposed to stop at Howland Island to refuel, but they never arrived. The pilot radioed compass readings hoping to be guided in. These, sadly, were the last words heard from Earhart. The plane was declared lost at sea after a long naval search. A number of theories have been advanced to explain Earhart's disappearance. Some say Earhart was spying for the United States. They say she was shot down over the Marshall Islands, which were held by Japan. Others say a navigational error caused Earhart to miss Howland Island and crash at sea. Still others say the plane ran out of gas and crash-landed. The real cause of Earhart's disappearance will probably never be learned, although people will always admire the courage of the first woman to fly across the ocean.

b.   Walter Gregg and his family should have taken a drive on the afternoon of March 11, 1958. They hung out at home instead. They were around to see their house demolished by an atomic bomb as a result. The bombing occurred when the bomb bay doors of a U.S. Air Force jet accidentally opened, and an atomic warhead fell out. The bomb crashed through the roof of the Greggs' house outside Florence, South Carolina. It obliterated the residence and gouged out a thirty-five-foot crater in the backyard. The explosion, luckily, was nonnuclear. What detonated was the TNT in the bomb's trigger device. The Greggs were slightly injured by flying debris. They accepted a $54,000 settlement from the government.

PARALLELISM: WORDS IN SERIES AND PAIRS

Parallelism refers to balance. For your sentences to have the necessary parallelism or balance, words that form pairs or series should all have the same form. Here is an example:

> Ian enjoys skating and reading.

Two words form a pair: *skating* and *reading*. Since both words have the same form (-*ing* verb forms), the sentence has the necessary parallelism or balance.

Here is another example of a sentence with parallelism. This time, there is balance among words that form a series:

> Janet and Rico found the movie fresh, funny, and surprising.

Three words form a series: *fresh*, *funny*, and *surprising*. Since each of these words has the same form (each is an adjective that describes *movie*), the sentence has the necessary parallelism.

Now here is a sentence that lacks parallelism:

> The doctor told the heart patient to avoid salt and that he should get more exercise.

In this example, two elements form a pair: *to avoid salt* and *that he should get more exercise*. The first element is a verb phrase; the second is a clause. Because the elements in the pair are different forms, the sentence lacks parallelism. To achieve the necessary balance, the sentence needs two verb phrases or two clauses:

> The doctor told the heart patient to avoid salt and to get more exercise. (two verb phrases)
>
> or
>
> The doctor told the heart patient that he should avoid salt and that he should get more exercise. (two clauses)

Here is another sentence that lacks parallelism:

> This course demands patience, dedication, and a student must know how to research.

In this example, three elements form a series: *patience, dedication,* and *a student must know how to research.* The first two elements are nouns, but the third element is a clause. Because all the elements in the series do not have the same form, the sentence lacks parallelism. Here is the sentence revised to achieve parallelism:

> This course demands patience, dedication, and research ability. (three nouns)

PRACTICE 18.11

The underlined element in the pair or series is not parallel. Rewrite the sentence to achieve parallelism.

Example: Joan's aptitude test revealed ability in math and <u>she was good at learning foreign languages.</u>

Joan's aptitude test revealed ability in math and foreign languages.

1. The citizens' committee criticized the mayor's proposal because of its complexity and <u>it was expensive</u>.

_____

_____

2. To save money on his living expenses, Gustav got a roommate, <u>ate out less</u> often, he fired his cleaning person, and he clipped coupons to use at the grocery store.

_____

_____

3. Before agreeing to the surgery, Delores decided she would get a second opinion and <u>to see if she feels better in two weeks</u>.

_____

_____

4. The proposal for renovating the downtown business district suggests eliminating one-way streets, instituting on-street parking, and <u>we should reface some of the other buildings</u>.

_____

_____

5. My family prefers a week at the ocean in a condominium to <u>spending a week in the mountains in a cabin</u>.

_____

_____

6. By three months, most infants will recognize their mother's voice, hold their heads up unassisted, and <u>three-month-old infants will grasp at objects placed within their reach</u>.

_____

_____

7. My piano teacher gave me a choice between playing one difficult piece or <u>I could play two less difficult ones</u>.

_____

_____

8. Geography 102 was canceled because the enrollment was low and <u>because of the illness of the instructor</u>.

_____

_____

PRACTICE 18.12

Complete each sentence with a parallel element.

Example: Tony swaggered in, tipped his hat, and ___*smiled at everyone*___

___*in the room.*_____

1. Most people expect Gregory to win the race for Student Government president because of his intelligence, integrity, and _____

_____

2. I like spending a quiet Saturday evening alone better than _____

_____

3. Marta approached the stage with her heart pounding, her palms sweating, and _____

_____

4. To pass the course, Professor Lloyd explained that we would have to write a research paper, that we would have to pass a midterm examination, and that _____

_____

5. Several committee members wanted to raise money with a rummage sale, but most wanted _____

_____

6. Chez enjoyed the novel, but I found it predictable, sluggish, and _____

_____

7. Lee has always liked small, informal weddings better than _____

_____

8. If you are not sure what courses to take next semester, you can consult the college catalog or _____

_____

PRACTICE 18.13

Find and correct the faulty parallelism in the following paragraph.

[1]Leonardo da Vinci, who lived from 1452 to 1519, was one of the world's great geniuses. [2]No one before him or who has lived after has achieved so much in so many fields. [3]He was an outstanding painter,

sculptor, and he was also an architect. [4]He designed bridges, highways, weapons, costumes, and he invented scientific instruments. [5]He also invented the diving bell and tank, and he designed flying machines, although they could not be built with the materials of the time. [6]Da Vinci approached science and art in the same methodical manner: He made sketches to help him solve problems. [7]He saw no difference between planning a machine and how he would plan a painting. [8]Probably the most famous painting in the world, the *Mona Lisa*, was painted by Leonardo da Vinci in Florence.

PARALLELISM: PAIRS OF CONJUNCTIONS

Some conjunctions work in pairs.

Conjunctions That Work in Pairs

either … or	not only … but [also]
neither … nor	whether … or
both … and	if … then

For parallelism, put the words that follow the second conjunction in the same form as the words that follow the first conjunction.

> Either I will earn enough money to pay my tuition, or I will ask my parents for a loan.

The words that follow *either* have the same form as the words that follow *or* (both word groups are clauses). Thus, parallelism is achieved.

Here is another example:

> Working full-time while going to school full-time is both tiring and foolish.

The word that follows *both* has the same form as the word that follows *and* (both words are modifiers). As a result, parallelism is achieved.

Now here is an example of a sentence that lacks parallelism:

> This stretch of beach is not only beautiful, but it is private.

In this example, *not only* is followed by *beautiful* (a descriptive word), and *but* is followed by *it is private as well* (a clause). Because the conjunctions are not followed by words in the same form, the sentence lacks parallelism. To achieve parallelism, follow each conjunction with words in the same form:

> This stretch of beach is not only beautiful but private.

PRACTICE 18.14

Complete each of the following sentences with a parallel element.

Example: To pass Calculus II either I must get a tutor, or

I must go to the math lab.

1. Luis will either trade his car in for a new model or _____

    _____

2. Either I will move to the city or _____

    _____

3. Professor Amin decided both to postpone the examination for a week

    and _____

    _____

4. Kwesi hopes not only to graduate a semester early but _____

    _____

5. The principal can neither enforce the dress code to the board of

    education's satisfaction nor _____

    _____

6. To improve economic conditions, the governor must not only attract new

    industry to our state but also _____

    _____

7. Jonathan is either helping those less fortunate than he or _____

    _____

8. Juanita is not only a good listener but _____

    _____

REVIEW PRACTICE 18.15

On a separate sheet, rewrite the following paragraph to eliminate problems
with parallelism.

¹Friendships at work have their own set of guidelines. ²You should understand the difference between work friends and friends who are personal. ³Conversations with work friends focus mostly on office personalities, politics, and they center on work-related problems. ⁴You should neither confide personal information nor problems to work friends. ⁵To avoid complications, try to socialize mostly with coworkers who are at your level in the hierarchy. ⁶Unequal status can lead to envy, suspicion, or sometimes cause favoritism. ⁷Proceed carefully with office friendships with members of the opposite sex. ⁸Avoid any hint of romance, either during work hours or there should be no hint after work hours. ⁹If you follow these guidelines, you can enjoy friendships at work without unpleasant complications.

POST TEST

On a separate sheet, revise the paragraph to improve parallelism and sentence variety.

¹Checkers is at least 5,000 years old. ²It was played in early Egypt, in ancient Greece, and it was played in early Rome. ³The earliest form of the game on record was played with twelve pieces on each side. ⁴The first known book about checkers was published in 1547 in Spain. ⁵The game was likely brought to Spain by the Moors. ⁶The Moors probably got the game in Arabia. ⁷Checkers is called "draughts" in England. ⁸Checkers is both fun and it is easy to play. ⁹It is popular all over the world. ¹⁰Many educators believe the game helps people develop foresight, think critically, and that it improves concentration.

SUCCEEDING IN COLLEGE

Keep a Learning Log

In Chapter 1, you learned about keeping a journal to discover ideas for your writing. Journaling in a learning log can also help you remember important content in your courses. A learning log is *not* the notebook where you record your class notes. It is a separate notebook in which you record your *reactions* to course content, class lectures, discussions, and reading. In a learning log, you relate course content in one class to course content in another class, to your own experience, and to your own thinking. For example, if you read something by Benjamin Franklin in your American literature class, you may be reminded about something you learned about him in a history class, and you can write that down in your learning log. Or if you learn about attention deficit disorder in your education class and you know someone with this disorder, you can compare your observations of that person with what you learned in class. Even if you disagree with something said in class, you can write about that disagreement in your log.

(continued on next page)

Keeping a learning log can "set" your learning so you better remember course content. It can also help you become a better learner by helping you discover which learning strategies work best for you. Keep track in your log of how you study and compare test results to your study strategy to determine if you should make changes. For example, note in your log that you studied for your psychology test in a study group. Keep track of how the group is doing. Note whether everyone gets down to business or whether there is off-task chatter, whether everyone participates or whether one person dominates. If you did not do well on the test, you may not want to use a study group to prepare for the next test, or you may want to join a different study group. If you are having trouble taking notes in physics class, write about the problem, perhaps noting that the instructor speaks too softly or too fast. Then you can devise a solution: sitting in front of the class and using a tape recorder, for example.

Write about It

Keep a learning log for three days. Then write about whether or not the log helps you learn content or become more informed about your study strategies. Be specific about why you find the log helpful or why you do not.

CHAPTER 19
Choosing Words Carefully

If you have problems with word choice, this chapter will help you learn what you need to know to express yourself more effectively. If you do not have problems with word choice, this chapter will reinforce what you already know and perhaps teach you a few new points. The following pretest will help you assess how much you currently know about choosing words carefully.

PRETEST

Place a checkmark next to the better sentence. Do not guess. If you are unsure, do not write anything. Check your answers in Appendix II.

1. a. _____ The movie was interesting and absorbing.

   b. _____ The movie was absorbing.

2. a. _____ After final exams are over, I am going to chill out for a week.

   b. _____ After final exams are over, I am going to relax for a week.

3. a. _____ After a massage, Jan no longer felt stiff.

   b. _____ After a massage, Jan no longer felt stiff as a board.

4. a. _____ Turn left at the house that is beige in color and travel two blocks north to find the house where my sister lives alone by herself.

   b. _____ Turn left at the beige house and travel two blocks north to find the house where my sister lives by herself.

5. a. _____ Because of the fog, I can't see anything more than five feet in front of me.

   b. _____ Because of the fog, I can't see nothing more than five feet in front of me.

WORDINESS

Unnecessary words—**wordiness**—weaken your style. When you revise, eliminate wordiness by pruning away words that add no meaning and words that are repetitious.

Words that add no meaning are **deadwood**, and you should revise to eliminate deadwood.

Sentences with Deadwood	Revisions
Two different kinds of cake were offered	Two different cakes were offered. (*Kinds of* adds no meaning.)
	or
	Two kinds of cake were offered.
Diane's new Corvette is brown in color.	Diane's new Corvette is brown. (Can *brown* be anything but a color?)
We rushed quickly to see what was wrong.	We rushed to see what was wrong. (*Rushing* has to be done quickly.)

Another form of wordiness is purposeless **repetition**. Consider this sentence:

To relax before my exam, I watched and viewed a movie.

Viewed repeats the idea included in *watched*, so *viewed* is purposeless repetition. Here is the sentence revised to eliminate the repetition:

To relax before my exam, I watched a movie.

Here are more examples to study:

Sentences with Repetition	Revisions
Carol finally came to the realization and understanding that she had to help herself.	Carol finally realized that she had to help herself.
	or
	Carol finally understood that she had to help herself. (*Realization* and *understanding* mean the same and either can be converted to an active verb.)

Some people think and believe that drug abuse is our nation's most serious problem.	Some people think that drug abuse is our nation's most serious problem.

or

Some people believe that drug abuse is our nation's most serious problem. (*Think* and *believe* mean the same.)

PRACTICE 19.1

Revise the following sentences to eliminate wordiness.

Example: In the year of 1912, Theodore Roosevelt was campaigning in the city of Milwaukee.

In 1912, Theodore Roosevelt was campaigning in Milwaukee.

_____

1. A would-be assassin who wanted to kill Roosevelt shot him on the right side part of his chest.

_____

_____

2. Much of the force of the bullet was absorbed by the President's eyeglasses case and by the fifty-page speech he was carrying double-folded in two in his breast pocket.

_____

_____

3. The end result was that the bullet lodged just short of his lung, and, dripping blood, the President pulled and tugged himself up to the podium.

_____

_____

4. In our modern world today, Secret Service agents would have whisked and rushed the President away, but Roosevelt was the type of person who carried on no matter what.

_____

_____

5. He announced and said he planned to deliver the speech as long as he still had life in his body.

_____

_____

6. He spoke for ninety minutes of time, but was unable to refer to or check his text.

_____

_____

7. There was a gaping, wide hole in the pages where the bullet had torn through them.

_____

_____

8. Roosevelt was luckily fortunate that he did not succumb to his wound.

_____

_____

PRACTICE 19.2

Cross out deadwood and unnecessary repetition to eliminate wordiness.

[1]The first metal coins were minted in about approximately 800 B.C. [2]Before that time in history, all trade had been done by barter. [3]For example, a toolmaker craftsman might barter and trade tools in exchange for meat or clothing to wear. [4]As civilization developed, trade became more intricately complex, and barter became too clumsily awkward. [5]A trader needed easily carried tokens that were small in size, but the tokens had to be valuable. [6]So the first coins were made of metal, in particular gold and silver metal. [7]This simple invention of money made trade much simpler.

DOUBLE NEGATIVES

These words are negatives (they communicate the idea of *no*):

Negatives

no	none	hardly
not	nowhere	scarcely
no one	nobody	
never	nothing	

any contraction form with *not* (*can't, don't, won't*, etc.)

In English, only one negative is used to express a single negative idea.

Incorrect (two negatives):	I *can't* see *no* reason to go.
Correct (one negative):	I can see *no* reason to go.
Correct (one negative):	I *can't* see any reason to go.

Incorrect (two negatives):	Dee would *never* tell *no one*.
Correct (one negative):	Dee would *never* tell anyone.
Correct (one negative):	Dee would tell *no one*.

Incorrect (two negatives):	The boys could *not hardly* eat.
Correct (one negative):	The boys could *hardly* eat.
Correct (one negative):	The boys could *not* eat.

The preceding examples show that eliminating one negative may mean changing *no one* to *anyone*, *nowhere* to *anywhere*, *never* to *ever*, and *no* or *none* to *any*.

PRACTICE 19.3

The following sentences contain double negatives. First underline each negative. Then revise each sentence by eliminating one negative.

Example: The board member came under attack because he is <u>not never</u> at the meetings.

The board member came under attack because he is never at the meetings.

1. Paul didn't do nothing to start the fight.

_____

_____

2. I gave the cashier $20.00, but I didn't get no change.

_____

_____

3. Mom couldn't find nowhere to hide the Christmas presents.

_____

_____

4. Some people won't ask nobody for nothing.

_____

_____

5. The street department hardly never swept the streets this fall.

_____

_____

FAQ

Q: How do I know if a word or phrase is slang?

A: Dictionaries often indicate whether an expression is a form of slang. You can also check with your instructor or a Writing Center tutor.

SLANG

Slang expressions are very informal usages unsuitable for most formal writing. Slang can originate with one group of people, say musicians or artists, and spread to the larger population. Slang often originates with young people and makes for colorful, vital speech. However, until a slang expression works its way into the language of the general population (if it ever does), avoid it in your college writing, unless you need it to create a special effect.

Here are examples of slang expressions. Because slang changes quickly, many of them may no longer be current by the time you read them.

dooced (getting fired for something written in a weblog)

drop the needle (play a vinyl record)

the 411 (the information)

pass the bone (share knowledge)

scope out (watch)

loose rap (lies told to impress member of the opposite sex)

party foul (something unacceptable done at a social gathering)

trick out (modify a car with parts and features after it is purchased)

whacked (crazy)

PRACTICE 19.4 WORKING TOGETHER

With some classmates, list as many slang expressions as you can think of. Limit your list to the slang you and your friends currently use. Next, with your group members, pick two of the slang expressions and use each of them in a separate sentence. Then rewrite the sentences, eliminating the slang and substituting language more appropriate to formal writing.

■

CLICHÉS

Clichés are overused expressions. At one time they were fresh and interesting, but years of overuse have made them tired and dull. Here is a partial list of clichés. Studying it will help you become sensitive to the kinds of expressions to avoid.

over the hill	sadder but wiser	crack of dawn
free as a bird	last but not least	busy as a beaver
cold as ice	fresh as a daisy	light as a feather
spring chicken	love conquers all	green with envy
hour of need	shadow of a doubt	slowly but surely
white as snow	call it quits	down in the dumps

PRACTICE 19.5

Write three clichés not on the list.

1. _____

2. _____

3. _____

PRACTICE 19.6

Rewrite the sentences, substituting fresh phrasings for the underlined clichés.

Example: I dread going shopping with Dotty because she is <u>like a bull in a china shop</u>.

I dread going shopping with Dotty because she is so clumsy, she is always

bumping into displays and breaking things.

1. If I were you, I would not <u>bet the rent</u> that Julian will keep his promise.

   _____

   _____

2. <u>In a nutshell</u>, the comedian is not very funny because his jokes are <u>as old as the hills</u>.

   _____

   _____

3. Trying to find my contact lens in the dark was like <u>looking for a needle in a haystack</u>.

   _____

   _____

4. It is a <u>crying shame</u> that more is not being done to help the homeless.

   _____

   _____

5. Nina and Jacob <u>worked their fingers to the bone</u> completing their wedding plans.

   _____

   _____

VOCABULARY BUILDING

The more words you know, the more precisely and effectively you can express yourself in both writing and speech. Vocabulary lists for study are available in any vocabulary-building book in your campus study skills center, bookstore, or library. You can also develop and learn your own list using the following procedures.

1. Using a notebook, index cards, or computer file, write down unfamiliar words you encounter in your textbooks and lectures. Also write down new words you discover in your reading of magazines and newspapers and that you hear on television or the radio. Write, too, the sentence you read or heard each word in.

2. In a paper or online dictionary, check the pronunciation of the word if you are uncertain of it and the meaning of the word. Copy these down. If there

is more than one meaning, copy the one that fits the use of the word in the sentence you read or heard.

3. Study your notebook, cards, or computer file each day. Learn the new words and review the old ones.

4. When possible, learn meanings through association. For example, to learn that *ostracize* means "to banish or expel," you may associate it with an ostrich, which banishes itself by poking its head in the sand. Also, learn clusters of words. For example, once you have learned what *luminous* means, learn *luminance, illuminate, luminary*, and *luminosity*. To discover word clusters, look for related words around each word you check in the dictionary.

5. Use the words you learn as you speak, write, and think, so they become a natural part of your vocabulary.

6. Many words share common **prefixes** (beginnings) and **suffixes** (endings). Study the meanings of prefixes and suffixes as an aid to learning meanings. To do this, consult a vocabulary book in the library or study skills center.

FAQ

Q: Are there any other ways I can increase my vocabulary?

A: If you use a computer, you can learn new words by having a different word and definition e-mailed to you each day. Visit this site to sign up: www.dictionary.com.

PRACTICE 19.7

1. For a day, record in a small notebook, on index cards, or in a computer file any words you see or hear that you do not know, following the directions given in the previous discussion.

2. Buy a copy of *Time* or *Newsweek* and read three articles, or read the articles online. List every word that is not familiar to you. Add some of these words to your notebook, index cards, or computer file. Read at least one article in the magazine each day and add unfamiliar words to your notebook, cards, or file.

REVIEW PRACTICE 19.8

Revise the paragraph to improve word choice by eliminating problems with wordiness, double negatives, slang, and clichés.

¹A man who was a chocolate maker and who went by the name of Clarence Crane tried to make a mint that would boost and increase his candy sales in summer when heat would melt his chocolate. ²To make a long story short, Crane was in a drugstore to get a bottle of flavoring. ³He didn't know nothing about how pills were made at the time. ⁴However, he noticed the druggist using a pill-making machine. ⁵It was manually operated by hand and made pills that were flat and round in shape. ⁶A

lightbulb went off in Crane's head. [7]He got an idea that became the bomb when he decided to use the pill-making machine to punch out the middle of his mints. [8]And that is how the lifesaver candy was created.

POST TEST

Underline problems with wordiness, double negatives, slang, and clichés, in the following passage. Then rewrite to eliminate the problems.

[1]In a class, I learned about the history of writing. [2]Nobody scarcely knows when writing originally began, although we do have a sense of how it developed. [3]Humans began making pictures to record hunting, wars, and tribal life. [4]Pictures and images were also used for messages. [5]A picture of the sun meant a day; two marks next to the picture meant two days. [6]Such signs are called *pictographs*. [7]Eventually pictographs were simplified. [8]For example, Egyptians used a wavy line to mean "a body of water," and the Chinese used an ear between two doors to mean "listen." [9]These markings are called *ideographs*.

[10]Eventually, the Egyptians, who were smart as a whip, developed a system of signs, called *hieroglyphics*, that included a phonetic system that was big-time cool. [11]With this writing, signs represented sounds rather than objects or ideas. [12]As civilization advanced and progressed, humans needed more signs, so they came up with the bright idea of a system of spelling words according to sound. [13]For example, the English word "belief" would be spelled with a picture of a bee and a leaf. [14]These signs are called *phonograms*.

[15]The next stage in the development of writing was the invention of the alphabet. [16]Both the Egyptians and the Babylonians eventually used alphabets of single letters. [17]From their writing came the Greek and Latin alphabets, which are used by most modern people of today who hang their hats outside Asia.

SUCCEEDING IN COLLEGE

Learn Specialized Vocabulary

Each subject you take will have its own specialized vocabulary, which you will need to learn, use, and spell correctly. In particular, you will notice that the introductory courses required of first- and second-year students include a great deal of terminology that will be new to you. As you encounter this vocabulary in your classes, make a point of mastering it.

- Listen for your instructor to shift tone of voice, slow down, or repeat a term to emphasize important vocabulary.

- Write down the terms your instructor mentions or writes on the board, along with the meanings of those terms. Be sure to get the spelling right.

- If your instructor does not define a term or if you have questions about the vocabulary, ask for help in class.

- Learn the words in your textbooks that are italicized, boldfaced, or printed in a second color.

- If your textbook has a glossary in the back, use it as a source of definitions for words you are unsure of.

- Use a notebook, index cards, or computer file to learn specialized vocabulary, following the procedures for vocabulary building explained on page 298.

- When you decide on a major, purchase a dictionary of specialized vocabulary in that discipline, such as *A Dictionary of Anthropology, A Dictionary of Economics*, or *The New Grove Dictionary of Music and Musicians*.

Write about It

Read the first chapter of one of your textbooks and write out the answers to these questions:

1. How many new, specialized vocabulary terms are there?

2. Are these terms italicized, boldfaced, or written in a different color?

3. Does the book have a glossary?

Write the definitions of the new, specialized vocabulary terms, and learn their meanings, spellings, and pronunciations.

PART FOUR Effective Sentences

COMPREHENSIVE POST TEST

■ Identifying Subjects and Verbs

1. Write the subject and verb for each sentence.

    a. The pile of dirty clothes in the laundry room is beginning to smell.

        subject _____ verb _____

    b. All of Mohammed's conversations focus on his interest in classical music.

        subject _____ verb _____

    c. By Friday, our American history class will have studied all the major battles of the Civil War.

        subject _____ verb _____

    d. Can you help me with dinner?

        subject _____ verb _____

    e. The mayor and her advisors plan to implement a new procedure for hiring city employees.

        subject _____ verb _____

■ Using Coordination and Subordination

2. Write a C if the sentence has coordination; write an S if it has subordination; write an N if it has neither coordination nor subordination.

    a. _____ Because heavy thunderstorms kept many people away from the polls, voter turnout was very light on election day.

    b. _____ Heavy thunderstorms kept many people away from the polls, so voter turnout was very light on election day.

    c. _____ Because of heavy thunderstorms, voter turnout was light on election day.

    d. _____ The eyes of a woodcock are on the top of its head; therefore, it can see backward and upward.

    e. _____ Since the eyes of the woodcock are on the top of its head, it can see backward and upward.

    f. _____ With eyes on the top of its head, the woodcock can see backward and upward.

g. _____ Jeff Bezos originally wanted to name his Web venture "Cadabra," but he decided on Amazon.com instead.

h. _____ Although he originally wanted to name his Web venture "Cadabra," Jeff Bezos decided on Amazon.com instead.

i. _____ Jeff Bezos originally wanted to name his Web venture "Cadabra," but decided on Amazon.com instead.

▓ Avoiding Sentence Fragments

3. If all the word groups are sentences, write *yes* on the blank. If some are fragments, write the number of fragments on the blank.

a. _____ The P.T.A. was founded in the United States in 1897. Originally called the National Congress of Mothers. It was expanded to include fathers, teachers, and other interested citizens. Today the P.T.A. being an important support group for the nation's public schools.

b. _____ The huddle formation used by football teams originated at Gallaudet University. Which is a liberal arts college for deaf people in Washington, D.C. The huddle was used to prevent other schools from reading players' sign language.

c. _____ Another interesting fact is that Alexander Graham Bell was originally an instructor for deaf children. Because he wanted to help his deaf wife and mother to hear. He invented the telephone. You may also be surprised to learn that in the United States, deaf people have safer driving records than hearing people.

d. _____ The first McDonald's opened in Des Plaines, Illinois, on April 15, 1955. This prototype restaurant offering hamburgers for 19 cents, fries and soft drinks, and coffee for a dime, and shakes for 20 cents. The Big Mac didn't arrive until 1968, and it cost 49 cents. The quarter-pounder arriving on the scene in 1971. It cost 53 cents.

▓ Avoiding Run-On Sentences and Comma Splices

4. If all the sentences are correct, write *yes* on the blank. If they include run-ons or comma splices, write the number of mistakes on the blank.

a. _____ Guion S. Bluford, Jr., was the first African-American to fly in space during the Space Shuttle Challenger mission STS-8 of August 30–September 5, 1983. Bluford, who holds a Ph.D. in aerospace engineering, flew a second time aboard the shuttle from October 30 to November 6. The first black man to fly in space was Cuban cosmonaut Arnaldo Tamayo-Mendez, he flew aboard Soyuz 38 and spent eight days on the Soviet space station.

P O S T   T E S T

b. _____ People get goose bumps when they are cold for a reason. These bumps are the result of the contraction of muscle fibers in the skin; the muscular activity produces more heat, which raises the body temperature. Thus, goose bumps are nature's way of helping us warm up.

■ Writing Sentences with Variety and Parallelism

5. Cross out and add words to revise the passage so that it has sentence variety.

Diamonds were considered lucky charms at one time. People wore diamonds for good fortune, thinking diamonds protected them from harm. We do not have this superstition today, but diamonds remain popular.

6. Place a check next to the sentences that are correct because they have parallel structure.

a. _____ The agenda for the meeting includes discussion on membership, a vote on the budget, and the nominating committee will present the new slate of officers.

b. _____ The agenda for the meeting includes discussion on membership, a vote on the budget, and the nominating committee's presentation of the new slate of officers.

c. _____ The loan officer wants not only to see a copy of my last pay stub, but he wants to see records of my credit card bills.

d. _____ The loan officer wants to see not only a copy of my last pay stub, but also records of my credit card bills.

e. _____ On Fridays, the special is either poached salmon or fried halibut.

f. _____ On Fridays, the special either is poached salmon or fried halibut.

■ Choosing Words Carefully

7. Fill in the blank with the correct word or phrase from the pair given in parentheses.

a. (hardly/not hardly) After running her first race, Mia could

_____ wait to run another one.

b. (anybody/nobody) I won't bring _____ with me to the concert.

8. Place a check next to the better sentence.

a. _____ After studying with the techniques she learned at the study skills center, Carlotta was chilling before her final exams.

b. _____ After studying with the techniques she learned at the study skills center, Carlotta felt confident before her final exams.

c. _____ On the first day of summer vacation, schoolchildren feel joyously liberated.

d. _____ On the first day of summer vacation, school children feel free as little birds.

e. _____ In my opinion, it seems to me that the housing market has cooled because interest rates have climbed.

f. _____ In my opinion, the housing market has cooled because interest rates have climbed.

DIAGNOSTIC SELF-ASSESSMENT

Note: To check your answers, turn to Appendix II.

■ **Using Verbs Correctly** If you make errors in this section, pay particular attention to Chapter 20.

1. If the underlined verb is correct, write *yes* on the blank; if it is incorrect, write *no*.

a. _____ Lee Jaworski <u>be</u> the person to beat in the 17th district congressional race.

b. _____ Santha <u>woked</u> up when the clock radio blared the morning news.

c. _____ I <u>expects</u> to get a summer job to help pay my tuition.

d. _____ Each day in class Marcel <u>ask</u> at least three questions.

e. _____ The flock of geese <u>migrate</u> across this region every year at this time.

f. _____ The cheerleading squad <u>have practice</u> as many hours a week as the football team.

g. _____ Each of the students <u>hopes</u> to earn a high grade.

h. _____ Either Jana or Harriet <u>drives</u> Grandma to the store every week.

i. _____ Each of the band members <u>wanted</u> to play a solo.

j. _____ The large committee <u>plans</u> every homecoming event.

k _____ When I finished my workout, I <u>walk</u> for five minutes to cool down.

l. _____ The nurse practitioner explained the side effects of the medication, and she <u>tells</u> me how to lessen those effects.

m. _____ The real estate agent <u>has list</u> the house for sale at $150,000.

n. _____ The dolphins <u>were swimming</u> closer to shore than I <u>have seen</u> them before.

■ **Using Pronouns Correctly** If you make errors in this section, pay particular attention to Chapter 21.

2. If the underlined pronoun is correct, write *yes* on the blank; if it is incorrect, write *no*.

a. _____ Douglass and <u>I</u> volunteer at the Seniors Center twice a week.

b. _____ At the climbing gym, Juanita climbed higher than <u>them</u>.

c. _____ Each of the ballerinas took <u>their</u> bow and smiled at the audience.

d. _____ The table server gave my date and <u>I</u> a coupon for a free dessert.

e. _____ The construction worker explained to the cab driver and <u>me</u> that the road was closed ahead.

f. _____ The jury believed that <u>its</u> verdict had been reached after an appropriate amount of deliberation.

h. _____ Professor Hayek is the instructor <u>whom</u> I told you about.

i. _____ Everybody should bring <u>their</u> notebooks to class.

■ **Using Modifiers Correctly** If you make errors in this section, pay particular attention to Chapter 22.

3. If the underlined modifier is correct, write *yes* on the blank; if it is incorrect, write *no*.

a. _____ The star at the top of the Christmas tree shone very <u>bright</u>.

b. _____ The speaker talked <u>briefly</u> and then answered questions.

c. _____ Once I got a satellite dish, my television picture was the <u>most clearest</u> it has ever been.

d. _____ <u>Noticing my depression</u>, Pablo's compassion was helpful.

e. _____ Darla plays the trumpet very <u>good</u>, so she is likely to get a music scholarship.

f. _____ After his third accident, Bob is <u>carefuler</u> than he used to be when he drives.

■ **Using Capitalization and Punctuation Correctly** If you make errors in this section, pay particular attention to Chapter 23.

4. If there are no capitalization errors, write *yes* on the blank. If capitals are missing, or if capitals are used incorrectly, write the number of errors on the blank.

a. _____ To reach Lake Milton, take route 44 to Bristolville and turn east.

b. _____ Last semester, I took American History 102 and learned about the Great Depression and World War II.

c. _____ The Fraternal Order of Police is sponsoring a Halloween party for children in the community.

5. If there are no punctuation errors, write *yes* on the blank. If punctuation is missing, or if punctuation is used incorrectly, write the number of errors on the blank.

a. _____ Before registering for the next semester, you must pay your library fine, and you must pay your parking tickets.

b. _____ Mother served the hot, apple pie with a choice of cheese, or ice cream.

c. _____ Angry and annoyed, the customer decided to speak to the store manager, a friendly, helpful man with a reputation for solving problems.

d. _____ Daylight Savings Time, it seems to me, should be mandatory in all states.

e. _____ Pablo who is originally from Spain; plans to apply to become a U.S. citizen, for he finds the people in this country friendly, ambitious and creative.

f. _____ The violin is called "the queen of instruments"; its rank is due to its beautiful tone and wide range of expression.

g. _____ My favorite daytime talk show host is Oprah Winfrey, who is not afraid to tackle controversial issues; my favorite nighttime talk show host is David Letterman, who is both funny, and topical.

h. _____ The best desserts on the menu are: the chocolate cheesecake, the bread pudding, and the homemade ice cream.

i. _____ Eleni wants only one thing for her birthday—a puppy.

j. _____ The new dean of education (Dr. Rayburn) was introduced at the faculty brunch.

k. _____ Phyllis's loan application was rejected because she forgot to sign it.

l. _____ The car in the driveway is her's.

m. _____ The children's doctor recommended that they get a flu shot.

n. _____ The dog buried all it's bones by the swing set.

o. _____ The mayor announced, "All city workers should contribute to the United Way campaign."

DIAGNOSTIC

■ **Eliminating Problems with Frequently Confused Words and Spelling**

If you make errors in this section, pay particular attention to Chapter 24.

6. Write the correct word in the blank.
   a. (advice/advise) Carla went to the Writing Center for _____ about her problem with sentence fragments.
   b. (their/there/they're) If I were you, I would not trust _____ motives.
   c. (argument/arguement) The neighbors' _____ was so loud that I could not sleep.

CHAPTER 20

Using Verbs Correctly

Verbs are vitally important to a sentence because they convey a great deal of meaning, and they can add considerable energy to writing. At the same time, verbs can be tricky because to use them correctly, you need to understand several grammar points, which this chapter will help you learn. If you currently know a great deal about using verbs, this chapter will reinforce your understanding and perhaps teach you a few new points. To assess your current level of understanding, take the following pretest.

PRETEST

A. If the underlined verb is correct, write *C* on the blank. If it is incorrect, write *I* on the blank. If you are unsure, do not guess; leave the space blank. Check your answers in Appendix II.

1. __C__ The sun <u>shone</u> so brightly I couldn't see to drive.
2. __I__ Maria <u>be</u> the one to ask about that.
3. __C__ We <u>had driven</u> two hundred miles when the fuel pump broke.
4. __I__ Larry explained, "A person <u>do</u> what he has to do."
5. __I__ I <u>hopes</u> I can get a part-time job this summer.
6. __I__ We <u>have did</u> everything you asked.
7. __C__ The teachers <u>began</u> their strike the day after Christmas.
8. __I__ They <u>has told</u> me they do not plan to go with us.
9. __C__ My sister Hannah <u>decided</u> to join the navy.
10. __I__ Olga <u>brang</u> her botany notes for me to copy.

(continued on next page)

b. Fill in the blank with the correct present tense form in parentheses.

1. (means/mean) My collection of shells from Ocean City __means__ a great deal to me.

2. (visits/visit) Either Mother or Aunt Harriet __visits__ Uncle Ned on his birthday.

3. (plans/plan) Both Hans and his best friend __plan__ to attend Ohio State University.

4. (likes/like) Everyone __likes__ a good mystery.

5. (practices/practice) The football team __practices__ twice a day in August.

6. (decides/decide) The personnel committee __decides__ whom to hire for the teaching positions.

7. (is/are) Here __are__ the papers you lost.

8. (wants/want) Each of the children __wants__ to take karate lessons.

9. (works/work) Stavros is one of those people who __works__ harder than necessary.

10. (sleeps/sleep) The cat, along with her kittens, __sleeps__ in the garage.

c. If the verb tenses change, write *TS* (for tense shift) on the blank. If the tenses are consistent, write *C* on the blank.

1. __TS__ The doctor explained that the child's tonsils were badly infected and that they had to be surgically removed when the infection was gone.

2. __C__ All of us are prepared for an emergency. We have first-aid kits, flashlights, waterproof clothing, and extra food.

3. _____ When the nature guide turned over the leaf, the scouts see the monarch butterfly egg.

4. _____ The killer whale feeds on seals, fish, and other whales. It did not attack human beings.

5. _____ The blue whale can grow to be 100 feet long, although it eats only microscopic animals.

VERB FORMS

As explained in Chapter 14, verbs often change their form to show different times, also called **tenses**. (To review, see page 207.) The next sections will tell you more about those verb forms and how to use them.

Regular Verbs

Most English verbs are **regular**, which means they form the past tense by adding *-d* or *-ed*. Here are examples of regular verbs:

Present Tense	Past Tense
love	lov<u>ed</u>
save	sav<u>ed</u>
walk	walk<u>ed</u>
yell	yell<u>ed</u>

Regular verbs ending in *y* often change the *y* to *i* before adding *ed*, like this:

Present Tense	Past Tense
study	stud<u>ied</u>
hurry	hurr<u>ied</u>
worry	worr<u>ied</u>

Present Tense Forms for Regular Verbs   When you write or speak of events that occur now, in the present time, you use the **present tense**. In the present tense, your regular verbs should have the forms shown in the chart below. Notice that whether the regular verb adds an *s* or *es* depends upon the subject of the sentence. One of the most common errors in English is omitting the *s* or *es* when it is needed, so pay attention to when the chart indicates these endings are required.

REGULAR VERB FORMS: PRESENT TENSE

Singular		Plural
I play.		We play.
You play.		You play.
		They play.
He plays.	Notice the *s* or *es*	The children play.
She plays.	ending here.	
It plays.		
The child plays.		

CAUTION: A common error is forgetting the *s* or *es* ending for a regular, present tense verb used with *he*, *she*, *it*, or any singular noun subject.

no: Mary *like* chocolate pudding.

yes: Mary *likes* chocolate pudding.

PRACTICE 20.1

On a separate sheet of paper, rewrite the paragraph, changing the past tense verbs to present tense forms. Be careful to use the *s* or *es* ending when needed. The first sentence is done as an example.

[1]African grasslands ~~supported~~ *support* large numbers of insect-eating and seed-eating birds. [2]The ostrich, one of these birds, survived on fruit, seeds, and small animals. [3]The Kori, the world's heaviest bird, also lived on the grasslands. [4]This bird weighed 110 pounds. [5]Oxpeckers, another grassland bird, perched on the backs of grazing animals and chewed ticks and other parasites they discovered there. [6]Still other grassland birds included bulbuls, shrikes, storks, cranes, and ground hornbills. [7]One of the most interesting birds, the weaverbird, designed elaborate hanging nests in trees. [8]Unfortunately, large flocks of these birds caused extensive damage to African trees. [9]Birds of prey on the grasslands included the vulture and the lanner falcon. [10]Indeed, birdwatchers often traveled to this part of the world to observe the rare and wonderful birds.

PRACTICE 20.2

Complete each of the sentences by using a present tense form of a regular verb from the list and any other words you want. Do not use the same verb twice, and be sure to use *s* or *es* endings where needed.

play	laugh	organize
smile	move	follow
study	practice	learn
worry	joke	collect

Example: The excited children *play happily in the school yard during recess.*

_____

1. My best friend _____

_____

2. Professor Bauer _____

_____

3. We _____

_____

4. The planning committee _____

_____

5. You _____

_____

6. I _____

_____

7. He _____

_____

8. My younger sister _____

_____

PRACTICE 20.3

Fill in the blanks with the correct present tense form of the verb in parentheses. The first blank is filled in as an example.

Because of my cold, my nose no longer (to function) ^1 *functions* _____ as part of my respiratory system. I (to inhale) ^2 _____ deeply, but no air (to penetrate) ^3 _____ the blocked passages. I (to race) ^4 _____ to the bathroom and (to grab) ^5 _____ a tissue before I (to sneeze) ^6 _____ myself to the floor. Pulling myself up, I (to head) ^7 _____ for the kitchen. My throat (to rust) ^8 _____ out, and my mouth (to enter) ^9 _____ the drought season. Switching on the light, I (to tug) ^10 _____ at the refrigerator door, which (to seem) ^11 _____ like wrenching a two-ton vault. Struggling for strength, I (to open) ^12 _____ the door, (to grab) ^13 _____ the orange juice, and (to pour) ^14 _____ the liquid. The juice (to burn) ^15 _____ my aching throat. I (to reach) ^16 _____ for a cold tablet and (to pop) ^17 _____ it in. To clear my nose, I (to reach) ^18 _____ for the nasal spray. I (to squirt) ^19 _____ twice in each nostril and (to tilt) ^20 _____ my head back. I (to walk)

²¹_____ back to bed, but I (to toss) ²²_____ and (to turn) ²³_____ for hours until exhausted. I (to drift) ²⁴_____ off to sleep, hoping not to awaken until the cold (to burn) ²⁵_____ itself out.

FAQ

Q: What is the problem with "incorrect" verb forms? I hear people use them all the time.

A: Many varieties of English exist. The "incorrect" forms can be acceptable for use with family and friends. They are inappropriate, however, in most school and work situations.

Past Tense Forms for Regular Verbs   When you write or speak of events that occurred in the past, you use the **past tense**. In the past tense, your regular verbs should have the forms shown in this chart. Notice that unlike the present tense forms, the past tense forms never change—they always end in *d* or *ed*, regardless of the subject.

REGULAR VERB FORMS: PAST TENSE

Singular	**Plural**
I played.	We played.
	You played.
You played.	They played.
He played.	The children played.
She played.	
It played.	
The child played.	

CAUTION: A common error is forgetting the *d* or *ed* ending for a regular, past tense verb.

No:	Yesterday I *walk* to work.
Yes:	Yesterday I *walked* to work.

PRACTICE 20.4

On a separate sheet, write a sentence using the regular verb in parentheses in its past tense form. Circle the past tense ending, and use a different subject for each sentence.

Example: (start) ___*The referee start(ed) the sudden death overtime play.*___

1. (look)

2. (want)

3. (talk)

4. (expect)

5. (discover)

On a separate sheet, rewrite Practice 20.3. This time fill in the blanks with past tense forms of the verbs given.

Past Participle Forms for Regular Verbs   The **past participle** is the verb form that can be used with the helping verbs *has, have,* and *had.* As shown in the chart, the past participle of regular verbs is formed in the same way the past tense of regular verbs is formed: by adding *d* or *ed.* Notice, however, that the subject of the sentence determines whether you use *has* or *have.*

REGULAR VERB FORMS: PAST PARTICIPLE

Singular	**Plural**
I have played.	We have played.
I had played.	We had played.
You have played.	You have played.
You had played.	You had played.
He has played.	They have played.
He had played.	They had played.
She has played.	The children have played.
She had played.	The children had played.
It has played.	
It had played.	
The child has played.	
The child had played.	

NOTE: As you can tell from the preceding examples, the past participle form does not change even though the form of the helping verb changes.

CAUTION: A common error is forgetting the *d* or *ed* ending for the past participle form of a regular verb.

No:	The union *has decide* to accept the wage offer.
Yes:	The union *has decided* to accept the wage offer.

PRACTICE 20.6

Find and correct the errors with the past participle and accompanying helping verbs. If you need help, consult the previous chart. The first one is done as an example.

planned
[1]Donna and Rico have ~~plan~~ their wedding for August 16, but suddenly Rico have decided that he wants to elope. [2]At one time, he had agreed that a big wedding would be desirable, but lately he have wonder if a big, splashy affair is too much trouble and expense. [3]Donna, surprisingly, has agree to think about eloping, even though she have wanted a big wedding all her life. [4]Fortunately, the caterer has agreed to return the couple's deposit if they cancel the reception.

PRACTICE 20.7

On a separate sheet, write a sentence using the helping verb and past participle form of the regular verb in parentheses.

Example: (has + walk) _For the past year, Jill has walked three miles a day._

1. (had + jump)

2. (has + change)

3. (had + open)

4. (has + work)

5. (had + apply)

Irregular Verbs

An **irregular verb** does not add *d* or *ed* to form the past and past participle forms. Instead, irregular verbs form the past and past participle in a variety of ways.

A list of some irregular verbs with their past and past participle forms follows. Study the list and place a star next to the forms you do not already know. Then learn these forms.

Present	Past	Past Participle
be (am/is/are)	was/were	been
become(s)	became	become
begin(s)	began	begun
bend(s)	bent	bent
bite(s)	bit	bitten

Present	Past	Past Participle
blow(s)	blew	blown
break(s)	broke	broken
bring(s)	brought	brought
buy(s)	bought	bought
catch(es)	caught	caught
choose(es)	chose	chosen
come(s)	came	come
cost(s)	cost	cost
do (does)	did	done
draw(s)	drew	drawn
drink(s)	drank	drunk
drive(s)	drove	driven
eat(s)	ate	eaten
fall(s)	fell	fallen
feed(s)	fed	fed
feel(s)	felt	felt
fight(s)	fought	fought
find(s)	found	found
fly (flies)	flew	flown
forget(s)	forgot	forgotten
forgive(s)	forgave	forgiven
freeze(s)	froze	frozen
get(s)	got	got *or* gotten
give(s)	gave	given
go (goes)	went	gone
grow(s)	grew	grown
hang(s)—a picture	hung	hung
hang(s)—a person	hanged	hanged
have(s)	had	had
hear(s)	heard	heard
hide(s)	hid	hidden
hold(s)	held	held
hurt(s)	hurt	hurt
keep(s)	kept	kept
know(s)	knew	known
lay(s)—to place	laid	laid

Present	Past	Past Participle
lead(s)	led	led
leave(s)	left	left
lend(s)	lent	lent
lie(s)—to rest	lay	lain
light(s)	lit	lit
lose(s)	lost	lost
make(s)	made	made
meet(s)	met	met
pay(s)	paid	paid
read(s)	read	read
ride(s)	rode	ridden
ring(s)	rang	rung
rise(s)	rose	risen
run(s)	ran	run
say(s)	said	said
see(s)	saw	seen
sell(s)	sold	sold
send(s)	sent	sent
set(s)	set	set
shake(s)	shook	shaken
shine(s)—to give light	shone	shone
shine(s)—to polish	shined	shined
shrink(s)	shrank	shrunk
sing(s)	sang	sung
sit(s)	sat	sat
sleep(s)	slept	slept
speak(s)	spoke	spoken
spend(s)	spent	spent
stand(s)	stood	stood
steal(s)	stole	stolen
sting(s)	stung	stung
strike(s)	struck	struck
swim(s)	swam	swum
take(s)	took	taken
teach(es)	taught	taught
tear(s)	tore	torn
tell(s)	told	told

Present	Past	Past Participle
think(s)	thought	thought
throw(s)	threw	thrown
wake(s)	woke *or* waked	woken *or* waked
wear(s)	wore	worn
win(s)	won	won
write(s)	wrote	written

FAQ

Q: Where can I find the forms for all the irregular verbs?

A: You can look up an irregular verb in a dictionary to find its past tense and past participle forms.

Present Tense Forms for Irregular Verbs   When you write or speak of events that occur now, use the **present tense**. In the present tense, your irregular verbs should have the form shown in the first column of the chart beginning on page 318. You will add *s* or *es* to that form, depending on the sentence subjects, as shown in the chart that follows. One of the most common errors in English is omitting the *s* or *es* when it is needed, so pay attention to when the chart indicates these endings are required.

IRREGULAR VERB FORMS: PRESENT TENSE

Singular	**Plural**
I drink.	We drink.
You drink.	You drink.
	They drink.
He drinks.	The dogs drink.
She drinks.	
It drinks.	
The dog drinks.	

Notice the *s* or *es* ending here.

CAUTION: A common error is forgetting the *s* or *es* ending for an irregular present tense verb used with *he*, *she*, *it*, or any singular noun subject.

No: Helga *sing* beautifully.

Yes: Helga *sings* beautifully.

PRACTICE 20.8

Rewrite the sentences, changing the underlined past tense verbs to present tense forms. Be careful to use the *s* or *es* ending when needed. If you are unsure of the correct form, check the chart beginning on page 318.

Example: The golden sun <u>rose</u> over the Atlantic Ocean.

The golden sun rises over the Atlantic Ocean.

1. Matteo always <u>forgot</u> to meet me at he library after class.

   _____

   _____

2. The thoughtful dinner guest <u>brought</u> the hostess a bottle of wine.

   _____

   _____

3. For a moment the centerfielder <u>lost</u> the ball in the sun, but he <u>caught</u> it anyway.

   _____

   _____

4. I <u>knew</u> you <u>drove</u> because I <u>saw</u> your car.

   _____

   _____

5. Jannine <u>left</u> her car keys in the ignition.

   _____

   _____

6. When the church bells <u>rang</u>, the congregation <u>rose</u> and <u>sang</u> a hymn.

   _____

   _____

PRACTICE 20.9

Complete each sentence with a present tense form of an irregular verb from the list beginning on page 318 and any other words you need. Use *s* or *es* endings where needed.

Example: The scouts and their leader *take a group of senior citizens shopping every week.*

1. She _____

   _____

2. During the meeting, Boris and I _____

   _____

3. Before leaving for work, Luis _____

   _____

4. They _____

   _____

5. The customer _____

   _____

Present Tense Forms for *Be, Have,* and *Do*   The present tense forms of the
irregular verbs *be, have,* and *do* are tricky. The following charts will help you
learn these forms.

PRESENT TENSE FORMS OF *BE*	
Singular	**Plural**
I am.	We are.
You are.	You are.
He is.	They are.
She is.	The toys are.
It is.	
The toy is.	

PRESENT TENSE FORMS OF *HAVE*	
Singular	**Plural**
I have.	We have.
You have.	You have.
He has.	They have.
She has.	The children have.
It has.	
The child has.	

PRESENT TENSE FORMS OF *DO*

Singular	**Plural**
I do.	We do.
You do.	You do.
He does.	They do.
She does.	The children do.
It does.	
The child does.	

CAUTION: Use the contraction forms *don't* and *doesn't* carefully. A common mistake is to use *don't (do not)* when *doesn't (does not)* is needed.

No:	The toy *don't* work anymore.
Yes:	The toy *doesn't* work anymore.
No:	He *don't* want to work outside.
Yes:	He *doesn't* want to work outside.

PRACTICE 20.10

Fill in the blank with the correct present tense form of the verb in parentheses.

Example: (be) This CD _____*is*_____ very popular among teenagers.

1. (have) He _____ an impressive stamp collection.

2. (be) New Year's Eve parties _____ always a disappointment to me.

3. (do) Many parents _____ not understand their teenage children.

4. (have) I _____ the information you asked for.

5. (do) Jamal _____ the best he can, but I _____ not always recognize that fact.

6. (be) I _____ here if you need help, and your parents

   _____ too.

Past Tense Forms for Irregular Verbs   When you write or speak of events that occurred in the past, you use the **past tense**. In the past tense, use the irregular verb forms in the second column of the chart beginning on page 318. Unlike the present tense forms, the past tense forms never change, as shown in the chart that follows.

IRREGULAR VERB FORMS: PAST TENSE

Singular	**Plural**
I drank.	We drank.
You drank.	You drank.
He drank.	They drank.
She drank.	The dogs drank.
It drank.	
The dog drank.	

CAUTION: A common error is using the past participle form (in the third column) for the simple past tense. Remember, the past participle appears with a helping verb (see page 317).

No:	Jim *done* the work. (past participle without helping verb)
Yes:	Jim *has done* the work. (helping verb with past participle)
Yes:	Jim *did* the work. (past tense form)

PRACTICE 20.11

Fill in the blank with the past tense form of the irregular verb in parentheses. If you are unsure of the form, check the chart beginning on page 318.

Example: (hold) As Grandma _____*held*_____ the quilt I made for her, she smiled gratefully.

1. (forget) Michael was embarrassed because he _____ his sister's birthday.

2. (hear) When Eleni _____ about the earthquake in California, she raced home to call her relatives in San Diego.

3. (lend) José is sorry he _____ Lenny $50 because Lenny never repaid the loan.

4. (begin) Once everyone was seated, the orchestra _____ the overture.

5. (steal) As Aaron Cohen released the pitch, Brett Butler _____ second base.

6. (wake) The alarm on the clock radio sounded at 6:45, and I

_____ with a start.

7. (teach) Yesterday Professor Morales _____ us several techniques for successful revising.

8. (buy) The angora sweater I _____ for Nuha is one size too large.

PRACTICE 20.12

Pick five irregular verbs that you do not already know the parts of (use the chart beginning on page 318). Then, on a separate sheet, use the past tense form of each of these verbs in a sentence.

Past Tense Forms for *Be* The irregular verb *be* is the only verb whose forms vary in the past tense according to the subject of the sentence. The following chart shows you the forms.

PAST TENSE FORMS OF *BE*

Singular	Plural
I was.	We were.
You were.	You were.
He was.	They were.
She was.	The toys were.
It was.	
The toy was.	

PRACTICE 20.13

Fill in the blank with *was* or *were*.

Example: The test results _____ *were* _____ surprising.

1. The doctor _____ certain that rest and a better diet

_____ all you needed.

2. I _____ eager to join you, but my roommates

_____ not available to go.

3. They _____ certain they passed the quiz, but you

_____ skeptical.

4. The children _____ excited when they found a puppy on the porch.

5. She _____ the first person in her family to go to college, so

her parents _____ very proud of her.

6. We _____ eager to help you stop smoking.

Past Participle Forms for Irregular Verbs.   The **past participle** is the verb form used with the helping verbs *has*, *have*, and *had*. The past participle of irregular verbs is the form in the third column of the chart beginning on page 318. As the following chart shows, the subject of the sentence determines whether you use *has* or *here*.

IRREGULAR VERB FORMS: PAST PARTICIPLE

Singular	Plural
I have drunk.	We have drunk.
I had drunk.	We had drunk.
You have drunk.	You have drunk.
You had drunk.	You had drunk.
He has drunk.	They have drunk.
He had drunk.	They had drunk.
She has drunk.	The dogs have drunk.
She had drunk.	The dogs had drunk.
It has drunk.	
It had drunk.	
The dog has drunk.	
The dog had drunk.	

NOTE: As you can tell from the preceding examples, the past participle form does not change even though the form of the helping verb changes.

(continued)

> **CAUTION:**   The past participle form must be used with a helping verb; it is not used alone.
>
> No: I *seen* Nancy. (past participle without helping verb)
>
> Yes: I *have seen* Nancy. (past participle and helping verb)
>
> Yes: I *had seen* Nancy. (past participle and helping verb)
>
> No: I *seen* her yesterday. (past participle without helping verb)
>
> Yes: I *saw* her yesterday. (past tense form)

PRACTICE 20.14

Fill in the blank with the past participle form of the irregular verb in parentheses.

Example: (bring) Fortunately, Gina has _____ *brought* _____ a first-aid kit

1. (blow) The strong winds have _____ since early this morning.

2. (choose) Lars has _____ to attend St. Bonaventure.

3. (go) The stray dogs had _____ by the time the dog warden arrived.

4. (lie) Doreen has _____ down for a while to try to get rid of her headache.

5. (ride) After Peter and Sondra had _____ the merry-go-round for the fifth time, they wanted some cotton candy.

6. (write) Thousands of angry consumers have _____ the Better Business Bureau to complain about the faulty appliance.

PRACTICE 20.15

Write a sentence using the helping verb and past participle form of the irregular verb in parentheses. If you are unsure, check the chart beginning on page 318.

Example: (has + teach)   *Dr. Yurak has taught both English and history for* _____

twenty years.

1. (had + wake) _____

    _____

2. (has + do) _____

3. (had + see) _____

    _____

4. (has + sting) _____

    _____

5. (had + stand) _____

    _____

6. (has + be) _____

    _____

7. (had + meet) _____

    _____

REVIEW PRACTICE 20.16

Rewrite each sentence twice, first using the past tense form of the under-lined irregular verb, then using a past participle form.

Example: The family <u>eats</u> a vegetarian supper of corn chowder and wheat rolls.

a. *The family ate a vegetarian supper of corn chowder and wheat rolls.*

b. *The family has eaten a vegetarian supper of corn chowder and wheat rolls.*

1. Mom and Dad <u>hide</u> the eggs for the annual Easter egg hunt.

    a. _____

    _____

    b. _____

    _____

2. Few people <u>understand</u> the significance of the governor's decision.

    a. _____

    _____

b. _____

_____

3. The honor guard <u>stands</u> at attention for an hour.

a. _____

_____

b. _____

_____

4. Jan <u>swims</u> five miles before breakfast.

a. _____

_____

b. _____

_____

5. The bypass *runs* all the way to Route 40.

a. _____

_____

b. _____

_____

FAQ

Q: Can I tell which verb form to use by how the sentence sounds?

A: How a sentence sounds is not a reliable guide for choosing a verb form. Instead, identify the subject and then decide on the appropriate singular or plural form.

SUBJECT-VERB AGREEMENT

A word that refers to one person or item is **singular**; a word that refers to more than one person or item is **plural**.

Singular (refers to one person or item)		Plural (refers to more than one person or item)	
dog	month	dogs	months
desk	I	desks	we
box	he	boxes	they
cup	she	cups	
	it		

To achieve **subject-verb agreement**, use a singular verb with a singular subject and a plural verb with a plural subject. Subject-verb agreement is only an issue with present tense verb forms and the past tense forms of *be—was* (singular) and *were* (plural).

Present tense verb forms add *s* or *es* when used with *he, she, it*, or a singular noun. *Was* is used with singular nouns and *I, he, she*, and *it*. The following charts summarize this subject-verb agreement rule.

PRESENT TENSE: MOST VERBS

Singular Subject/Singular Verb   **Plural Subject/Plural Verb**

I move slowly.   We move slowly.

You move slowly.   You move slowly.

He moves slowly.   They move slowly.

She moves slowly.   The dogs move slowly.

It moves slowly.

The dog moves slowly.

NOTE: Add *s* or *es* to the verb only when the subject is *he, she, it*, or a singular noun.

PAST TENSE: *WAS/WERE*

Singular Subject/Singular Verb   **Plural Subject/Plural Verb**

I was here.   We were here.

You were here.   You were here.

He was here.   They were here.

She was here.   The dogs were here.

It was here.

The dog was here.

NOTE: Use *was* only when the subject is *I, he, she, it*, or a singular noun.

PRACTICE 20.17

1. Fill in each blank with the correct present tense form of the verb in parentheses.

From time to time, you probably (wake up) ¹_____ with dark circles under your eyes. These circles (indicate) ²_____ that you (need) ³_____ more sleep.

Blood vessels under the eyes (drain) ⁴_____ blood from your head. However, blood circulation (slow) ⁵_____ when you are tired. This slow-down (cause) ⁶_____ the blood vessels to swell. Under the eyes, the skin (thin) ⁷_____. When blood vessels (swell) ⁸_____, you (see) ⁹_____ right through the skin. The darkness you (notice) ¹⁰_____ is actually blood.

2. Fill in the blanks with either *was* (singular) or *were* (plural).

a. We _____ certain that Jamal _____ not here yet.

b. You _____ the best person for the job because Joyce _____ not available.

c. This class _____ difficult, but they _____ able to handle it.

d. Jane _____ new in town, but she _____ making friends easily.

e. It _____ too early to leave, but we _____ too tired to stay.

f. The spring rains _____ over, but the summer heat _____ not here yet.

PRACTICE 20.18

Eliminate the faulty subject-verb agreement in the following paragraph.

¹Lighthouses guide sailors to safe anchorages. ²They also warns them of danger. ³The most famous ancient lighthouse was the Pharos of Alexandria, built in Egypt about 300 B.C. ⁴Early lighthouses was just wooden towers with metal baskets of burning wood or coal hung from poles on the top. ⁵Today, the most powerful light shine from the Créac'h d'Ouessant lighthouse. ⁶It warn of treacherous rocks of northwest France. ⁷Most lighthouses have sirens that blare out coded fog warnings. ⁸However, some lighthouses emits radio signals to guide ships with radio direction finders. ⁹Without lighthouses, the sea would be even more treacherous than it already is.

Compound Subjects

A **compound subject** is a two-part subject with the parts connected by *and, or, either … or, neither … nor,* or *not only … but [also].*

1. If the subjects are joined by *and,* the verb will usually be plural.

> My best friend and I <u>spend</u> spring break in Florida.

2. When the subjects are considered one unit, like *ham and eggs* and *rock and roll,* use a singular verb:

> Rock and roll <u>is</u> here to stay.

3. If the subjects are joined by *or, either … or, neither … nor,* or *not only … but [also],* the verb agrees with the closer subject.

> Either my brothers or my sister <u>is</u> going. (singular verb to agree with the singular *sister*)

> Neither my hat nor my gloves <u>are</u> where I left them. (plural verb to agree with the plural *gloves*)

NOTE: If you do not like the sound of "Either my brothers or my sister is going," reverse the order to place the plural subject second, so you can use a plural verb:

> Either my sister or my brothers <u>are</u> going.

PRACTICE 20.19

Follow each compound subject with the correct present tense form of the verb in parentheses. Then finish the sentence with any other words you care to add.

Example: (taste) The meat and the potatoes ___*taste overcooked and bland.*___

1. (know) Neither the club president nor the treasurer _____

   _____

2. (grow) Cotton and tobacco _____

   _____

3. (sing) The choir or the choirmaster _____

   _____

4. (visit) The children and their teacher _____

_____

5. (have) Neither the encyclopedia nor the dictionaries _____

_____

6. (plan) Not only Sue but also Helen _____

_____

7. (volunteer) Either Mr. Chen or his wife _____

_____

8. (hope) The teacher and her principal _____

_____

Collective Noun Subjects

Collective nouns refer to groups. They are words like these:

congregation	committee	band	faculty
group	team	jury	flock
herd	audience	family	class

1. If the collective noun is considered one group acting as a whole, a singular verb is used.

> At noon, the <u>band</u> <u>boards</u> the bus for the trip to the Rose Parade. (The singular verb is used because *band* is acting as a whole.)

2. If the members of the group are acting individually, the collective noun takes a plural verb.

> The <u>faculty</u> <u>have</u> debated that issue for years. (The plural verb is used because the individual members of the faculty are acting individually.)

PRACTICE 20.20

On a separate sheet, write sentences using the given collective nouns as subjects and the correct present tense forms of the verbs in parentheses. Be prepared to explain why you used the verb form that you did.

Example: flock (migrate) *The flock migrates to a warmer climate for the winter.*

1. army (attack)

2. family (eat)

3. jury (argue)

4. committee (decide)

5. team (practice)

Indefinite Pronoun Subjects

An **indefinite pronoun** refers to a group without specifying the particular members.

1. These indefinite pronouns always take a singular verb:

anyone	anybody	anything	each
everyone	everybody	everything	one
no one	nobody	nothing	none
someone	somebody	something	

<u>Anyone</u> <u>is</u> welcome to attend the open house.

<u>Everything</u> <u>works</u> out eventually.

<u>Each student</u> <u>writes</u> a term paper during the senior year.

<u>Somebody</u> <u>helps</u> Grandma clean her house every week.

2. These indefinite pronouns always take a plural verb:

both	many	few	several

<u>Many</u> <u>believe</u> that Congress will defeat the budget proposal.

3. These indefinite pronouns take either a singular or plural verb, depending on whether the sense of the subject is singular or plural:

all	more	some
any	most	

<u>Some</u> of my homework <u>is</u> missing. (The verb is singular because the sense of the subject is that one unit is missing.)

<u>Some</u> of the puzzle pieces <u>are</u> missing. (The verb is plural because the sense is that more than one unit is missing.)

PRACTICE 20.21

Circle the indefinite pronoun subjects and fill in the blanks with the correct present tense form of the verb in parentheses.

Example: (be) (All) of the lost money _____ *is* _____ in the back of the drawer

1. (believe) Each of us _____ the tax increase will improve the economy.

2. (find) Many of the band members _____ the new director enthusiastic and creative.

3. (be) Everyone _____ invited to the tailgate party before the homecoming game.

4. (be) All of the hem _____ torn from the skirt.

5. (seem) None of the proposals _____ adequate to solve the problem.

6. (be) Some of the desserts _____ low in fat and sugar.

7. (go) Everything _____ wrong when I am in a hurry.

8. (taste) All of the items _____ underseasoned to me.

9. (expect) Nobody _____ you to be perfect.

10. (feel) All of the clothes _____ soft.

Phrases between the Subject and Verb

Phrases, particularly prepositional phrases (see page 214), often come between the subject and verb. Do not be fooled by these phrases, for they do not affect subject-verb agreement.

The <u>theme</u> of the stories <u>is</u> middle-class greed. (A singular verb is used to agree with the singular subject *theme*. The phrase *of the stories* does not affect agreement.)

PRACTICE 20.22

After each subject and phrase, write a present tense verb and any other words you want to add. (Use forms of the verb *to be* no more than twice.) Underline the subject once and the verb twice; draw a line through the phrase between the subject and verb.

Example: The <u>carton</u> ~~of records~~ <u>is blocking</u> the entrance to the room.

_____

1. The people on the bus _____

_____

2. Many paintings by that artist _____

_____

3. The students from Sri Lanka _____

_____

4. The scouts, along with their scoutmaster, _____

_____

5. The group of children _____

_____

6. The mistakes on the last page of the essay _____

_____

7. The seats in the tenth row _____

_____

8. The ragweed in the fields _____

_____

9. One of the kittens _____

_____

10. The container of sewing materials _____

_____

Inverted Order

When a sentence has **inverted order**, the subject comes *after* the verb. (See page 216 for more on inverted order.) Inverted order often occurs when a sentence begins with *here* or *there*. The following sentences have inverted order. The subjects are underlined once, and the verbs are underlined twice.

Here <u>are</u> the <u>items</u> for the charity garage sale.

There <u>is</u> only <u>one movie</u> suitable for children.

Even if a sentence has inverted order, the subject and verb must agree. (See page 207 and page 213 on identifying subjects and verbs.)

PRACTICE 20.23

Complete the following sentences, being sure your subjects and verbs agree.

Example: Here is _an unusual painting._ _____

_____

1. Here are _____

_____

2. There is _____

_____

3. There are _____

_____

4. There were _____

_____

5. There was _____

_____

■

Who, Which, That

Who, which, and *that* are **relative pronouns** that refer to nouns. (See page 241.) Use a singular verb when *who, which,* or *that* refers to a singular noun. Use a plural verb when *who, which,* or *that* refers to a plural noun. Study these two examples:

Peter is one of those students *who study* constantly. (The plural verb is used because *who* refers to the plural noun *students.*)

This is the book *that has* the surprise ending. (The singular verb is used because *that* refers to the singular noun *book.*)

PRACTICE 20.24

Draw an arrow from *who, which*, or *that* to the noun it refers to. Then fill in the blank with the correct present tense form of the verb in parentheses.

Example: (follow) Vashti is a person who _____ *follows* _____ every rule to the letter.

1. (do) A person who _____ not understand trigonometry will have trouble with physics.

2. (support) The beams that _____ this section of roof are beginning to rot.

3. (believe) Dr. Perni is one of those instructors who _____ her students can succeed.

4. (divide) This is the lake that _____ the property in half.

5. (scare) This is the kind of movie that always _____ me.

REVIEW PRACTICE 20.25

Find and eliminate the subject-verb agreement problems in the following passage, drawing on everything you have learned.

¹Beluga whales live in groups called pods, which are social units that may consists of two to twenty-five whales. ²Both males and females makes up a pod, although mothers with calves often form separate pods during calving season. ³A pod of belugas hunt and migrate together as one group.

⁴The behavior of belugas are interesting to observe. ⁵One of their most common behaviors are vocalizing. ⁶Also, during calving season, adult belugas at sea have been observed carrying objects such as planks, nets, and even caribou skeletons on their heads and backs. ⁷Females in zoological habitats have also been seen carrying floats or buoys on their backs after losing a newborn. ⁸Experts thus theorize that this carrying is surrogate behavior. ⁹Belugas, which exhibits a great deal of curiosity toward humans, often swim up to boats. ¹⁰They seem as interested in us as we are in them.

TENSE SHIFTS

As you have learned, verb tenses express different times. If you move from one verb tense to another without a good reason to indicate a different time, you create a problem called **tense shift**.

tense shift:	When I *left* the house this morning, I *go* to school.
explanation:	The first verb *(left)* is in the past tense to show that an event occurred before the present. However, the second verb *(go)* shifts to the present tense for no reason.
correction:	When I *left* the house this morning. I *went* to school.
explanation:	Both verbs are now in the past tense, so the tense shift is eliminated.

Some tense shifts are not a problem because a change of time is called for. Consider the following example:

appropriate tense shift:	"Frankfurters" *are* named for the city where they *were* first made: Frankfurt, Germany.
explanation:	The present tense *are* is used because frankfurters are named *in the present*. The past tense *were* is used because frankfurters were first made *in the past*.

PRACTICE 20.26

Underline the verbs and then eliminate each inappropriate tense shift by crossing out the problem verb and writing the correct form above it.

Example: After 1 <u>completed</u> my research paper for sociology class, I ~~treat~~ *treated* myself to dinner and a movie.

1. My high school teachers always asked for an outline whenever I submit my final essay.

2. As I drive into my old neighborhood, I saw that the house I grew up in was no longer standing.

3. Painting the walls in my bedroom went quickly, but painting the ceiling takes most of the day.

4. The eager science students collect specimens in the park. Then they mounted them on slides and view them under the microscope.

5. Before leaving the house, I make sure the stove is turned off, and then I checked the security locks.

PRACTICE 20.27

Eliminate inappropriate tense shifts by changing verb tenses where necessary. Remember not all tense changes are a problem. Eliminate only the inappropriate shifts.

[1]In 1937, pilot Amelia Earhart and Fred Noonan, her navigator, were attempting an around-the-world flight. [2]They planned to land and refuel on Howland Island. [3]However, Earhart's plane is lost over the Pacific Ocean, although she gave compass readings over the plane's radio, hoping to be guided to a safe landing. [4]"We're on the line of 157–337…. We are running north and south," the pilot says. [5]These were the last words the outside world heard Earhart speak. [6]The ground crew on Howland listens in vain for the twin-engine plane, but Earhart and Noonan are never heard from again. [7]Still, Earhart lives in the memory of millions of Americans who admire her as a pioneer who, as the first woman to fly the ocean alone, is not afraid of adventure.

REVIEW PRACTICE 20.28

Edit to eliminate the problems with verbs in the following paragraph. You will need to draw on everything you learned in this chapter.

[1]A team of scientists raise fleas in laboratories to learn more about how these pests caused disease in humans and to learn about effective ways to control the insects. [2]The fleas be kept in special jars that contain sieves. [3]These fleas lay eggs in the jars, and the eggs drops through the sieves. [4]The scientists collects the eggs so they can raise more fleas from them. [5]Each of the jars also have tubes that carries warm water to heat blood that is contained underneath a skin-like sheath. [6]The fleas bite through this sheath to drink the blood, which is served as their food. [7]Interestingly, these laboratory breeding grounds for fleas are called *fake pups*.

Finding and Eliminating Verb Errors in Your Writing

Finding and eliminating verb errors is best saved for editing. If you check earlier, you may be checking sentences that you later decide to delete or change. The following tips can help you edit for problems with verbs.

- Study each irregular verb you have used; if you are unsure whether your form is correct, check a dictionary.
- Do not rely on your ear to check for subject-verb agreement because the sound of your sentence is not always a reliable test.
- Pay special attention if you are writing in the present tense. Look especially for subjects that are compound, collective nouns, or indefinite pronouns. Check to be sure you have used the correct verb. If you have any phrases between the subject and verb, mentally cross them out before checking the verb.
- If you use *was* or *were*, follow the suggestions in the previous bullet.
- Identify the verb tense that you start out with. Then read to be sure you have maintained that tense. If you change tense, be sure you mean to alter the time referred to.
- If you like to compose at the computer, your computer's grammar checker may flag incorrect verb forms. However, grammar checkers are not completely reliable, so be sure to learn the forms

POST TEST

1. Find and correct the verb errors in the following paragraph.

[1]Henry Louis Aaron, known as "Hank," be American baseball's all-time champion home run hitter. [2]He enters the record books on April 8, 1974, when he breaked Babe Ruth's record of 714 home runs. [3]Aaron then went on to hit a total of 755 homers before he complete his 23-year major-league career. [4]Aaron begun playing professionally for all-black teams in Mobile and Indianapolis, but he sign with the National League's Milwaukee Braves when he be 18. [5]He had reach the major leagues when he were only 20 and quickly become one of the game's finest players. [6]He play for the Braves almost exclusively, first in Milwaukee and then in Atlanta. [7]Along with a lifetime batting average of .305, Aaron had 2,297 runs batted in. [8]He was the National

League's most valuable player in 1957 and lead the league in home runs and runs batted in. [9]A favorite with fans, Aaron done much to generate enthusiasm for the game he loved to play.

2. Change the underlined past tense verbs to present tense verbs.

[1]After the noon rush hour, Leo's Pizzeria <u>was</u> a mess. [2]The once clean stainless-steel table where pizzas <u>were</u> made <u>was</u> splattered with sauce and flooded with oil. [3]On the table, crusty dough and hardening strands of mozzarella <u>contributed</u> to the mess, which included crumbled plastic dough bags dripping with oil. [4]A mountain of dirty dishes <u>sat</u> in wait, threatening to topple if someone <u>did</u> not come soon to wash them. [5]A collection of torn pizza boxes, strewn across the counter, <u>hid</u> spatulas, used and abandoned. [6]Blackened pizzas, burned and forgotten during the rush, <u>filled</u> the air with the scent of charcoal. [7]Added to this smell <u>were</u> the watering onions near the ovens. [8]The flour used to make the crusts <u>covered</u> everything in the room with a fine dust. [9]Anyone who <u>entered</u> the kitchen would surely think twice before eating at Leo's.

SUCCEEDING IN COLLEGE

Ask Questions and Engage in Class Discussions

When you ask questions in class, you have the opportunity to clear up problems for yourself and for others. You can make sure you fully understand important material, and you may even raise a point that otherwise might not be mentioned. When you engage in class discussions, you become part of a community of learners and an active participant in academic dialogue. You make a contribution to your class, sharpen your critical thinking skills, and set your learning. And in very large classes, you help your instructor remember you.

Despite the importance of asking questions and engaging in class discussions, some students are reluctant to speak in class. Sometimes students are shy, or they may be fearful. If you hesitate to speak in class, you should work to overcome your reluctance because there is much to gain from class participation. The following tips can help.

- Sit in the front of the room. Asking questions from the front of the room is easier because you can make eye contact with your instructor. You won't see students sitting behind you; so you will be less likely to feel intimidated.

- Listen thoughtfully. Pay attention to the questions and comments already made, so you do not duplicate them. If you do need to ask a question asked previously, acknowledge that you heard the answer but need more explanation.

- Think first. Form your question or comment, reflect on it a moment, and then raise your hand. If it helps, write down your question or make a note about the comment you wish to make.

- If questions or comments occur to you while you are doing your homework, write them down to ask in class.

- Do not hesitate. If you wait to ask a question or make a comment, thinking that someone else will do it for you, you may find that the class ends, and you missed your opportunity.

Write about It

Explain how you feel about asking questions and speaking in class. If you like, you can consider the following questions: Do you speak often? Are you comfortable or uncomfortable? Are you more comfortable in some classes than others? Have you always felt the way you do now? What kinds of classes make it easy for you to speak up? What kinds of classes make it hard?

CHAPTER 21
Using Pronouns Correctly

To use pronouns correctly, you need to understand several grammar points. If you do not currently know all of them, do not be concerned because this chapter will help you learn them. On the other hand, you may currently know a great deal about using pronouns correctly, in which case this chapter will reinforce your understanding and perhaps teach you a few new points. To assess your current level of understanding, take the following pretest.

PRETEST

Fill in the blanks with the correct pronoun form in parentheses, and then check your answers in Appendix II. Do not guess; if you are unsure, do not put anything in the blank.

1. (I, me) My sister and ___I___ are attending the same college.

2. (they, them) Each morning I walk farther than ___they___.

3. (I, me) Because there was a fly in the soup, the manager gave my date and ___me___ a free dinner.

4. (her, their) Each of the mothers complained that ___Her___ children watched too much television.

5. (his or her, their) All of the students were instructed to bring ___their___ books and notes to the examination.

(continued on next page)

6. (its, their) The book of old photographs fell off _____*its*_____ shelf.

7. (its, their) The committee felt _____*its*_____ authority should be extended to making and enforcing rules.

8. (who, whom) That is the person _____*whom*_____ I told you about.

9. (I, me) The police officer told the other driver and _____*me*_____ that she could not determine who caused the accident.

10. (its, their) One of the dresses has lost _____*its*_____ shape.

PRONOUN-ANTECEDENT AGREEMENT

A **pronoun** takes the place of a noun or refers to a noun (a noun names a person, place, idea, emotion, or item).

The noun the pronoun stands for or refers to is the **antecedent**. In the following examples, an arrow is drawn from the pronoun to the noun antecedent:

Some <u>consumers</u> do not understand <u>their</u> legal rights.

<u>Michelle</u> understood that if <u>she</u> did not find a suitable babysitter, <u>she</u>

would not be able to return to college.

The oak <u>tree</u> must be diseased, for <u>it</u> is dropping <u>its</u> leaves.

A pronoun must be singular if the word it refers to (the antecedent) is singular. The pronoun must be plural if the antecedent is plural. Matching singular pronouns with singular antecedents and plural pronouns with plural antecedents creates **pronoun-antecedent agreement.**

singular pronoun/singular antecedent: The <u>child</u> cried because <u>she</u> broke <u>her</u> favorite toy.

plural pronoun/plural antecedent: The basketball <u>players</u> cheered when <u>they</u> won the game in double overtime.

Here is a chart of singular and plural pronouns.

PRONOUNS

Singular   **Plural**

I, me, my, mine   we, us, our, ours

he, she, it, him, her they, them, their, theirs

his, hers, its

Pronouns That Are Both Singular and Plural

   you, your, yours

PRACTICE 21.1

Fill in each blank with a pronoun from the above chart. Then draw an arrow from the pronoun to its antecedent. The first one is done as an example.

At 4:00 A.M., Gregory was awakened by the blare of 1 _his_ smoke detector. 2 _____ was dazed at first, but quickly 3 _____ realized that the house was on fire. Gregory's roommates downstairs had also been awakened, and 4 _____ were shouting to Greg to get out of the house. However, Greg realized that Mike and his sister Darla were still asleep in the attic, so 5 _____ ran upstairs to get 6 _____. Greg pounded on 7 _____ door to wake 8 _____ up. Then, the three of them began descending the stairs to the front door. Before they reached 9 _____, Darla was overcome by smoke and Mike had to carry 10 _____ part of the way. The three of them escaped just in time, for as they exited there was an explosion upstairs and fire shot through the windows. Firefighters blame the fire on a space heater. 11 _____ was placed too close to some rags and ignited 12 _____. 13 _____ said the boys are fortunate that 14 _____ detector was working. Everyone is safe, but Darla suffered from smoke inhalation, so 15 _____ had to be hospitalized.

Compound Subject Antecedents

A **compound subject** is a two-part subject with the parts connected by *and, or, either … or,* or *neither … nor, not only … but [also].* Follow these rules when a pronoun refers to all or part of a compound subject.

1. When the noun antecedents are joined by *and,* the pronoun will usually be plural.

   My *father and mother* sold <u>their</u> house and moved into an apartment. (*Their* is plural because it refers to two people, *father and mother.*)

2. If the noun antecedents are joined by *or, either … or,* or *neither … nor,* the pronoun agrees with the closer antecedent.

   Ivan or Ralph will lend me <u>his</u> car to use while mine is in the shop. (The singular *his* is used to agree with *Ralph,* the closer antecedent.)

   Neither the president nor his <u>advisors</u> believe <u>they</u> can get the disarmament bill through Congress. (The plural *they* is used to agree with *advisors,* the closer antecedent.)

   Either Jeff or his brothers will bring <u>their</u> extension ladder over so I can clean the gutters around the house. (The plural *their* is used to agree with *brothers,* the closer antecedent.)

NOTE: To avoid an awkward-sounding (but grammatically correct) sentence, place the plural part of a compound subject last.

Awkward:	Either the scouts or the scout leader will bring *his* leaf identification manual.
Natural sounding:	Either the scout leader or the scouts will bring *their* leaf identification manual.

PRACTICE 21.2

Fill in the blank with the correct pronoun.

Example: Neither the mayor nor city council members are spending <u>their</u> own money for reelection campaigns.

1. The students and their teacher decorated _____ classroom for the Martin Luther King, Jr., memorial celebration.

2. Joyce and Burt handed in _____ research papers early.

3. Either my mother or my grandmother will make _____ chocolate chip cookie recipe for the family reunion.

4. Neither the teachers nor the school board members changed _____ positions after hours of negotiating.

5. I thought Rico or Elliot would offer to bring _____ Coleman stove on the camping trip.

6. The Hummel figurine and the Royal Copenhagen plate were carefully removed from the _____ gift box.

■

Collective Noun Antecedents

A **collective noun** refers to a group. These words are collective nouns:

audience	faculty	herd
band	family	jury
committee	group	team

1. If the sense of the collective noun is that the group is acting as one unit, the pronoun that refers to the collective noun should be singular.

The <u>committee</u> was unsure of <u>its</u> assignment.

> **NOTE:** If you find it awkward to use the singular *its*, add "members of" before the collective noun and use a plural verb and pronoun:
>
> The members of the committee were unsure of their assignment.

2. If the members of the group are acting individually, the pronoun that refers to the collective noun should be plural:

The <u>committee</u> argued about <u>their</u> differing opinions.

PRACTICE 21.3

Circle the collective noun antecedent. Then fill in the blank with the singular *its* or the plural *their*.

Example: The women's softball (team) scored _____*its*_____ third upset of the season against the top-ranked team in the league.

1. The jury debated all night in order to resolve _____ different views of the evidence.

2. The audience shouted _____ approval by calling for an encore.

3. After the curtain fell on the third act, the cast came out and took _____ bow.

4. The coach reminded the team to bring _____ playbooks to every practice.

5. The orchestra lifted _____ instruments, signaling that the concert was about to begin.

6. At the general membership meeting, the committee reported _____ findings.

Indefinite Pronoun Antecedents

An **indefinite pronoun** refers to a group without specifying the particular members. An indefinite pronoun can be an antecedent for another pronoun.

1. These indefinite pronouns are always singular, so pronouns that refer to them should also be singular:

anyone	everybody	nothing
everyone	nobody	something
no one	somebody	each
someone	anything	one
anybody	everything	none

Everyone should bring <u>his or her</u> notebook to the lecture.

Each of the priests is volunteering <u>his</u> time to help at the battered persons' shelter.

None of the mothers brought <u>her</u> children to the meeting.

> **NOTE:** As the last two examples illustrate, a prepositional phrase that comes after the indefinite pronoun does not affect pronoun-antecedent agreement. (See also "Phrases after the Antecedent" on page 353.)

2. These indefinite pronouns are always plural, so pronouns that refer to them should also be plural:

both   many   few   several

Few understand all <u>their</u> rights under the law.

Many believe <u>their</u> educational backgrounds are not adequate.

3. These indefinite pronouns are either singular or plural. Pronouns that refer to one of them should be singular if the meaning of the indefinite pronoun is singular, and plural if the meaning of the indefinite pronoun is plural.

all   more   some

any   most

All of the class finished <u>their</u> research papers. (The plural pronoun is used because the antecedent *all* has a plural sense.)

All of the report fell out of <u>its</u> folder. (The singular pronoun is used because the antecedent *all* has a singular sense.)

FAQ

Q: Is there an easy way to remember which indefinite pronouns are singular and which are plural?

A: Notice that many of the singular indefinite pronouns end in forms you can easily recognize as singular: *-one, -body,* and *-thing.*

PRACTICE 21.4

Fill in the blanks with the correct pronoun; choose *his, her, its, they,* or *their*:

Example: All of the contestants hoped _____*their*_____ entries would be judged the best of the show.

1. Most of the curtain has slipped off _____ rod.

2. Many of the protesters shouted that _____ civil rights had been violated.

3. To pass inspection, you must be sure that everything is in

   _____ place.

4. Each of the boys on the varsity basketball team is expected to keep

   _____ grades up to a B average.

5. The salesclerk was alarmed because one of the expensive designer dresses

   was missing from _____ hanger.

6. Very few of the contestants believed _____ had much of a chance to win.

Nonsexist Usage

In the past, writers would use the masculine forms *he, his, him,* and *himself,* to refer to nouns and indefinite pronouns that included both males and females. Thus, sentences like the following were frequently written and spoken:

Each student is expected to bring <u>his</u> book to class.

Every person has <u>his</u> own opinion.

Everybody described <u>his</u> career goals.

FAQ

Q: Can I use *he, him,* and *his* with singular antecedents that include females?

A: Using masculine pronouns to refer to singular antecedents that include females is grammatically correct, but many readers will consider this usage sexist.

Although this use of the masculine pronoun is grammatically correct, it excludes women. To avoid using a masculine pronoun to refer to groups that include both men and women, you have three options.

1. Use *he* or *she, him* or *her, his* or *hers, himself* or *herself.*

   Everybody described his or her career goals.

   Using pairs of pronouns works in many situations. However, if this solution becomes cumbersome, use one of the two solutions that follows.

2. Use plural forms.

   All the students described their career goals.

3. Reshape the sentence to avoid the pronoun.

   Every person described a career goal.

PRACTICE 21.5

Rewrite each sentence to eliminate sexist pronoun usage. Refer to the three preceding suggestions for how to do this, and try to use each suggestion twice.

Example: None of the people who entered the writing contest had his manuscript returned.

The people who entered the writing contest did not have their manuscripts returned.

1. Anyone who cannot reach his goal is sure to feel frustrated.

_____

_____

2. Everyone who entered the poetry contest is convinced that his poem will win the $500 prize.

_____

_____

3. Anyone who puts his money in a money market fund now will earn an average of 4 percent interest.

_____

_____

4. None of the audience felt the play was worth the price he paid.

_____

_____

5. Each of the investment brokers advised his clients to avoid the risks of penny stocks.

_____

_____

6. Someone has left his chemistry book and notes on the desk.

_____

_____

Phrases after the Antecedent

Sometimes a prepositional phrase comes after the antecedent (see page 214 for an explanation of prepositional phrases). When this happens, the phrase will not affect pronoun-antecedent agreement.

> The can of sardines sits on <u>its</u> side in the cupboard. (The prepositional phrase *of sardines* does not affect agreement. The singular *its* is used to agree with the singular *can*.)

> Each of the windows had slipped off <u>its</u> track. (The prepositional phrase *of the windows* does not affect agreement. The singular *its* is used to agree with the singular *each*.)

> The students in the class asked if <u>their</u> test would be given on Wednesday. (The prepositional phrase *in the class* does not affect agreement. The plural *their* is used to agree with the plural *students*.)

Draw a line through each prepositional phrase. Then fill in the blanks with the correct pronoun (choose *its* or *their*).

Example: Each ~~of the birds~~ spread _____*its*_____ wings and flew from the nest.

1. The last two cars in the caravan lost _____ way after taking a wrong turn north of Cincinnati.

2. Each of the items for the experiment is in _____ proper place on the counter.

3. The baby birds in the nest opened _____ mouths to be fed.

4. The box of Christmas presents fell from _____ hiding place on the shelf in the back of the closet.

5. Two of the women sold _____ stereo systems to buy a one-way ticket to Toronto.

Circle the letter of the correct sentence.

1.   a. Because hypertension (high blood pressure) is the cause of 1.5 million heart attacks a year, everyone should learn if <u>he or she has</u> it.

     b. Because hypertension (high blood pressure) is the cause of 1.5 million heart attacks a year, everyone should learn if <u>they have</u> it.

2.   a. Most people with hypertension have no symptoms, so <u>they do</u> not know they are afflicted.

     b. Most people with hypertension have no symptoms, so <u>he or she does</u> not know they are afflicted.

3.   a. For example, neither my uncle nor my father discovered <u>their</u> high blood pressure until it was almost too late—after having a major heart attack.

     b. For example, neither my uncle nor my father discovered <u>his</u> high blood pressure until it was almost too late—after having a major heart attack.

4. a. As a result, our family has <u>their</u> blood pressure checked regularly.

 b. As a result, our family has <u>its</u> blood pressure checked regularly.

5. a. One of my family members discovered <u>her</u> hypertension after experiencing vision changes.

 b. One of my family members discovered <u>their</u> hypertension after experiencing vision changes.

6. a. Other people discover <u>their</u> high blood pressure when they investigate chest pains, shortness of breath, or swollen ankles.

 b. Other people discover <u>his or her</u> high blood pressure when they investigate chest pains, shortness of breath, or swollen ankles.

PRONOUN REFERENCE

When a pronoun does not refer clearly to its antecedent, confusion can occur. The next sections help you avoid such confusion.

Unclear Reference

When the reader cannot tell which antecedent a pronoun refers to, the problem is **unclear reference**. Here is a sentence that has unclear reference because the pronoun could refer to two nouns:

> Kathy was having lunch with Sasha when she heard the news.

Because the pronoun reference is unclear, the reader cannot tell whether Kathy or Sasha heard the news. Here is another example:

> After I put the cereal and orange juice on the table, my dog jumped up and spilled it.

What was spilled, the cereal or the orange juice? Because the pronoun reference is unclear, the reader cannot tell for sure.

To solve a problem with unclear reference, you may have to use a noun instead of a pronoun:

> Kathy was having lunch with Sasha when Sasha heard the news.

> After I put the cereal and orange juice on the table, my dog jumped up and spilled the juice.

Rewrite the following sentences to solve problems with unclear pronoun reference.

Example: Lenny told Jake that he would have to return the book by Friday.

Lenny told Jake to return the book by Friday.

1. I put the chicken in the oven and the broccoli in the microwave. An hour later it burned.

   _____

   _____

2. Tatiana carefully removed the vase from the coffee table before dusting it.

   _____

   _____

3. My mother explained to my sister that she had to leave for school in an hour.

   _____

   _____

4. Before Jack could give Marvin his class notes, he fell asleep.

   _____

   _____

5. As I was placing the ceramic bowl on the glass table, it broke.

   _____

   _____

Unstated Reference

Unstated reference occurs when a pronoun refers to an unspecified antecedent. To solve the problem, add the unstated form.

unstated reference:	Joel is known as a patient tutor. It is a trait the other tutors admire. [*It* is meant to refer to *patience*, but that word does not appear—*patient* does.]
correction:	Joel is known as a patient tutor. <u>His patience</u> is a trait the other tutors admire.
unstated reference:	Because Anika is so insecure, she has very few friends. It causes her to seek constant approval. [*It* is meant to refer to *insecurity*, but that word does not appear—*insecure* does.]
correction:	Because Anika is so insecure, she has very few friends. <u>Her insecurity</u> causes her to seek constant approval.

Unstated reference also occurs when *this*, *that*, *which*, *it*, or *they* has no specified antecedent. To solve the problem, add the missing word or words.

unstated reference:	During my last physical examination, the doctor urged me to lower my salt intake. This means my food tastes bland. [*This* has no stated antecedent.]
correction:	During my last physical examination, the doctor urged me to lower my salt intake. <u>This change</u> means my food tastes bland.
unstated reference:	The auto workers and GM negotiated all night, but it failed to produce a contract. [*It* has no stated antecedent.]
correction:	The auto workers and GM negotiated all night, but <u>the session</u> failed to produce a contract.

Unstated reference will occur when *they* or *you* has no stated antecedent. To solve the problem, add the missing word or words.

unstated reference:	I called the billing office to complain about my bill, but they said it was correct. [<u>They</u> has no stated antecedent.]
correction:	I called the billing office to complain about my bill, but <u>the clerk</u> said it was correct.
unstated reference:	Worker dissatisfaction occurs when you do not let employees participate in decision making. [*You* has no stated antecedent.]
correction:	Worker dissatisfaction occurs when <u>employers</u> do not let employees participate in decision making.

> **NOTE:** *You* and *your* address the reader directly. Use these pronouns only when you mean to address the reader; do not use them for general statements that apply to more people than the reader.
>
> no: At election time, <u>you</u> always see politicians promising things they can't deliver.
>
> yes: At election time, voters always see politicians promising things they can't deliver.
>
> yes: At election time, politicians are always promising things they can't deliver.

PRACTICE 21.9

Revise the sentences to eliminate the unstated reference problems.

Example: Because he had a tension headache, Nick was irritable. It made him very difficult to be around.

Because he had a tension headache, Nick was irritable.

His irritability made him very difficult to be around.

1. The comedian told several ethnic jokes. It annoyed most of the audience.

   _____

   _____

2. The movie was excessively violent and too long. This caused most of the critics to review it badly.

   _____

   _____

3. The paint had a few blisters in it near the ceiling, but for the most part, they did an excellent job.

   _____

   _____

4. I went to see my advisor, but they said that he was sick.

   _____

   _____

5. Ivan felt nervous about the upcoming examination. It made sleep difficult for him.

_____

_____

6. During finals week, you always know that students are working hard.

_____

_____

7. The police officer explained to the suspects that they had a right to an attorney, which is guaranteed by law.

_____

_____

8. Corrine is a very talented artist. It helped her earn a scholarship to the state art institute.

_____

_____

REVIEW PRACTICE 21.10

Eliminate the problems with pronoun reference in the following paragraph. The first one is done as an example.

[1]Saturn, the second largest planet in the solar system, is the least dense [2]~~It~~ *Its density* is the reason Saturn would float in an ocean, if there were one big enough. [3]They say that the planet's mass is 95 times the mass of the Earth. [4]Saturn radiates about 80 percent more energy than it receives from the sun. [5]However, you cannot attribute the excess energy to a particular cause just yet. [6]Saturn's diameter is almost 75,000 miles, but the planet is 10 percent narrower at its poles. [7]It is a consequence of its rapid rotation. [8]Saturn and Jupiter are similar in atmospheric appearance, but it has dark and light cloud markings and swirls and curling ribbons. [9]A thick haze mutes these markings.

[10]Helium and hydrogen compose most of the atmosphere, with about 80 percent composed by it. [11]The most remarkable feature of Saturn, however, is its rings, made up of billions of water-ice particles orbiting around the planet. [12]With winds measured at 1,100 miles per hour near its equator and temperatures ranging between 176 degrees and –203 degrees, the planet is far from hospitable.

SUBJECT, OBJECT, AND POSSESSIVE PRONOUNS

Pronouns can be used as subjects, as objects, or as possessive forms.

SUBJECT, OBJECT, AND POSSESSIVE PRONOUNS

Subject	Object	Possessive
I	me	my/mine
we	us	our/ours
you	you	your/yours
he	him	his
she	her	her/hers
it	it	its
they	them	their/theirs

Subject Pronouns

A pronoun is the ***subject*** of a sentence or clause when it tells who or what the sentence is about (see page 213 for more on identifying subjects).

> *He* slammed the car door on John's finger.
>
> Because *I* am ill, *they* must go alone.
>
> During summer school, *she* took a word-processing course.
>
> *They* ate quickly and left.
>
> In the spring and summer, *I* walk five miles a day.

When a pronoun functions as the subject, you must use one of the subject pronouns in the chart above.

Object Pronouns

A pronoun can be the **object of a verb**. The object of a verb is the word that receives the action the verb expresses.

> Daniela carried *it* upstairs.

The verb is *carried*. *It* receives the action of the verb *carried* and is, therefore, the object of that verb.

To find the object of a verb, ask "whom or what?" *after* the verb. Here are some examples:

> Pat ate *it*. (Ask "ate whom or what?" and the answer is *it*, so *it* is the object of the verb.)
>
> Ida always understands *him*. (Ask "understands whom or what?" and the answer is *him*, so *him* is the object of the verb.)
>
> The ending of the book surprised *me*. (Ask "surprised whom or what?" and the answer is *me*, so *me* is the object of the verb.)

A pronoun can also be the **object of a preposition**. The object of a preposition follows a preposition. A preposition is a word like *to*, *in*, *at*, *near*, *around*. (See page 214 on prepositions.) In the sentences that follow, the italicized pronouns function as objects of prepositions:

> Janine put the chair next to *us*. (The preposition is *to*.)
>
> The annoyed pitcher threw the ball at *me*. (The preposition is *at*.)
>
> Raul always wants to be near *her*. (The preposition is *near*.)

Sometimes the preposition is not stated; instead, it is understood to be *to* or *for*. This often happens after the verbs *give*, *tell*, *buy*, *bring*, and *send*.

> The instructor gave *him* the answer. (The instructor gave the answer to *him*.)
>
> Mother sent *me* a rose for my birthday. (Mother sent a rose *to me* for my birthday.)
>
> I bought *him* the book. (I bought the book *for him*.)

When a pronoun functions as an object, use one of the object pronouns in the chart on page 360.

FAQ

Q: What is an indirect object?

A: An indirect object is the object of the preposition *to* or *for*. These prepositions may be unstated, as in I gave *him* a cookie.

Possessive Pronouns

A pronoun can also be possessive; that is, it can show ownership, as in these sentences:

Diane lets *her* cat sleep in bed with *his* cat toys.

Wise investors never put all of *their* money in one stock.

NOTE: Notice that *its* is the possessive pronoun, not *it's*. *It's* is a contraction form that means "it is" or "it has."

possessive: The dog buried *its* bone.

contraction: I believe *it's* too late to call Vincenzo.

Who and Whom

Who is a subject pronoun and *whom* is an object pronoun. Thus, use *who* for a subject of a sentence or clause and *whom* for the object of a verb or preposition.

subject of sentence: *Who* wants to eat dinner now?

subject of clause: Josef is the one *who* can help you.

object of verb: The person *whom* you need works in this office.

object of preposition: To *whom* should I mail the form?

PRACTICE 21.11

Above each underlined pronoun, write *S* if it is a subject pronoun, *O* if it is an object pronoun, or *P* if it is a possessive pronoun.

[1]Danny is someone <u>whom</u> I could never trust. [2]<u>I</u> lent <u>him</u> my car because <u>his</u> was in the shop, but little did <u>I</u> know that <u>I</u> would never see <u>it</u> again. [3]Danny drove <u>my</u> car to the gas station, but when <u>he</u> went inside to pay, <u>he</u> foolishly left the keys in the ignition and the door unlocked. [4]While he was inside, a thief jumped in and drove off. [5]Unfortunately, the guy was more than a car thief, for he used my car in an armed robbery an hour later. [6]The police caught up with <u>him</u>, but a high-speed chase ensued, followed by a crash. [7]<u>My</u> car ended up down a ravine. [8]It has been two years since the inci-

dent, and the car still has not been returned to <u>me</u>. ⁹My father and I have tried to get it back, but the police told <u>us</u> that <u>they</u> need <u>it</u> for the upcoming trial. ¹⁰<u>We</u> can try again when the trial is over. ¹¹The wheels of justice may turn slowly, but the wheels of my car are not turning at all.

PRACTICE 21.12

Fill in the blanks with a correct subject, object, or possessive pronoun. Write *S* if you have used a subject pronoun, *O* if you have used an object pronoun, or *P* if you have used a possessive pronoun. In the first and last sentences, choose *who* or *whom*.

Roy was a high school quarterback for ¹_____ the future looked bright. As a sophomore, ²_____ broke the school passing records, and as a junior ³_____ led ⁴_____ team to a conference championship. Many college scouts were watching ⁵_____, and ⁶_____ were ready to offer ⁷_____ rather impressive scholarships. Unfortunately, an incident occurred in Roy's senior year. Two hefty players on an opposing team sacked Roy at the line of scrimmage. ⁸_____ tackled ⁹_____ so hard that ¹⁰_____ was knocked unconscious and rushed to the hospital. He had a concussion, but ¹¹_____ came out of it just fine. However, when I went to see Roy in the hospital, he told ¹²_____ that he had no desire to play football again. When Roy got out of the hospital, ¹³_____ friends and coaches tried to change his mind, but ¹⁴_____ were unable to persuade ¹⁵_____ to go back to the game. Roy was just too afraid of getting hurt again. Roy went to college, but ¹⁶_____ had to give up his athletic scholarship. He does not seem to have any regrets, though. In fact, when I last spoke to ¹⁷_____ he told ¹⁸_____ he was sure he had done the right thing. ¹⁹_____ would have thought Roy could be happy without football?

Subject and Object Pronouns in Compounds

And or *or* can link a pronoun to a noun to form a **compound**.

Bob and *me*   the children and *us*   the children or *I*

the boy and *I*   Gloria and *he*   Conchetta or *them*

If the pronoun is part of a compound that acts as a subject, use a subject pronoun. If the pronoun is part of a compound that acts as the object of a verb or the object of a preposition, use an object pronoun.

> *Bob and I* bought season tickets to the Steelers' games. (The italicized compound is the subject of the sentence, so the subject pronoun is used.)

> The car almost hit *Bob and me*. (The italicized compound is the object of the verb, so the object pronoun is used.)

> The coach was angry with *Bob and me*. (The italicized compound is the object of the preposition *with*, so the object pronoun is used.)

To decide if a subject or object pronoun is needed in a compound, mentally cross out everything in the compound except the pronoun. Then decide if the remaining pronoun is a subject or an object.

> ~~The children and~~ I went to the movie.

> ~~The children and~~ me went to the movie.

When everything but the pronoun is crossed out in each compound, you can tell that the pronoun is part of the subject. Thus, the subject form *I* is needed:

> The children and I went to the movies.

Here is another example:

> Professor Hernandez explained to ~~Colleen, Louise, and~~ I that our project was well researched and informative.

> Professor Hernandez explained to ~~Colleen, Louise, and~~ me that our project was well researched and informative.

With everything in the compound except the pronoun crossed out, you can see that the pronoun is part of the object of the preposition *to*. Therefore, an object pronoun is needed:

> Professor Hernandez explained to Colleen, Louise, and me that our project was well researched and informative.

NOTE: When a noun and pronoun form a compound, place the pronoun at the end of the compound.

No:	I and the teacher disagreed about the correct answer.
Yes:	The teacher and I disagreed about the correct answer.
No:	The boat belongs to me and Joyce.
Yes:	The boat belongs to Joyce and me.

FAQ

Q: Can I tell which pronoun to use according to how the sentence sounds?

A: Sound is an unreliable way to choose a pronoun.

PRACTICE 21.13

Fill in each blank with the correct subject or object pronoun in parentheses.

Example (she, her) Kurt and _____she_____ ran a mile in the snow.

1. (I, me) The salesclerk gave Jim and _____me_____ the wrong packages.

2. (we, us) The band was too loud for Dikla and _____us_____, so we left.

3. (I, me) Sora and _____I_____ searched the piles of sweaters for my size.

4. (we, us) The movers or _____ will pack the dishes in the kitchen.

5. (they, them) I gave you and _____ the directions to the farm that sells fresh produce.

6. (he, him) Dr. Amin wants Julia and _____ as lab assistants.

7. (she, her) To make money for college, Wanda and _____ worked all summer as table servers.

8. (I, me) Give the library books to Hans or _____ to return for you.

Subject and Object Pronouns Paired with Nouns

When a pronoun is paired with its noun antecedent, you can decide whether a subject or object pronoun is needed by mentally crossing out the noun and deciding whether the remaining pronoun is a subject or object. For example, crossing out the nouns in the following sentences will help you choose the correct pronoun:

> We ~~nonsmokers~~ favor banning smoking in public places.

> Us ~~nonsmokers~~ favor banning smoking in public places.

With the nouns crossed out, you can see that the pronoun acts as a subject, so the subject pronoun *we* is needed. This makes the first example the correct sentence. Now look at these sentences:

> Smokers are sometimes inconsiderate of we ~~nonsmokers~~.

> Smokers are sometimes inconsiderate of us ~~nonsmokers~~.

With the nouns crossed out, you can see that the pronoun is the object of the preposition *of,* so the second sentence is correct because it uses the object pronoun *us.*

PRACTICE 21.14

For each pair of sentences, cross out the paired noun and decide if a subject or object pronoun is needed. Then place a check next to the correct sentence.

Examples: __✓__ We ~~students~~ believed that the tuition hike was unfortunate but necessary in light of increasing costs.

_____ Us ~~students~~ believed that the tuition hike was unfortunate but necessary in light of increasing costs.

1. _____ Some of we golfers were unhappy with the condition of the course.
   _____ Some of us golfers were unhappy with the condition of the course.

2. _____ None of the legislators considered the impact of the tax increase on we, the middle-class property owners.
   _____ None of the legislators considered the impact of the tax increase on us, the middle-class property owners.

3. _____ Dr. Wren asked I, the only one who did not understand the problem, to put my answer on the board.
   _____ Dr. Wren asked me, the only one who did not understand the problem, to put my answer on the board.

4. _____ We new pledges must stick together if we are going to make it through the fraternity initiation.

_____ Us new pledges must stick together if we are going to make it through the fraternity initiation.

5. _____ The club charter prevents we new members from holding office for a year.

_____ The club charter prevents us new members from holding office for a year.

Subject and Object Pronouns in Comparisons

The words *than* and *as* can be used to show comparisons.

> Marta is friendlier *than* Lorraine. (Marta's friendliness is compared to Lorraine's friendliness.)

> Larry is not as good at math *as* John. (Larry's math ability is compared to John's math ability.)

Notice that when *than* or *as* is used to show comparison, words that could finish the comparison go unstated.

> Marta is friendlier than Lorraine.

> > *could be*

> Marta is friendlier than Lorraine *is*.

> Larry is not as good at math as John.

> > *could be*

> Larry is not as good at math as John *is*.

When a pronoun follows *than* or *as* in a comparison, decide whether to use a subject or object pronoun by mentally adding the unstated words. Which sentence uses the correct pronoun?

> Marcus is a better basketball player than *I*.
> Marcus is a better basketball player than *me*.

To decide which pronoun is correct, mentally add the unstated word or words:

> Marcus is a better basketball player than I am.
> Marcus is a better basketball player than me am.

With the unstated *am* added, you can see that the pronoun functions as the subject of the verb *am*. Since *I* is a subject pronoun, the first example is correct. Here is another example:

> The news report disturbed Harriet as much as *I*.
> The news report disturbed Harriet as much as *me*.

To decide on the correct pronoun, add the unstated words:

> The news report disturbed Harriet as much as it disturbed *I.*
>
> The news report disturbed Harriet as much as it disturbed *me.*

With the unstated words *it disturbed* added, you can see that the pronoun functions as the object of the verb *disturbed.* Since *me* is an object pronoun, the second example is correct.

Correct pronoun choice in comparisons is important because the pronoun can affect meaning. Here is an example:

> Carol always liked Julio more than I.
>
> Carol always liked Julio more than me.

The first sentence means that Carol liked Julio more than I liked Julio. The second sentence means that Carol liked Julio more than she liked me.

FAQ

Q: I always hear sentences like "Larry is not as good at math as me." Why is that wrong?

A: In informal speech and writing, "Larry is not as good at math as me" is common. For formal writing and speech, use "Larry is not as good at math as I."

PRACTICE 21.15

Fill in the blank with the correct pronoun in parentheses. If you are unsure, mentally rewrite each sentence, supplying the unstated words.

Example (they, them) Juanita and I do not enjoy NASCAR racing as much as ___*they*___.

1. (we, us) Carol and I were annoyed to discover that Ted and Janet had

   better seats for the concert than _____.

2. (I, me) Making friends has always been easier for Eleni than _____.

3. (he, him) Studying together helps you as much as _____.

4. (she, her) I believe in the power of positive thinking more than _____.

5. (we, us) On opening night, Francis was less nervous than _____.

6. (I, me) Since you do not care for classical music as much as

   _____, you should meet me after the concert for dinner.

PERSON SHIFT

When you write or speak about yourself, you use these pronouns: *I, we, me, us, my, mine, our,* and *ours.* They are called **first-person pronouns.**

> *I* hated to leave, but *I* had to get *my* car home by 10:00.

When you write or speak directly to a person, you use these pronouns: *you*, *your*, and *yours*. They allow you to address directly the person you are writing or speaking to. These pronouns are **second-person pronouns**.

> *You* should bring *your* dictionary to class on Thursday.

To write about people or things that do not include yourself or a person you are addressing, you use *he*, *she*, *it*, *they*, *him*, *her*, *them*, *his*, *hers*, *its*, *their*, and *theirs*. These are **third-person pronouns**.

> *She* told *him* to pick *her* up at 7:00.

Here is a chart of first, second, and third person pronouns.

FIRST-, SECOND-, AND THIRD-PERSON PRONOUNS		
First-Person	**Second-Person**	**Third-Person**
I	you	he
we		she
me	your, yours	it
us		they
my, mine		him
our, ours		her
		it
		them
		his
		her, hers
		its
		their, theirs

If you move unnecessarily from one person to another person within a sentence or longer passage, you create a problem called **person shift**:

> *I* attend aerobics classes three times a week. The exercise helps *you* relax. (The shift is from the first person *I* to the second person *you*.)

Here is the example rewritten to eliminate the person shift:

> *I* attend aerobics classes three times a week. The exercise helps *me* relax. (Both *I* and *me* are first person pronouns.)

To avoid person shifts, remember that nouns are always third person, so pronouns that refer to nouns should also be third person.

person shift:	*Salesclerks* have a difficult job. *You* are on *your* feet all day dealing with the public. (The shift is from the third-person *salesclerks* to the second-person *you* and *your*.)
shift eliminated:	*Salesclerks* have a difficult job. *They* are on *their* feet all day dealing with the public. (The third-person pronouns *they* and *their* refer to the third person *salesclerks*.)

NOTE: The most frequent problems with person shift occur when writers shift from the first person or third person to the second person *you* as illustrated in the previous example. For this reason, be sure when using *you* that you are really addressing the reader and not shifting from a first- or third-person form.

PRACTICE 21.16

Rewrite the sentences to eliminate troublesome person shifts.

Example: Chemistry was not as hard as I thought it would be. You just had to keep up with the reading and ask questions when you did not understand.

Chemistry was not as hard as I thought it would be. I just had to keep up with the reading and ask questions when I did not understand.

1. It was a mistake for me to try to teach my son to drive because you lose patience quickly when working with your own children.

   _____

   _____

2. Learning to use a computer was time-consuming for me. You had to study the user's manual and practice often.

   _____

   _____

3. I realize too much sun is not good for your skin, but every summer I neglect to use sunscreen.

   _____

   _____

4. Before high school seniors select a college, you should visit several campuses and speak to the admissions counselors.

_____

_____

5. Many doctors believe women should take calcium supplements. Doing so can help you guard against osteoporosis.

_____

_____

PRACTICE 21.17

Cross out pronouns that create troublesome person shifts and write the correction above the line.

[1]Some people are saying that men are less willing to mentor women in the workplace because they fear charges of sexual harassment. [2]However, male employees can still coach and support women to help them advance their careers. [3]First, companies should have formal mentor programs. [4]You should assign experienced employees to show newer employees the ropes. [5]That way, no one will suspect that the mentoring is anything other than a professional work arrangement. [6]Second, employers should draw up rules for people in the mentoring program. [7]Then, you do not have to wonder if your behavior will be seen as inappropriate. [8]You just follow the rules for mentoring and you will know that your behavior is acceptable. [9]Finally, new employees should have more than one mentor when possible to avoid the suspicion that people are pairing up. [10]If these guidelines were introduced into the workplace, both employees and employers would be comfortable with mentoring. [11]You would not have to worry that charges of sexual harassment would be leveled.

REVIEW PRACTICE 21.18

Fill in the blanks with the correct pronoun in parentheses.

1. (its, their) After days of discussion, the jury felt confident

    _____ its _____ verdict was the correct one.

2. (his or her, their) The instructor told everyone to bring

    _____ dictionary to class each day for the next two weeks.

3. (her, their) Several of the mothers agreed that _____
    preschool children would benefit from a play group.

4. (its, their) Some of the essay strays from _____ topic.

5. (its, their) When he was through playing, Tommy put his bag of marbles in

    _____ drawer.

6. (her, their) Each of the kindergarten girls brought _____
    favorite toy for sharing day.

7. (I, me) Between you and _____, I am sure that Janet is plan-
    ning to break up with Phil.

8. (he, him) Carla and _____ are sure to take first prize in the
    science fair, just as they did last year and the year before that.

9. (I, me) Even though Eduardo is stronger than _____, he
    rarely pins me in a wrestling match.

10. (we, us) Some of _____ fans felt the official's call was
    incorrect.

11. (we, us) _____ students should insist that the administra-
    tion explain why tuition was raised 20 percent.

12. (we, you) Last weekend I went camping with three of my friends.

    However, it was not very relaxing because _____ had to
    work too hard setting up and maintaining the camp.

13. (who, whom) For _____ did Antonio buy the book?

14. (who, whom) I cannot recall _____ is bringing the extra
    chairs for the party.

Finding and Eliminating Pronoun Errors in Your Writing

Finding and eliminating pronoun errors is best saved for editing. If you check earlier, you may be checking sentences that you later decide to delete or change. The following tips can help you edit for problems with pronouns.

- Memorize which indefinite pronouns are singular, which are plural, and which can be either singular or plural, so you can more easily use pronouns to refer to these words.

- Be sure every pronoun has a stated antecedent.

- Check your use of *it*, *they*, and *you*. Be sure these pronouns have stated antecedents.

- If you compose at the computer, use the Search or Find function to locate these common indefinite pronouns: *anyone*, *anybody*, *anything*, *someone*, *somebody*, *something*, *everybody*, *everyone*, *everything*, *no one*, *nobody*, *nothing*, and *each*. If a pronoun refers to one of these words, be sure it is singular.

POST TEST

a. Cross out each incorrect pronoun, and write in the correction.

   [1]Most volunteer youth coaches find it a rewarding experience because you can make an important contribution to the lives of young people. [2]To make coaching a positive experience, coaches must remember several points. [3]First, successful coaches' priorities should be having fun and learning—they should not emphasize winning above all. [4]You should remember that the players are kids first and athletes second. [5]Coaches should know the players and respect their limits. [6]For example, ten-year-olds should not be asked to lift weights. [7]This could harm young bodies. [8]They say that successful coaches allow for a wide range of abilities and resist the temptation to field only the best players. [9]Most important of all, however, is making sure that the kids feel they are a valued part of a team.

b. Cross out each incorrect pronoun and write the correct one above it.

(continued on next page)

[1]A person who lives in constant fear of becoming a victim of crime can solve their problem easily—by turning off their television. [2]Several years ago, a set of studies was done. [3]They showed that when people watch a great deal of television, they suffer an exaggerated sense of fear. [4]Apparently, all the murder and mayhem on the small screen make frequent TV viewers feel at risk. [5]Thus, someone who spends most of their time in front of the set will worry far more about being victimized by crime than someone who watches little or no television. [6]Women and children may find his or her fears even greater. [7]It is because women on television are most often shown as the victims of violent crime, and young children do not recognize the unrealistic nature of much programming. [8]Thus, you feel more threatened than other viewers. [9]Obviously, the studies show that parents of a young child should limit his or her child's viewing time.

SUCCEEDING IN COLLEGE

Know How to Write on a Deadline

In college and on the job, you will often need to produce a satisfactory piece of writing in a limited amount of time. When faced with a deadline, you may feel stress, and that stress can make it even harder for you to write well. The trick to meeting a deadline is to get organized and use the time you do have to best advantage.

Above all, do not panic and do not delay. Get going immediately by making a schedule. Work backwards from your deadline date. For example, if your deadline date is next Friday, schedule editing and proofreading on Thursday, revising on Wednesday, and so on. The closer your deadline is, the tighter your schedule will be and the more you will do in a single day.

Under the pressure of a deadline, you may be tempted to skip steps in the writing process, but that is a mistake. You will not be able to spend as much time generating ideas, drafting, revising, and editing, but you should work through each of these steps to whatever extent time allows, so be sure to include all of them in your schedule. Furthermore, you should not abandon resources that have helped you in the past. If reliable readers help you evaluate your draft, use them in deadline situations—just give them less to do and less time to do it in.

Write about It

Discuss the role deadlines play in your life. You may consider the following questions if you like, or any others you think lend insight into how deadlines affect you:

- In general, are deadlines (not just for writing projects) present in your life very often?

- Are the deadlines for important projects?

- How do deadlines make you feel?

- How well do you perform when faced with a deadline?

CHAPTER 22
Using Modifiers Correctly

Modifiers are descriptive words that help you express yourself in a precise and interesting way. If you do not currently use modifiers well, this chapter will explain what you need to know. If you already use modifiers correctly, this chapter will reinforce your understanding and perhaps teach you some new points. Before getting under way, you should assess your current level of understanding by taking the following pretest.

PRETEST

If the underlined modifier is used correctly, write *yes* on the blank. If the underlined modifier is not used correctly, write *no* on the blank. Do not guess; if you are unsure, do not write anything. You can check your answers in Appendix II.

1. _____ Whistling <u>soft</u>, Chuyen worked in the kitchen.

2. _____ Professor Smith <u>quickly</u> explained the directions before he passed out the exam questions.

3. _____ The splinter in Fluffy's paw caused her to limp <u>bad</u>.

4. _____ The <u>frustrated</u> toddler pounded her fists against the floor and screamed in rage.

5. _____ Les is <u>more happier</u> now that he has changed his major to physical therapy.

6. _____ Diana plays the cello <u>good</u>.

7. _____ Ivan felt his history midterm was the <u>easiest</u> test he had taken this semester.

8. _____ <u>Whistling as he walked down the street</u>, Tom's mood could not have been better.

9. ____ <u>Wondering which route to take</u>, Katrina pulled to the side of the road and studied the map.

10. ____ The second day I had the flu, I felt <u>worser</u> than I did the day before.

ADJECTIVES AND ADVERBS

A word or word group that describes another word or word group is a **modifier**. In the following sentences, the modifiers are italicized. An arrow points to the word the modifier describes.

The *cloudy* sky threatened rain.

The pitcher threw a *sinker* ball.

The *marathon* runner was breathing *heavily.*

Modifiers that describe nouns and pronouns are **adjectives**. In the following sentences, the adjectives are italicized and an arrow is drawn from the adjective to the word it describes:

Janet spilled *hot* coffee.   (*Hot* describes the noun *coffee.*)

Michael is *shy*   (*Shy* describes the noun *Michael.*)

She seems *angry.*   (*Angry* describes the pronoun *she.*)

Adverbs are modifiers that describe verbs, adjectives, or other adverbs. Adverbs often tell *how, when,* or *where.*

The lecturer spoke *briefly.* (*Briefly* describes the verb *spoke*; it tells *how* the lecturer spoke.)

The lecturer spoke *very* briefly. (*Very* describes the adverb *briefly*; it tells *how* briefly.)

I just finished an *extremely* difficult job. (*Extremely* describes the adjective *difficult*; it tells *how* difficult.)

I just finished an extremely difficult job *yesterday.* (*Yesterday* describes the verb *finished*; it tells *when* the job was finished.)

The car stalled *there.* (*There* describes the verb *stalled*; it tells *where* the car stalled.)

PRACTICE 22.1

Draw an arrow from each bracketed modifier to the word described. Above each bracketed modifier, write *adj* if the modifier is an adjective or *adv* if the modifier is an adverb.

Example: [Frightened by the dark,] Leo sang [loudly] all the way home.

1. The [experimental] therapy relieved Jan's [painful] symptoms [quickly].

2. [Briefly] the waiter explained the specials of the day, and then he turned and walked away [quickly].

3. The [silver] tinsel sparkled [brightly] in the [colorful] lights of the Christmas tree.

4. The [elderly] man spoke [fondly] of his [childhood] days on a [dairy] farm.

5. The [high] [academic] standards of the university are [well] known throughout the country.

-ly Adverbs

Many adjectives can be made into adverbs by adding an *-ly* ending.

Adjective	Adverb
glad	gladly
painful	painfully
quick	quickly
loud	loudly
quiet	quietly

The *painful* tooth kept me awake all night. (*Painful* is an adjective describing the noun *tooth*.)

The dog limped *painfully* into the garage. (*Painfully* is an adverb describing the verb *limped*.)

NOTE: Be careful to use the adverb form when the modifier describes a verb, adjective, or adverb.

No: Marvin ran quick into the house.

Yes: Marvin ran *quickly* into the house. (Use the adverb form because the modifier is describing a verb.)

PRACTICE 22.2

Circle the correct form in each set of parentheses. Then draw an arrow to the word described.

Example: Archaeologists study the pyramids (frequent/(frequently)).

Egyptian tombs were not always as grand as the pyramids. The first
Egyptians were buried (shallow/shallowly) under a pile of rocks in
desert pits. The bodies were wrapped (tight/tightly) in goatskin or reed
mats, and the desert's hot sand preserved them rather (adequate/adequately). Personal goods were placed (close/closely) around the body.
Then around 3000 B.C., kings and officials began to build large, flat-topped tombs made of sunbaked mud and bricks, which provided protection against the (harmful/harmfully) effects of nature. Each of these
tombs had a (vast/vastly) burial chamber and (large/largely) rooms
filled with goods. Around 2700 B.C. came the invention of stone architecture and the first pyramid, called the Step Pyramid. The tomb of
King Djoser lies buried under the structure. Like later pyramids, it had
two purposes. It was both a royal tomb and a temple for worshipping
the dead king. The pyramids of Egypt are a (massive/massively)
reminder of the pharaohs' power and a creative ancient civilization.

PRACTICE 22.3

On a separate sheet, use each adjective and adverb in its own sentence.
Draw an arrow from the adjective or adverb to the word it describes.

1. easy

2. easily

3. comfortable

4. comfortably

5. fearful

6. fearfully

Good/Well

Good is an adjective, so it describes nouns and pronouns. *Well*—except when it means "healthy"—is an adverb, so it describes verbs, adjectives, and other adverbs.

It saddens me that Felipe is moving because he is a *good* friend. (*Good* is an adjective describing the noun *friend*.)

Two weeks after my surgery, I felt *well* again. (Here, *well* means "healthy" and is an adjective describing the pronoun *I*.)

For a beginner, you skate very *well*. (*Well* is an adverb describing the verb *skate*.)

Be careful not to use *good* as an adverb.

No: Marla did good on her test.

Yes: Marla did well on her test. (*Well* is an adverb describing the verb *did*.)

Good is also used as an adjective after verbs like *seem*, *feel*, *look*, and *taste*:

I feel good today. (Here, *good* suggests "in good spirits" and describes the pronoun *I*.)

The food tastes good. (*Good* describes the noun *food*; no action is being described.)

The cool breeze feels good. (Again, no action is described; *good* describes *breeze*.)

FAQ

Q: What's the difference between "I feel well" and "I feel good"?

A: "I feel good" means "I am in a good mood." "I feel well" means "I feel healthy." Remember that *well* rhymes with the first syllable of *healthy*.

PRACTICE 22.4

Fill in each blank with *good* or *well*, whichever is correct.

1. The children's production of *Hansel and Gretel* was _____

   staged, and the sets were particularly _____ .

2. The horse I bet on ran _____ until the home stretch, and then

   she did not do very _____ .

3. Although I have been taking my allergy medicine, I still do not feel

   _____.

4. Nao plays the clarinet _____ enough to have his first recital, even though he has had only a dozen lessons.

5. With her red hair, Marsha looks _____ in green.

Comparative and Superlative Forms

Adjectives and adverbs can be used to show how two or more things compare to each other.

Katherine is *thinner* than Mario. (The adjective *thinner* compares how thin Katherine and Mario are.)

The audience is cheering *more loudly* now. (The adverb *more loudly* compares how loudly the audience is cheering now with how loudly it cheered at some point in the past.)

Lee is the *tallest* member of the basketball team. (The adjective *tallest* compares Lee's height with the height of the other team members.)

The **comparative** form of an adjective or adverb compares two things. The **superlative** form compares more than two things. The comparative form of adjectives and adverbs is usually made by adding *-er* or using the word *more* before the modifier. The superlative form is usually made by adding *-est* or using the word *most* before the modifier.

FAQ

Q: Does the dictionary give comparative and superlative forms?

A: If you look up the base form of an adjective, the comparative and superlative forms will also be given.

COMPARATIVE AND SUPERLATIVE FORMS

Modifier	Comparative	Superlative
loud	louder	loudest
heavy	heavier	heaviest
young	younger	youngest
annoyed	more annoyed	most annoyed
beautiful	more beautiful	most beautiful
intelligent	more intelligent	most intelligent

modifier:	Joy and Ned bought a *large* house. (no comparison here)
comparative:	Joy and Ned bought a *larger* house than Kay and Tom. (two houses are compared)
superlative:	Joy and Ned bought the *largest* of the three houses they looked at. (more than two houses are compared)
modifier:	Etty spoke *persuasively* (no comparison here)
comparative:	Etty spoke *more persuasively* than Carl did (two people are compared)
superlative:	Etty spoke the *most persuasively* of all the candidates. (more than two candidates are compared)

Keep the following guidelines in mind when you form the comparative and superlative forms of modifiers:

1. With one-syllable modifiers, *-er* and *-est* are usually used.

sad	sadder	saddest
loud	louder	loudest
near	nearer	nearest

2. With three-syllable words, use *more* and *most*.

usual	more usual	most usual
rapidly	more rapidly	most rapidly
important	more important	most important

3. With adverbs of two or more syllables, use *more* and *most*.

quickly	more quickly	most quickly
clearly	more clearly	most clearly
freely	more freely	most freely

4. With two-syllable adjectives ending in *-y*, change the *y* to *i* and add *-er* and *-est*.

happy	happier	happiest
angry	angrier	angriest
easy	easier	easiest

5. Some two-syllable adjectives that do not end in *-y* use *-er* and *-est*, and some use *more* and *most*.

foolish	more foolish	most foolish
careful	more careful	most careful
quiet	quieter	quietest

6. Never use an *-er* form with *more* or an *-est* form with *most*.

no:	Maria is *more happier* now that she quit her job.
yes:	Maria is *happier* now that she quit her job.
no:	Lionel is the *most foolhardiest* child I know.
yes:	Lionel is the *most foolhardy* child I know.

The following comparative and superlative forms are irregular. Memorize them or check this chart each time you use them.

IRREGULAR COMPARATIVE AND SUPERLATIVE FORMS

Modifier	Comparative	Superlative
good	better	best
well	better	best
bad	worse	worst
badly	worse	worst
many	more	most
much	more	most
some	more	most
little	less	least

PRACTICE 22.5

The base form of a modifier appears in parentheses. Fill in the blank with the correct comparative or superlative form (whichever is called for).

> *Example:* (expensive) The Toyota is ___*more expensive*___ than the comparably equipped Jetta.

1. (young) My sister is two years _____ than I.

2. (loud) When I banged on the wall to request quiet, the person in the next apartment turned the radio up _____ .

3. (quickly) Of all the runners in the race, Dana is expected to run the

   _____ .

4. (talented) Of the two actors auditioning for the role, Stavros is the

   _____ .

5. (easy) John drew Henry a map showing an _____ way to get to the lake than taking Route 11.

6. (bad) Christmas is the _____ holiday for those who have no friends or family.

PRACTICE 22.6

The base form of a modifier appears in parentheses. Fill in the blank with the correct comparative or superlative form.

> Example: (good) I like studying in the library ___*better*___ than studying in my room.

1. (bad) Of all the movies playing in town this week, you selected the _____ one to see.

2. (well) Since I began to exercise regularly, I feel _____ than I ever did before.

3. (some) _____ of us are going to our twenty-year reunion than went to the ten-year reunion.

4. (good) The score Jamie got on his third algebra quiz was the

    _____ one he has earned this term.

5. (bad) Lying to a friend is bad; refusing to admit the lie is _____ .

6. (good) John believes that the movie version of *The Da Vinci Code* is

    _____ than the book.

DANGLING MODIFIERS

A modifier without a logical sentence subject to describe is a **dangling modifier**. Dangling modifiers are a problem because they create silly or confusing sentences like this:

> *Standing at the street corner*, a car splashed mud all over my new coat. (*Standing at the street corner* has no logical sentence subject to describe. Therefore, it seems that the *car* was standing at the street corner.)

Because *standing at the street corner* has no sensible subject to describe, it is a dangling modifier. Here is another example:

> *Tired after a hard day of classes*, sleep was needed. (Tired after a hard day has no logical subject to describe, so it seems that *sleep* was tired.)

Dangling modifiers can be eliminated two ways. First, you can supply a logical sentence subject for the modifier to describe just after the modifier.

dangling modifier:	Feeling depressed, an evening with friends was needed. (Was the evening depressed?)
correction:	Feeling depressed, Colleen needed an evening with friends. (Now *feeling depressed* has a logical subject to describe—*Colleen*.)

dangling modifier:	Unsure of which choice to make, an academic advisor was needed. (Was the advisor unsure of which choice to make?)
correction:	Unsure of which choice to make, I needed an academic advisor. (Now *unsure of which choice to make* has a logical subject to describe—*I.*)

A second way to eliminate a dangling modifier is to change the modifier to a subordinate clause. (Subordinate clauses are discussed on page 224.)

dangling modifier:	Walking across the street, a truck turned the corner and narrowly missed me. (Was the truck walking across the street?)
correction:	While I was walking across the street, a truck turned the corner and narrowly missed me. (The opening modifier is rewritten as a subordinate clause.)
dangling modifier:	When entering the bar, an ID must be shown. (Does the ID enter the bar?)
correction:	When a person enters the bar, an ID must be shown. (The opening modifier is rewritten as a subordinate clause.)

PRACTICE 22.7

On a separate sheet, rewrite each sentence to eliminate the dangling modifier.

Example: Wondering what to do, an idea struck me.

Wondering what to do, I was struck by an idea.

1. Exhilarated by the sunny day, a walk in the park sounded like a good idea.

2. Feeling the chill in the air, a roaring fire in the fireplace sounded perfect.

3. Before beginning to make the Mississippi mud cake, all the ingredients were assembled on the kitchen counter.

4. Frightened by the menacing dog, my knees began to shake.

5. Unsure of the best course of action, the decision was difficult.

6. Making no errors in the field and batting the best they have all season, the game was easily won by the Meadville Tigers.

MISPLACED MODIFIERS

A modifier placed too far away from the word it describes is a **misplaced modifier**. Misplaced modifiers are a problem because they create confusing or silly sentences. (As you will see in the first example below, prepositional phrases can be modifiers.)

misplaced modifier:	Andrea bought a silk dress at a thrift shop with a broken zipper. (Did the thrift shop have a broken zipper? It seems so because *with a broken zipper* is too far from *dress*, the word the modifier is meant to describe.)
misplaced modifier:	The litterbug threw a plastic wrapper out of the car window driving down Route 81. (Was the car window driving down Route 81? It seems so because *driving down Route 81* is too far from *litterbug*, the word the modifier is meant to describe.)

To eliminate a misplaced modifier, move the modifier as close as possible to the word it describes:

Andrea bought a silk dress with a broken zipper at a thrift shop. (*With a broken zipper* is now next to *dress*, the word the modifier describes.)

Driving down Route 81, the litterbug threw a plastic wrapper out of the car window. (*Driving down Route 81* is now next to *litterbug*, the word the modifier describes.)

PRACTICE 22.8

Rewrite the sentences to eliminate the misplaced modifiers.

Example: Lydia said she wanted a hamburger on the phone.

On the phone, Lydia said she wanted a hamburger.

1. The children stuck in the hospital for Halloween got candy from the visiting clown that was chocolate.

2. Carlo asked Henry to help him fix his flat tire in the restaurant.

_____

_____

3. At a garage sale, I bought a lovely end table for my apartment with drawers.

_____

_____

4. Gregory gave an electronic keyboard to his brother with a memory and playback functions.

_____

_____

5. For the New Year's Eve celebration, Jorge borrowed noise makers from his roommate with colored streamers.

_____

_____

REVIEW PRACTICE 22.9

Eliminate the errors with modifiers by crossing out and writing above the line. You will have to draw on everything you learned in this chapter. The first one is done as an example.

[1]Sybil Bauer (1903–1927), one of the ~~most~~ best backstroke swimmers, won the Olympic gold medal and eleven national championships. [2]She probably would have won more championships if there had been more events when she was swimming competitive. [3]Going into the 1924 Olympics, world records for every backstroke distance were held by Bauer. [4]In fact, in an informal meet in 1922, she swam four seconds more fast than the men's record. [5]Unfortunately, that time was not recognized because the meet was not sanctioned. [6]In the 1925 Olympics, Bauer won

the only backstroke event, the 100-meter, easy. [7]Her time was more than four seconds more fast than the silver medalist's. [8]Sadly, Bauer was stricken with cancer and died premature at twenty-four. [9]In six years of competitive swimming, she set twenty-four records. [10]Imagine what she could have accomplished had she lived even longer.

Finding and Eliminating Modifier Errors in Your Writing

Try the following tips to find and correct errors with modifiers when you edit. If you check earlier, you may check sentences that you later decide to delete or change.

- Check your *-ly* modifiers. Convert any that describe nouns or pronouns into adjectives.
- Check modifiers that describe verbs, adjectives, and adverbs to be sure they are adverbs.
- Mentally draw an arrow from *good* or *well* to the word it describes. If the word is a noun or pronoun, use *good*; otherwise, use *well*. Remember, though, that *good* is used after *seem*, *feel*, *look*, and *taste*.
- Check sentences opening with an *-ing* or *-ed* form. Be sure each of these forms is closely followed by a sentence subject it can logically describe.
- Each time you use *more* or *most*, be sure the word does not appear with a modifier ending in *-er* or *-est*.

POST TEST

Eliminate the errors with modifiers by crossing out and writing above the line.

[1]Johnny Heisman, for whom the Heisman Trophy is named, was one of football's inventivest coaches. [2]One of his most odd inventions was the hidden-ball trick. [3]Once a player asked him if it was illegal to hide a ball during a play in 1895. [4]Heisman knew it was not against the rules, and he wondered how it could be done. [5]Thinking the ball could be hidden under a running back's jersey, a play was devised by Heisman and two of his players. [6]As the ball was snapped to "Tick" Tichenor, the rest of the team would drop back and form a circle around him. [7]Then Tichenor

would drop to one knee and slip the ball quick under his jersey. [8]The team would run to the right, and the defenders would follow them. [9]Then Tichenor would get up quick and run the other way. [10]Trying the trick against Vanderbilt, a touchdown was scored. [11]More tighter uniforms and more faster play have made the hidden-ball trick more hard to perform. [12]The bizarre play is rarely used today.

SUCCEEDING IN COLLEGE

Study Visual Aids

You may be tempted to skip over visual aids such as photographs, charts, graphs, and tables in your textbooks, but don't. By offering a visual depiction of important points, photographs, charts, graphs, and tables can help you understand and remember important information.

The following strategies can help you make the most of visual aids in your textbooks:

- Identify the main point the visual aid is making. Is a chart showing that more women than men have undiagnosed heart disease? Is a table of data showing you which states spend the most money on education? Is a photograph showing you the conditions in a nineteenth-century New York tenement apartment?

- Read the caption of the visual aid for the main point or explanatory information.

- Study the details by identifying the people, scenes, and moods in photographs; the headings on columns in charts and tables; and the labels for horizontal and vertical axes of graphs.

- Connect the information in the visual aid to the material you read in the textbook chapter. Does the visual aid illustrate a point made in the text, or does it introduce a new point?

Write about It

Find one photograph and one other visual aid in one or two of your textbooks. Using the above strategies, explain what can be learned from each of these visual aids. If you like, you can answer these questions to generate ideas:

1. What is the main point of the visual aid?

2. What other information does the visual aid provide?

3. How does the information connect to the information in the text?

4. Does the visual aid help you understand or learn information in the textbook? Why or why not?

CHAPTER 23

Using Capital Letters and Punctuation Correctly

When used correctly, capital letters and punctuation marks help writers convey meaning. Therefore, the more you know about how to capitalize and punctuate, the better able you are to use these tools to help express your ideas. This chapter will help you learn what you need to know to capitalize and punctuate to the best advantage. First, to assess your current level of understanding, take the following pretest.

PRETEST

A. If all the necessary capital letters appear, write *yes* on the blank; if one or more capitals are missing, write *no*. Do not guess; if you are unsure, do not write anything. Check your answers in Appendix II.

1. _____ My dog, Laddie, ran away last week, but he was seen near lake jewel.

2. _____ My favorite holiday is memorial day because it signals the start of summer.

3. _____ This semester my favorite class is psychology, although I am also enjoying Western Civilization 303.

4. _____ Ever since I was a child, I have eaten Kellogg's Rice Krispies for breakfast along with Minute Maid orange juice.

5. _____ Last summer, I was sure the Cleveland indians would be in the pennant race.

B. Add a period, question mark, or exclamation point, whichever is most appropriate. Check your answers in Appendix II.

6. My advisor asked me when I planned to graduate

7. The hysterical child screamed, "My dog has been hit by a car" (Put the punctuation inside the quotation mark.)

8. I wondered why Janie never introduced me to her family

9. How many eggs do you add to the cake batter

10. Joey was voted the most valuable player in the game

C. If the sentence is punctuated correctly with commas, write *yes* in the blank; if not, write *no*. Do not guess; if you are unsure, do not write anything. Check your answers in Appendix II.

11. _____ After storming onto the floor and arguing with the referee Coach Bennett received a technical foul.

12. _____ The withered, ivy plant could not be saved, so I tossed it in the trash.

13. _____ I left for Nashville, Tennessee, on August 22, 1983.

14. _____ Uncertain yet eager, Josh began his first day as a camp counselor.

15. _____ When we have children of our own we come to understand how our own parents worried, sacrificed, and planned to ensure our own futures.

16. _____ Without telling the children where they were going, we picked them up at school, put them in the car, and headed for Virginia Beach Virginia.

17. _____ Rosa was well prepared for the test and feeling confident, so she was sure she did well.

18. _____ Suddenly, and unexpectedly, the string snapped, and the kite drifted off.

19. _____ George in my opinion is trustworthy, and he is certainly a hard worker.

20. _____ Because the spring was unusually dry the crop yield was low, and produce prices rose.

D. If the semicolon is used correctly, write *yes* in the blank; if it is not used correctly, write *no*. Do not guess; if you are unsure, do not write anything. Check your answers in Appendix II.

21. _____ I told you not to go; it's too bad you didn't listen to me.

22. _____ People who do not vote; do not understand how a democracy functions.

23. _____ My mother was born in Alexandria, Virginia; my father was born in Denver, Colorado; my sister was born in Tucson, Arizona; and I was born in Detroit, Michigan.

24. _____ The wedding was a disaster; by the end of the evening, the bride and groom were not speaking to each other.

25. _____ When the lifeguard put up the gale warning flags; everyone left the beach.

(continued on next page)

E. If the sentence is punctuated correctly with a colon, parentheses, or dash, write *yes* in the blank. If not, write *no.* If you are unsure, do not write anything. Check your answers in Appendix II.

26. _____ We went to the restaurant at eight o'clock; but it was closed. (I'm not really sure why.)

27. _____ The topic of my research paper is: why eating disorders are more common among females than males.

28. _____ Franklin Roosevelt said this: "The only thing we have to fear is fear itself."

29. _____ My earliest memory of my father—and it is indeed a pleasant one—is of him putting me on his shoulders and parading around the house.

30. _____ Drexel (what an unusual name) has a sister named Drexine (good grief!).

F. If the sentence is punctuated correctly with apostrophes, write *yes* in the blank; if not, write *no.* If you are unsure, do not write anything. Check your answers in Appendix II.

31. _____ The hat I found belongs to one of the boy's.

32. _____ I can't understand why Carmen is so angry at Ralph.

33. _____ Its' been quite some time since I've had a vacation.

34. _____ In the '50s life was simpler.

35. _____ Both senators' bills died in committee.

36. _____ Someone's car is double-parked and sure to be ticketed.

37. _____ My boss's top priority right now is increasing efficiency in all departments.

38. _____ All of her *e*'s look like *i*'s to me.

CAPITAL LETTERS

Most often, capital letters are used to identify something specific. The capital letters in *Fifth Avenue* signal that Fifth Avenue is a *specific* street: the capital letters in *General Motors* signal that General Motors is a *specific* car manufacturer.

1. Capitalize the names of people and animals.

Lucy	Fido	Madonna
Douglas	Rover	George Bush

but

Do not capitalize words such as *man, boy, girl, woman, cat, rock star, collie,* and *child.*

Mohan bought a sheepdog he named Hairy.

2. Capitalize the first word of a sentence.

The door slammed shut on Henry's finger.

3. Capitalize the first word of a direct quotation.

Doreen explained, "You must get an advisor's signature before you can register for this course."

but

"You must get an advisor's signature," Doreen explained, "before you can register for this course." (Do not capitalize *before* because it does not begin a sentence that is a direct quotation.)

4. Always capitalize *I.*

Curt and I felt I had a good chance of winning the competition.

5. Capitalize titles before people's names.

Mayor Morales	Judge Fulks	Senator Glenn
Reverend Jones	Rabbi Mendel	Captain McKenna
Professor O'Brien	Uncle Raymond	President Bush

but

Do not capitalize titles used without the names.

a mayor	the judge	a senator
a reverend	a rabbi	the captain
a professor	my uncle	a president

The instructor, Professor Chang, introduced the guest lecturer, Councilman Luntz, who used to be a senator.

6. Capitalize months, days of the week, and holidays.

January	Tuesday	Easter
May	Saturday	Labor Day

The first Monday in September is Labor Day.

7. Capitalize specific geographic locations, including specific cities, states, countries, bodies of water, roads, and mountains.

Georgia	Columbus, Ohio	Lake Erie
Route 86	Stark County	Atlantic Ocean
Mt. Rushmore	Grand Canyon	France
Colorado River	Northwest Territory	Pike's Peak

but

Do not capitalize general geographic locations.

state	city	the country
a lake	the mountain	north of town
the ocean	a river	my county

We left the city at ten and headed west. By late afternoon, we had arrived in St. Louis to see the Mississippi River.

8. Capitalize the names of nationalities, religions, languages, and the adjective forms of these words.

English	Judaism	Spanish
Catholic	Thai food	Chinese
African dance	French restaurant	Latin American music

This town has excellent Japanese restaurants and art galleries with extensive European collections.

9. Capitalize names of organizations, companies, colleges, and buildings.

Fraternal Order of Police	General Foods
Democratic Party	Yale University
Empire State Building	American Cancer Society

but

organization	university
political party	building

When I was in New York for the Modern Language Association conference, I stayed near the Empire State Building.

10. Capitalize historic events and documents.

Gettysburg Address   the Roaring Twenties

the Reformation   Battle of the Bulge

the Declaration of Independence   the Korean War

World War I   the Constitution

The television show M*A*S*H was set during the Korean War, but it was first shown during the Vietnam War.

FAQ

Q: Can I omit capital letters in e-mail?

A: Informal e-mail between friends and family is often written without capital letters. However, follow the capitalization rules in more formal e-mail, such as that written for school or work.

11. Capitalize the names of sacred books, and words referring to God. Also capitalize pronouns that refer to God.

the Lord	the Talmud	the Scriptures
the Trinity	the Koran	Jehovah
the Old Testament	the Torah	the Bible

The man prayed to the Almighty for His help.

12. Capitalize the names of specific course titles, but not the general names of courses unless they are languages.

History 101	French	Survey of English Literature
Chemistry 709	Italian	Business Management

but

sociology	accounting	mathematics

My geography course was not as difficult as I expected it to be, but Child Psychology 210 and German were very hard.

13. Capitalize the brand names of products but not the general names of product types.

Aim toothpaste	Jell-O	Tretorn sneakers
Marlboro	Toyota	London Fog raincoat

but

toothpaste	gelatin	tennis shoes
cigarettes	car	raincoat

At the grocery store, I remembered to get the Roman Meal bread, but I forgot the ice cream and Hershey's syrup.

14. Always capitalize the first and last word of a title. In between, capitalize everything except articles (*a, an,* and *the*), conjunctions (words like *and,*

but, or, for, so, if, as), and prepositions (words like *of, at, in, near, by*). If the title has a colon, capitalize the first word after the colon.

Gone with the Wind	*Star Trek II: The Wrath of Khan*
"A Modest Proposal"	*Around the World in Eighty Days*
A Farewell to Arms	"Politics and the English Language"

In English class we read *Tender Is the Night*

15. Capitalize words that show family relationships if names can be substituted for these words.

Ask Mother what she wants for her birthday. (We can say, *Ask Lucille what she wants for her birthday.*)

During World War II, Grandpa was a medic. (We can say, *During World War II, Charles was a medic.*)

but

Ask my mother what she wants for her birthday. (We do not say *Ask my Lucille what she wants for her birthday.*)

During World War II, my grandpa was a medic. (We do not say *During World War II, my Charles was a medic.*)

PRACTICE 23.1

a. Fill in the blanks according to the directions given in parentheses.

Example: (Use a street.) For most of my life, I lived on <u>Elm Avenue.</u>

1. (Use the title of a television show or movie; underline the title to indicate italics.) If you are interested in good entertainment, be sure to see

   _____.

2. (Use the title of a book; underline the title.) In literature class, I read

   _____.

3. (Use the specific title of a course.) Besides composition, this term I am

   taking _____.

4. (Use the general name of a course other than a language.) So far in

   college, my favorite course has been _____.

5. (Use a holiday.) The holiday that I enjoy the least is _____.

6. (Use a date.) My birthday is _____.

7. (Use the brand names of three specific products and use the general name of one other product.) At the grocery store, I spent $20.00 on

_____.

8. (Use a specific geographic location.) This summer, I would very much

like to see _____.

9. (Use a specific historic period or event.) In history, I enjoyed studying

about _____.

10. (Use a congressperson's title and last name.) When I learned that the legislature was considering raising the speed limit, I wrote a letter of

protest to _____.

11. (Use mother or father as a substitute for a name.) As I was growing up,

_____ taught me to take responsibility for my actions.

12. (Use mother or father.) As I was growing up, my _____ taught me to take responsibility for my actions.

b. Add necessary capital letters, and omit unnecessary ones.

1. Roberto Walker Clemente (1934–1972) was one of Major League Baseball's greatest players. In fact, he was the first latin American player to be admitted into the national baseball hall of fame.

2. Born in Carolina, Puerto Rico, on august 18, 1934, Clemente was the youngest child of Melchor and Luis Clemente. Clemente's Father was a foreman for the local Sugar Company, while his Mother worked at the plantation house.

3. Clemente played baseball during High School, but he also pursued track and javelin. He was considered a potential olympic competitor in track and field. Local businessman Roberto Marin recruited Clemente to play for the brooklyn dodgers. Over the course of his career, Clemente accumulated 3,000 hits. His 3,000th hit came on september 30, 1972.

4. About his career, Clemente said, "i am convinced that god wanted me to be a baseball player." In addition to his induction into the national

baseball hall of fame, Clemente was inducted into the black athletes hall of fame, and he was pictured on a u.s. postage stamp. He was even asked to run for the Mayor of San Juan.

5. Clemente was also known for his acts of charity and for mentoring young hispanic ballplayers. In 1972, he decided to visit Managua, Nicaragua, to help earthquake victims. Moments after his plane took off, it crashed and sank into the atlantic ocean, killing everyone on board. Thousands of memorial gifts were sent, generating enough money to build Ciudad Deportiva, where Puerto Rican boys could cultivate their athletic ability under the guidance of professional athletes.

THE PERIOD, QUESTION MARK, AND EXCLAMATION POINT TO END SENTENCES

The period (.), question mark(?), and exclamation point(!) are all used to signal the end of sentences.

The Period

Use a period to end a sentence that makes a statement, makes a request, or issues an order.

a statement:	Because of the heavy rains, the lowlands are flooded.
a request:	Bring me the evening paper, please.
an order:	Leave me alone so I can study.

The Question Mark

Use a question mark to end a sentence that asks a direct question.

Will you lend me your history notes?

Is this seat taken?

How can I help you if you refuse my advice?

However, use a period—not a question mark—to end a sentence with an indirect question. An **indirect question** is a statement, even though it notes that someone asked a question.

indirect question:	I wonder where I will be in ten years.

direct question:	Where will I be in ten years?
indirect question:	The waiter asked whether we wanted dessert.
direct question:	The waiter asked, "Do you want dessert?"
indirect question:	Kevin wanted to know whether he could borrow my car.
direct question:	May I borrow your car?

The Exclamation Point

Use an exclamation point after a statement or command that shows strong feeling or surprise.

a command with strong feeling:	Get out of the car before the engine catches on fire!
a statement with strong feeling:	I will get even with you if it is the last thing I do!
a statement with surprise:	I couldn't believe I earned the highest grade ever scored on the exam!

NOTES:

1. Do not overuse exclamation points. If you must use them often, your words are not conveying the message.

2. Do not use an exclamation point with a period or question mark.

no:	Are you sure you want to go?!
yes:	Are you sure you want to go?
no:	I am amazed at her nerve.!
yes:	I am amazed at her nerve.
yes:	I am amazed at her nerve!

FAQ

Q: Can I use more than one exclamation point at the end of a sentence if I want to show very strong emotion?

A: Use only one exclamation point at the end of a sentence.

PRACTICE 23.2

On a separate sheet, write sentences according to the directions given, ending each sentence with a period, question mark, or exclamation point—whichever is appropriate.

1. Write a sentence you might hear spoken on campus; be sure the sentence makes a statement.

2. Write a direct question you might ask a waiter in a restaurant.

3. Write a sentence that asks an indirect question. Begin the sentence with "Shelly asked whether."

4. Write a sentence that expresses great anger or fear.

5. Write a sentence that expresses a request a parent might make of a child.

6. Write a sentence that expresses a command a fire chief might give to fire-fighters; the command should express strong emotion.

COMMAS

The comma is the most frequently used punctuation mark. Commas are important because they separate sentence elements to make the reader's job easier.

Commas with Dates

With dates, use a comma to separate the day and the year.

I expect to graduate June 14, 2008.

On June 14, 2008. I will graduate.

NOTE: One form of writing dates does not use commas. Do not use commas if the day precedes the month and year.

I expect to graduate 14 June 2008.

If no day is given, there is no comma between the month and the year.

Julia began working for the United Parcel Service in January 2000.

Do not use a comma between the month and the day.

no: My birthday is May, 4, 1969.
yes: My birthday is May 4, 1969.

Commas with Places and Addresses

Use commas to separate the names of cities and states.

When they retired, my parents moved to Naples, Florida.

or

My parents moved to Naples, Florida, when they retired.

Place a comma between the street address and the city. There is no comma before the zip code.

> Garth's Flower Shop is located at 311 West Palm Lane, Warren, Ohio 44484.

PRACTICE 23.3

On a separate sheet, write sentences as directed.

1. Write a sentence that begins with "I live at." Include your complete street address, city, state, and zip code.

2. Write a sentence that gives the city and state of a place you want to visit. Begin the sentence with "I would like to visit."

3. Write a sentence that gives the month and year you began college. Begin the sentence with *I began college.*

4. Write a sentence that gives your complete date of birth. Begin the sentence with *I was born.*

Commas with Words, Phrases, and Clauses in a Series

A **series** is three or more words, phrases, or clauses. All but the last item in a series should be followed by a comma.

words in a series:	I realized I had forgotten my *shampoo, brush, and pajamas.*
phrases in series:	I have *lost weight, toned my muscles, and increased my flexibility.*
clauses in a series:	*You can take these books back to the library, you can pick up my dry cleaning, and you can wash the car.*

FAQ

Q: Can I place a comma wherever I pause or draw a breath in speech?

A: This method is an unreliable way to use commas. The only reliable method is to learn the rules.

NOTE: When all the items in a series are separated by *and* or *or,* no comma is used.

The dessert cart held fancy *pies and cakes and tortes.*

Place the plant *in the kitchen window or on the television or coffee table.*

PRACTICE 23.4

Use each series or pair in a sentence, being careful to use commas correctly.

Example: the spaghetti the veal and the broiled chicken

The waiter explained that the specials of the day were the spaghetti, the veal, and the broiled chicken.

1. the hardback or the paperback

2. the noise the pollution and the crowds

3. a fever a sore throat a stuffy nose and body aches

4. the food was overpriced the service was slow and the seating was uncomfortable

5. a relaxing bath or an invigorating shower

6. swept the downstairs and washed the clothes and cleaned the garage

Commas with Coordination

Coordination means that two word groups that can stand alone as sentences (**main clauses**) are joined by *and, but, or, for, so, nor,* or *yet* (**coordinating conjunctions**). Coordination is explained more fully on page 225.

Place a comma before a coordinating conjunction that joins two main clauses.

> Jillian gently picked up the baby chick, and she stroked it lovingly.
>
> I would ask you to join me, but I know that you are busy.
>
> Our current basketball coach will probably be fired, for he has won only a fourth of his games the past two years.
>
> The corporate offices of Raphael Industries will move to our town, so we can expect a decrease in our unemployment rate.

NOTE: Do not place a comma every time you use a coordinating conjunction. Many times these conjunctions do not connect main clauses. When they do not, no comma is used.

> The Corvette raced down the street and sped around the corner. (No comma is used because *and* does not join two main clauses, only two verb phrases.)

NOTE: Remember that main clauses cannot be joined by a comma alone— the comma must be used with the coordinating conjunction, or you will have written a comma splice. (See page 263.)

PRACTICE 23.5

Circle every coordinating conjunction. When the conjunction joins main clauses, add a comma before it. The first one is done as an example.

[1]You will never find the pot of gold at the end of the rainbow(for) rainbows do not end. [2]They are actually circles and the arc of color you see is just a small part of the rainbow. [3]In order for a rainbow to

form, sunshine and air loaded with water are needed. [4]The sunlight looks white but white light really is made up of all colors. [5]The water in the air bends the light and separates it into the colors so you see a rainbow. [6]How much of the rainbow you see depends on where the sun is in the sky. [7]When the sun is high, most of the rainbow is below the horizon yet when the sun is lower, more of the rainbow is visible. [8]When the sun is near the horizon, an observer on a high mountain or in an airplane may be lucky enough to see the whole rainbow circle. [9]Occasionally, the light of the moon forms a rainbow. [10]However, the moon's light is faint so the lunar rainbow's colors are faint and difficult to see.

Commas with Introductory Elements

An **introductory element** is a word, phrase, or clause that comes before the sentence subject. You should follow an introductory element with a comma. In the following examples, the subjects are underlined as a study aid.

comma after introductory word:	Carefully, <u>the child</u> placed the precious china doll on the shelf.
	Whistling, <u>Kobina</u> sanded the cupboard doors.
comma after introductory phrase:	Playing both offense and defense, <u>Mario</u> was the most valuable member of the football team.
	In the middle of the night, <u>the smoke alarm</u> went off and roused all of us from our beds.
comma after introductory subordinate clause:	When the steel mills closed, <u>over a thousand people</u> were out of work.
	If the union does not get a pay raise, <u>its members</u> will take a strike vote.

PRACTICE 23.6

Add commas after introductory elements in the following paragraph and cross out any incorrect commas.

[1]In Babylon some 4,000 years ago the first paved roads appeared. [2]As people, began living in town and trading with their neighbors they

needed better means of transport. ³A cart could not cross wild country because it could break an axle or sink into mud or sand. ⁴Thus paved roads were developed in response to a need. ⁵Undoubtedly, the greatest road-builders were the ancient Romans. ⁶Built by army engineers Roman roads were made of stones and gravel and ran straight from town to town. ⁷The roads were sloped so that rain would drain away to the sides. ⁸A marvel of engineering these roads were used by Roman armies to march across the empire and keep the peace.

Commas with Interrupters

An **interrupter** is a word or phrase that interrupts the flow or main idea of a sentence. Some common interrupters are

I believe	it seems to me
incidentally	as a matter of fact
in fact	to tell the truth
believe it or not	I am sure
by all means	if you ask me
by the way	without a doubt

Interrupters are set off from the rest of the sentence with commas.

The physical education requirement, *if you ask me,* should be abolished. (The interrupter comes in the middle of the sentence, so there is a comma *before and after* it.)

By the way, Kwame has decided to run for a seat on the student council. (The interrupter comes at the beginning of the sentence, so a comma is placed *after* it.)

Mayor Juarez has no choice but to lay off some city workers, *it seems to me.* (The interrupter comes at the end of the sentence, so a comma is placed *before* it.)

Transitions are often considered interrupters and are set off from the rest of the sentence with commas. (Transitions are explained on page 67.)

As a result, Donofrio won the election by a 50 percent margin. (The transition comes at the beginning of the sentence, so a comma is placed *after* it.)

Dr. Wright, *however,* disagrees with my view. (The transition comes in the middle of the sentence, so a comma is placed *before and after* it.)

Nonessential elements are also interrupters and set off from the rest of the sentence with commas. A **nonessential element** is a word, phrase, or clause that is not necessary for identifying the person, item, or place referred to. Here are examples of sentences with nonessential elements:

> Asa, *my oldest brother,* joined the Air Force. (*My oldest brother* is nonessential because it is not needed to identify who joined the Air Force; *Asa* does that.)

> The woman next door, *determined to strike out on her own,* quit her job and moved to Tennessee. (*Determined to strike out on her own* is nonessential because it is not needed to identify who quit her job and moved to Tennessee; *the woman next door* does that.)

> Xenia, Ohio, *which was once devastated by a tornado,* is now thriving. (*Which was once devastated by a tornado* is nonessential because it is not needed to identify what is now back on its feet; *Xenia, Ohio,* does that.)

The same word group can be nonessential in one sentence and essential in another. Here is an example:

> Alexis Ellington, *who won three major poetry contests*, will read some of her poems on campus this Friday night. (*Who won three major poetry contests* is nonessential for identifying who will read her poems, so commas are used.)

> A woman *who won three major poetry contests* will read some of her poems on campus this Friday night. (*Who won three major poetry contests* is now essential for identifying who will read her poems; therefore, no commas are used.)

PRACTICE 23.7

Insert commas where they are needed to set off interrupters.

[1]To my way of thinking Mississippi has a number of interesting places to visit. [2]In northeastern Mississippi for example there is the site of the Chickasaw fort that was attacked by the French in 1736. [3]Jackson, Mississippi which is the state capital offers many reminders of the state's history. [4]The Old Capital now the State Historical Museum was built chiefly by slave labor. [5]It was here that Mississippi voted to secede from the Union. [6]It is also the place where Jefferson Davis who was president of the Confederacy made his last speech. [7]A traveler who has the time may want to visit Delta and Pine Land Company Plantation which is one of the largest cotton plantations in the world. [8]It covers 38,000 acres near Scott. [9]For those who enjoy nature, Mississippi has sixteen state parks and six national forests. [10]If you find yourself in Mississippi, you will discover much to keep you occupied I am sure.

Commas with Coordinate Modifiers

Use a comma to separate coordinate modifiers not already separated by *and.* **Coordinate modifiers** describe the same word equally.

> Be careful on the *wet, slippery* floor. (*Wet* and *slippery* are coordinate modifiers because they both describe *floor,* so a comma is placed between them.)

Modifiers are coordinate, if you can place *and* between them.

> Davey could not part with his *old, faded* shorts because he wore them in the state basketball championships. (You can say *old and faded shorts,* so the modifiers are coordinate, and a comma is used.)

> I asked the waiter for *fresh apple* pie for dessert. (You would not say *fresh and apple pie,* so the modifiers are not coordinate, and no comma is used.)

Another way to test if modifiers are coordinate is to reverse their order. If you can reverse their order, the modifiers are coordinate. In the preceding examples, *old, faded shorts* can be changed to *faded, old shorts,* so the modifiers are coordinate. However, *fresh apple pie* cannot be changed to *apple fresh pie,* so the modifiers are not coordinate.

NOTE: Do not use a comma between coordinate modifiers separated by *and*.

no:	The speaker was given a warm, and enthusiastic welcome.
yes:	The speaker was given a warm and enthusiastic welcome.

PRACTICE 23.8

On a separate sheet, use each pair of modifiers and the noun in a sentence of your own. If the modifiers are coordinate and *not* already separated by *and,* place a comma between them.

1. hot blinding sun

2. cut bleeding knee

3. elegant silk scarf

4. steaming chicken soup

5. sensitive and caring nurse

6. warm gentle breeze

Commas with Direct Address

In **direct address,** you use the name of the person or animal you are speaking to. Names used in direct address are set off with commas.

> *Marvin,* I need to borrow your class notes.
>
> If you ask me, *Harriet,* we should leave now.
>
> Stop rolling in the clean laundry, *you silly cat.*

Do not set off the name of a person or animal spoken *about;* set off only the names of persons or animals spoken *to.*

direct address:	Carla, let me use your car for an hour. (Carla is spoken *to.*)
no direct address:	Carla will let me use her car for an hour. (Carla is spoken *about.*)

PRACTICE 23.9

On a separate sheet, write six sentences of your own. Two sentences should have direct address at the beginning, two should have direct address in the middle, and two should have direct address at the end. Remember, a comma is used *after* direct address at the beginning, *before* direct address at the end, and *before and after* direct address in the middle.

REVIEW PRACTICE 23.10

Place commas where they are needed in the following paragraphs.

1. ¹When I woke up I knew it was going to be "one of those days." ²First I heard my roommate cry, "Ryan come quickly." ³I sprinted to the living room and saw the cause of Ralph's scream. We had been robbed. ⁴Amazed I scanned the room. ⁵The stereo was gone the television was gone and the DVD player was gone. ⁶The couch was gone and the coffee table was gone. ⁷In fact the only thing that was not taken was the laundry basket which stood alone in the middle of the room. ⁸Ralph and I just looked at each other in disbelief. ⁹Not knowing what else to do we started to laugh for we both realized at the same moment that this was the day we were going to put new locks on the doors. ¹⁰Timing I guess is everything.

2. ¹Paul Revere was born on January 1 1735 in Boston Massachusetts. ²He was the third child of a silversmith Apollos De Revoire. Apollos a French Huguenot had come to Boston as a boy. ³When he was older he changed

his name to the simpler Revere. [4]Young Paul became an excellent crafts-man in fine metals. [5]In 1757 he married Sarah Orne. [6]When she died in 1773 Revere married Rachel Walker. [7]He had eight children by each wife but five of them died in infancy. [8]Revere was an early member of the Sons of Liberty and he was one of the leaders of the Boston Tea Party in 1773. [9]On the night of April 15 1775 Paul Revere rode to warn American patri-ots northwest of Boston that the British intended to raid Lexington and Concord. [10]As a result of Revere's warnings the Lexington Minutemen were ready for the British and for the important historic battle that launched the American Revolution. [11]During the war Revere engraved the printing plates for the first currency for Massachusetts set up a powder mill and served in the local militia. [12]In 1792 he opened a foundry to cast cannons and bells. [13]At sixty-five he learned how to roll sheet copper and became the first man in the United States to do this. [14]His copper sheets in fact were used on the famous ship *Old Ironsides*. [15]Revere died in Boston on May 10 1818.

SEMICOLONS

The semicolon is also a mark used to signal separation among sentence ele-ments. It most often separates main clauses, but it can also be used to avoid confusion in certain series.

Semicolons to Separate Main Clauses

Semicolons can separate **main clauses** (word groups that can stand alone as sentences). For a discussion of main clauses, see page 224.

> The table has been in my family for four generations; it was given to me by my mother.

> The fund-raising drive was a success; we collected enough pledges to keep the soup kitchen open another year.

When you use a semicolon, be sure you have main clauses on *both* sides. A semicolon cannot separate a main clause from a word group that is not a main clause.

no:	Because Hank was having trouble with math; he decided to hire a tutor. (The word group before the semicolon is not a main clause that can stand alone as a sentence.)

Semicolons can also be used with conjunctive adverbs to join main clauses. This rule is discussed in detail on page 231. Common conjunctive adverbs are:

Conjunctive Adverbs

; however,	; furthermore,	; thus,
; nevertheless,	; therefore,	; consequently,
; nonetheless,	; moreover,	

> Some people agreed with the speaker's remarks; however, most seemed to disagree.
>
> State aid to public schools has been cut drastically; therefore, it will be necessary to pass a school levy.

PRACTICE 23.11

Place semicolons where they are needed in the following sentences.

Example: The December snowfall set a record, however, it was never necessary to close the schools.

1. A person who runs for public office must endure considerable scrutiny every facet of a politician's life is subject to examination.

2. Louisa was finally realizing her dream she was about to open her own toy and hobby shop.

3. I took my complaint to three company officials nonetheless, no one was sure how to help me.

4. The driver failed to see the stop sign partially hidden by the bushes as a result, he narrowly missed hitting an oncoming van.

5. My son studied ecology in his fourth-grade science class he then convinced me to recycle aluminum and paper.

Semicolons with Items in a Series

A semicolon can separate items in a series when the series already has commas in it.

> The menu featured omelets, pancakes, and sausage for breakfast; hero sandwiches, soup, and burgers for lunch; and pasta, steak, and fish for dinner.

PRACTICE 23.12

Place semicolons where they are needed in the following sentences. In some cases, you will replace commas with semicolons.

Example: The City Council voted to create tax incentives, which will attract new businesses; to build a new high school, which will alleviate crowding; and to increase pay for safety forces, which will attract more police officers.

1. The team's infield is strong: Jakes, a senior, plays first base Juarez, a sophomore, plays second base Wallace, a junior, plays third base and Sniderman, a freshman, plays shortstop.

2. Tony looked for his Christmas presents in the linen closet, where they were hidden last year, in the attic, where years of castoffs were stored and in the garage, where Dad has his workroom.

3. At the flea market, I bought an old chair, which should fit in my living room a weathered porch swing, which I plan to refinish and a broken record player, which I have no use for at all.

4. On the cruise, my parents met a couple from Juneau, Alaska, a woman from Nashville, Tennessee, and a family from Great Neck, New York.

5. The model home has a gourmet kitchen, which includes stainless steel appliances, an open floor plan, which was designed by a famous architect, and a large lot, which sits on a cul-de-sac.

REVIEW PRACTICE 23.13

In the following paragraph, add semicolons where they are needed and strike out semicolons that are incorrectly used.

[1]Every summer I go to the beach, and usually there is some mishap. [2]I have cut myself on shells, which is always a danger because I walk barefoot, received a severe sunburn, which made me very sick, and gotten sand in my eye, which caused a nasty abrasion on my cornea. [3]Last summer for the first time, I was stung by a jellyfish. [4]I was standing in shallow water; when I felt the painful sting. [5]Fortunately, I had just read an article about how to deal with jellyfish stings; so I knew just what to do. [6]Quickly, I scooped up some sand, then rubbed it on the sting under water. [7]This helped wash away any remaining jellyfish nettles. [8]Next, I went to my room and applied alcohol this neutralized the majority of the toxins. [9](I could have also used vinegar or meat tenderizer.) [10]Finally, I washed the area with soap and fresh water. [11]In the case of a severe jellyfish sting, especially if there are allergic

reactions, I would have consulted a physician or gone to an emergency ward; additional help may have been necessary. [12]For the next 24 hours, I felt a bit nauseated, somewhat headachy, and a little feverish however, after that, I was fine.

COLONS, PARENTHESES, AND DASHES

The **colon** (:) introduces a long list, a quotation, or an explanation. **Parentheses** [( )] enclose material that is downplayed. The **dash** (—) signals a long pause for emphasis or dramatic effect.

The Colon

1. Use a colon to introduce a list.

> The doctor told me to avoid the following: salt, chocolate, caffeine, and artificial preservatives.

> I got a job for these reasons: bills, bills, and more bills.

2. Use a colon to introduce material that explains something in the main clause.

> The evening ended on a bad note: A prankster pulled the fire alarm, and the building had to be evacuated.

3. Use a colon to introduce an example of something in the main clause.

> Jake has become a compulsive buyer: Just yesterday he spent a hundred dollars on a silk shirt and fifty dollars on a leather belt.

4. Use a colon to introduce a quotation.

> Herman Melville wrote one of the most famous opening sentences in literature: "Call me Ishmael."

NOTE: Do not use a colon after a linking verb (see page 208), after a preposition (see page 214), or between a verb and its object (see page 360).

no:	Michael is: bright, motivated, and talented. (The colon appears after a linking verb.)
yes:	Michael is bright, motivated, and talented.
no:	I looked for my lost wallet in: the house, the car, and the office. (The colon appears after a preposition.)

yes:	I looked for my lost wallet in the house, the car, and the office.
no:	At the outlet mall, Karen bought: pottery, baskets, and shoes. (The colon comes between the verb and its object.)
yes:	At the outlet mall, Karen bought pottery, baskets, and shoes.

Parentheses

Use parentheses to enclose material that you want to downplay or deemphasize. Often material in parentheses is a side comment.

> My physics teacher (Dr. Garner) has agreed to give me extra help before the final exam.

> Translators (the unsung heroes of the literary world) must preserve the meaning and intent of the original work.

> Before beginning assembly, check to be sure you have all the parts (twelve in all).

The Dash

Use a dash to signal a long pause for emphasis or dramatic effect.

> My flight was canceled because of bad weather—what an annoyance that proved to be.

> Eight of us—all wearing heavy winter coats—squeezed into the car. Carla—an extremely talented violinist—is the youngest member of the symphony orchestra.

NOTE: If you want to downplay material, parentheses can sometimes be used in place of a colon. If you want to emphasize the material, dashes can sometimes be used.

colon:	Harvey cares about just one person: himself.
parentheses to downplay:	Harvey cares about just one person (himself).
dash to emphasize:	Harvey cares about just one person—himself.

PRACTICE 23.14

Add colons, parentheses, and dashes to the following passage, and be prepared to explain your reason for each addition. (The passage can be punctuated correctly in several different ways.)

[1]The elevator is the product of centuries of development, beginning with the ancient Greeks. [2]The Greeks knew how to lift objects using pulleys grooved wheels that ropes can slide over and winches machines that have broad drums with ropes fastened to them. [3]Turning the drum with a crank winds the rope up on the drum or lets it out; running the rope over a pulley allows a load to be raised or lowered.

[4]In the seventeenth century came the "flying chair," which was designed to carry people to the top floors of a building by means of a system of weights and pulleys. [5]Because it operated outside the building, the flying chair never became popular a fact that does not surprise most people.

[6]During the last half of the nineteenth century, elevators were in existence, but they were mostly used for freight. [7]Steam power was used to turn the hoisting drums of these elevators. [8]People did not use these elevators much for one reason they were afraid the rope holding the elevator might snap, and the elevator would go crashing down. [9]Then Elisha Otis invented a safety device that prevented this accident from happening, and elevators became popular. [10]Also, at this time, hydraulic power fluid under pressure began to be used to raise and lower elevators. [11]Finally, the electric elevator, which is what is used today, was developed by the German engineer, Werner von Siemens.

APOSTROPHES

Apostrophes serve two main purposes: They signal ownership, and they signal that letters or numbers have been omitted in contractions and other forms.

Apostrophes for Possession

Possession means ownership. One way to show possession is with a phrase beginning with *of,* and the other way is with an apostrophe.

The brightness *of the sun* makes it difficult to drive. (The brightness belongs to the sun.)

The *sun's* brightness makes it difficult to drive. (The brightness belongs to the sun.)

The office *of the vice president* is on the second floor. (The office belongs to the vice president.)

The *vice president's* office is on the second floor. (The office belongs to the vice president.)

The paw *of the dog* is badly cut. (The paw belongs to the dog.)

The *dog's* paw is badly cut. (The paw belongs to the dog.)

A number of rules govern how to use the apostrophe to show possession.

1. Add an apostrophe and an *s* to all singular nouns and to plural nouns that *do not* end in *s*.

Singular Noun or Plural Noun that Does Not End in *s*	Add *'s*	Possessive Form
Bill	Bill's	Bill's coat
car	car's	car's driveshaft
children	children's	children's toys
teacher	teacher's	teacher's desk
men	men's	men's clothing
Doris	Doris's	Doris's job

2. Add an apostrophe to plural nouns ending in *s*.

Plural Noun Ending in *s*	Add an Apostrophe	Possessive Form
brothers	brothers'	brothers' room
shoes	shoes'	shoes' laces
babies	babies'	babies' diapers

3. When a word is hyphenated, add the apostrophe after the last part of the word.

> This is my mother-in-law's car.

> All of my editor-in-chief's decisions were carefully made.

4. With two or more nouns, use the apostrophe after the last noun to show joint possession. Use the apostrophe after each noun to show individual possession.

> Carol and Dan's son will go to Italy this summer as part of the Children's International Summer Village program. (The son belongs to both Carol and Dan; this is joint ownership.)

> Carol's and Dan's businesses are enjoying excellent growth. (Carol and Dan each have a business; this is individual ownership.)

5. Use an apostrophe and *s* to make indefinite pronouns possessive. An **indefinite pronoun** refers to members of a group without specifying the particular members. (Indefinite pronouns are explained more fully on page 335.)

Someone's car is parked so closely to mine that I cannot get in on the driver's side.

Everyone's responsibility is to help the poor.

6. Do not use apostrophes with possessive pronouns. These words already show ownership, so no apostrophe is needed.

Possessive Pronouns

Singular	Plural
my, mine	our, ours
your, yours	your, yours
his	their, theirs
her, hers	
its	
yes:	The winning number is his.
no:	The winning number is his'.

NOTE: *Its* is a possessive pronoun, so no apostrophe is needed to show ownership. *It's* is a contraction form of "it is" or "it has." There is no form *its'*.

Possessive: The dog keeps licking *its* paw as if something is wrong.

Contraction: *It's* difficult to give up sugar.

PRACTICE 23.15

Fill in the blank with the correct possessive form; use the information in parentheses as a guide.

Example: (The dog belongs to Mona.) _____Mona's_____ dog will weigh over a hundred pounds when it is grown.

1. (The questions belong to the students.) The instructor was careful to

   answer all the _____ questions.

2. (The mattress belongs to the bed.) I have trouble sleeping in the dorm

   because my _____ mattress is too soft.

3. (The blades belong to the knives.) All of the steak _____ blades are too dull to cut easily.

4. (The paycheck belongs to Phyllis.) A mistake was made in _____ paycheck, and she was shorted $20.00.

5. (The laces belong to the shoes.) Both of the _____ laces broke when I tried to tie them.

6. (The ring belongs to my sister-in-law.) My _____ square-cut emerald ring is a family heirloom worth a great deal of money.

7. (The help belongs to everyone.) _____ help is needed if the fund-raiser is to be a success.

8. (Rhonda and Helen made different mistakes.) _____ and _____ mistakes are easy to correct.

9. (Rhonda and Helen have the same expectations.) _____ and _____ expectations are too high.

10. (The van belongs to Morris.) _____ van has 100,000 miles on it, but he has no plans to trade it in.

11. (The fillings belong to the teeth.) Most of my _____ fillings are loose.

12. (The natural resources belong to the country.) The _____ natural resources must be protected.

13. (The leg belongs to the table.) The _____ leg is marred because the cat uses it as a scratching post.

14. (The gloves belong to several boys.) The _____ gloves were left in a pile to dry by the radiator.

15. (The book belongs to the teacher) The _____ book was left on the desk.

Apostrophes for Contractions

A **contraction** is formed when two words are joined to make one. When the words are joined, at least one letter is omitted. An apostrophe stands for the missing letter or letters.

FAQ

Q: Some teachers don't like students to use contractions. Why?

A: Contractions are not suitable for formal academic writing. However, many teachers will allow them in writing that is not formal. Ask your teacher whether you can use them, if you are unsure.

Common Contractions

Two Words	Contraction	Missing Letter(s)
are not	aren't	o
Two Words	**Contraction**	**Missing Letter(s)**
is not	isn't	o
does not	doesn't	o
have not	haven't	o
can not	can't	no
could not	couldn't	o
they will	they'll	wi
she will	she'll	wi
he will	he'll	wi
who is	who's	i
who has	who's	ha
will not	won't	irregular: ill/o
would not	wouldn't	o
we are	we're	a
they are	they're	a
she had	she'd	ha
he would	he'd	woul

PRACTICE 23.16

Fill in the blank with the contraction form of the words in parentheses.

Example: _____*I'm*_____ changing my major to computer technology because the job opportunities are excellent in that field.

1. (we are) Although Higgins is a longshot candidate, _____ still planning to campaign for him.

2. (do not; you are) _____ look now, but the person

_____ talking about just walked in the room.

3. (do not; I am) If I _____ get at least a *C* in my circuits class,

_____ going to change my major to computer science.

4. (would not) Juanita turned down the job offer because she knew she

_____ like the hours.

5. (he has; does not) Now that _____ had a year of physical

therapy, Lee _____ have trouble with his back.

6. (it is) _____ possible to be happy living anywhere as long as you have good friends.

7. (she will) Pilar called to say _____ be an hour late.

8. (I will) _____ help you in any way I can as long as you cooperate with me.

9. (who is) Jamison is the attorney _____ likely to be appointed a municipal judge.

10. (who has) _____ been borrowing my tapes without my permission?

Other Uses for the Apostrophe

1. The apostrophe can stand for missing numbers.

> I graduated with the class of '91. (The apostrophe stands for the missing *19*.)

2. The apostrophe can stand for missing letters in informal speech or dialect.

> Grandpa always said, "Feelin' sorry fer yerself is a waste of time."
> "Bring 'em wit' ya," Mike shouted.

3. The apostrophe is used with an *s* to form the plural of letters. No apostrophe is used to form the plural of numbers, words used as terms, symbols, and abbreviations.

Plural of letters:	How many *s*'s are in *embarrass?*
Plural of numbers:	Be more careful about how you make your *4s.*
Plural of words used as terms:	All your *theres* are used incorrectly.
Plural of symbols:	Write out the word *percent* instead of using *%s.*
Plural of abbreviations:	There are three *M.D.s* here tonight.

PRACTICE 23.17

Place apostrophes where needed. Some sentences are correct.

1. In the 90s, a computer revolution occurred.
2. The second grader was having trouble learning how to make *rs*.
3. Gary announced, "The best things in life are eatin, sleepin, and partyin."
4. The English department hired three new Ph.D's to teach full time.
5. Marta was having trouble with her *thens* and *thans*.

REVIEW PRACTICE 23.18

Place apostrophes where they are needed in the following sentences. One sentence requires an apostrophe and an *s*.

1. The quarterbacks spectacular pass sparked the offenses scoring drive.
2. Once youve owned a car with a CD player, youll never buy a car without one again.
3. Chris short story was accepted for publication by one of this countrys leading magazines.
4. The *C*s that Dana earned kept her off of the deans list.
5. Johns and Marthas problems arent going to be solved overnight; it will take years of counseling before theyre able to understand and alter their behavior.
6. Three companies employees were honored with Chamber of Commerce awards of excellence.
7. My sister-in-laws business, which she started in the late 70s, is now grossing over two hundred thousand dollars a year.
8. Angelo snapped, "Were comin; dont be so impatient."
9. The teams locker room was jammed with reporters, following the upset victory over the Division I champs.
10. The cab drivers strike is a problem for those visiting the city.

QUOTATION MARKS

Quotation marks most frequently signal that someone's spoken or written words are being reproduced. They also indicate titles of short published writings.

Quotation Marks with Exact Spoken or Written Words

When you reproduce the exact words someone spoke or wrote, enclose the words in quotation marks. A sentence with someone's exact words usually has two parts: a statement of who spoke or wrote the words and the words themselves. The sentence is punctuated according to where in the sentence the exact words appear, as the following examples show.

1. Exact words after the statement of who spoke or wrote the words:

> Judy warned me, "Be sure to study hard for the chemistry exam because it's a real killer."
>
> *A Tale of Two Cities* begins, "It was the best of times."
>
> I asked Mario, "Will you join me for lunch tomorrow?"

   a. A comma separates the statement of who spoke from the exact words.

   b. The first word of the exact words is capitalized.

   c. The period or question mark appears inside the final quotation marks.

2. Exact words before the statement of who spoke or wrote the words:

> "There is a reason for everything," Eleni always said.
>
> "Take me to your leader," the alien ordered.
>
> "Will I ever be promoted?" the weary office worker wondered.

   a. If the exact words do not ask a question, a comma appears before the final quotation marks.

   b. If the exact words ask a question, a question mark appears before the final quotation marks.

   c. The first word after the exact words is not capitalized unless it is a person's name.

3. Exact words before and after the statement of who spoke or wrote the words:

> "Before we begin today's lecture," said Dr. Sanchez, "let's review yesterday's material."
>
> "I think we can go now," I said. "The rain has stopped."
>
> "Are you sure," I asked, "that we can come along?"

   a. A comma appears after the first group of exact words, inside the quotation marks.

   b. If the first group of exact words does not form a sentence, a comma appears after the statement of who spoke or wrote the words. The second group of exact words does not begin with a capital letter.

   c. If the first group of exact words forms a sentence, a period appears after the statement of who spoke or wrote the words. The second group of exact words begins with a capital letter.

   d. A period or question mark appears inside the final quotation marks.

4. A person's thoughts are punctuated like exact words:

> I asked myself, "How did I get into this mess?"

> "I know I can do it," I thought.

5. Before using quotation marks, be sure you really have someone's exact words.

use quotation marks:	Jane said, "I hate snow."
do not use quotation marks:	Jane said that she hates snow. (No one's exact words are repeated here.)
use quotation marks:	The lawyer said, "I will settle the case."
do not use quotation marks:	The lawyer said that he would settle the case. (No one's exact words are repeated here.)

PRACTICE 23.19

On a separate sheet, write sentences according to the directions given.

1. Write a sentence that you recently heard spoken on campus. Place the exact words after the statement of who spoke.

2. Write a sentence you recently spoke to a friend. Place the exact words after the statement of who spoke.

3. Write a sentence that includes a question a teacher has asked you. Place the exact words before the statement of who spoke.

4. Write a sentence that includes words a waiter might say. Place the exact words before the statement of who spoke.

5. Write two sentences that you might speak to a classmate before an exam. Place the exact words before and after the statement of who spoke.

6. Write a sentence a grandparent might speak. Use the words "When I was young" to begin the exact words. Place the exact words before and after the statement of who spoke.

7. Write a sentence that includes a question you might ask your doctor. Place the exact words after the statement of who spoke.

8. Write a sentence that includes words you would think to yourself after waiting for fifteen minutes in a traffic jam.

Quotation Marks with Titles of Short Published Works

Quotation marks enclose the titles of short published works: the titles of magazine and newspaper articles, essays, short stories, short poems, songs, and book chapters.

Titles of longer works, such as books, magazines, newspapers, record albums, television shows, plays, and movies are underlined or placed in italics (slanted type).

Use Quotation Marks	Underline
"Araby" (a short story)	<u>Gone with the Wind</u> (a novel/film)
"That Lean and Hungry Look" (an essay)	<u>Arsenic and Old Lace</u> (a play)
"Art at Its Best" (newspaper article)	<u>Wall Street Journal</u> (a newspaper)
"Ode to the West Wind" (a short poem)	<u>Twentieth-Century American Poets</u> (a book)
"Rootbeer Rag" (a song)	<u>Streetlife Serenade</u> (an album)

PRACTICE 23.20

On a separate sheet, write two sentences. Each one should include the title of a magazine or newspaper article.

REVIEW PRACTICE 23.21

Add the missing punctuation and capitalization in the following sentences.

1. The Reading Labs speed-reading class is designed for students with a low reading rate and its study skills class is designed for students with poor study habits.

2. The three doctors opinions were the same my tonsillectomy cant be postponed.

3. After Brian graduated with his degree in Spanish he went to central america to work with the poor.

4. Exhausted and discouraged I could not finish the marathon but I will try again next year.

5. Kevin wondered out loud is all this effort going to pay off?

6. After borrowing ten thousand dollars from investors Alma opened her own childrens clothing store.

7. At the student gallery there is a new exhibition of african art that will be on display until january.

8. Thomas Jefferson died fifty years after the signing of the declaration of independence.

9. Slow down the pace the coach shouted from the sidelines.

10. My favorite short story is Young Goodman Brown yet I also admire Flannery O'Connor's short story, Good country People.

Finding and Eliminating Capitalization and Punctuation Errors in Your Writing

Find and correct errors with capitalization and punctuation when you edit. If you check earlier, you may check sentences that you later decide to delete or change. The following strategies can help.

- Use your dictionary to check capitalization and contractions. While a dictionary will not tell you every time you should capitalize or use an apostrophe, it will tell you when a word is always capitalized and where the apostrophe goes in a contraction.

- Identify the subject of a sentence and look in front of it. Words before a subject are introductory elements and should be followed by a comma.

- Look left and right of coordinating conjunctions. If a main clause appears on *both* sides, place a comma before the conjunction.

- If you are unsure whether an element is an interrupter, read the sentence without it. If the sentence is still grammatically correct, the element is probably an interrupter that can be set off with commas.

- Check each semicolon you use to be sure a main clause appears on *both* sides or that a series exists that already has commas in it.

- If you compose at the computer, use the Search or Find function to locate these conjunctions: *and, but, or, nor, for, so, yet.* If there is a main clause on both sides of the word, use a comma before the conjunction.

POST TEST

Drawing on everything you have learned in this chapter, add the missing capitalization and punctuation in the following passage.

[1]Although she died in the early 60s, Marilyn Monroe continues to fascinate the american public. [2]The actress combined glamour with wholesomeness and sex appeal with innocence to create a legend summed up in a single word Marilyn. [3]As Carl Sandburg explained, she

wasnt the usual movie idol.

[4]Born as Norma Jeane Mortenson on June 1 1926 in Los Angeles California the actress first called herself Norma Jeane Baker and then Marilyn Monroe. [5]Her film debut was in Scudda-Hoo! in 1948 and her career blossomed with small parts in all about eve in 1950 and the <u>asphalt jungle</u> in the same year. [6]Her gift for comedy became apparent in Gentlemen prefer blondes 1953 and How to Marry a millionaire 1953. [7]Part of her humor lay in the idea that her gorgeous blonde character didnt seem to understand why people thought she was beautiful or funny.

[8]Monroes life was scrutinized by the press her marriages to baseball great Joe DiMaggio and playwright Arthur Miller were widely publicized. [9]She was always troubled by her lack of privacy. [10] To convince the world that she was more than a blonde bombshell Monroe took acting lessons and starred in complex films like Bus Stop 1956 and The Misfits 1961.

[11]Monroes career was cut short when she died in Los Angeles from an overdose of sleeping pills on August 5 1962. [12]However her sudden death seemed only to enhance the mystique of the actress.

SUCCEEDING IN COLLEGE

Improve Your Concentration

To study successfully, you must be able to concentrate so you can comprehend material, analyze it, and recall it as necessary. If you need to improve your ability to concentrate, here are some simple steps to take.

- Eliminate distractions. You may think you can study with the television on or with your roommate practicing yoga postures in the same room, but visual and auditory distractions interfere with concentration. Take advantage of quiet hours in your residence hall, find a quiet place on campus to study, or rent a study carrel at the library.

- Respect your concentration span. If your mind regularly begins to wander after a half hour of reading, schedule five minute breaks every thirty minutes. If you get restless after an hour at your desk, take a short walk and come back to your work.

(continued on next page)

- Respect your personal rhythms. If you are more alert in the morning, study early. If you concentrate better before a meal, study then. Know your rhythms and schedule study time accordingly.

- Build your concentration span gradually. Study for thirty minutes before taking a break, and add five minute blocks until you can concentrate for an hour.

- Create variety. Try studying two subjects, each for thirty minutes, rather than one subject for an hour. Do some work that requires writing, and follow it with work that requires reading.

- Use the clock and set goals. Tell yourself you will concentrate on a subject for a specific amount of time and do not stop until the clock reaches that time. If possible, set an alarm to sound when time is up.

- Take a meditation class. Meditating aids relaxation, but it also helps you learn to concentrate. You may find a meditation class on campus or at your local community center.

Write about It

Explain how well you currently concentrate. Is your ability to concentrate sufficient for your academic tasks this term? Why or why not?

CHAPTER 24
Eliminating Problems with Frequently Confused Words and Spelling

Some English words are so similar that people often mistake them for each other. However, these mistakes, along with spelling errors, can distract a reader, so this chapter is designed to help you avoid them. But first, to help you assess your current level of recognition, take the following pretest.

PRETEST

If the underlined word is correct, write *yes* on the blank; if it is not, write *no*.

1. _____ I bought <u>an</u> historical novel to read on vacation.
2. _____ Emil would <u>of</u> joined us, but he had to work.
3. _____ There were six <u>misspelled</u> words in the paragraph.
4. _____ Jane has lied so often that no one <u>believes</u> her any longer.
5. _____ The <u>effect</u> of the tax increase will not be known right away.
6. _____ The factory <u>use</u> to employ twice as many people as it does now.
7. _____ The speeding truck <u>passed</u> me at over 80 miles an hour.
8. _____ We are <u>suppose</u> to have a midterm exam on Friday.
9. _____ The <u>less</u> problems we have, the happier I am.
10. _____ Of all the items on the menu, Jake can't decide <u>among</u> the salmon, prime rib, and chicken marsala.

FREQUENTLY CONFUSED WORDS

The words given here sometimes present problems for writers.

A/An

1. *A* is used before a consonant sound. (See page 448 on vowels and consonants.)

> *a* tree, *a* friendly face, *a* unicycle (despite the opening vowel, this word
> begins with a consonant sound)

2. *An* is used before a vowel sound.

> *an* apple, *an* ice cream cone, *an* hour (despite the opening consonant,
> this word begins with a vowel *sound*)

PRACTICE 24.1

FAQ

Q: Will my computer's grammar or spellchecker find errors with frequently confused words?

A: Your spellchecker will not distinguish between soundalikes such as *here* and *hear.* Your grammar checker may find some errors with frequently confused words, but you cannot rely on it to find all of them. You must, therefore, learn the frequently confused words.

1. Fill in the blanks with *a* or *an.*

   a. _____ friendly stranger gave us directions.

   b. Ivan gave _____ interesting interpretation of the short story.

   c. _____ uncle of mine is _____ sheriff in

   _____ county west of here.

   d. Laughter is _____ universal language.

   e. _____ sink full of dirty dishes awaited me when I returned

   from _____ meeting of the Art Guild.

   f. _____ unicorn is _____ mythical beast.

2. On a separate sheet, write two sentences using *a* and two using *an.*

Accept/Except

1. *Accept* means "to receive."

> I *accept* your offer of help with thanks.

2. *Except* means "leaving out" or "excluding."

> All the votes *except* those from Precinct Z have been counted.

TIP:
Think of the *ex* in except and excluding.

PRACTICE 24.2

1. Fill in the blanks with *accept* or *except.*

   a. I cannot _____ your explanation.

   b. It is not easy to _____ defeat with dignity.

   c. Everyone _____ Joanie found the movie dull.

   d. No teacher will _____ a paper as sloppy as this.

   e. _____ for the first number, the concert was very good.

   f. The examination was easy _____ for the last essay question.

2. On a separate sheet, write two sentences using *accept* and two using *except.*

Advice/Advise

1. *Advice* is a noun meaning a suggestion or opinion.

   > In her column, Ann Landers gave *advice.*

2. *Advise* is a verb meaning to give advice.

   > The doctor *advised* Harriet to quit smoking.

TIP:
If you have a vice, you need *advice.*

PRACTICE 24.3

1. Fill in the blanks with *advice* or *advise.*

   a. You should follow my _____ and go back to school.

   b. Why should I _____ you if you won't do as I say?

   c. If you reject my _____, I will offer no more help.

d. Anton's _____ is always sound because he thinks problems through so carefully.

e. I cannot _____ you without more information.

f. No one can _____ you on matters of the heart.

2. On a separate sheet, write two sentences with *advice* and two with *advise*.

Affect/Effect

1. *Affect* is a verb meaning "to influence."

   The steelworkers' strike has begun to *affect* the local economy.

2. *Effect* is usually a noun meaning "result."

   The *effects* of the plant layoffs will be serious.

3. *Effect* is sometimes a verb meaning "to bring about."

   Councilman Page will try to *effect* a change in the city charter.

PRACTICE 24.4

1. Fill in the blanks with *affect* or *effect*.

   a. The _____ of the drought will be felt in the marketplace early this fall.

   b. I hope my decision to resign from the committee will not have a

      negative _____ on the committee's work.

   c. The store owners petitioned the mall management to _____ a change in Christmas shopping hours.

   d. What people eat for breakfast can _____ how they perform all morning.

   e. An _____ of an oil shortage is higher gasoline prices.

   f. Childhood traumas _____ us as adults.

2. On a separate sheet, write two sentences using *affect* as a verb, two using *effect* as a noun, and two using *effect* as a verb.

All Ready/Already

1. *All ready* means "all set," or "prepared."

   The crew was *all ready* to set sail.

2. *Already* means "by this time."

   Do not apply for the job because the position has *already* been filled.

TIP:
The expressions *all ready* and *all set* both have two words.

PRACTICE 24.5

1. Fill in the blanks with *all ready* or *already.*

   a. The party was _____ over, and the guest of honor had not arrived.

   b. I just cleaned this closet, and _____ it is cluttered.

   c. The water skier waved his hand to the driver to signal he was

   _____.

   d. Harry and Pilar were _____ to go, but I still had to make a phone call.

   e. _____ Hank is whining, and we just got here.

   f. As soon as Lateefa completes her last economics course, she will be

   _____ to graduate.

2. On a separate sheet, write two sentences using *all ready* and two using *already.*

All Right/Alright

In formal usage, *all right* is considered the acceptable form. *Alright* is not acceptable in college papers.

Among/Between

1. Use *between* for two people or things.

   There are many differences *between* working in a fast-food restaurant and working in a fancy restaurant.

2. Use *among* for more than two people or things.

> The argument *among* the students lasted most of the class period.

PRACTICE 24.6

1. Fill in the blanks with *among* or *between.*

    a. _____ the students in the class, only Mario earned an A on the final exam.

    b. It is difficult for me to choose _____ teaching and research for my career.

    c. The competition _____ the three teams is friendly.

    d. My antique necklace is _____ my most prized possessions.

    e. Ten-year-old Anna could not decide _____ the red bicycle and the green one.

    f. Just _____ you and me, I do not trust Lee.

2. On a separate sheet, write two sentences using *among* and two using *between.*

◼

Been/Being

1. *Been* is the past participle of *be.* It is usually used after *have, has,* or *had.*

> It has *been* years since I have seen Joel.

2. *Being* is the *-ing* (present participle) form of *be.* It is usually used after *am, is, are, was,* or *were.*

> Wanda is *being* careless when she leaves her purse there.

NOTE: Do not use *been,* without *have, has,* or *had.*

Incorrect: I been working hard.

Correct: I have been working hard.

PRACTICE 24.7

1. Fill in the blanks with *being* or *been.*

    a. Although I have _____ absent, I studied the assignments.

    b. The child does not understand that she is _____ rude.

    c. The Chens had _____ gone a week before they remembered they forgot to stop their mail.

    d. I am _____ inducted into the honor society tonight.

    e. Ned has _____ more than patient.

    f. Six families are _____ relocated to make way for the new road.

2. On a separate sheet, write two sentences with *been* and two with *being.*

Beside/Besides

1. *Beside* means "alongside of."

    Park the car *beside* the garage.

2. *Besides* means "in addition to."

    Besides being too small, the house was poorly located.

PRACTICE 24.8

1. Fill in the blanks with *beside* or *besides.*

    a. _____ the coffee cup was a stale donut.

    b. _____ the creek, the collie lay sleeping peacefully.

    c. Mother hid the children's Christmas presents in the chest _____ the bed.

    d. Few people _____ you and me realize that Randy is insecure.

e. _____ having a headache, I feel sick to my stomach.

f. What is the restaurant's specialty, _____ pasta?

2. On a separate sheet, write two sentences using *beside* and two using *besides*.

Can/Could

1. *Can* is used for the present tense to mean "am/is/are able to."

   If I get an income tax refund, I *can* buy a stereo.

2. *Could* is used for the past tense to mean "was/were able to."

   I thought I *could* finish by noon, but I was wrong.

PRACTICE 24.9

1. Fill in the blanks with *can* or *could*. To determine if you need present or past tense, check the tense of the other verb in the sentence, or look for clues such as *yesterday* or *now*.

   a. Before I _____ walk, I was reading.

   b. When I was sixteen, I _____ stay up all night and feel great the next day; now I _____ sleep for eight hours and still be tired.

   c. The photographer was certain he _____ restore the old family picture I found in Grandma's steamer trunk.

   d. I _____ never be sure if Sam is telling the truth or lying.

   e. Jenny is sure she _____ help us draft a newsletter.

   f. Last year I _____ not afford a vacation, but this year I _____ manage a week at the ocean.

2. On a separate sheet, write two sentences using *can* and two using *could*.

Fewer/Less

1. Use *fewer* for items that can be counted.

> *Fewer* than half the class passed the midterm.

2. Use *less* for something considered as a unit, and for something that cannot be counted.

> There is *less* concern for the homeless than there should be.

TIP:
Think of the word *countless*. It contains *count* and *less*. Then remember that *less* is used for things that are not counted.

PRACTICE 24.10

1. Fill in the blanks with *fewer* or *less*.

   a. The older I get, the _____ I worry about minor matters.

   b. If you take vitamin C, you may get _____ colds.

   c. _____ accidents occurred on Fifth Avenue this year than last year.

   d. The movie had _____ violent scenes than I expected.

   e. If more people would exercise, there would be _____ depression in the world.

   f. With _____ sex discrimination in the workplace, more women are executives.

2. On a separate sheet, write two sentences using *fewer* and two using *less*.

Good/Well

1. *Good* is an adjective, so it only describes nouns and pronouns.

> Lester is a *good* drummer. (*Good* describes the noun *drummer.*)

2. *Good* is used as an adjective after *seem, feel, look,* and *taste.*

> The steaming soup tasted *good.* (*Good* describes the noun *soup.*)

3. *Well* is an adverb, so it describes verbs.

> Bonnie sings *well*. (*Well* describes the verb *sings*.)

4. *Well* also refers to health.

> Tanya does not feel *well* enough to join us.

See also page 380.

PRACTICE 24.11

1. Fill in the blanks with *good* or *well.*

   a. This is a _____ time to plant a garden.

   b. I hope I do as _____ as you did in the time trials.

   c. I did not do very _____ on my chemistry exam because I did

   not understand covalent bonding _____ enough.

   d. The movie was not as _____ as I expected it to be.

   e. Isabella played a _____ tennis match today; I wish I had

   played as _____.

   f. The _____ behavior of the children earned them a treat.

   g. After eating five cookies, I do not feel _____.

   h. The warm sun feels _____ on my face.

2. On a separate sheet, write two sentences with *good* and two with *well.*

It's/Its

TIP:

Do not use *it's* unless you can substitute *it is* or *it has.*

1. *It's* is the contraction form and means "it is" or "it has."

   > *It's* time to head for home.
   >
   > *It's* been a pleasure serving you.

2. *Its* is the possessive form, so it shows ownership.

   > The rubber tree plant is dropping *its* leaves.

PRACTICE 24.12

1. Fill in the blanks with *it's* or *its*.

   a. _____ a sure bet that the store will close if _____ merchandising policies don't improve.

   b. The head librarian announced that the library has increased

   _____ holdings by 30 percent.

   c. _____ hard to believe, but _____ been three years since we met.

   d. If _____ work you want, you have come to the right place.

   e. _____ a shame, but Cinema Sixty has changed

   _____ policy of showing only first-run features.

   f. The company decided to reduce _____ costs by switching from television to direct-mail advertising.

2. On a separate sheet, write two sentences using *it's* and two using *its*.

Of/Have

Do not substitute *of* for *have*. *Have* is a helping verb (see page 209), and *of* is a preposition (see page 215).

Incorrect	Correct
could of	could have
will of	will have
would of	would have
should of	should have
may of	may have
must of	must have
might of	might have

Passed/Past

1. *Past* refers to a previous time. It can also mean "by."

   It is not possible to change the *past*.

Past experiences affect us in the present.

I drove *past* your house yesterday.

TIP:
Think of the letters *p* and *t*, as in *past* and *previous time*.

2. *Passed* is the past tense of the verb *to pass*, and means "went by" or "handed."

   As Rico *passed* Cathy's desk, he gave her a rose.

   The teacher *passed* the specimen around so all could see it.

PRACTICE 24.13

1. Fill in the blanks with *past* or *passed*.

   a. When the police officer _____ the warehouse, she saw the flames.

   b. The _____ too often intrudes on the present.

   c. As the marching band _____ the reviewing stand, thunderous applause erupted.

   d. We should forgive Kurt for his _____ mistakes.

   e. The relay runner _____ the baton to his teammate, who

      quickly _____ the runner in first place.

   f. In times _____ it was safe to walk at night.

2. On a separate sheet, write two sentences with *past* and two with *passed*.

Quiet/Quit/Quite

1. *Quiet* means "silence/silent" or "calm."

   Some people can work with a radio on, but I need *quiet*.

2. *Quit* means "stop" or "give up."

   Even if I wanted to *quit* school, my parents would not let me.

3. *Quite* means "very" or "exactly."

   I am *quite* sure no one lives here.

   That is not *quite* the point I am making.

PRACTICE 24.14

1. Fill in the blanks with *quiet, quit,* or *quite.*

   a. If you are _____ certain you can remain _____ for an hour, I can get my work done.

   b. If you do not _____ smoking soon, you will _____ likely have health problems.

   c. The _____ in this room is almost eerie.

   d. Martha returned the paint because it was not _____ the color she wanted.

   e. If you are not _____ certain that you can finish this project, you should probably _____.

   f. Alonzo _____ his fraternity because the parties were too

   _____.

2. On a separate sheet, write two sentences using *quiet,* two using *quit,* and two using *quite.*

Suppose/Supposed

1. *Suppose* means "assume" or "guess."

   I *suppose* I can be done by six if I hurry.

2. *Supposed* is the past tense form of *suppose.*

   The mayor *supposed* he would win the election by a large margin.

3. *Supposed* means "ought" or "should." In this case, it is preceded by a form of *be* and is always followed by *to.*

   We are *supposed* to clear the cafeteria tables when we are finished eating.

TIP:
Always use *supposed* (with the *-ed*) to mean "ought" or "should." *I am suppose to go* is an incorrect form written when the *t* in *to* is allowed to function as the *d* in *supposed.*

PRACTICE 24.15

1. Fill in the blanks with *suppose* or *supposed.*

   a. Franz is _____ to drive everyone to the party, but where do

   you _____ he will get a car?

b. We all _____ Matthew would go on to graduate school.

c. What do you _____ will happen if the research council does

not get the grant it is _____ to?

d. Cathy was _____ to meet me here an hour ago.

e. Lorenzo is _____ to bring the chips to the party, but I

_____ he will forget.

f. Do you _____ it is possible to finish the cleaning before our
guests arrive?

2. On a separate sheet, write two sentences using *suppose* and two using
supposed.

■

Then/Than

TIP:

Then and *time* have an *e:*
than and *compare* have
an *a.*

1. *Then* refers to a certain time.

> I asked Sylvia what she meant; *then* she yelled at me.

2. *Than* is used to compare.

> The chicken is tastier *than* the veal.

PRACTICE 24.16

1. Fill in the blanks with *then* or *than.*

a. My new apartment is less noisy _____ my previous
one.

b. If you arrive _____, you will be able to meet my
sister.

c. _____ she said that she would rather arrive late

_____ not at all.

d. You asked for my advice and _____ refused to take it.

e. Diana would rather quit school _____ sell her stamp
collection for tuition money.

      f. Getting a campus job is easier _____ people realize.

2. On a separate sheet, write two sentences using *then* and two using *than*.

There/Their/They're

1. *There* shows direction. It can also come before *are, was, were, is,* or *will be.*

    Put the boxes down over *there.*

    There are twelve of us helping out at the senior citizens' center.

2. *Their* is a possessive form; it shows ownership.

    The students opened *their* test booklets and began to work.

3. *They're* is the contraction form of *they are.*

    If *they're* leaving now, I should go with them.

TIP:
Use *they're* only when you can substitute *they are.*

PRACTICE 24.17

1. Fill in the blanks with *there, their,* or *they're.*

    a. According to the evening paper _____ will be a wheat shortage next year.

    b. Henri and Tom said _____ not going unless they can bring

       _____ video games with them.

    c. If you put the couch over _____, then _____ will

       be enough room for _____ record collection.

    d. The police officers are concerned because the referendum that would

       grant _____ pay raises may not get on the November ballot.

    e. _____ asking five hundred dollars for _____ used piano.

    f. I looked _____ but I couldn't find _____ coats.

2. On a separate sheet, write two sentences using *there,* two using *their,* and two using *they're.*

Through/Though/Threw

1. *Through* means "in one side and out the other." It also means "finished."

> It was hard for Grandma to pass the thread *through* the needle.
>
> I will be *through* proofreading my essay in an hour.

2. *Though* means "although"; *as though* means "as if."

> *Though* Alan has never taken lessons, he plays the piano well.
>
> Maria acts *as though* she is mad at the world.

3. *Threw* is the past tense of *throw*.

> The quarterback *threw* an incomplete pass.

PRACTICE 24.18

1. Fill in the blanks with *through, though,* or *threw.*

   a. When she was _____ studying, Eleni rested for an hour.

   b. _____ Hank pretends he does not care, anyone can see

      _____ his act.

   c. Cal won a stuffed rabbit when he _____ the baseball at the milk bottles on the midway.

   d. _____ Toni made a basket, the shot did not count because

      he _____ the ball after the buzzer.

   e. Diane strolled _____ the park as _____ she did not have any worries.

   f. If we elect Smith, we will have a better chance to work

      _____ the police labor dispute.

2. On a separate sheet, write two sentences using *through,* two using *though,* and two using *threw.*

To/Too/Two

1. *To* means "toward." It can also be part of a verb, as in *to run.*

> I was going *to* class when I saw Rhonda.
>
> I wanted *to* ask you a favor.

2. *Too* means "excessively" or "also."

> The movie was *too* violent for me.
>
> I would like a piece of that cake *too.*

3. *Two* is the number.

> Only *two* candidates for the school board have experience.

PRACTICE 24.19

1. Fill in the blanks with *to, too,* or *two.*

   a. Before beginning _____ exercise, stretch for ten minutes.

   b. _____ much smoking and _____ little exercise

   make Dan a prime candidate _____ get a heart attack.

   c. The car needed _____ new tires and a water pump

   _____.

   d. _____ tell you the truth, I was not _____ pleased

   _____ be headed _____ the mall _____
   days before Christmas.

   e. The highlight of the trip was going _____ Disney World for

   _____ days.

   f. A week is _____ long for me _____ be gone.

2. On a separate sheet, write two sentences using *to,* two using *too,* and two
   using *two.*

Use/Used

1. *Use* is a noun that means "purpose." It is also a verb that means "make use of."

> What possible *use* could this have?
>
> How do you *use* this gadget?

2. *Used* is the past tense and past participle form of the verb *to use*. It also means "adjusted" or "accustomed"; in this case, it is followed by *to*.

> The child *used* the towel and threw it on the floor.
>
> I have *used* this product successfully before.
>
> I am not *used* to this kind of treatment.

PRACTICE 24.20

1. Fill in the blanks with *use* or *used*.

   a. I am not _____ to the idea that I am now an adult.

   b. I _____ that shampoo, but I did not like the results.

   c. This school does not make sufficient _____ of computers.

   d. A person _____ to feel safe walking alone at night.

   e. We have _____ that textbook in our English class.

   f. I _____ to wear braces on my teeth.

2. On a separate sheet, write two sentences using *use* and two using *used*.

Where/Were/We're

1. *Where* refers to location.

> Home is *where* a person should feel safe.

2. *Were* is the past tense form of *are*.

> The Raiders *were* ahead until the third quarter.

3. *We're* is the contraction form of *we are*.

> *We're* certain that Mom will do well in school.

PRACTICE 24.21

1. Fill in the blanks with *where, were,* or *we're*.

   a. If you ask me, we do not know _____ we are going.

   b. The plans _____ changed because _____ uncertain about how long it will take us to drive to Cleveland.

   c. The new federal building will be built _____ the old courthouse now stands.

   d. _____ all uncertain about what the future holds and

      _____ we will be this time next year.

   e. Debbie and Lenny _____ the best-behaved children at the party.

   f. _____ going, but _____ not happy about it.

2. On a separate sheet, write two sentences using *were,* two using *where,* and two using *we're*.

Will/Would

1. *Will* looks to the future from the present tense.

> Dr. Schwartz believes [present tense] he *will* [at a later date] get his book published.

2. *Would* looks to the future from the past tense.

> Dr. Schwartz believed [past tense] he *would* [at a later date] get his book published.

1. Fill in the blanks with *will* or *would*.

    a. Councilwoman Drucker promised that she _____ not vote to raise city taxes.

    b. The regional basketball tournament _____ be played on our campus this spring.

    c. If you do not stop snapping at people, no one _____ want to be around you.

    d. The fans wondered who _____ pitch the last inning.

    e. The Academic Council plans to announce that graduation

    requirements _____ change in the near future.

    f. The child _____ not leave unless he could take his toy.

2. On a separate sheet, write two sentences using *will* and two using *would*.

Whose/Who's

TIP:
Use *who's* only when you can substitute *who is* or *who has*.

1. *Whose* is a pronoun that indicates possession.

> The person *whose* car is double-parked got a ticket.

2. *Who's* is the contraction form of *who is* or *who has*.

> *Who's* on the telephone?
>
> *Who's* been watching the game?

1. Fill in the blanks with *whose* or *who's*.

    a. _____ umbrella was left on the desk?

    b. Dr. Berringer is a teacher _____ lectures are always stimulating.

  c. It is impossible to know _____ been here in the last hour.

  d. They are the couple _____ children broke our window.

  e. _____ the instructor for this course?

  f. I cannot be sure _____ coming to Luis's surprise party.

2. On a separate sheet, write two sentences using *whose* and two using *who's.*

Your/You're

1. *Your* is a possessive pronoun and, therefore, shows ownership.

   Remember to bring *your* ticket when you come.

2. *You're* is the contraction form of *you are.*

   You're the only person I can trust with this secret.

TIP:
Use *you're* only when you can substitute *you are.*

1. Fill in the blanks with *your* or *you're.*

   a. If you really don't want _____ bicycle anymore, Jane will buy it from you.

   b. _____ never really certain what _____ future holds.

   c. _____ best bet is to give Luigi a gift certificate because

      _____ never going to find something he doesn't already have.

   d. The key to _____ success will be hard work, not

      _____ parents' money.

   e. _____ my best friend, so I know you will help me.

   f. I felt _____ prose was too wordy, so I took the liberty of

      revising some of _____ phrasing.

2. On a separate sheet, write two sentences with *your* and two with *you're.*

SPELLING

Spelling errors distract readers, and they can be annoying. If spelling is a serious problem for you, the tips and rules that follow will help.

Spelling Rules

To apply many of the spelling rules, you must know the difference between vowels and consonants.

Vowels:	*a, e, i, o, u*
Consonants:	*b, c, d, f, g, h, j, k, l, m, n, p, q, r, s, t, v, w, x, z*

Y can be a vowel or a consonant, depending on how it sounds.

y as a vowel:	*funny, shy*
y as a consonant:	*yellow, yes*

Rule 1:

I comes before *e* except after *c,* or when sounding like long *a* as in *neighbor* and *weigh.*

The *i* comes before the *e:*

niece, field, grief, believe, friend, relieve, belief

The *e* comes before the *i* because the letters are after *c:*

conceive, ceiling, deceive, receipt, conceit, receive

The *e* comes before the *i* because of the long *a* sound:

neighbor, weight, weigh, sleigh

Words with a *shin* sound are spelled *ie* after *c:*

ancient, conscience, efficient, sufficient

Some exceptions to the rule:

either, neither, seize, weird, height, foreign, society.

TIP:

The following nonsense sentence contains five of the most common exceptions to the ie/ei rule: Either foreigner seized weird leisure.

Rule 2:

Before adding an ending other than *-ing,* change *y* to *i* if there is a conso-nant before the *y.*

Change *y* to *i* if there is a consonant before the *y:*

study	+	ed	= studied	plenty	+	ful	= plentiful
happy	+	ness	= happiness	cry	+	ed	= cried
pretty	+	est	= prettiest	lovely	+	er	= lovelier

Keep the *y* if there is a vowel before it:

enjoy	+	ment	=	enjoyment	stay	+	ed	=	stayed
play	+	s	=	plays	toy	+	s	=	toys
employ	+	ed	=	employed	destroy	+	er	=	destroyer

Keep the *y* if the ending is *-ing:*

hurry	+	ing	=	hurrying	study	+	ing	=	studying
employ	+	ing	=	employing	cry	+	ing	=	crying
fly	+	ing	=	flying	imply	+	ing	=	implying

Some exceptions to the rule:

day	+	ly	=	daily	lay	+	ed	=	laid
pay	+	ed	=	paid	sly	+	ness	=	slyness
shy	+	ly	=	shyly	gay	+	ly	=	gaily
say	+	ed	=	said					

Rule 3:

When you add an ending to a word that ends with a silent *e,* drop the *e* if the ending begins with a vowel, but keep the *e* if the ending begins with a consonant.

Drop the *e* if the ending begins with a vowel:

hope	+	ing	=	hoping	dine	+	ing	=	dining
pleasure	+	able	=	pleasurable	write	+	er	=	writer
dine	+	er	=	diner	dense	+	ity	=	density
praise	+	ing	=	praising	rhyme	+	ed	=	rhymed
time	+	ed	=	timed					

Keep the *e* if the ending begins with a consonant:

hope	+	ful	=	hopeful	complete	+	ly	=	completely
loose	+	ly	=	loosely	state	+	ment	=	statement
hate	+	ful	=	hateful	home	+	less	=	homeless
time	+	less	=	timeless	move	+	ment	=	movement
rude	+	ness	=	rudeness					

Some exceptions to the rule:

acknowledge	+ ment	=	acknowledgment
judge	+ ment	=	judgment
mile	+ age	=	mileage
notice	+ able	=	noticeable
argue	+ ment	=	argument
nine	+ th	=	ninth
acre	+ age	=	acreage
awe	+ ful	=	awful
true	+ ly	=	truly
courage	+ ous	=	courageous

Rule 4:

When adding an ending that begins with a vowel to a one-syllable word, double the final consonant if the last three letters of the word are consonant-vowel-consonant (c-v-c).

Double the final consonant if the one-syllable word ends c-v-c:

swim	+ ing	= swimming	fat	+ est	=	fattest
thin	+ er	= thinner	skip	+ ing	=	skipping
drop	+ ed	= dropped	run	+ er	=	runner

Do not double the final consonant if the one-syllable word does not end c-v-c:

eat + ing = eating   burn + er = burner   boil + ed = boiled

Rule 5:

When adding an ending that begins with a vowel to a word of more than one syllable, double the final consonant if the last three letters of the word are consonant-vowel-consonant (c-v-c) *and* if the stress is on the last syllable.

Double the final consonant if the word ends c-v-c and the stress is on the last syllable:

begin	+ er	= beginner	regret + ed	= regretted
admit	+ ing	= admitting	prefer + ed	= preferred

Do not double the final consonant if the stress is not on the last syllable:

pardon	+ ed	= pardoned	ripen + ing = ripening
labor	+ er	= laborer	

Do not double the final consonant if the word does not end c-v-c:

evict   +   ing = evicting   pretend + er = pretender

ordain   +   ed = ordained

Do not double the consonant if the stress shifts from the last syllable when the ending is added.

prefer   +   ence = preference

confer   +   ence = conference

but

preference (stress shifts from last to first syllable)

conference (stress shifts from last to first syllable)

Rule 6:

Most nouns form the plural by adding *s*. However, if the noun ends in *ch, sh, s, x, z,* or *o*, add *es* to form the plural.

genius + es   =   geniuses   mix   + es   = mixes

potato + es   =   potatoes   church + es   = churches

Some exceptions to the rule:

memos   radios   solos

Rule 7:

When you change the final *y* to *i,* add *es* to form the plural (see Rule 2).

candy + es   = candies   party + es   = parties   fly + es = flies

but

key   + s   = keys   boy   + s   = boys   toy + s   = toys

PRACTICE 24.25

1. To check your understanding of spelling rule 1, fill in the blanks with either *ie* or *ei.* If you are unsure, check a dictionary.

    a. ch _____ _____ f   g. perc_____ _____ ve

    b. br_____ _____ f   h. sh_____ _____ ld

c. fr____ ____ ght   i. r____ ____ gn

d. ach____ ____ ve   j. v____ ____ n

e. w____ ____ gh   k. th____ ____ r

f. s____ ____ ge

2. To check your understanding of spelling rules 2–5, add the given endings to the words below. If you are unsure, consult the rule given in parentheses or look up the word in a dictionary.

a. sorry + er _____ (rule 2)

b. bat + er _____ (rule 4)

c. make + s _____ (rule 3)

d. hammer + ing _____ (rule 5)

e. hop + ed _____ (rule 4)

f. enjoy + able _____ (rule 2)

g. advertise + ment _____ (rule 3)

h. ask + ing _____ (rule 4)

i. sense + ible _____ (rule 3)

j. slip + ed _____ (rule 4)

k. gossip + ed _____ (rule 5)

l. omit + ing _____ (rule 5)

m. wealthy + er _____ (rule 2)

n. rake + ing _____ (rule 3)

o. ship + ment _____ (rule 4)

p. permit + ed _____ (rule 5)

q. bite + ing _____ (rule 3)

r. marry + ed _____ (rule 2)

s. big + er _____ (rule 4)

t. lazy + ness _____ (rule 2)

3. To check your understanding of rules 6 and 7, write the plural of each noun. If you are unsure, check a dictionary.

a. toy _____

b. brush _____

c. jelly _____

d. mosquito _____

e. television _____

f. veto _____

g. tax _____

h. girl _____

i. enemy _____

j. match _____

Frequently Misspelled Words

The following seventy-five words are often misspelled. Learn to spell every word on the list by making flash cards to study. Have someone quiz you until you can spell all of these words with ease.

1. absence	14. committee	27. grammar
2. across	15. criticism	28. guarantee
3. actually	16. definitely	29. guidance
4. a lot	17. dependent	30. height
5. analyze	18. develop	31. hoping
6. appreciate	19. discuss	32. immediately
7. argument	20. eighth	33. independent
8. athlete	21. embarrass	34. intelligence
9. awkward	22. especially	35. knowledge
10. beginning	23. existence	36. laboratory
11. belief	24. February	37. leisure
12. business	25. foreign	38. length
13. coming	26. government	39. library

40. marriage	52. physical	64. safety
41. mathematics	53. planned	65. scene
42. meant	54. pleasant	66. schedule
43. medicine	55. preferred	67. separate
44. necessary	56. prejudice	68. severely
45. neither	57. privilege	69. success
46. ninety	58. pursue	70. surprise
47. ninth	59. receipt	71. thoroughly
48. occasionally	60. receive	72. through
49. opinion	61. religious	73. until
50. parallel	62. rhythm	74. weight
51. persuade	63. sacrifice	75. written

The Hyphen

Hyphens are most often used to form compound words and to show that a word continues from the end of one line to the beginning of the next. For some word-processing programs, use one horizontal line for the hyphen (-) and two lines for the dash (–).

1. Use a hyphen between words that form a single adjective before a noun.

state-of-the-art stereo	well-known speaker
comparison-contrast essay	run-of-the-mill Sunday
strong-willed child	so-called advice

Do not use a hyphen when the compound comes after the noun:

Fran is a success because she is strong willed.

Do not use a hyphen with an *-ly* word:

The slowly moving traffic made me an hour late.

2. Use hyphens between compound numbers from twenty-one through ninety-nine.

thirty-six	seventy-seven
forty-two	fifty-eight

3. Use a hyphen between the numerator and denominator in written fractions.

one-fourth	two-thirds

4. Do not use hyphens with most **prefixes** (word beginnings) like *un, inter, mis,* and *dis.*

unnoticed	interrelated	misspell	disengage.

5. Use a hyphen after the prefixes *self-, all-, ex-* (meaning *former*), and before the **suffix** (word ending) *-elect.*

self-assured	ex-governor
all-inclusive	mayor-elect

6. Use a hyphen with a prefix before a word that begins with a capital letter.

un-American	pro-Cuban	mid-January

7. Use a hyphen to divide a word at the end of a line, but remember these cautions:

   a. Do not divide one-syllable words.

   b. You should not leave a single letter at the end of the line, so do not divide a word such as *a-void.*

PRACTICE 24.26

Add hyphens where they are needed in the following paragraph.

[1]My mother in law is a first rate artist who will show her paintings at a gallery on the twenty first of the month. [2]Her show will last until mid May. [3]In addition to being a highly acclaimed artist, my mother in law is the ex chair of the United Way campaign in our city and an energetic fund raiser for anti drug campaigns. [4]At sixty seven, she is a remarkable, self possessed, high powered woman whom I admire greatly.

REVIEW PRACTICE 24.27

Eliminate the eleven errors with frequently confused words and spelling in the following paragraph.

[1]Sadly, more and more young children are developing negative body images and starting to diet as a result. [2]However, young children are not suppose to diet. [3]Instead, it's much better if their encouraged to develop healthy attitudes toward food, exercise, and body types. [4]If overwieght children could develop good eating habits and maintain there weight during their formative years, than they will have a good chance of slimming down once they hit the growth spurts of puberty. [5]Its true that the habits children learn at a young age will stay with them long passed childhood and into adulthood. [6]There would be far less eating disorders if children were taught proper nutrition and self acceptance. [7]As a country, were so concerned with being skinny that we teach children—unconsciously or otherwise—to have unrealistic and unhealthy expectations for desireable weight.

Finding and Eliminating Errors with Frequently Confused Words and Spelling in Your Writing

FAQ

Q: Why do I need to learn how to spell? Can't I just use my computer's spellchecker?

A: Computer spellcheckers have limitations. They do not, for example, distinguish between the frequently confused words and soundalikes, and they include fewer words than most dictionaries. Also, you must know how to spell for those times you are not writing at the computer.

Look for errors with frequently confused words and spelling when you edit. If you check earlier, you may check sentences that you later decide to delete or change. The following strategies can help.

- Study your draft word by word, very slowly. Each time you encounter a word that might be misspelled or confused, check it in a dictionary. Never overlook a word even if your suspicion is very slight.

- Keep a list of words you misspell and confuse, and study it daily. You may find it helpful to underline the troublesome parts of words like this.

  for<u>eig</u>n

- Learn the correct pronunciation of words. You may misspell *disastrous* if you pronounce it incorrectly as *disasterous*.

- Break words into parts when you spell, like this:

  with ∗ hold   class ∗ room   under ∗ standing

under ⋆ statement   break ⋆ fast   table ⋆cloth

room ⋆ mate   shoe ⋆ lace   beach ⋆front

- Some words may be easier to handle if you spell them syllable by syllable. For example, *organization* may be easier to spell if you say each syllable as you go: "or ● gan ● i ●za ● tion."

  Be aware of **prefixes** (word beginnings) like *un, inter, mis,* and *dis.* When they are added to words, the spelling of the base word is not likely to change.

  dis ⋆ satisfaction   inter ⋆ related   un ⋆ nerve

  mis ⋆ shapen

- Use tricks to help you remember correct spellings and confusing words. For example, *instrument* contains the word *strum,* and you strum a guitar, which is an instrument; *tragedy* contains the word *rage.*

POST TEST

Find and correct the thirteen errors with frequently confused words and spelling.

[1]The practice of wearing wedding rings goes back to the anceint Egyptians and there habit of sealing a pact with a show of trust. [2]Since a signet ring has the crest of it's owner, such rings were exchanged as a show of trust. [3]If a person excepted the ring, he or she was enterring into a relationship of shared trust. [4]Eventualy, the practice moved from politics to business. [5]Now it is a part of marriage ceremonys signifying love and trust among two people.

[6]The practice of using the forth finger of the left hand as the ring finger dates back to the third century B.C. [7]At that time, physicains believed that a nerve was suppose to run directly passed this finger and than on to the heart.

SUCCEEDING IN COLLEGE

Use Memory Tricks

In this chapter, you learned that memory tricks can help you spell some words and avoid confusing others. For example, above you read that spelling *instrument* may be easier if you remember that it contains the word *strum,* and you strum a guitar, which is an instrument.

You can also use memory tricks to learn content in your other courses. One particularly useful trick is **association** or connecting new material to something you already know. For example, say that for your economics class, you must learn that *laissez-faire* is a form of capitalism whereby people compete with minimal government intervention. You might associate *laissez* with "lazy" and remember that lazy people like to be left alone to loaf, just as government leaves business alone to regulate itself in a *laissez-faire* system.

Another memory trick is to use a **mnemonic device,** which is a saying or name that jogs your memory. Music students often use the mnemonic device, "Every good boy does fine," to remember the lines on a music staff are E, G, B, D, F. Say, for example, you must remember that the structure of a cell nucleus includes the chromatin, nucleolus, and nuclear envelope—CNN, easy to remember if you think of the cable news channel. If you must remember that the parts of a bacteria cell are the flagellum, cytoplasm, capsule, plasma membrane, and ribosome, you might devise a sentence like this, "Funny Cindy captures pink rats."

Write about It

Go to your textbooks and find five sets of facts you need to learn or will need to learn in the future. Then write out five different memory tricks to help you remember those sets of facts.

COMPREHENSIVE POST TEST

■ **Using Verbs Correctly**

1. If the underlined verb is correct, write *yes* on the blank; if it is incorrect, write *no*.

   a. _____ We <u>been</u> the ones who told Donald that the test was postponed.

   b. _____ The children <u>drunk</u> their milk and then ran outside to play.

   c. _____ Both of the television documentaries <u>discusses</u> the aftermath of the Vietnam War.

   d. _____ Before the sun comes up each morning, everyone in the family <u>exercise</u> for thirty minutes.

   e. _____ The box of canned goods <u>are</u> ready to take to the food bank.

   f. _____ After receiving a standing ovation, the cast of the play <u>was</u> called on stage for another bow.

   g. _____ Each of the aspiring journalists <u>hopes</u> to get a job on the student newspaper.

   h. _____ Neither the book nor the movie <u>is</u> suitable for a young audience.

   i. _____ Each of the puppies <u>have</u> black spots on white fur.

   j. _____ The a capella choir <u>expects</u> to tour Europe this spring.

   k. _____ After Henri turned in his midterm exam, he <u>checks</u> two answers in his notes.

   l. _____ The newspaper reporter double-checked his sources and then <u>decides</u> to write the front-page story.

■ **Using Pronouns Correctly**

2. If the underlined pronoun is correct, write *yes* on the bank; if it is incorrect, write *no*.

   a. _____ Katrina and <u>him</u> believe in reincarnation.

   b. _____ Because Josef trained all summer, he ran the Thanksgiving marathon faster than <u>I</u>.

   c. _____ None of the radio stations had <u>their</u> license renewed by the Federal Communications Commission.

   d. _____ Because they were talking during the play, someone asked Lee and <u>she</u> to be quiet.

   e. _____ One of the sweaters slid off <u>their</u> hanger.

POST TEST

f. _____ The flock of geese spends several days at the pond behind my house before continuing <u>its</u> southern migration.

g. _____ Mario is the artist <u>who</u> painted my portrait.

h. _____ Everybody loses <u>his or her</u> way once in a while.

■ Using Modifiers Correctly

3. If the underlined modifier is correct, write *yes* on the blank; if it is incorrect, write *no.*

a. _____ Doris sneezed so <u>loudly</u> that everyone gasped.

b. _____ The ivy needs a trim <u>bad</u>; it is growing across the walkway and up the steps.

c. _____ Now that I have contact lenses, I can see small print <u>more better</u> than I could with glasses.

d. _____ <u>Understanding the need for review</u>, exercises were an important part of every class.

e. _____ I did surprisingly <u>good</u> at the audition, considering I hadn't performed for two years.

f. _____ When he was unjustly accused of lying, Jake was the <u>most angry</u> I have ever seen him.

■ Using Capital Letters and Punctuation Correctly

4. If there are no capitalization errors, write *yes* on the blank. If capitals are missing, or if capitals are used incorrectly, write the number of errors on the blank.

a. _____ At the town meeting, mayor McKelvey spoke about the city's efforts to lure Associated Electronics into the Mahoning Industrial Park.

b. _____ The Independence Day celebration at Oak Hill Park is now an annual event.

c. _____ If you travel west on Route 46, you will find Mosquito Lake.

d. _____ General Motors corporation announced plans to build its new cobalt at its plant in Lordstown, Ohio.

e. _____ Jon and Kat asked reverend Simon to marry them in Fifth Avenue Baptist Church.

5. If there are no punctuation errors, write *yes* on the blank. If punctuation is missing, or if punctuation is used incorrectly, write the number of errors on the blank.

a. _____ The congressional candidate spoke in five cities in three days, and made an appearance on two television programs.

b. _____ Awake, but tired, I managed to pull myself out of bed, stumble down the stairs, and make breakfast.

c. _____ Unaware that the street was being repaved, Tasha turned onto Market Street and found herself in slow moving dense traffic.

d. _____ Computer grammar checkers, in my opinion, are not very reliable, for they flag errors that do not exist, and fail to flag errors that do exist.

e. _____ I ordered the chicken marsala, which was tough and bland; my date ordered the prime rib, which was served cold.

f. _____ Many states require schools to administer competency tests to students; some educators object to these high stakes tests.

g. _____ Because of declining revenue, the postal service wants to eliminate Saturday deliveries; this plan worries many people.

h. _____ My favorite search engines are: Alta Vista, Google, and Yahoo.

i. _____ Two issues divide this country more than any others—gun control and abortion.

j. _____ Two issues divide this country more than any others (gun control and abortion).

k. _____ Marcus's car won't start because it has a dead battery.

l. _____ They're the ones to ask because the ladder you want to borrow is their's.

m. _____ To stimulate holiday sales, the store manager reduced all the toys' prices.

n. _____ The computer technician explained that the repair would be expensive; my machine needed it's motherboard replaced.

o. _____ "If we do not increase the sales tax," the mayor explained, "we will have a serious budget deficit in six months."

■ Eliminating Problems with Frequently Confused Words and Spelling

6. Write the correct word in the blank.

a. (your/you're) _____ the one who has lost

_____ way.

b. (to/too/two) I would like _____ go with you, but you

already have _____ many people in the car.

c. (achieved/acheived) You should be proud of what you have

_____ this term.

d. (mispent/misspent) Because I _____ my savings, I have no money for a vacation.

e. (happiness/happyness) Money does not buy _____.

CHAPTER 25

Editing for One Kind of Error

You may think editing is important only in your writing class. Although professors in your other classes may not specifically mention editing, they will expect you to find and correct your errors. In fact, they may be less tolerant of mistakes than your writing teacher, who understands that mistakes are part of learning to write. Similarly, employers, supervisors, and business colleagues will expect your e-mails, reports, memos, and other job-related writing to be error-free.

This chapter and the next one help you practice your editing skills. In this chapter, you will edit for one kind of error at a time, and in the next chapter, you will edit for multiple errors.

PRACTICE 25.1: SENTENCE FRAGMENTS

For editing strategies, see "Finding and Eliminating Sentence Fragments in Your Writing" on page 259.

1. Some of the following are correct sentences, and some are sentence fragments. On a separate sheet, edit to eliminate the fragments.

   a. Kittens are born blind and deaf. However, the vibration of their mother's purring is a physical signal. That the kittens can feel.

   b. Cats purr at a speed equal to an idling diesel engine. However, a cat's purring being far more pleasant to listen to than a diesel engine.

   c. A cat arches its back for a reason. Usually indicating that the cat feels threatened. The arch is part of the animal's body language.

   d. A cat can arch its back very high because its spine has almost sixty vertebrae that fit loosely together. Humans, on the other hand, have only thirty-four vertebrae. The difference being significant.

e. Cats can remember things for up to sixteen hours. Unlike dogs, whose memory lasts only five minutes or less. In fact, cats' memories are even better than those of monkeys and orangutans.

f. Cats also hear well. They can hear in all directions without moving their heads. This is because thirty muscles in their ears can rotate 180 degrees.

g. When cats scratch the furniture. It isn't because they are destructive. They walk on their claws. And are the only animals that do so.

h. Cats have a reputation for finickiness. However, they eat about 127,750 calories a year. In other words, approximately 28 times their body weight.

i. Only three animals walk by moving the two legs on one side of their body first. These animals are the giraffe, the camel, and the cat. All other animals walk by moving alternate legs.

j. Although most cats hate water. The Bengali Mach-Bagral cat swims to catch fish. A wild cat, this animal is found in Nepal, Burma, India, and Southern China.

2. On a separate sheet, edit to eliminate the fragments.

[1]Many animals got their names in surprising ways. [2]Consider the gorilla, for example. [3]When he was sailing along the west coast of Africa around the fifth or sixth century B.C. [4]A navigator named Hanno reported seeing something rather odd. [5]Later writing about his travels. [6]Hanno reported seeing "a tribe of hairy women." [7]He further reporting that his African guides called these women "gorillai." [8]Centuries later, historians decided that Hanno was observing from a distance, and he really saw gorillas.

[9]More than 2,000 years after Hanno navigated the coast of Africa. [10]American missionary and naturalist T. S. Savage discovered great apes in the wild. [11]Writing of his discovery in a natural history journal, Savage remembered Hanno's reference to the large, hairy women. [12]And called these creatures "gorillas."

PRACTICE 25.2 RUN-ON SENTENCES AND COMMA SPLICES

For editing strategies, see "Finding and Eliminating Run-on Sentences and Comma Splices in Your Writing" on page 269.

1. Some of the following are correct sentences, and some are run-ons or comma splices. On a separate sheet, edit to eliminate the errors.

a. If you are left-handed, you might be particularly interested in these "lefty facts"; even if you are right-handed, you will find them interesting.

b. The word *left* comes from the Latin *laevus,* which means "unlucky," in ancient Rome, however, the word "left" meant "sinister."

c. In ancient Peru, the Incas believed that being left-handed was a sign of good luck the Egyptians thought it was good luck to enter a house with the left foot first.

d. In the United States, lefties are called "southpaws" and "wrong-way drivers" in Australia, they are called "molly-dookers" and "sissy-fisted."

e. It was Charles Seymour, a sportswriter, who coined the term "southpaw" when he noticed left-handed pitchers threw from the south side of the pitcher's mound.

f. In North American sign language, a raised right hand means "powerful" and "brave," but a left hand over a right hand means "burial" and "death."

g. Left-handed brains are often musical but have trouble with language. For example, left-handed Bob Dylan wrote the music for "Blowin' " in the Wind" in fewer than five minutes; however, it took him a month to write the lyrics.

h. James Garfield, Harry Truman, Gerald Ford, George Bush, and Bill Clinton were the U.S. presidents who were left handed, Ronald Reagan was born left-handed but was forced to switch.

i. Benjamin Franklin signed the Declaration of Independence with his left hand Michelangelo used both hands to paint the Sistine Chapel.

j. Wally Schirra was the only astronaut to fly in all three space programs (Mercury, Gemini, and Apollo), he too was left-handed.

2. Edit to eliminate the run-on sentences and comma splices.

[1]If you are a baseball fan, you may have wondered about the origin of the "bullpen," which is the place where relief pitchers warm up. [2]There actually is a game called bull pen perhaps you think the name comes from that. [3]However, the term actually comes from newspaper reporters, they would write that a pitcher whose ball was hit particularly hard was "slaughtered." [4]Eventually, this led to comparing pitchers with bulls and the game with a bullfight. [5]When a pitcher was taken out of the game and another sent in, the reporters wrote, "Another bull was led to slaughter." [6]In bullfighting, a pen is kept near the arena this pen is called the "bullpen." [7]Thus, the place where relief pitchers warm up and wait to be called into the game was dubbed the bullpen.

PRACTICE 25.3 VERB FORMS

For editing strategies, see "Finding and Eliminating Verb Errors in Your Writing" on page 342.

1. Write a sentence for each verb form.

   a. the present tense of *do*

   b. the past tense of *swim*

   c. the past participle of *throw*

   d. the past tense of *think*

   e. the present tense of *understand*

   f. the past participle of *play*

   g. the past tense of *drink*

   h. the past participle of *know*

   i. the present tense of *volunteer*

   j. the past tense of *forgive*

2. Find and correct the verb form errors.

   [1]Every once in a while, newspapers print "stupid criminal" stories. [2]This one run in the Tallahassee *Democrat.* [3]A police officer in Tallahassee, Florida, been on routine patrol when he heard music blaring from a car parked at a convenience store. [4]He pulled in to tell the driver to turn the volume down. [5]Then he noticed the car be parked in a handicapped space. [6]The officer told the driver to move, but the man said he only need a minute. [7]Of course, before approaching the car, the officer has began a license check, and about this time it came back: The man had stole the car. [8]The police officer arrested the man on charges of grand theft auto, drug possession, and parking in a handicapped spot. [9]Clearly, this man had forgot that he was not a criminal mastermind.

PRACTICE 25.4 SUBJECT-VERB AGREEMENT

For editing strategies, see "Finding and Eliminating Verb Errors in Your Writing" on page 342.

1. Circle the correct verb.

   a. Either Naomi or Daniel plan/plans the annual family reunion every Thanksgiving weekend.

b. A committee of notable artists determine/determines the winner of the prestigious Duane Ricci Art Scholarship.

c. The union president and two shop stewards meet/meets with the company president this afternoon to begin contract negotiations.

d. Rico is one of those students who take/takes the most challenging classes possible.

e. Here are/is the papers you have been looking for all morning.

f. To graduate with a master's degree, each of the English majors write/writes a thesis.

g. Many believe/believes that the booming housing market is keeping the economy afloat.

h. The first thirty minutes of the movie were/was very violent.

i. One of the school board candidates want/wants to charge students to participate in extracurricular activities.

j. The surgeon general and the American Medical Association support/supports regulating herbal remedies.

2. Cross out the incorrect verbs and write the correct forms above.

[1]Animals that produce poison uses it for self-defense or to attack prey. [2]The poisons come in different toxicities. [3]Some does not kill. [4]A few of the animals produces just enough poison to stun the enemy long enough to escape. [5]For example, frogs with poisonous skin tastes unpleasant, so the predators release them. [6]One of the South American frogs have poison under the skin. [7]Indian hunters use this poison to tip their arrows. [8]For this reason, this variety of frogs are called "arrow-poison frogs."

[9]Not all poisonous animals are seriously harmful to humans. [10]However, there are a variety of ants that can give people a nasty sting. [11]The North American harvester ants are one of those animals that harms humans. [12]Living in desert regions, they feeds on grass seeds, but if they encounter people, they will bite. [13]Some kinds of scorpion has a sting so powerful that it can kill humans. [14]In addition, box jellies, which lives off the coast of Australia, is the most dangerous jellyfish. [15]Their sting kills a person in less than three minutes. [16]Anyone swimming near these sea creatures are in grave danger. [17]Perhaps the most poisonous of all spiders are the American black widow. [18]The female of the species is more dangerous than the male. [19]Its bite, which is extremely painful, sometimes causes death. [20]There is also the stonefish, which live in warm seas. [21]It

lies hidden on coral reefs. [22]If one of its spines are touched, it gives out a poison that can kill a person in a few hours.

PRACTICE 25.5 PRONOUN-ANTECEDENT AGREEMENT

For editing strategies, see "Finding and Eliminating Pronoun Errors in Your Writing" on page 373.

1. Fill in the blank with the correct pronoun.

a. Someone in the band's trumpet section needs to tune

_____ instrument.

b. At the police officers' benefit luncheon, the chief of police and the

mayor delivered _____ speeches on the same topic: the importance of handgun control.

c. Each of the nuns chose to relinquish _____ traditional habit in favor of more contemporary clothing.

d. All of the nuns chose to relinquish _____ traditional habit in favor of more contemporary clothing.

e. Because they were so dissatisfied, the store manager gave my sisters

and my mother _____ money back.

f. The flock of Canadian geese makes _____ summer home at the pond in my backyard.

g. The board of trustees reached _____ decision on new personnel policies after months of discussion.

h. Anyone who wants to tutor in the math lab should bring

_____ transcript and three recommendations to the math office by Tuesday.

i. When the teacher asked for an honest opinion, the class expressed

_____ reactions to the new textbook.

j. Antonio or his father will volunteer _____ time at the nursing home on Christmas morning.

2. Cross out the incorrect pronouns and write the correct forms above.

[1]We are accustomed to seeing women wearing earrings in their ears, and it's not unusual for a man to pierce one or both of their ears. [2]Both a man and a woman will pierce his or her ears for the same reason: decoration. [3]Pirates, however, wore earrings for a different reason. [4]Believe it or not, some people theorize that a pirate pierced their ears for health reasons.

[5]According to acupuncturists, a person has pressure points just above their earlobe which help to improve eyesight, increase energy, and reduce appetite. [6]Obviously, everybody on a long sea voyage would want his or her eyesight and energy bolstered and appetite suppressed. [7]Some of the pirates also had waxy lumps dangling from the bottom of his earrings. [8]Each of these waxy lumps had their specific purpose—to protect the pirates' hearing. [9]During exchanges of cannon fire, the pirates used the wax as their earplugs.

PRACTICE 25.6 SUBJECT, OBJECT, AND POSSESSIVE PRONOUNS

For an editing strategy, see "Finding and Eliminating Pronoun Errors in Your Writing" on page 373.

1. Circle the correct pronoun.

   a. Susan and she/her are surprising choices to star in the winter holiday musical.

   b. From the day after Thanksgiving until the week before Christmas, Gregory, Jeffrey, Denny, and I/me are volunteering to work for Habitat for Humanity.

   c. My decision worried Carlotta more than he/him.

   d. The police officers who/whom rescued the child refused to be interviewed by the media.

   e. Although he is only sixteen, Raul is already a better carpenter than either his father or they/them.

   f. Before unveiling the new city public relations campaign, the mayor showed it to we/us business leaders, who/whom helped finance the effort.

g. To who/whom should I address this letter?

h. Because of our different work schedules, Kelly and she/her were able to leave for the country several hours before Dom and we/us.

i. In my opinion, we/us cross-country runners do not get the same respect other athletes do.

j. I am dismayed that advertisers are more interested in teenage shoppers than we/us senior citizens.

2. Cross out the incorrect pronouns and write the correct forms above.

[1]I have always been fascinated by the people who developed computers and computer applications. [2]They are capable of considerably more abstract thinking than me. [3]For example, consider something as small as the computer mouse. [4]We computer users may not realize that the computer mouse was invented by Douglas Engelbart, who was a leader of Stanford Research Institute's oNLine System project. [5]Interestingly, other researchers and him thought the mouse would increase the intellect of we humans.

[6]The first mouse was a wooden box with one button. [7]People whom wanted to use it had to tilt it so that one wheel was in the air. [8]Engelbart's rather clunky wooden mouse has evolved over the years to the sleek machine that you and me now use. [9]However, the evolution continues. [10]Researchers have developed prototypes that are easier for you and me to use. [11]For example, one invention is a glove that allows users to click and move the cursor by waving their hands.

PRACTICE 25.7 MODIFIERS

For editing strategies, see "Finding and Eliminating Modifier Errors in Your Writing" on page 388.

1. Correct the errors with modifiers. One sentence is already correct.

a. As Kareem played the last notes of the concerto, he knew he had performed the difficult piece good, but he didn't know how good until the audience jumped to its feet and began clapping enthusiastically.

b. The screeching cat woke the baby trapped in the furnace room, causing him to cry very loud.

c. Paula had only forty-five seconds between scenes, so she had to make her costume change as quick as possible, and she had to do it in a dim lit hallway.

d. At 6 feet, 9 inches, Roy is the most tall member of the basketball team, but he is certainly not the most fast.

e. Of the two of you, Karen is the best singer, but you are the best dancer.

f. The pickup truck swerved dangerously close to the workers who were repairing the curbs along the east side of the street.

g. I concentrated on what the doctor was saying, but I did not understand his instructions very good.

h. Concerned about the approaching snowstorm, taking the train is safer than driving.

i. Because Grandpa needs a new battery in his hearing aid, the radio is turned up more louder than usual, and the neighbors are complaining bitterly to the landlord.

j. Dinner will be late because the roast is cooking too slow, and Dad has not started making the potatoes yet.

2. Eliminate the problems with modifiers.

[1]Because Julius Caesar wrote so extensive, historians know much about the life of a Roman soldier on the march in 60 B.C. [2]A soldier was awakened at dawn by bugles on the march. [3]His breakfast consisted of wheatcake made from grain and wine ground by the soldier himself. [4]He ate the breakfast very fastly and then took down his tent, which he shared with other soldiers. [5]He also took down the camp wall, which was made of the most sharp stakes available.

[6]Marching along in armor, the soldier's possessions were carried for a distance of about 23 miles. [7]Around midday, the soldiers stopped and ate their lunch (another wheatcake) very quick. [8]The soldier spent the afternoon building a new camp. [9]To make the camp, soldiers dug into the earth about six feet and piled up the dirt to make a wall inside the trench. [10]They stuck their stakes into the top of the wall and lashed them together good. [11]With the wall made, the soldiers could set up their own tents and eat supper (more wheatcakes and watered-down wine). [12]After eating supper, recreation was allowed. [13]However, it got dark soon after supper,

so there was little the soldiers could do except sit around the fire, exchange stories, and play dice. [14]Of course, the men had to take turns standing a four-hour watch as sentries.

PRACTICE 25.8 COMMAS

For editing strategies, see "Finding and Eliminating Capitalization and Punctuation Errors in Your Writing" on page 424.

1. Add the missing commas, and cross out the ones that do not belong. Some sentences are correct.

   a. Without using a telescope or binoculars a person can see about 3,000 stars in the night sky, but that is only true when the sky is not overcast.

   b. The biggest zipper ever made is 2,047 feet long, and has 119,007 teeth.

   c. The world's heaviest insect is the goliath beetle, which can weigh up to 4 ounces, about as much as a tennis ball.

   d. Surprisingly, garden snails have 14,157 teeth, and giraffes have tongues that are 17 inches long.

   e. Ohio State University and the University of Michigan, have a fierce long-standing rivalry. In fact it is the biggest rivalry in college athletics believe it or not.

   f. The reason I called you Carmine is to ask you to work my shift on Sunday. To return the favor, I will be happy to work for you sometime.

   g. Jonathan was offered a sales job in Tacoma Washington but he does not want to move. He is hoping to find a job in a nearby city that is, interesting challenging and well-paid.

   h. If you decide to change your major to education you will have to maintain a 3.0 grade average, and you will have to pass a proficiency test in your junior year.

   i. Professor Pontutti by all accounts is a caring creative teacher who welcomes controversy and open discussion in his classroom.

   j. Slowly, and deliberately, the elderly woman made her way across the street and she smiled at every pedestrian she passed.

2. Add the missing commas, and cross out the ones that do not belong.

   [1]Peterborough New Hampshire high school student Colin Rizzio was taking the SAT exam in October, 1997. [2]He noticed something unusual about an algebra problem. [3]He copied the problem down, and showed it

to his math teacher the next week. ⁴As Rizzio suspected the teacher confirmed that there was a flaw in the problem, and he advised Rizzo to report it to the Educational Testing Service which is the organization that develops and administers the test. ⁵Five months later Rizzio found out he was right and history was made. ⁶He had found the first defective question on the SAT in fourteen years.

⁷As a result of Rizzio's discovery the scores of more than 45,000 students were increased. ⁸Most were increased by ten points but some were increased by twenty or thirty points. ⁹Rizzio was interviewed for many newspapers and appeared on *Good Morning America, CBS Morning News* and *Today.* ¹⁰"I'm glad I did it" Rizzo said. ¹¹"I didn't think it would be this big."

PRACTICE 25.9 SEMICOLONS

For editing strategies, see "Finding and Eliminating Capitalization and Punctuation Errors in Your Writing" on page 424.

1. Add the missing semicolons, and cross out the ones that do not belong. If appropriate, replace unnecessary semicolons with commas, and replace unnecessary commas with semicolons. Some sentences are correct.

   a. The giant stegosaurus was as long as a school bus, yet its brain was very small.

   b. The triceratops had three horns on its head, two of the horns were over three feet long; which helped to scare off attackers.

   c. The brachiosaurus was the heaviest dinosaur; it weighed as much as twenty elephants.

   d. The Federal Reserve cut interest rates by half a point however, many analysts fear the cut will not be enough to stimulate the economy.

   e. Although they are more expensive; organic fruits and vegetables are becoming increasingly popular.

   f. The reason for the increased popularity is the belief that organic food is both healthier and tastier.

   g. This year's fine and performing arts scholarships were awarded to Mina Jaffee, who plans to study voice at Baldwin-Wallace College, Eleni Petrakis, who plans to study violin at Oberlin College, and David Coolidge, who plans to study painting at Youngstown State University.

h. In 1948, American scientists Walter Brattain, John Bardeen, and William Shockley invented the transistor nevertheless, it was the Japanese who used the invention to revolutionize radio.

i. The forerunner of the modern computer was invented in 1835 by English mathematician Charles Babbage; his machine used punch cards borrowed from a weaving machine.

j. Because he was impressed that hole-punched cards in weaving machines could be used to give instructions; Babbage adapted the idea to handle math problems and remember information.

2. Add the missing semicolons, and cross out the ones that do not belong. If appropriate, replace unnecessary semicolons with commas, and replace unnecessary commas with semicolons.

[1]The now extinct mammoth roamed the earth until as recently as 10,000 years ago. [2]The mammoth was 12 feet high, it could weigh as much as 14,450 pounds. [3]Slightly larger than today's elephants, but with far longer tusks—up to 16 feet long—mammoths survived arctic temperatures thanks to extra fat stores and hairy coats. [4]Although you might guess otherwise because of their size; mammoths were plant-eaters. [5]Their teeth became well-worn from chewing stringy plants; in fact, mammoths' teeth were almost identical to those of today's elephants. [6]Mammoths living farthest north had a more difficult time finding plants to feed on; primarily because of the frozen ground of the arctic region. [7]Their fat, which was especially thick around the shoulders, was used as an emergency store of food.

[8]Because of the enormous size of the full-grown mammoth; only the most fearless creatures attacked it; and that included saber-toothed tigers and humans. [9]Saber-toothed tigers primarily attacked mammoth young however, humans hunted full-grown mammoths with spears and axes, putting the carcasses to a variety of uses. [10]First they would use the flesh, which was a good food source, then they would use the hide which made excellent clothing, finally they would use the bones and tusks, which were building materials for huts.

PRACTICE 25.10 APOSTROPHES

For an editing strategy, see "Finding and Eliminating Capitalization and Punctuation Errors in Your Writing" on page 342.

1. Correct the sentences by doing the following, as needed: Add an apostrophe, add an apostrophe and an *s,* eliminate incorrect apostrophes, or move incorrectly placed apostrophes.

   a. Nearly one-third of the Earths land is covered by deserts.

   b. The submarine was invented over 250 years' ago by Cornelius van Drebbel.

   c. The mens' basketball team has'nt won a regional championship for five years, but they're confident that under Coach Harris' leadership they'll win one this year.

   d. Everyones answer on the third test question was wrong, so Professor Solomonson promised to consider dropping the question from his' test.

   e. My father-in-law's decision to move into an assisted living facility surprised everyone, but its his decision to make.

   f. Tim and Phyllis's apartments have each been sublet for the fall term, so if they return early, they'll each have to find a place to stay.

   g. William Butler Yeats's poetry is difficult but rewarding.

   h. The teachers union has decided to accept the school boards offer, but teachers are not happy with their current negotiating team's eagerness to strike over health care benefit's.

   i. The three students frequent absence is the reason they are not doing well in Professor Marks course.

   j. Now is'nt the time to tell Juan that he cant borrow the Smith's car next weekend.

2. Correct the sentences by doing the following, as needed: Add an apostrophe, add an apostrophe and an *s,* eliminate incorrect apostrophes, or move incorrectly placed apostrophes.

   [1]When the people of Texas severed ties with Mexico, the Mexican government sent in 4,000 troops under General Santa Anas direction. [2]As the Mexican army approached, 150 men who were determined to defend the city of San Antonio retreated to the Alamo, one of Spains missions built in the previous century. [3]They were joined by fifty other men, but they werent any match for the superior numbers. [4]After a thirteen-day siege, all the Texans died.

   [5]When General Sam Houston assembled his forces', he set out to face the Mexican army to secure independence. [6]Houstons' rallying cry— indeed, Texans rallying cry—in the war for independence from Mexico

was "Remember the Alamo." [7]The Mexican's defeat at Houston's hands was quick and decisive. [8]Texas gained its independence.

[9]From 1846 to 1848, Mexico and the United States fought a war over the Texas boundary. [10]The war ended with the Senates ratification of the Treaty of Guadalupe Hidalgo, and Mexicos loss of half of it's territory. [11]Thats how New Mexico and California fell within this countrys borders.

CHAPTER 26
Editing for Multiple Kinds of Errors

Because the practice exercises in this chapter require you to edit paragraphs to correct more than one kind of error, they are more like editing your own papers than the exercises in the previous chapter.

PRACTICE 26.1 TRANSITIONS, COORDINATION, SUBORDINATION, AND PARALLELISM

The following paragraph is choppy, it lacks transitions, and it has an error in parallelism. On a separate sheet, rewrite the paragraph so it includes transitions, coordination, subordination, and appropriate parallelism.

[1]A catcher-outfielder named Michael Joseph "King" Kelly was one of the most popular baseball players of the 1880s. [2]Kelly played for Cincinnati, Chicago, New York, and he also played for Boston. [3]He was a good hitter and a great base runner. [4]Kelly was an alert ballplayer. [5]He was always looking for a way to get an advantage over the other team. [6]He was sitting on the bench one day. [7]An opposing batter hit a high foul ball. [8]None of Kelly's teammates would be able to catch the ball. [9]Kelly leaped off the bench. [10]He went after the ball. [11]He was shouting to the umpire at the same time, "Kelly now catching!" [12]Kelly caught the ball. [13]The umpire refused to allow the catch. [14]Kelly insisted the catch was not against the rules. [15]The rules allowed substitutions at any time. [16]The umpire still would not call the batter out. [17]Kelly was right. [18]A new rule was written into the rule book that winter. [19]The new rule said that a player could not enter the game while the ball is in play.

PRACTICE 26.2 SENTENCE FRAGMENTS, RUN-ON SENTENCES, AND COMMA SPLICES

Edit the paragraph to eliminate five sentence fragments, one run-on sentence, and three comma splices.

[1]Although most colleges and universities are on a semester system. [2]Many schools favor an academic year divided into quarters. [3]And with good reason. [4]The quarter system offers students more flexibility. [5]They have an opportunity to take more classes they change their schedules three times a year, four with summer school. [6]Therefore, students can sample a greater variety of courses and instructors. [7]Students who have trouble deciding on a major appreciate this variety, it provides them exposure to more courses. [8]Thus helping them make up their minds. [9]Also, students who find themselves in courses they do not like need only endure a ten or eleven week quarter, not a fifteen or sixteen week semester. [10]Another advantage of quarters being that they often do not begin until after Labor Day. [11]This fact means students have a more traditional summer break. [12]One criticism of the quarter system is that it goes too fast, thus, students cannot take the time they need to learn many subjects. [13]Quarters do progress quickly, but students adjust to the pace and learn efficient study habits. [14]Nonetheless, the semester system is likely to remain the dominant pattern. [15]It is cheaper to administer, there are only three registrations a year, rather than the four registrations that occur with the quarter system. [16]Colleges always looking for ways to save money.

PRACTICE 26.3 SUBJECT-VERB AGREEMENT, TENSE SHIFTS, AND VERB FORMS

The following paragraph has six subject-verb agreement errors, four tense shifts, and one incorrect verb form. Cross out the incorrect verbs and write the correct ones above the line.

[1]Either elaborate rituals or simple copulation mark the courtship of spiders. [2]Some crab spiders, for example, showed almost no

courtship behaviors other than actual copulation. [3]Others wrap the female in silk threads. [4]The threads does not immobilize the female but communicate the intentions of the male. [5]Then there is wolf spiders. [6]When a female wolf spider passes a male, the male begins a series of exhausting courtship behaviors. [7]These included crouching, foreleg extension and waving, drumming, and abdominal vibrations. [8]Similarly, jumping male spiders used visual signals to communicate with females. [9]Although some lifts a leg or two, others perform a complex dance to attract the female. [10]If one of the females are receptive, she assumes a crouching posture. [11]The male then extends his forelegs, touches the female, and climbs on her back to begin copulation. [12]Because the webs of a spider is used for prey capture, it is essential that males who are courting web spinners vibrate the female's web in a way that is distinct from the vibrations of a trapped insect. [13]One group of male spiders approaches the female only after she has eaten and thus is unlikely to gobble up a suitor. [14]Despite his best efforts, however, the male spider often be in big trouble. [15]In certain species, the females, which are commonly larger than the males, kill and eat the male after mating. [16]Although this fate is not always what occurred, most males live only long enough to mate once or twice before they die.

PRACTICE 26.4 SUBJECT-VERB AGREEMENT AND PRONOUN-ANTECEDENT AGREEMENT

The following paragraph has eight errors with subject-verb agreement and six errors with pronoun-antecedent agreement. Cross out the incorrect verbs and pronouns and write the correct forms above the line.

[1]Computer technology makes life more convenient for students. [2]Any student who can take advantage of e-mail, the Internet, and word processing programs will find that their productivity is increased and that their time is used efficiently. [3]For example, instead of spending hours in the library looking for books and articles, students is using

the Internet for research. [4]At some schools, a class of students receive questions via the Internet and debate the answers with students at other schools. [5]At other schools, a cluster of courses are offered online, and students can take these courses with his or her peers from other institutions, even ones out of the country. [6]Another one of the electronic conveniences are e-mail, which makes it possible for a student to communicate with their instructor, friends, and family quickly, easily, and cheaply. [7]Anyone who want to check their grades, ask a professor a question, register, or find out what is happening on campus can do so with e-mail. [8]Both students and professors benefits from this technology. [9]Finally, word processing allows every student to turn their paper into a professional-looking piece in record time. [10]It also allow for efficient editing, saving of manuscript, and collaboration. [11]Yes, technology is not without its problems, but on college campuses, it sure makes life easier.

PRACTICE 26.5 TENSE SHIFT AND PERSON SHIFT

The following paragraph has four inappropriate tense shifts and four person shifts. Cross out the incorrect verbs and pronouns and write the corrections above the line.

[1]The productivity of the land of medieval Europe was limited by inadequate technology. [2]The farmers of this land were so poorly equipped that you cannot efficiently cultivate and harvest your crops. [3]Almost all agricultural tools were made of wood, a weak and impractical material for use on the thick European soil. [4]These tools were so limiting that much work is invariably accomplished with bare hands, a technique that caused the soil to lose fertility. [5]As a result, you have to rest large portions of land for entire growing seasons, a fact that decreased the output of your farm. [6]The lack of technology and equipment allowed the unpredictable weather to wreak havoc on farm productivity. [7]Without advanced drainage systems, fields are flooded during an excessively wet season. [8]Similarly, without irrigation technology, fields were dried up by droughts. [9]Because of

the lack of advanced technology, medieval Europe often suffered severe food shortages.

PRACTICE 26.6 FORMS OF ADJECTIVES, ADVERBS, AND DANGLING MODIFIERS

The following paragraph contains seven errors with forms of adjectives and adverbs, and two with dangling modifiers. Cross out the errors and make corrections above the line.

[1]Some people are just natural funny. [2]They manage to find humor in even the most commonest situations. [3]My friend Peggy, for example, is one of the most funniest people I know. [4]In fact, she has been funny for as long as I have known her good. [5]I remember all the way back to junior high school when Peggy got up to sharpen her pencil. [6]Wearing her pencil down in math class, the pencil sharpener located in the closet on the wall was needed. [7]Peggy walked to the closet, and some perverse impulse must have taken over because she entered the closet, closed the door behind her, and stayed there for the rest of class. [8]Wondering if she was missed, the door was cracked from time to time and she peeked out. [9]No one, apparently, noticed but me. [10]It was all I could do to keep from falling on the floor laughing hysterical. [11]When the bell sounded, Peggy just walked out of the closet casual and headed for her next class, sharpened pencil in hand. [12]Of all of the stunts Peggy has pulled, that is one of the memorablest.

PRACTICE 26.7 COMMAS AND CAPITAL LETTERS

The following paragraph has seventeen comma errors as a result of missing or misplaced commas. It also has eight errors in capitalization as a result of missing or incorrect capitals. Make the necessary corrections directly on the page.

[1]The Toll House cookie an american favorite has an interesting origin. [2]In 1930 Ruth Wakefield and her husband bought the Toll House inn which was located in whiteman Massachusetts. [3]While she was making a batch of brown sugar dough for her butter cookies Ruth cut

a chocolate bar into chunks mixed the chunks in and hoped the chunks would melt during baking to create chocolate cookies. [4]That did not happen. [5]Instead the chocolate did soften slightly and history was made: the chocolate chip cookie was born. [6]When she served these surprise creations the response was to say the least enthusiastic. [7]Pleased with her success Ruth named the cookies after her Inn. [8]Subsequently the nestle company bought the toll house name, and developed the little chocolate chip. [9]If nothing else this story reminds us that sometimes, the best discoveries are the result of happy accidents.

PRACTICE 26.8 ALL PUNCTUATION

Using everything you have learned about commas, semicolons, dashes, parentheses, colons, apostrophes, and quotation marks, add missing punctuation and cross out incorrect punctuation in the following paragraph.

[1]You probably know that Benjamin Franklin was a statesman publisher and public servant. [2]Did you know that as an inventor and scientist Franklin had few equals. [3]First Franklin and his kite showed the world that lightning is actually electricity then he invented the lightning rod which saved many buildings from fires caused by lightning. [4]His Franklin stove gave more heat than other stoves and used much less fuel. [5]Also Franklins bifocal lenses were invented for both reading and distance use. [6]One of Franklins discoveries was of particular importance the discovery that disease flourishes in poorly ventilated rooms. [7]In addition Franklin showed Americans how to improve acid soil by using lime something vitally important to a society dependent upon farming. [8]Interestingly Franklin refused to patent any of his inventions, or use them for profit he preferred to have them used freely for the benefit of society. [9]As a result of his' discoveries and generosity Franklin was elected to membership in the Royal Society of London a rare honor for someone living in the colonies. [10]The great English statesman William Pitt said, "Franklin is an honor to the English nation and to human nature."

PRACTICE 26.9 RANGE OF ERRORS

The following paragraph contains:

1 incorrect verb form	1 run-on sentence
2 errors in subject-verb agreement	1 comma splice
1 error in pronoun-antecedent agreement	4 comma errors
1 sentence fragment	1 dangling modifier
2 errors in parallelism	2 errors in capitalization

Edit directly on the page to correct the errors. In some cases, more than one correction is possible.

[1]Thunderstorms be most likely to happen in the spring and summer months and during the afternoon and evening hours, however, they can occur year-round and at all hours. [2]Along the gulf coast and across the southeastern and western United States, most thunderstorms occurring during the afternoon. [3]In the Plains states, thunderstorms frequently occurs in the late afternoon and at night. [4]Occasionally thunder and lightning accompanies snow or freezing rain. [5]For example lightning resulted in power outages near Washington D.C. during the blizzard of 1993. [6]A person should never take a thunderstorm lightly, for they are at risk from lightning, flooding, and tornadoes can pose a threat. [7]People who are outdoors, in or on water, and people on or near hilltops are at risk from lightning associated with thunderstorms. [8]During heavy thunderstorms, people in cars are at risk from flash flooding also people in mobile homes are at risk from tornadoes. [9]When learning of an approaching thunderstorm, reasonable caution should be exercised.

PRACTICE 26.10 RANGE OF ERRORS

The passage below contains:

1 semicolon error	1 frequently confused word
3 errors in sets of quotation marks	3 spelling errors

6 errors in capitalization	3 apostrophe errors
2 comma errors	1 comma splice
1 error in end punctuation	1 sentence fragment
2 errors in subject-verb agreement	1 incorrect verb form

Editing directly on the page, correct the errors. In some cases, more than one correction is possible.

[1]When someone sneezes; do you say god bless you. [2]You probably do but may not no why. [3]One explanation relates to superstition. [4]It is said that early people beliefed that a persons spirit existed in the form of breath contained in the head, thus a sneeze might acidentally expel it. [5]Saying god bless you was an appeal to god not to let the spirit escape.

[6]On the other hand, there is some experts who claim the custom isnt based on superstition. [7]They beleive it started during a great plague that took place in anceint athens. [8]A sneeze being the first sign that a person had became ill. [9]Saying god bless you meant asking for gods blessing for someone who were going to die.

PRACTICE 26.11 RANGE OF ERRORS

The following passage contains:

1 spelling error	1 unstated antecedent
1 semicolon error	1 frequently confused word
4 comma errors	1 sentence fragment
3 errors with apostrophes	1 incorrect modifier form
2 tense shifts	1 comma splice
1 incorrect noun form	5 errors in capitalization

Editing directly on the page, correct the errors. In some cases, more than one correction is possible.

[1]Susan B. Anthony who was born in 1820 and died in 1906 was an american pioneer of womens rights. [2]The daughter of a quaker abolitionist she became a teacher after being educated in New York. [3]Disatisfaction with it caused her to except the position of assistant

manager of the family farm in upstate New York. [4]Here she being exposed to the strong held views of such men as William Lloyd Garrison and Frederick Douglass. [5]As a result, she becomes an advocate of reform. [6]Her early efforts in this area failed, she was not taken seriously because she was a women. [7]Eventually, she teamed up with Elizabeth Cady Stanton and together they found the American equal rights association to work for womens' suffrage. [8]For the remainder of her life; she was devoted to this cause. [9]As a result of her tireless work and ceasless travel, womens' suffrage became a recognized cause in both America and Europe.

CHAPTER 27

Writing in Response to Reading

A a college student, you read a great deal, including textbooks, library materials, Web pages, novels, supplemental books, and assigned articles. Interestingly, that reading can help you improve your writing. If you pay attention to the characteristics of what you read, noting how other writers develop details, use words, write openings and closings, create transitions, and craft sentences, you can learn strategies to try in your own writing.

The focus of this chapter is on reading because reading is an important part of college life and because reading improves writing. Also, much of your college writing will be in response to reading material, so this chapter takes up writing in response to reading. First you will learn a procedure for reading, and then you will have an opportunity to put the process into action. Finally, you will read sample essays written in the patterns you learned when you studied paragraphs. With these samples, you can see how the patterns are used for essays, and you can practice your reading skills.

ACTIVE READING

When you read for your own enjoyment, all that matters is that you have a good time. You can skip a paragraph or fail to understand a word or read with the television on—as long as you are enjoying yourself. However, when you read for your college classes, more is expected of you. You must read attentively for full comprehension. To do this, you must follow a reading procedure different from the one you follow when you read for pleasure alone; you must follow a process called **active reading.**

Active reading gets you involved. It helps you to understand what you read and form judgments about the material by answering the questions in the following box.

Questions an Active Reader Asks

1. What is the author's thesis (central point)?
2. What main ideas support the thesis?
3. Is the support for the thesis adequate and convincing?
4. Is the author expressing facts, opinions, or both?
5. What is the author's tone or attitude (serious, sarcastic, preachy, humorous, angry, insulting, etc.)?
6. What is the author's purpose (to share, inform, entertain, and/or persuade)?
7. Who is the author's intended audience?
8. What is the source of the author's detail (observation, personal experience, research, and/or reasoning)?

To be an active reader, you must do more than let the words sound in your ears. You must become actively involved by focusing on what you are reading. The steps described in the following pages will show you how to do this.

Step 1: Surveying

Survey your reading material to get an idea of what to expect. First check the title. What does it suggest the reading will be about? Who is the author? Have you read anything by this person before? If so, what can you expect based on your past experience? Has your instructor said anything about this material? If so, what can you expect based on these comments?

Now look through the material. Are there headings, boldface type, italics, lists, or pictures with captions? If so, what do these suggest you can expect from the reading?

Now read the opening and closing paragraphs quickly. What clues do these provide to content and the writer's purpose? Read the first sentence of each paragraph. What clues to content do these provide?

Once you have surveyed the material, you will have a sense of what to expect when you read. You will probably know what the writer's general subject is and whether the author is expressing feelings, explaining something, or trying to convince you of something. Just as important, you will form some questions about the reading. When you are through surveying and move on to reading, you should look for the answers to your survey questions.

Step 2: Reading without Interruption

Read the material quickly but attentively. If you encounter a word you do not understand, circle it to check later; if you do not understand a passage, place a question mark next to it. The important thing is to keep going, getting as much as you can without laboring over anything. As you read, try to determine the writer's thesis.

After this reading, answer as many of the active-reader questions as you can. Then look up every word you circled and write the meanings in the margin near the circled word. Now take a break if you need one.

Step 3: Reading and Studying

Pick up your pen and read again. This time underline the author's thesis (if it is stated) and the main ideas to support the thesis (often found in topic sentences). Do not underline too much—just go for the thesis and main points. As you read, use your pen to write your reactions in the margins. Record your observations (even personal ones like "This makes me think of Chris"); note strong agreement or disagreement ("how true" or "absolutely not"); indicate where more detail is needed ("This isn't proven."). In addition, put stars next to passages you particularly like and question marks next to parts you do not understand. (See page 490 for an example of how to mark an essay.) After this reading, return to the active-reading questions and answer the ones that remain.

If the material is long or difficult, take a break and then read it one more time, again using your pen to record your observations and underline main points. If you are unable after this reading to answer all the questions an active reader asks, or if there is anything you do not understand, write your questions down and ask your teacher.

FAQ

Q: I don't read very fast. Is that a problem?

A: Do not confuse active reading with speed-reading. Speed is not the issue. Your goal is to understand the form and content of what you read and to make judgments about its truth and effectiveness.

Step 4: Testing Yourself

Close the book after your studied reading and write a brief summary of the material. Or recite a summary to yourself or to another person. This testing helps lock the main points in your memory.

A Sample Active Reading

The following essay has been marked the way an active reader might mark it. After the essay are the answers to the questions an active reader asks. Studying this material will help you appreciate how an active reader interacts with a text.

Students in Shock

John Kellmayer

In the following essay, the author explains that colleges are becoming increasingly aware of the pressures students face, and they are trying to help students manage their stress. As you read the essay and notice the active reading comments, think about how *you* would mark the text.

1   If you feel overwhelmed by your college experiences, you are not alone—many of today's college students are suffering from a form of shock. <u>Going to college has always had its ups and downs, but today the "downs" of the col-</u>*thesis* <u>lege experience are more numerous and difficult, a fact that the schools are responding to with increased support services.</u>

2   Lisa is a good example of a student in shock. She is an attractive, intelligent twenty-year-old college junior at a state university. Having been a straight-A student in high school and a member of the basketball and softball teams there, she remembers her high school days with fondness. Lisa was popular then and had a steady boyfriend for the last two years of school.

3   Now, only three years later, Lisa is miserable. She has changed her major
good, realistic examples four times already and is forced to hold down two part-time jobs in order to pay her tuition. She suffers from sleeping and eating disorders and believes she has no close friends. Sometimes she bursts out crying for no apparent reason. On more than one occasion, she has considered taking her life.

4   Dan, too, suffers from student shock. He is nineteen and a freshman at a local community college. He began college as an accounting major but hated that field. So he switched to computer programming because he heard the job prospects were excellent in that area. Unfortunately, he discovered that he had little aptitude for programming and changed majors again, this time to psychology. He likes psychology but has heard horror stories about the difficulty
Howie is like Dan. of finding a job in that field without a graduate degree. Now he's considering switching majors again. To help pay for school, Dan works nights and weekends as a sales clerk at Kmart. He doesn't get along with his boss, but since he needs the money, Dan feels he has no choice except to stay on the job. A few months ago, his girlfriend of a year and a half broke up with him.

Source: Reprinted with permission of Townsend Press.

Not surprisingly, Dan has started to suffer from depression and migraine   5
headaches. He believes that in spite of all his hard work, he just isn't getting
anywhere. He can't remember ever being this unhappy. A few times he con-
sidered talking to somebody in the college psychological counseling center.   *Common reaction to*
He rejected that idea, though, because he doesn't want people to think there's   *idea of counseling*
something wrong with him.

What is happening to Lisa and Dan happens to millions of college stu-   6   *A frightening statistic.*
dents each year. <u>As a result, roughly one-quarter of the student population at</u>   *How was it learned?*
<u>any time will suffer from symptoms of depression.</u> Of that group, almost half
will experience depression intense enough to ⬭warrant⬭ professional help. At   *call for*
schools across the country, psychological counselors are booked up months
in advance. Stress-related problems such as anxiety, migraine headaches,   *an eating disorder*
insomnia, ⬭anorexia⬭ and ⬭bulimia⬭ are epidemic on college campuses.   *involving starvation*

Suicide rates and ⬭self-inflicted⬭ injuries among college students are higher   7   *an eating disorder*
now than at any other time in history. The suicide rate among college youth is   *involving binge eating*
fifty percent higher than among nonstudents of the same age. It is estimated   *followed by forced*
that each year more than five hundred college students take their own lives.   *vomiting*

College health officials believe that these reported problems represent   8
only the tip of the iceberg. They fear that most students, like Lisa and Dan, suf-   *caused by one's self*
fer in silence.

There are three reasons today's college students are suffering more than   9
in earlier generations. First is a weakening support structure. The transition   *Why blame families for*
from high school to college has been difficult, but in the past there was more   *problems schools*
family support to help get through it. Today, with divorce rates at a historical   *create?*
high and many parents experiencing their own psychological difficulties, the
traditional family is not always available for guidance and support. And when
students who do not find ⬭stability⬭ at home are bombarded with numerous new   *permanence*
and stressful experiences, the results can be devastating.

Another problem college students face is financial pressure. In the last   10
decade tuition costs have skyrocketed—up about sixty-six percent and ninety   *I know several people*
percent at private schools. For students living away from home, costs range   *who had to drop out*
from five thousand dollars to as much as twelve thousand a year and more.   *because of lack of*
And at the same time that tuition costs have been rising dramatically, there   *money.*
has been a cutback in federal aid to students. College loans are now much
harder to obtain and are available only at near-market interest rates. Consequently, most college students must work at least part-time. And for some students, the pressure to do well in school while holding down a job is too much
to handle.

A final cause of student shock is the large selection of majors available.   11
Because of the magnitude and difficulty of choosing a major, college can prove   *This school does a*
a time of great indecision. Many students switch majors, some a number of   *terrible job of advising*
times. As a result, it is becoming commonplace to take five or six years to get   *on majors and careers.*
a degree. It can be depressing to students not only to have taken courses that
don't count towards a degree but also to be faced with the added tuition costs.
In some cases these costs become so high that they force students to drop
out of college.

12   While there is no magic cure-all for student shock, colleges have begun
to recognize the problem and are trying in a number of ways to help students
cope with the pressures they face. First of all, many colleges are upgrading
their psychological counseling centers to handle the greater demand for services. Additional staff is being hired, and experts are doing research to learn
more about the psychological problems of college students. Some schools
even advertise these services in student newspapers and on campus radio
stations. Also, upperclassmen are being trained as peer counselors. These

*This school could use
better RAs in the
dorms.*

peer counselors may be able to act as a first line of defense in the battle for
students' well-being by spotting and helping to solve problems before they
become too big for students to handle.

13   In addition, stress-management workshops have become common on college campuses. At these workshops, instructors teach students various techniques for dealing with stress, including biofeedback, meditation, and exercise.

*Technique for
monitoring & controlling
body functions*

14   Finally, many schools are improving their vocational counseling services.
By giving students more relevant information about possible majors and career
choices, colleges can lessen the anxiety and indecision often associated with
choosing a major.

15   If you ever feel that you're in shock, remember that your experience is not
unique. Try to put things in perspective. Certainly, the end of a romance or an
exam is not an event to look forward to. But realize that rejection and failure
happen to everyone sooner or later. And don't be reluctant to talk to somebody
about your problems. The useful services available on campus won't help you
if you don't take advantage of them.

*What about
unreasonable profs &
difficult classes as
causes of shock?*

ANSWERS TO ACTIVE-READER QUESTIONS FOR "STUDENTS IN SHOCK"

1. **What is the author's thesis?**

   *"Going to college has always had its ups and downs, but today the 'downs'
   of the college experience are more numerous and difficult, a fact that the
   schools are responding to with increased support services."*

2. **What main ideas support the thesis?**

   *About a quarter of the student population will experience depression; half
   of that group will need professional help.*

   *Stress-related problems are epidemic. Suicide and self-inflicted injuries
   are at an all-time high.*

   One cause of the student shock is decreased family support.

   *A second cause is financial pressure as a result of higher tuition and less
   financial aid.*

   A third cause is difficulty choosing a major.

Colleges are addressing the problem of shock by upgrading counseling services, offering stress-management workshops, and improving vocational counseling.

3. **Is the support for the thesis adequate and convincing?**

The opening examples are well detailed and convince me that shock is a problem, but I think the reasons for the shock given are sketchy and incomplete.

Other causes exist, such as difficult classes, unreasonable professors, and unprepared students. I'd also like to know where the author got his information. That would make the piece more convincing.

4. **Is the author expressing facts, opinions, or both?**

both

5. **What is the author's tone or attitude (serious, sarcastic, preachy, humorous, angry, insulting, etc.)?**

The author seems serious, concerned, and objective.

6. **What is the author's purpose (to share, to inform, to entertain, and/or to persuade)?**

The author wants to inform the reader about the problem of student shock and explain how the problem is being addressed. He seems to do this to help students who suffer from shock.

7. **Who is the author's intended audience?**

The you in the last paragraph indicates that the author is addressing students.

8. **What is the source of the author's detail (observation, personal experience, research, and/or reasoning)?**

The author must have done some research to learn about the extent of the problem and what colleges are doing. It's hard to know if any personal experience or observation was involved.

NARRATION

Did I Save Lives or Engage in Racial Profiling?

Lori Hope

When the author traveling on an airplane with her son became suspicious of a man who appeared to be Middle Eastern, she wrestled with whether to report her suspicions or keep quiet. As you read this 2002 essay from *Newsweek*'s "My Turn" column, ask yourself what you would do in a similar situation—and why.

Like most narratives, "Did I Save Lives or Engage in Racial Profiling?" answers these questions: What happened? Who was involved? When did it happen? Where did it happen? Why did it happen? How did it happen? Pay attention to the answers to these questions and decide which ones are emphasized most.

You will notice that the thesis comes at the end of the essay, rather than the beginning. You will also notice that some paragraphs lack topic sentences. Often, topic sentences are not needed when the narration's time sequence provides a sufficient organizational framework.

Before reading the essay, review the following vocabulary:

racial profiling—singling out people because of their ethnicity; in the essay, racial profiling refers to identifying males who look Middle Eastern as possible terrorists

Richard Reid—called the "shoe bomber" because in 2001 on a flight from Paris to Miami, he tried to light an explosive devise hidden in his shoe

avowed—confirmed, publicly stated

reeled—to be in a whirl or go round and round

jettisoned—thrown off

1   Half a lifetime ago, I read a magazine essay that took deep root within me, and still sprouts whenever I find myself tempted to react to someone based on skin color. The author, an African-American, described what it was like to see people cross the street when he walked toward them on a sidewalk.

Source: From *Newsweek*, April 1, 2003. All rights reserved. Reprinted by permission.

When racial profiling became an issue in the war against terrorism, I—an avowed liberal—found myself wondering what I would do if I saw someone who appeared to be of Middle Eastern descent behaving in a way that could be considered "suspicious." A few months ago I stopped wondering.   2

A plane my 16-year-old son and I were scheduled to board was swapped with another because of mechanical problems. Although I was relieved to know we were boarding an aircraft that checked out, I still felt uneasy about flying because of the "shoe bomber" incident three days earlier. I hadn't noticed security checking anyone's shoes.   3

Once settled into the aisle seat, with my son next to the window, I learned there could be another delay because of weather. Before opening my novel I noticed a man in the exit row two seats ahead, looking toward the rear of the plane. He was olive-skinned, black-haired and clean-shaven, with a blanket covering his legs and feet. I thought that was strange, because I felt so warm. No one else was using a blanket.   4

Nine-C, as I called him, sat motionless for 10 minutes, except for glancing nervously down the aisle every few minutes. Then his leg started to shake, and he seemed to be reaching for something under his blanket. He bent over. Adrenaline coursed through my body. I sensed something horrible. The plane was still on the ground, but I felt airsick.   5

"You're being ridiculous," I told myself. "Nine-C just wants to get home. He's cold; he has to use the bathroom. Just relax and keep your water bottle handy, in case he lights a match."   6

But he was very big, and the people sitting near him were not. And I wondered, "What if he goes to the bathroom to light his bomb?" Then I looked at my son—I thought of his potential, his brilliance as a musician and mathematician. How could I tell if 9-C was a terrorist? I couldn't.   7

I forced myself to walk to the rear of the plane. "What should a passenger do if she sees someone behaving in a way she considers odd?" I asked the flight attendant.   8

"Tell me about it."   9

"I'm probably just being paranoid," I started, and described what I'd seen. When I got back to my seat, I tried to forget my suspicions, having turned them over to an expert. A few minutes later, a flight attendant asked the passengers in row nine how they were doing. Another attendant came down the aisle, looking carefully at both sides.   10

"We need to de-ice the wings," announced the captain, apologizing for yet another delay. He emerged from the cockpit, walked back to 9-C's row and looked out to examine the wings. The other pilot did the same.   11

Soon afterward, we learned we were returning to the gate because of "another minor mechanical problem." Absorbed in my book, I hardly paid attention. When I looked up a chapter later, I saw that 9-C was gone. Was he in the bathroom?   12

We took off, and once at cruising altitude, I walked to the rear to see if he'd changed seats. But he was nowhere. I asked the flight attendant where he was. "We don't know what happens once security gets them. After the shoe-bomber, we're glad to get rid of anyone suspicious."   13

14   I felt awful. I didn't mean for 9-C to be taken away. I had probably ruined an innocent traveler's day, not to mention delaying an already late flight. And I hadn't even noticed he'd gone. I vowed not to scare my son; I'd keep the story to myself.

15   But I couldn't. The head flight attendant asked me to come to the front of the plane. My heart pounded and my cheeks burned; I felt ashamed and afraid. "Thank you for alerting us to that man," he said, smiling. "We all observed him, including our pilots. He seemed depressed, but also very nervous. Security did a background check and decided to question him. If he's OK, we'll compensate him. You did the right thing. Once we're in the air, it's too late."

16   We were moved to first class, and I wrote an incident report. Later, while waiting for our luggage, I reeled with questions: Had other passengers wondered about 9-C? Where was he now? Would I ever know whether he was a danger? Most important, had I become a racial profiler, bulldozing the roots of that powerful essay that had shaped me in my youth?

17   Perhaps I had. But I'm not sure I regret it. I can live with the guilt, grief and anger. Even though I lost a part of myself and may have gotten an innocent man jettisoned from the plane, it's not the same world it was half a lifetime ago.

STUDY QUESTIONS

1. The best statement of the thesis comes at the end of the essay. In your own words, write out that thesis. Why does it come at the end of the essay?

2. What purpose does the dialogue in paragraphs 6 and 7 serve? In paragraphs 8–10, 11, 13, and 15?

3. Which of the who? what? when? where? why? how? questions does Hope answer in the most detail? Why does she use so much detail? Which does she answer in the least detail? Why does she use so little detail?

4. Which paragraphs open with transitions that show chronological order?

5. **Other Patterns** In addition to narration, what other writing patterns did you notice? What description appears in paragraphs 4 and 5? What purpose does that description serve? How is cause-and-effect analysis part of the essay?

WRITING TOPICS

1. Narrate an account of a time you were suspicious of someone. Explain what you did and whether you now believe you did the right thing.

2. Narrate an account of a time someone was suspicious of you. Explain what happened and why you think it happened.

3. Tell a story about something that caused you to wonder about what you should do. Tell what you decided to do and why.

4. Tell a story that reveals how your behavior has changed since the terrorist attacks of September 11, 2001.

5. Tell a story about a time you judged someone on the basis of that person's appearance. Alternatively, tell about a time someone judged you on the basis of your appearance.

6. Use your imagination and retell Hope's story from the point of view of the passenger in seat 9-C.

DESCRIPTION

A Link to the Living

Patsy Garlan

A visit to her daughter's human anatomy laboratory prompted Patsy Garlan to write this description, which first appeared in *The Atlantic Monthly* (2000). If you think the description is likely to be ghoulish, you will be surprised by the author's respectful tone. As you read, pay particular attention to the sensory details and specific word choice. Also notice that Garlan describes two subjects.

Before reading the essay, review the following vocabulary:

cavernous—vast; spacious

formaldehyde—a gas used as a disinfectant and preservative

Dante—in his epic poem, *The Inferno,* Dante acts as narrator, guided through Hell by the Roman poet Virgil.

gurney—wheeled cart or stretcher

1   You can imagine how startling it was when my daughter the medical student inquired, "Would you like to see my cadaver?" A glance at her eager young face filled with cheerful expectancy made me soften the fervor of my denial to "Oh, no, darling, no—I don't think so. No. No."

2   But then I thought, How often does a person, a layperson, have an opportunity like this—to look inside the body of another human being? You'll be forever sorry if you pass up this chance. I glanced at her again. She was waiting for me to come round. As she always did—as kids do. "Well," I said, "what would it be like?"

3   So off we went, in the warm dusk of the New Hampshire evening. I found myself fighting off my apprehension and hoping I would be able to control my queasiness. As we descended the stairs heading deep into the cavernous basement of the medical-school building where the anatomy lab was housed, she began to prepare me. It will be cold, because—you know. And there will be a smell of formaldehyde—don't mind it; you get used to it.

4   We entered the dimly lit lab. I want to say, we crossed the threshold— "Abandon all hope, ye who enter here." I put my trust in her, like Dante follow-

Source: Copyright © 2000, as first published in *The Atlantic Monthly.*

ing Virgil into the underworld. We wound our way among the sleek gurneys with their sheet-shrouded burdens. Not another soul breathed in that vast space. The smell of formaldehyde was an assault. The silence was thick, as if the bodies had absorbed all the sound, like flannel, like blankets, like snow.

5

She showed me first the trays of parts, stainless-steel basins of raw things—one full of kidneys, another of livers—like offerings in a meat market. She spoke in hushed tones, as if we were in an intensive-care room or a nursery. We approached the gurney that bore the cadaver she had been dissecting. Slowly, gently, she turned back the cover from the thin white feet and legs. "We'll start here," she said. "The head is so very personal." I knew she was allowing me time to prepare for the intimacy of that encounter.

6

She pointed to a clipboard on a low wall, where the history of the cadaver was detailed. He was an old man—and an old cadaver, having been in storage for many months. I don't remember why he died. She told me that in some medical-school labs the students make dark jokes and horse around, probably in an effort to handle their feelings. She was grateful that the attitude here was different.

7

She raised the sheet from the lower torso, which was laid open like a display package. I was astonished to see that our bodies' essential parts are all neatly organized, many in their own little membranes like plastic-wrapped leftovers in a well-maintained refrigerator. I had always assumed that the coils of intestines, the stomach, the liver, the spleen, would be jumbled up together. The tidy reality was strangely satisfying.

8

She had been working on a section of colon, I think it was. I watched in fascination as she carefully removed the covering from the head. She said. "It is so important to us students to have this experience. And if people are willing to donate their bodies for us, we must, must give them due respect."

9

I gazed at the small face of an old man, an old man who somehow linked my daughter and me and all human flesh together, in the semi-dark, in this timeless moment.

10

Outside, green, growing leaves were gleaming softly under a star-studded sky. Up into the freshness of evening we came, full of a sense of the enduring connectedness of all living things, and of the child who becomes the parent and the parent the child.

STUDY QUESTIONS

1. Garlan describes two subjects. What are they?

2. What is the dominant impression of each subject that Garlan describes?

3. Cite an example of each of the following: sensory detail of smell, sensory detail of sound, and sensory detail of sight.

4. A **simile** is a comparison of two unlike items, using the word *like* or the word *as*. For example, in paragraph 7, Garlan says that body parts were "like plastic-wrapped leftovers in a well-maintained refrigerator." Cite another simile in the essay. Are the similes an effective descriptive strategy? Explain.

5. What strategy does Garlan use to conclude her essay? Does the conclusion provide a satisfying finish? Explain.

6. **Other Patterns** In addition to description, what other writing patterns did you notice? How does Garlan use narration in the essay?

WRITING TOPICS

1. Like Garlan, describe a place that is very quiet. Alternatively, describe a place that is very noisy. Try to select a place that you can visit to select your sensory details.

2. Describe a friend or relative. Be sure to have a dominant impression, such as "trendy," "dainty," or "imposing."

3. Describe a laboratory or some other specialized classroom on campus. Remember to include a dominant impression.

4. Like Garlan, describe a place most people do not see, such as the kitchen of a local restaurant, the stockroom where you work, the basement of your house, or the broadcast booth of the campus radio station. Remember to include your dominant impression.

5. Write an editorial for your local or campus newspaper to encourage people to donate their bodies to medical schools for use in anatomy labs.

6. In the last paragraph, Garlan mentions "the child who becomes the parent and the parent the child." Tell about a time a parent and child reversed roles.

ILLUSTRATION

Words That Wound

Kathleen Vail

In this 1999 article from *American School Board Journal,* Kathleen Vail addresses the serious issue of bullying in our schools, using examples to illustrate both its devastating effects and our lack of an appropriate response. As you read, think about the fact that Vail's original audience was public school managers. Consider her purpose for writing and whether she achieves that purpose. Also, notice that Vail combines illustration with narration and cause-and-effect analysis in order to achieve her purpose for writing.

Before you read, review the following vocabulary:

Columbine High School—in 1999, two students killed thirteen people and wounded twenty-three others at this school in Colorado

crusader—a person who works for a cause

condoning—approving

battery—a beating

lobby—to try to influence a legislator to pass a law

Brian Head saw only one way out. On the final day of his life, during economics class, the 15-year-old stood up and pointed a semi-automatic handgun at himself. Before he pulled the trigger, he said his last words: "I can't take this anymore." 1

Brian's father, William Head, has no doubt why his only child chose to take his life in front of a classroom full of students five years ago. Brian wanted everyone to know the source of his pain, the suffering he could no longer endure. The Woodstock, Ga., teen, overweight with thick glasses, had been systematically abused by school bullies since elementary school. Death was the only relief he could imagine. "Children can't vote or organize, leave or run away," says Head. "They are trapped." 2

For many students, school is a torture chamber from which there is no escape. Every day, 160,000 children stay home from school because they are afraid of being bullied, according to the National Association of School Psychologists. In a study of junior high and high school students from small Midwestern towns, nearly 77 percent of the students reported they'd been victims of bullies at school—14 percent saying they'd experienced severe reactions 3 to the abuse. "Bullying is a crime of violence," says June Arnette, associate director of the National School Safety Center. "It's an imbalance of power, sustained over a period of time."

4   Yet even in the face of this suffering, even after Brian Head's suicide five years ago, even after it was revealed this past spring that a culture of bullying might have played a part in the Columbine High School shootings, bullying remains for the most part unacknowledged, underreported, and minimized by schools. Adults are unaware of the extent and nature of the problem, says Nancy Mullin-Rindler, associate director of the Project on Teasing and Bullying in the Elementary Grades at Wellesley College Center for Research on Women. "They underestimate the import. They feel it's a normal part of growing up, that it's character-building."

5   After his son's death, William Head became a crusader against bullying, founding an effort called Kids Hope to prevent others from suffering as Brian had. Unfortunately, bullying claimed another victim in the small town of Woodstock: 13-year-old Josh Belluardo. Last November, on the bus ride home from school, Josh's neighbor, 15-year-old Jonathan Miller, taunted him and threw wads of paper at him. He followed Josh off the school bus, hit the younger boy in the back of the head, and kicked him in the stomach. Josh spent the last two days of his life in a coma before dying of his injuries. Miller, it turns out, had been suspended nearly 20 times for offenses such as pushing and taunting other students and cursing at a teacher. He's now serving a life sentence for felony murder while his case is on appeal.

6   Bullying doesn't have to result in death to be harmful. Bullying and harassment are major distractions from learning, according to the National School Safety Center. Victims' grades suffer, and fear can lead to chronic absenteeism, truancy, or dropping out. Bullies also affect children who aren't victimized: Bystanders feel guilty and helpless for not standing up to the bully. They feel unsafe, unable to take action. They also can be drawn into bullying behavior by peer pressure. "Any time there is a climate of fear, the learning process will be compromised," says Arnette.

7   A full 70 percent of children believe teachers handle episodes of bullying "poorly," according to a study by John Hoover at the University of North Dakota at Grand Forks. It's no wonder kids are reluctant to tell adults about bullying incidents. "Children feel no one will take them seriously," says Robin Kowalski, professor of psychology at Western Carolina University, Cullowhee, N.C., who's done research on teasing behavior.

8   Martha Rizzo, who lives in a suburb of Cincinnati, calls bullying the "dirty little secret" of her school district. Both her son and daughter were teased in school. Two boys in her son's sixth-grade class began taunting him because he wore sweatpants instead of jeans. They began to intimidate him during class. Once they knocked the pencil out of his hand during a spelling test when the teacher's back was turned. He failed the test. Rizzo made an appointment with the school counselor. The counselor told her he could do nothing about the behavior of the bullies and suggested she get counseling for her son instead. "Schools say they do something, but they don't, and it continues," says Rizzo. "We go in with the same problem over and over again."

Anna Billoit of Louisiana went to her son's middle school teachers when   9
her son, who had asthma and was overweight, was being bullied by his classmates. Some of the teachers made the situation worse, she says. One male
teacher suggested to her that the teasing would help her son mature. "His attitude was 'Suck it up, take it like a man,'" says Billoit.

Much bullying goes on in so-called transition areas where there is little or   10
no adult supervision: hallways, locker rooms, restrooms, cafeterias, play-
grounds, buses, and bus stops. When abuse happens away from adult eyes,
it's hard to prove that the abuse occurred. Often, though, bullies harass their
victims in the open, in full view of teachers and other adults. Some teachers
will ignore the behavior, silently condoning it. But even when adults try to deal
with the problem, they sometimes make things worse for the victim by not han-
dling the situation properly. Confronting bullies in front of their peers only
enhances the bullies' prestige and power. And bullies often step up the abuse
after being disciplined. "People know it happens, but there's no structured way
to deal with it," says Mullin-Rindler. "There's lots of confusion about what to do
and what is the best approach."

Societal expectations play a part in adult reactions to childhood bullying.   11
Many teachers and administrators buy into a widespread belief that bullying
is a normal part of childhood and that children are better off working out such
problems on their own. But this belief sends a dangerous message to children,
says Head. Telling victims they must protect themselves from bullies shows
children that adults can't and won't protect them. And, he points out, it's an
attitude adults would never tolerate themselves. "If you go to work and get
slapped on the back of the head, you wouldn't expect your supervisor to say,
'It's your problem — you need to learn to deal with it yourself,'" says Head. "It's
a human-rights issue."

Ignoring bullying is only part of the problem. Some teachers go further by   12
blaming the victims for their abuse by letting their own dislike for the victimized
child show. "There's a lot of secret admiration for the strong kids," says Eileen
Faucette of Augusta, Ga. Her daughter was teased so badly in the classroom
that she was afraid to go to the blackboard or raise her hand to answer a question. The abuse happened in front of her teacher, who did nothing to stop it.

Head also encountered a blame-the-victim attitude toward his son. Brian   13
would get into trouble for fighting at school, but when Head and his wife investigated what happened, they usually found that Brian had been attacked by other
students. The school, Head said, wanted to punish Brian along with his attackers. "The school calls it fighting," Head says. "But it's actually assault and battery."

And changes are coming. This past April, five months after Josh Bellu-   14
ardo's death, the Georgia State Legislature passed an anti-bullying law. The
law defines bullying as "any willful attempt or threat to inflict injury on another
person when accompanied by an apparent present ability to do so" or "any
intentional display of force such as would give the victim reason to fear or
expect immediate bodily harm." Schools are required to send students to an
alternative school if they commit a third act of bullying in a school year. The
law also requires school systems to adopt anti-bullying policies and to post the
policies in middle and high schools.

15   Head was consulted by the state representatives who sponsored the bill, but he believes the measures don't go far enough. He urges schools to treat bullying behavior as a violation of the state criminal law against assault, stalking, and threatening, and to call the police when the law is broken.

16   He knows it's too late for Brian, too late for Josh, too late for the teens who died in Littleton. But he continues to work, to educate and lobby on the devastating effects of bullying so that his son's death will not have been in

17   vain.

"We should come clean and say what we've done in the past is wrong," says Head. "Now we will guarantee we'll protect the rights of students."

STUDY QUESTIONS

1. In your own words, write out the thesis of "Words That Wound." Where in the essay is the thesis stated?

2. For what reason do you think Vail wrote "Words That Wound"? Do you think she achieves her purpose? Why or why not?

3. Which paragraphs include examples? How do the examples help Vail achieve her purpose for writing?

4. In the introduction, how does Vail stimulate readers' interest in her essay?

5. **Other Patterns** In addition to illustration, what other writing patterns did you notice? Which paragraphs include narration? How does that narration help Vail achieve her writing purpose? How does Vail use cause-and-effect analysis to achieve her purpose?

WRITING TOPICS

1. Bullying is not the only problem that students face in elementary, middle, and high school. Identify another problem and use examples to illustrate it.

2. Identify a problem that college students face, and use examples to illustrate it.

3. Bullying also occurs outside of school—in the workplace and on the athletic field, for example. Give examples of bullying that occurs outside of school.

4. If you have witnessed or been the victim of bullying, give your own examples of it, being sure to mention the effects.

5. Pick a hurtful behavior besides bullying and use examples to illustrate it and its effects.

6. Give examples of ways students, teachers, and parents can prevent bullying.

PROCESS ANALYSIS

Dumpster Diving

Lars Eighner

"Dumpster Diving" is a shortened form of an essay first published in *Threepenny Review* in 1991, then published in *Utne Reader,* and later published in Eighner's *Travels with Lizbeth,* which is his memoir about the three years he spent as a homeless person with his dog Lizbeth. As you read, notice that the process Eighner explains—searching dumpsters for useful items, especially food—makes points about materialism and what is important. Notice, too, the elements of definition, contrast, and illustration in the essay.

Before reading the essay, review the following vocabulary:

scavenging—taking discarded material

foraging—searching for provisions

niche—a place or position

bohemian—unconventional

dilettanti—those who just dabble in something

qualms—misgivings

transience—impermanence

sated—full

I began Dumpster diving about a year before I became homeless. 1

I prefer the term *scavenging.* I have heard people, evidently meaning to be polite, use the word *foraging,* but I prefer to reserve that word for gathering nuts and berries and such, which I also do, according to the season and opportunity. 2

I like the frankness of the word *scavenging.* I live from the refuse of others. I am a scavenger. I think it a sound and honorable niche, although if I could I would naturally prefer to live the comfortable consumer life, perhaps—and only perhaps—as a slightly less wasteful consumer owing to what I have learned as a scavenger. 3

Except for jeans, all my clothes come from Dumpsters. Boom boxes, candles, bedding, toilet paper, medicine, books, a typewriter, a virgin male love doll, coins sometimes amounting to many dollars: all came from Dumpsters. And, yes, I eat from Dumpsters, too. 4

Source: From *Travels With Lizbeth* by Lars Eighner, copyright © 1993 by the author and reprinted by permission of St. Martin's Press, LLC.

5 There is a predictable series of stages that a person goes through in learning to scavenge. At first the new scavenger is filled with disgust and self-loathing. He is ashamed of being seen.

6 This stage passes with experience. The scavenger finds a pair of running shoes that fit and look and smell brand-new. He finds a pocket calculator in perfect working order. He finds pristine ice cream, still frozen, more than he can eat or keep. He begins to understand: people do throw away perfectly good stuff, a lot of perfectly good stuff.

7 At this stage he may become lost and never recover. All the Dumpster divers I have known come to the point of trying to acquire everything they touch. Why not take it, they reason, it is all free. This is, of course, hopeless, and most divers come to realize that they must restrict themselves to items of relatively immediate utility.

8 The finding of objects is becoming something of an urban art. Even respectable, employed people will sometimes find something tempting sticking out of a Dumpster or standing beside one. Quite a number of people, not all of them of the bohemian type, are willing to brag that they found this or that piece in the trash.

9 But eating from Dumpsters is the thing that separates the dilettanti from the professionals. Eating safely involves three principles: using the senses and common sense to evaluate the condition of the found materials; knowing the Dumpsters of a given area and checking them regularly; and seeking always to answer the question "Why was this discarded?"

10 Yet perfectly good food can be found in Dumpsters. Canned goods, for example, turn up fairly often in the Dumpsters I frequent. I also have few qualms about dry foods such as crackers, cookies, cereal, chips, and pasta if they are free of visible contaminants and still dry and crisp. Raw fruits and vegetables with intact skins seem perfectly safe to me, excluding, of course, the obviously rotten. Many are discarded for minor imperfections that can be pared away.

11 A typical discard is a half jar of peanut butter—though nonorganic peanut butter does not require refrigeration and is unlikely to spoil in any reasonable time. One of my favorite finds is yogurt—often discarded, still sealed, when the expiration date has passed—because it will keep for several days, even in warm weather.

12 No matter how careful I am I still get dysentery at least once a month, oftener in warm weather. I do not want to paint too romantic a picture. Dumpster diving has serious drawbacks as a way of life.

13 I find from the experience of scavenging two rather deep lessons. The first is to take what I can use and let the rest go. I have come to think that there is no value in the abstract. A thing I cannot use or make useful, perhaps by trading, has no value, however fine or rare it may be.

14 The second lesson is the transience of material being. I do not suppose that ideas are immortal, but certainly they are longer-lived than material objects.

15 The things I find in Dumpsters, the love letters and rag dolls of so many lives, remind me of this lesson. Now I hardly pick up a thing without envisioning the time I will cast it away. This, I think, is a healthy state of mind. Almost

everything I have now has already been cast out at least once, proving that what I own is valueless to someone.

I find that my desire to grab for the gaudy bauble has been largely sated. 16 I think this is an attitude I share with the very wealthy—we both know there is plenty more where whatever we have came from. Between us are the rat-race millions who have confounded their selves with the objects they grasp and who nightly scavenge the cable channels for they know not what.

I am sorry for them. 17

STUDY QUESTIONS

1. In which paragraph does the process analysis begin? What is the purpose of the paragraphs before the process analysis?

2. Where does the author mention what *not* to do? Why does he do so?

3. Does Eighner write his process analysis solely because he wants to explain how to scavenge, or does he have another purpose for writing? That is, why does the author find it important to explain the process he writes about?

4. How does the last sentence relate to the point the process analysis is making?

5. **Other Patterns** In addition to process analysis, what other writing patterns did you notice? Examples appear in paragraphs 6, 10, and 15. How do those examples help the author achieve his writing purpose? What patterns are used in paragraph 2? What purpose do those patterns serve?

WRITING TOPICS

1. Explain a process for finding useful items at a garage sale or flea market.

2. Explain a process related to buying, growing, or preparing food.

3. Explain a process for deciding what to discard and what to keep. If you like, you can limit your discussion to the contents of a closet, desk, backpack, wallet, or purse.

4. Explain a process for getting along on limited resources. For example, you can explain how to eat on twenty dollars a week, how to cook on a hot plate in a dorm room, or how to survive without a car.

5. Eighner says that a "thing [he] cannot use or make useful … has no value" [paragraph 13]. Agree or disagree with the idea that to be valuable, an item must be useful.

6. Eighner says he feels sorry for the "rat-race millions" [paragraph 16]. Do you feel sorry for them? Explain why or why not.

DEFINITION

Supermodel?

Jenny Bradner

In this 2001 essay that first appeared in the newspaper supplement *Family Style,* Jenny Bradner objects to the popular definition of a super-model and offers her own definition as a replacement. The essay refers to a fairy tale called "The Emperor's New Clothes," which is about an emperor who was approached by two swindlers who promised to make him the most beautiful suit of clothes in the world—and one that would appear invisible to anyone who was stupid or incompetent. The swindlers pre-tended to weave the clothes, and the people, including the emperor him-self, were afraid to admit that they saw nothing.

Before reading the essay, review the following vocabulary:

accolades—honors; praise

emulation—imitation

paradox—contradiction

lemmings—small rodents known to migrate into the sea where many are drowned; a reference to following a trend or leader, even if doing so leads to disaster

Rothschild—a wealthy banking family

Michael Jordan—a famous basketball player

Claudia Schiffer—a supermodel

---

1   I'm scanning the pages of *Cosmopolitan* magazine and I'm offended. I'm offended that these airbrushed women—women of cosmetic surgery and eat-ing disorders, women caked with cosmetics and enhanced by lights and wardrobe—are the members of a segment of society that we have deemed both super and models.

2   Maybe you're thinking I am some overweight, miserable housewife with nothing better to do than pick on the beautiful elite. Not so. I'm just frustrated by the accolades these magazine images receive when I am surrounded by examples of real people who truly are both super and models.

3   The dictionary describes *super* this way: "a generalized term of approval," and "being of a high grade or quality, very large or powerful, or exhibiting the

characteristics of its type to an extreme or excessive degree." It defines *model* like this: "an example for imitation or emulation or one who is employed to display clothes." So, while I see how such a pairing of words does describe Cindy Crawford and her cohorts, I am also left to ponder the paradox of identifying this clique as both super and models.

I wonder if we have trouble calling a person either super or a model if he or she bears any resemblance to ourselves. That is, we don't believe that others would consider us to be super or models, and, thus, the term must only refer to those who bear no resemblance to us. And models certainly fit *that* bill. In general, they are taller and thinner, and have features more striking than many other individuals. But does that really make them supermodels? Or does it just make them freaks of nature?

Maybe you'll argue that the *super* in supermodel refers not to what they look like, but rather to their careers—to the unbelievable fees they command. And that *model* refers simply to the act of displaying clothes. Either way, the message is obscene: If you are tall, thin, and strangely attractive, and if you can make more money and last longer in the business than other models, then you are deemed a supermodel.

And truthfully, *model* no longer refers only to displaying clothes. It actually and quite frighteningly has come to mean *role model* in a truly shocking way: If during your career you inspire thousands of little girls to put stock in their beauty instead of their brains, and if your work helps lead them to self-destructive behaviors, including eating disorders and abusive relationships brought on by low self-esteem, then you have truly made it to the top. That's super? That's a model?

Do we really believe this, or have we fallen prey to the same thinking that got the emperor to walk naked through the streets and all of his people to exclaim and congratulate him on his fine new suit of clothes? Are we these lemmings? In some ways, sadly, yes.

But there is still hope. We know who our role models should be. We know that parents are super for reaching within and beyond themselves solely for the well-being of another human being. We know that teachers are super for working with children and adults to better their lives while getting little more than some personal satisfaction as compensation. Gandhi was super. Mother Theresa was super. People who commit their lives to improving the lives of others are super. *They* are models.

Cliché? Call it what you will. But if you ask me, we've got the wrong bunch up on pedestals. We know who our role models should be, but in our own reversion to our awkward middle-school days, we just can't bring ourselves to stand up and shout, "The Emperor's naked!" And until we can do that, supermodels will continue to reign as our super models, and teenagers will continue to develop eating disorders.

I use supermodels as the examples and not the rule only because the phrase fits so neatly. But they aren't the sole offenders. Professional athletes, actors, the painfully wealthy. None of these bear resemblance to the truest meaning of the term supermodel, but they have captured our love and admiration seemingly for no other reason than that they are bigger than life. They, too, contribute to making regular people feel like failures, causing children and adults alike to suffer in pursuit of the unattainable.

11   Let's roll out the red carpet to honor those who deserve honoring. And while we're at it, let's rein in the salaries of professional athletes and fashion models, and beef up those of teachers and social workers. Not possible? Well, let's at least remember to thank our parents and teachers and not covet Carol Alt's thighs or Cal Ripken's swing. Besides, who among us really wants to give up chocolate glazed donuts and lazy coffee dates with friends?

12   I can't be a Rothschild. I can't be Michael Jordan or Claudia Schiffer. I can, however, be honest and kind, intelligent and generous. Not very glamorous, I know. But far more valuable.

STUDY QUESTIONS

1. What is Bradner defining, and what is her assertion about the term she is defining?

2. Generally, definition paragraphs and essays should not include dictionary-style definitions. However, "Supermodel" includes two dictionary definitions in paragraph 3. Are those definitions a problem? Why or why not?

3. Bradner uses sentence fragments intentionally in paragraphs 9 and 12 in order to create a special effect. Identify the fragments. Why do you think she uses them? (If you want to use fragments for special effect, consult with your instructor.)

4. How does explaining what her term is *not* help the author achieve her purpose for writing?

5. For what purpose do you think Bradner wrote "Supermodel?"

6. **Other Patterns** In addition to definition, what other writing patterns did you notice? How does the author use examples to develop her definition? How does she use contrast?

WRITING TOPICS

1. Write a definition of *supermodel* that explains what most people think a supermodel is.

2. Bradner says in paragraph 8, "We know who our role models should be." Pick one person you think of as a role model. In a paragraph, tell why that person is a role model for you.

3. Explain how you respond to the models you see in a magazine. Why do you have that reaction?

4. Write a definition of *role model.* As an alternative, write a definition of *hero.*

5. In paragraph 11, Bradner says that we should "rein in the salaries of professional athletes." Do you agree? Argue for or against Bradner's view.

6. Why do you think we look up to supermodels, athletes, actors, and rock stars?

COMPARISON
AND CONTRAST

They Shut My Grandmother's Room Door

Andrew Lam

Pacific News Service editor Andrew Lam is a short-story writer and journalist who lives in San Francisco. In the following essay, Lam draws on experiences in Vietnam and the United States to contrast the two cultures' views of death. Be sure to determine which culture's view he prefers.

Before reading the essay, review the following vocabulary:

convalescent home—nursing home

Tet—the Vietnamese new year

disjointed—disconnected

escrow—money held as part of a contract

filial piety—the respect of a son or daughter

wafting—floating through air

1   When someone dies in the convalescent home where my grandmother lives, the nurses rush to close all the patients' doors. Though as a policy death is not to be seen at the home, she can always tell when it visits. The series of doors being slammed shut remind her of the firecrackers during Tet.

2   The nurses' efforts to shield death are more comical to my grandmother than reassuring. "Those old ladies die so often," she quips in Vietnamese, "everyday's like new year."

3   Still, it is lonely to die in such a place. I imagine some wasted old body under a white sheet being carted silently through the empty corridor on its way to the morgue. While in America a person may be born surrounded by loved ones, in old age one is often left to take the last leg of life's journey alone.

4   Perhaps that is why my grandmother talks now mainly of her hometown, Bac-Lieu; its river and green rich rice fields. Having lost everything during the war, she can now offer me only her distant memories: life was not disjointed back home; one lived in a gentle rhythm with the land; people died in their homes surrounded by neighbors and relatives. And no one shut your door.

Source: Copyright © by Andrew Lam. Andrew Lam is the author of *Perfume Dreams: Reflections on the Vietnamese Diaspr*oora.

So it goes. The once gentle, connected world of the past is but the language of dreams. In this fast-paced society of disjointed lives, we are swept along and have little time left for spiritual comfort. Instead of relying on neighbors and relatives, on the river and land, we deal with the language of materialism: overtime, escrow, stress, down payment, credit cards, tax shelter. Instead of going to the temple to pray for good health, we pay life and health insurance religiously.

My grandmother's children and grandchildren share a certain pang of guilt. After a stroke which paralyzed her, we could no longer keep her at home. And although we visit her regularly, we are not living up to the filial piety standard expected of us in the old country. My father silently grieves and my mother suffers from headaches. (Does she see herself in such a home in a decade or two?)

Once, a long time ago, living in Vietnam we used to stare death in the face. The war in many ways had heightened our sensibilities toward living and dying. I can still hear the wails of widows and grieving mothers. Though the fear of death and dying is a universal one, the Vietnamese did not hide from it. Instead we dwelt in its tragedy. Death pervaded our poems, novels, fairy tales, and songs.

But if agony and pain are part of Vietnamese culture, pleasure is at the center of America's culture. While Vietnamese holidays are based on death anniversaries, birthdays are celebrated here. American popular culture translates death with something like nauseating humor. People laugh and scream at blood and guts movies. The wealthy freeze their dead relatives in liquid nitrogen. Cemeteries are places of big business, complete with colorful brochures. I hear there are even drive-by funerals where you don't have to get out of your own car to pay your respects to the deceased.

That America relies upon the pleasure principle and happy endings in its entertainments does not, however, assist us in evading suffering. The reality of the suffering of old age is apparent in the convalescent home. There is an old man, once an accomplished concert pianist, now rendered helpless by arthritis. Every morning he sits staring at the piano. One feeble woman who outlived her children keeps repeating, "My son will take me home." Then there are those mindless, bedridden bodies kept alive, through a series of tubes and pulsating machines.

But despair is not newsworthy. Death itself must be embellished or satirized or deep-frozen in order to catch the public's attention.

Last week on her eighty-second birthday I went to see my grandmother. She smiled her sweet sad smile.

"Where will you end up in your old age?" she asked me, her mind as sharp as ever.

The memories of monsoon rain and tropical sun and relatives and friends came to mind. Not here, not here, I wanted to tell her. But the soft moaning of a patient next door and the smell of alcohol wafting from the sterile corridor brought me back to reality.

"Anywhere is fine," I told her instead, trying to keep up with her courageous spirit. "All I am asking for is that they don't shut my door."

1. What subjects is Lam contrasting?

2. For what purpose do you think Lam wrote "They Shut My Grand-mother's Room Door"?

3. Explain the difference between the way Americans and Vietnamese view death. How does the closed door reflect the difference?

4. Lam uses both a point-by-point organization and a subject-by-subject organization. (See page xxx for more on these organizational strategies.) Which paragraphs are organized with a subject-by-subject pattern? Which paragraphs are organized with a point-by-point pattern?

5. **Other Patterns** In addition to comparison and contrast, what other writing patterns did you notice? Which paragraph includes examples? How does illustration help Lam achieve his purpose for writing?

6. Lam concludes his essay by saying. " 'All I am asking for is that they don't shut my door,' " What does he mean? How does that statement bring the essay to a satisfying finish?

WRITING TOPICS

1. In paragraphs 4 and 5, Lam contrasts the present time in the United States and an earlier time in Vietnam. Contrast some aspect of your life now with that aspect at an earlier time. For example, you can consider your attitude toward school, the way you view friendship, what you do to relax, or your idea of a good time.

2. If you have lived with or cared for an elderly relative, tell what the experience was like.

3. Lam accuses Americans of avoiding aging and death. Agree or disagree with him, citing examples to support your view.

4. Compare or contrast the rituals surrounding death in your culture or religion with those of some other culture or religion. To learn about the rituals of another culture or religion, interview one or more people.

5. Despite her age, her stroke, and her confinement to a nursing home, Lam's grandmother had a "courageous spirit" (paragraph 14). Tell about an elderly person you know or knew and explain the nature of that person's spirit. As an alternative, tell about the spirit of someone you know who lives with adversity.

6. In paragraph 8, Lam says that "pleasure is at the center of America's culture." Agree or disagree, using examples to support your view.

CAUSE-AND-EFFECT
ANALYSIS

Sometimes Honesty Is the Worst Policy

Judy Mandell

Judy Mandell has experienced age discrimination. In this 2002 essay, which first appeared in *Newsweek*'s "My Turn" column, she discusses the effects of that discrimination as well as what causes some women to lie about their age. As you read, consider how the author uses contrast and examples to support her points.

Before reading the essay, review the following vocabulary:

fabricate—make up

naïve—inexperienced and lacking sophistication

prone—having a tendency toward something

For as long as I've known her, an elderly relative of mine has lied about how old she is. She lives in a retirement community in the South. She looks great for her age—but I can't tell you what it is. I'm sworn to secrecy. Her friends think she's three years younger. "What's a few years among friends?" I asked her. "No one wants to be with an old lady," she answered.   1

She takes lying about her age to the extreme. Several years ago, when she was the only survivor of an automobile accident, she had the presence of mind to fabricate her age to the emergency medical technicians as they wheeled her into the ambulance. She was nearly arrested by U.S. Immigration officers because she crossed off and changed her birth date on her passport. For her, tampering with official documents is a way of life; she recently made me promise not to put her true age in her obituary.   2

I, on the other hand, had never lied about my age. I was proud, in fact, even when I turned 50. Why should I lie? I was told I looked good, and I felt great. My kids were grown, my marriage was fine, and I had a great job. I loved it when people said, "Your kids are *that* old? I can't believe it!" I thought that people who wouldn't reveal their age suffered from low self-esteem. That is, until my boss, the new, thirtysomething school headmaster, found out how old I was.   3

Source: From *Newsweek,* October 21, 2002. All rights reserved. Reprinted by permission.

4   I taught part time and did fund-raising for a small private school. I was the second oldest person on the faculty. I never imagined that it could matter until the morning I met with the headmaster in his office. We chatted about the school, the students and me. "How old are you?" he asked. When I answered 50, he seemed to stop breathing. He definitely stopped talking. There was a long, strange silence.

5   "Why are you asking?" I said.

6   "Never mind," he answered.

7   I should have lied.

8   I was angry that my boss had asked that question, but I didn't want to rock the boat, so I let it pass.

9   Several weeks later the headmaster informed me that the school was having financial difficulties. They "just couldn't afford me," he said. I was let go.

10   Sure, there were age-discrimination laws 10 years ago, but I had no proof that age was the reason I was fired. I just took it on the chin, telling myself this guy was a jerk, I'd have more time for my writing and, anyhow, I must look pretty good if he was so shocked that I was 50.

11   My friend PJ, a book editor, never cared about who knew her age—until recently. "I don't look my age, but that doesn't matter anymore," she told me. "When younger people know I'm in my mid-50s, they treat me differently. They realize I'm their parents' age.

12   Another friend, a mother of three, lies about her age or avoids the subject. When her husband left her for a younger woman, she had a tummy tuck and a face-lift. She's dating, but it's hard to find a man interested in a 45-year-old woman. She says she'll tell her age if she finds someone she wants to settle down with. In the meantime, she's keeping it a secret.

13   After I lost my job, I decided to keep quiet, too. I even requested that my date of birth be dropped from the Library of Congress data on the copyright page of my books.

14   Then last month I accepted an invitation to have lunch with a New York book editor. We had had several phone conversations but never met in person. I knew she was under 30, but of course I had never told her how old I am.

15   I worried, even obsessed, about how she would react when she saw me. But when we finally met, I detected no disappointment. In fact, we had fun, chatting and laughing like a couple of teenagers. After a while, I told her my age and asked her how she viewed women over 50.

16   Her answer surprised me. She confided that women over 50 made her nervous because she was afraid that they would perceive her as young. And to her, being young meant being naïve and prone to errors. She viewed older women as worldly, seasoned, deserving of respect. Although I envied her age, she seemed to envy mine.

17   Since that lunch, I've felt a lot better about my age. Sure, there are things about getting older that aren't terrific, like memory lapses and sagging skin, but in many ways, being mature is an advantage.

18   Not everyone agrees, so I still avoid the subject. But the next time I'm nervous or self-conscious about telling a younger person my age, I'll try to remember that she may be questioning how she will measure up to me.

STUDY QUESTIONS

1. According to the essay, what are the effects of being perceived as old?

2. What caused the author to change her mind about telling people her true age?

3. Explain the significance of the title. Do you think the title is a good one? Why or why not?

4. Give the transition that opens each of the following paragraphs, and state what relationship the transitions signal:

   a. paragraph 3

   b. paragraph 12

   c. paragraph 14

5. **Other Patterns** In addition to cause-and-effect analysis, what other writing patterns did you notice? How does Mandell use comparison-contrast to help make her point? How does she use illustration?

WRITING TOPICS

1. Using cause-and-effect analysis, explain why we value youth more than age.

2. Mandell focuses on the effects of age discrimination on women. Explain the effects on men.

3. Discuss the effects of being the age that you are.

4. Explain how age affects the way you perceive and react to people.

5. Explain how some aspect of the media, such as movies, television, advertising, or magazines affects the way we perceive age.

6. Tell about another time when honesty is not always the best policy.

CLASSIFICATION

Mother Tongue

Amy Tan

The daughter of Chinese immigrants, Amy Tan is a writer whose works include *The Joy Luck Club* (1987), *The Kitchen God's Wife* (1991), *The Bone-setter's Daughter* (2001), and *Saving Fish from Drowning* (2005). In "Mother Tongue," which first appeared in *Three-penny Review* in 1990, Tan discusses the different "Englishes" she uses with her Chinese-speaking mother as well as how she has been affected by her mother's imperfect English. Be sure to notice the way Tan classifies (groups) the kinds of English she uses.

Before you read, review the following vocabulary:

wrought—worked or shaped

transcribed—wrote out

belies—proves false

mother tongue—native language

guise—false appearance

impeccable—perfect

insular—isolated

semantic—referring to word meanings

1   I am not a scholar of English or literature. I cannot give you much more than personal opinions on the English language and its variations in this country or others.

2   I am a writer. And by that definition, I am someone who has always loved language. I am fascinated by language in daily life. I spend a great deal of my time thinking about the power of language—the way it can evoke an emotion, a visual image, a complex idea, or a simple truth. Language is the tool of my trade. And I use them all—all the Englishes I grew up with.

3   Recently, I was made keenly aware of the different Englishes I do use. I was giving a talk to a large group of people, the same talk I had already given to half a dozen other groups. The nature of the talk was about my writing, my life, and my book, *The Joy Luck Club*. The talk was going along well enough,

until I remembered one major difference that made the whole talk sound wrong. My mother was in the room. And it was perhaps the first time she had heard me give a lengthy speech, using the kind of English I have never used with her. I was saying things like, "The intersection of memory upon imagination" and "There is an aspect of my fiction that relates to thus-and-thus"—a speech filled with carefully wrought grammatical phrases, burdened, it suddenly seemed to me, with nominalized forms, past perfect tenses, conditional phrases, all the forms of standard English that I had learned in school and through books, the forms of English I did not use at home with my mother.

Just last week, I was walking down the street with my mother, and I again found myself conscious of the English I was using, the English I do use with her. We were talking about the price of new and used furniture and I heard myself saying this: "Not waste money that way." My husband was with us as well, and he didn't notice any switch in my English. And then I realized why. It's because over the twenty years we've been together I've often used that same kind of English with him, and sometimes he even uses it with me. It has become our language of intimacy, a different sort of English that relates to family talk, the language I grew up with.

So you'll have some idea of what this family talk I heard sounds like, I'll quote what my mother said during a recent conversation which I videotaped and then transcribed. During this conversation, my mother was talking about a political gangster in Shanghai who had the same last name as her family's, Du, and how the gangster in his early years wanted to be adopted by her family, which was rich by comparison. Later, the gangster became more powerful, far richer than my mother's family, and one day showed up at my mother's wedding to pay his respects. Here's what she said in part:

"Du Yusong having business like fruit stand. Like off the street kind. He is Du like Du Zong—but not Tsung-ming Island people. The local people call putong, the river east side, he belong to that side local people. That man want to ask Du Zong father take him in like become own family. Du Zong father wasn't look down on him, but didn't take seriously, until that man big like become a mafia. Now important person, very hard to inviting him. Chinese way, came only to show respect, don't stay for dinner. Respect for making big celebration, he shows up. Mean gives lots of respect. Chinese custom. Chinese social life that way. If too important won't have to stay too long. He come to my wedding. I didn't see, I heard it. I gone to boy's side, they have YMCA dinner, Chinese age I was nineteen."

You should know that my mother's expressive command of English belies how much she actually understands. She reads the *Forbes* report, listens to *Wall Street Week,* converses daily with her stockbroker, reads all of Shirley MacLaine's books with ease—all kinds of things I can't begin to understand. Yet some of my friends tell me they understand 50 percent of what my mother says. Some say they understand 80 to 90 percent. Some say they understand none of it, as if she were speaking pure Chinese. But to me, my mother's English is perfectly clear, perfectly natural. It's my mother tongue. Her language, as I hear it, is vivid, direct, full of observation and imagery. That was the

4

5

6

7

language that helped shape the way I saw things, expressed things, made sense of the world.

8   Lately, I've been giving more thought to the kind of English my mother speaks. Like others, I have described it to people as "broken" or "fractured" English. But I wince when I say that. It has always bothered me that I can think of no way to describe it other than "broken," as if it were damaged and needed to be fixed, as if it lacked a certain wholeness and soundness. I've heard other terms used, "limited English," for example. But they seem just as bad, as if everything is limited, including people's perceptions of the limited English speaker.

9   I know this for a fact, because when I was growing up, my mother's "limited" English limited *my* perception of her. I was ashamed of her English. I believed that her English reflected the quality of what she had to say. That is, because she expressed them imperfectly her thoughts were imperfect. And I had plenty of empirical evidence to support me: the fact that people in department stores, at banks, and at restaurants did not take her seriously, did not give her good service, pretended not to understand her, or even acted as if they did not hear her.

10   My mother has long realized the limitations of her English as well. When I was fifteen, she used to have me call people on the phone to pretend I was she. In this guise, I was forced to ask for information or even to complain and yell at people who had been rude to her. One time it was a call to her stockbroker in New York. She had cashed out her small portfolio and it just so happened we were going to go to New York the next week, our very first trip outside California. I had to get on the phone and say in an adolescent voice that was not very convincing, "This is Mrs. Tan."

11   And my mother was standing in the back whispering loudly. "Why he don't send me check, already two weeks late. So mad he lie to me, losing my money."

12   And then I said in perfect English, "Yes, I'm getting rather concerned. You had agreed to send the check two weeks ago, but it hasn't arrived."

13   Then she began to talk more loudly. "What he want, I come to New York tell him front of his boss, you cheating me?" And I was trying to calm her down, make her be quiet, while telling the stockbroker, "I can't tolerate any more excuses. If I don't receive the check immediately, I am going to have to speak to your manager when I'm in New York next week." And sure enough, the following week there we were in front of this astonished stockbroker, and I was sitting there red-faced and quiet, and my mother, the real Mrs. Tan, was shouting at his boss in her impeccable broken English.

14   We used a similar routine just five days ago, for a situation that was far less humorous. My mother had gone to the hospital for an appointment, to find out about a benign brain tumor a CAT scan had revealed a month ago. She said she had spoken very good English, her best English, no mistakes. Still, she said, the hospital did not apologize when they said they had lost the CAT scan and she had come for nothing. She said they did not seem to have any

sympathy when she told them she was anxious to know the exact diagnosis, since her husband and son had both died of brain tumors. She said they would not give her any more information until the next time and she would have to make another appointment for that. So she said she would not leave until the doctor called her daughter. She wouldn't budge. And when the doctor finally called her daughter, me, who spoke in perfect English—lo and behold—we had assurances the CAT scan would be found, promises that a conference call on Monday would be held, and apologies for any suffering my mother had gone through for a most regrettable mistake.

I think my mother's English almost had an effect on limiting my possibilities in life as well. Sociologists and linguists probably will tell you that a person's developing language skills are more influenced by peers. But I do think that the language spoken in the family, especially in immigrant families which are more insular, plays a large role in shaping the language of the child. And I believe that it affected my results on achievement tests, IQ tests, and the SAT. While my English skills were never judged as poor, compared to math, English could not be considered my strong suit. In grade school I did moderately well, getting perhaps B's, sometimes B-pluses, in English and scoring perhaps in the sixtieth or seventieth percentile on achievement tests. But those scores were not good enough to override the opinion that my true abilities lay in math and science, because in those areas I achieved A's and scored in the ninetieth percentile or higher.

This was understandable. Math is precise; there is only one correct answer. Whereas, for me at least, the answers on English tests were always a judgment call, a matter of opinion and personal experience. Those tests were constructed around items like fill-in-the-blank sentence completion, such as, "Even though Tom was _____, Mary thought he was _____." And the correct answer always seemed to be the most bland combinations of thoughts, for example, "Even though Tom was shy, Mary thought he was charming," with the grammatical structure "even though" limiting the correct answer to some sort of semantic opposites, so you wouldn't get answers like, "Even though Tom was foolish, Mary thought he was ridiculous." Well, according to my mother, there were very few limitations as to what Tom could have been and what Mary might have thought of him. So I never did well on tests like that.

The same was true with word analogies, pairs of words in which you were supposed to find some sort of logical, semantic relationship—for example, "*Sunset* is to *nightfall* as _____ is to _____." And here you would be presented with a list of four possible pairs, one of which showed the same kind of relationship: *red* is to *stoplight, bus* is to *arrival, chills* is to *fever, yawn* is to *boring.* Well, I could never think that way. I knew what the tests were asking, but I could not block out of my mind the images already created by the first pair, "*sunset* is to *nightfall*"—and I would see a burst of colors against a darkening sky, the moon rising, the lowering of a curtain of stars. And all the other pairs of words—red, bus, stoplight, boring—just threw up a mass of

15

16

17

confusing images, making it impossible for me to sort out something as logical as saying: "A sunset precedes nightfall" is the same as "a chill precedes a fever." The only way I would have gotten that answer right would have been to imagine an associative situation, for example, my being disobedient and staying out past sunset, catching a chill at night, which turns into feverish pneumonia as punishment, which indeed did happen to me.

18   I have been thinking about all this lately, about my mother's English, about achievement tests. Because lately I've been asked, as a writer, why there are not more Asian Americans represented in American literature. Why are there few Asian Americans enrolled in creative writing programs? Why do so many Chinese students go into engineering? Well, these are broad sociological questions I can't begin to answer. But I have noticed in surveys—in fact, just last week—that Asian students, as a whole, always do significantly better on math achievement tests than in English. And this makes me think that there are other Asian-American students whose English spoken in the home might also be described as "broken" or "limited." And perhaps they also have teachers who are steering them away from writing and into math and science, which is what happened to me.

19   Fortunately, I happen to be rebellious in nature and enjoy the challenge of disproving assumptions made about me. I became an English major my first year in college, after being enrolled as pre-med. I started writing nonfiction as a freelancer the week after I was told by my former boss that writing was my worst skill and I should hone my talents toward account management.

20   But it wasn't until 1985 that I finally began to write fiction. And at first I wrote using what I thought to be wittily crafted sentences, sentences that would finally prove I had mastery over the English language. Here's an example from the first draft of a story that later made its way into *The Joy Luck Club,* but without this line: "That was my mental quandary in its nascent state." A terrible line, which I can barely pronounce.

21   Fortunately, for reasons I won't get into today, I later decided I should envision a reader for the stories I would write. And the reader I decided upon was my mother, because these were stories about mothers. So with this reader in mind—and in fact she did read my early drafts—I began to write stories using all the Englishes I grew up with: the English I spoke to my mother, which for lack of a better term might be described as "simple"; the English she used with me, which for lack of a better term might be described as "broken"; my translation of her Chinese, which could certainly be described as "watered down"; and what I imagined to be her translation of her Chinese if she could speak in perfect English, her internal language, and for that I sought to preserve the essence, but neither an English nor a Chinese structure. I wanted to capture what language ability tests can never reveal: her intent, her passion, her imagery, the rhythms of her speech and the nature of her thoughts.

22   Apart from what any critic had to say about my writing, I knew I had succeeded where it counted when my mother finished reading my book and gave me her verdict: "So easy to read."

STUDY QUESTIONS

1. How is the author affected by her mother's "limited" English? How is Tan's mother herself affected?

2. What kinds of English does Tan classify (group) in the essay?

3. Does Tan explain each category in her classification in the same amount of detail? If not, why doesn't she?

4. A **topic sentence** states the focus of a supporting paragraph. Which paragraphs open with topic sentences? Do these topic sentences help the reader? Explain.

5. Do you agree that the "terrible line" in paragraph 20 is really not very good? Why or why not?

6. **Other Patterns** In addition to classification, what other writing patterns did you notice? Which paragraphs include brief narrations? What purpose do these narrations serve?

WRITING TOPICS

1. Classify three kinds of English you use and give examples of each kind. You might consider the English you use in class, at work, with friends, and with family.

2. Discuss one way our speech influences the opinions people form about us.

3. Tan says she became a writer because teachers were steering her away from English and toward math. As a result, she wanted to prove she could be a writer. Tell about a time you did something just to prove that you could.

4. Classify the kinds of problems faced by students who speak English as a second language. If necessary, interview international students on your campus for ideas.

5. Tan was greatly affected by her mother's English. Tell about a significant effect a parent or other caregiver had on you.

6. Classify the kinds of problems a person who speaks "limited" English is likely to encounter.

ARGUMENT

Money for Morality

Mary Arguelles

Mary Arguelles has written for several magazines, including *New Mother, Baby Talk,* and *Reader's Digest.* In "Money for Morality," which first appeared in *Newsweek* in 1991, she uses examples to argue that we have misplaced our most important virtues because we seek incentives and rewards for doing the right thing. As you read, ask yourself whether Arguelles makes a convincing case.

Before you read, review the following vocabulary:

good Samaritan—a person who helps people in distress

presumption—assuming something is true

legacy—something handed down

ubiquitous—existing everywhere

mercenary—money-oriented

catapulted—hurled

kowtowing—touching the head to the floor while kneeling; worshiping

1   I recently read a newspaper article about an 8-year-old boy who found an envelope containing more than $600 and returned it to the bank whose name appeared on the envelope. The bank traced the money to its rightful owner and returned it to him. God's in his heaven and all's right with the world. Right? Wrong.

2   As a reward, the man who lost the money gave the boy $3. Not a lot, but a token of his appreciation nonetheless and not mandatory. After all, returning money should not be considered extraordinary. A simple "thank you" is adequate. But some of the teachers at the boy's school felt a reward was not only appropriate, but required. Outraged at the apparent stinginess of the person who lost the cash, these teachers took up a collection for the boy. About a week or so later, they presented the good Samaritan with a $150 savings bond, explaining they felt his honesty should be recognized. Evidently the

Source: Originally appeared in the "My Turn" column of *Newsweek,* October 28, 1991.

virtues of honesty and kindness have become commodities that, like everything else, have succumbed to inflation. I can't help but wonder what dollar amount these teachers would have deemed a sufficient reward. Certainly they didn't expect the individual who lost the money to give the child $150. Would $25 have been respectable? How about $10? Suppose that lost money had to cover mortgage, utilities, and food for the week. In light of that, perhaps $3 was generous. A reward is a gift; any gift should at least be met with the presumption of genuine gratitude on the part of the giver.

3

What does this episode say about our society? It seems the role models our children look up to these days—in this case, teachers—are more confused and misguided about values than their young charges. A young boy, obviously well guided by his parents, finds money that does not belong to him and he returns it. He did the right thing. Yet doing the right thing seems to be insufficient motivation for action in our materialistic world. The legacy of the '80s has left us with the ubiquitous question: what's in it for me? The promise of the golden rule—that someone might do a good turn for you—has become worthless collateral for the social interactions of the mercenary and fast-paced '90s. It is in fact this fast pace that is, in part, a source of the problem. Modern communication has catapulted us into an instant world. Television makes history of events before any of us has even had a chance to absorb them in the first place. An ad for major-league baseball entices viewers with the reassurance that "the memories are waiting," an event that has yet to occur has already been packaged as the past. With the world racing by us, we have no patience for a rain check on good deeds.

4

Misplaced virtues are running rampant through our culture. I don't know how many times my 13-year-old son has told me about classmates who received $10 for each A they receive on their report cards—hinting that I should do the same for him should he ever receive an A (or maybe he was working on $5 for a B). Whenever he approaches me on this subject, I give him the same reply: "Doing well is its own reward. The A just confirms that." In other words, forget it! This is not to say that I would never praise my son for doing well in school. But my praise is not meant to reward or elicit future achievements, but rather to express my genuine delight in the satisfaction he feels at having done his best. Throwing $10 at that sends out the message that the feeling alone isn't good enough.

5

Kowtowing to ice cream: As a society, we seem to be losing a grip on our internal control—the ethical thermostat that guides our actions and feelings toward ourselves, others, and the world around us. Instead, we rely on external "stuff" as a measure of our worth. We pass this message to our children. We offer them money for honesty and good grades. Pizza is given as a reward for reading. In fact, in one national reading program, a pizza party awaits the entire class if each child reads a certain amount of books within a four-month period. We call these things incentives, telling ourselves that if we can just reel them in and get them hooked, then the built-in rewards will follow. I recently saw a television program where unmarried teenaged mothers were featured as the participants in a parenting program that offers a $10 a week "incentive" if these young women don't get pregnant again. Isn't the daily struggle of being a single, teenaged mother enough of a deterrent? No, it isn't, because we as a society won't allow it to be. Nothing is permitted to succeed or fail on its own merits anymore.

6   I remember when I was pregnant with my son I read countless child-care books that offered the same advice: don't bribe your child with ice cream to get him to eat spinach; it makes the spinach look bad. While some may say spinach doesn't need any help looking bad, I submit it's from years of kowtowing to ice cream. Similarly, our moral taste buds have been dulled by an endless onslaught of artificial sweeteners. A steady diet of candy bars and banana splits makes an ordinary apple or orange seem sour. So too does an endless parade of incentives make us incapable of feeling a genuine sense of inner peace (or inner turmoil).

7   The simple virtues of honesty, kindness and integrity suffer from an image problem and are in desperate need of a makeover. One way to do this is by example. If my son sees me feeling happy after I've helped out a friend, then he may do likewise. If my daughter sees me spending a rainy afternoon curled up with a book instead of spending money at the mall, she may get the message that there are some simple pleasures that don't require a purchase. I fear that in our so-called upwardly mobile world we are on a downward spiral toward moral bankruptcy. Like World War II Germany, where the basket holding the money was more valuable than the money itself, we too may render ourselves internally worthless while desperately clinging to a shell of appearances.

STUDY QUESTIONS

1. What is the purpose of the first three paragraphs of the essay?

2. What is the thesis of "Money for Morality"? Where is that thesis expressed?

3. What is the topic sentence (statement of focus) of paragraph 3? paragraph 4? paragraph 5?

4. Do you think the teachers should have taken up the collection? Explain.

5. Does Arguelles write a convincing argument? Explain.

6. **Other Patterns** In addition to argument, what other writing patterns did you notice? What examples does Arguelles use? What is the purpose of those examples? How does she use cause-and-effect analysis?

WRITING TOPICS

1. Arguelles believes that "misplaced virtues are running rampant through our culture." Use examples to help argue that this statement is or is not true.

2. Write a definition of *virtue*.

3. Tell a story that shows how you imagine the boy reacted to the three-dollar reward.

4. Should students be rewarded for good academic performance? Argue your opinion.

5. Argue for or against Arguelles's thesis.

6. Many of Arguelles's examples are related to school. Using examples from your own experience and observation, argue that schools do or do not do a good job teaching positive values.

SUCCEEDING IN COLLEGE

Use Active Reading When You Read Your Textbooks

Use the active reading strategies you learned in this chapter when you read your textbooks, keeping the following points in mind.

- You may not be able to locate a thesis in textbook material so concentrate on underlining or highlighting main ideas and important examples—the ones you want to be sure to learn for your examinations.

- Be careful not to underline or highlight too much, or you will end up memorizing most of the textbook when you study for your exams.

- Make sure you fully understand everything you underline or highlight. If you have any questions, write them down to ask in class.

- Pay particular attention to boldface terms; they are probably important vocabulary words you should learn.

- Carefully read summaries at the ends of chapters, and be sure you can answer any end-of-chapter questions.

Write about It

Select a textbook chapter you must know for one of your classes and read it with the active reading strategies. Then write up an explanation of how well you think the procedure worked for you, noting why you think the way you do.

CHAPTER 28

Writing Summaries and Essay Examination Answers

As a college student, you will often write summaries and essay examination answers to demonstrate that you have read and comprehended assigned materials. In this chapter, you will learn how to handle these important writing tasks.

WRITING A SUMMARY

A **summary** is a restatement—*in your own words*—of an author's most important ideas. When you summarize, you record an author's central point and major supporting details using your own wording and style.

You may be asked to summarize readings or chapters in textbooks so an instructor can check whether you understand reading assignments. In addition, when you write research papers, you may have to include summarized material.

The Characteristics of a Summary

To write a successful summary, keep the following points in mind:

1. *Include only the author's central point (the thesis) and major supporting details.* Do not include minor details, examples, or explanations unless these are necessary for clarification.

2. *Include only the author's ideas.* Do not comment on something the author has said, because a summary focuses exclusively on what the author said.

3. *Keep the summary significantly shorter than the original.* Because you are including only the most important ideas, your summary is bound to be shorter than the original.

4. *Preserve the author's meaning.* Do not alter the author's meaning in any way. Here are two examples:

original:	Some states still have not enacted legislation mandating barrier-free structures.
unacceptable restatement:	No laws require barrier-free buildings in many states.
explanation:	*Many* in the restatement changes the meaning of the original because the author said *some.*
acceptable restatement:	In a number of states no laws require barrier-free buildings.
explanation:	Use of *a number of* does not alter the author's meaning.
original:	States that did not raise the drinking age to 21 would lose their federal highway funds.
unacceptable restatement:	States were being pressured to make 21 the legal age to drink.
explanation:	The restatement alters meaning by omitting important information: the fact that states that did not raise the drinking age would lose federal highway funds.
acceptable restatement:	Failure to make 21 the legal drinking age would cost states their federal highway funds.
explanation:	All the important information is in the restatement.

5. *Use your own wording and sentence style.* You must preserve the author's meaning, but you should restate the author's ideas in your own way. Here is an example:

original:	The trouble with Little League is that the coaches have emphasized winning at the expense of skill acquisition and having fun.

restatement: Little League coaches stress winning rather than enjoyment and learning, thus creating problems.

When you summarize, do not merely substitute synonyms (words with similar meaning) for the original words. Substituting synonyms is *not* restating in your own style because sentence structure is not altered. Here is an example:

original: The trouble with Little League is that the coaches have emphasized winning at the expense of skill acquisition and having fun.

unacceptable restatement: The problem (synonym) with Little League is that the managers (synonym) have stressed (synonym) beating the opponent (synonym) at the cost of (synonym) acquiring skills (synonym) and having a good time (synonym).

explanation: The preceding restatement is unacceptable because sentence structure has not been changed. Instead, synonyms have been substituted for words in the original.

6. *Use some of the author's words when there is no acceptable substitute, or when you particularly like the author's phrasing.* In the Little League example, a restatement may include the words *Little League* because no other words will do. However, if you use original words that are not part of your normal vocabulary or that are part of the author's distinctive phrasing, use quotation marks around the words. Here is an example:

original: The trouble with Little League is that the coaches have emphasized winning at the expense of skill acquisition and having fun.

restatement: Little League coaches stress winning but do not stress "skill acquisition" and the enjoyment of the game.

explanation: "Little League," "coaches," and "winning" are used without quotation marks because there is no substitute and the words are part of most people's vocabulary. "Skill acquisition" appears with quotation marks because the phrase is part of the author's distinctive phrasing.

Use quotations when necessary, but do not overuse them. Most of the summary should be in your own words.

7. *Open with the author's name, the title of the material being summarized, and the author's topic, purpose, and/or thesis.* Here are sample openings for a summary of "Students in Shock" on page 490.

> <u>author's name, title, and topic presented</u>: In "Students in Shock," John Kellmayer warns students about the stress associated with college and advises them to cope with the stress by taking advantage of certain campus resources.

> <u>author's name, title, and thesis presented</u>: John Kellmayer's "Students in Shock" explains that colleges are doing more to help students who are having problems.

> <u>author's name, purpose, and thesis presented</u>: To make college students aware of some of the challenges they might face and how to deal with them, John Kellmayer discusses common student problems and campus resources for solving those problems.

Notice that in each example, the verb that functions with the author's name or essay title is in the present tense. Even though the work was written in the past, use the present tense:

> John Kellmayer *warns*…
>
> "Students in Shock" *explains*…
>
> John Kellmayer *discusses*…

8. *To achieve coherence, repeat the author's name with a present tense verb.* Use phrases like these:

> Kellmayer also explains…
>
> Kellmayer continues by describing…
>
> Kellmayer goes on to show…

How to Write a Summary

Step 1   Read the material as many times as necessary to understand everything. Look up unfamiliar words.

Step 2   Underline the thesis, topic sentences, and major supporting details.

Step 3   On a separate sheet, write the underlined ideas in your own words.

Step 4   Write a first draft, opening with a sentence that includes the author, title, and the author's thesis, topic, and/or purpose. Use a present tense verb with the author's name. Then go to your list of restatements and write these in the same order the ideas appear in the original.

Step 5   Read your summary out loud. If you hear an awkward gap, add a transition and/or repeat the author's name with a present tense verb.

Step 6   Review the summary to be sure you can answer *yes* to the questions in the checklist that follows.

Step 7   Edit your summary carefully for mistakes.

FAQ

Q: What can I do if I have trouble summarizing a passage?

A: Read the section several times until you understand it. Then imagine yourself explaining what you read to a friend, and write the summary the same way you would explain it.

> ## ✔ Checklist for a Summary
>
> Before submitting your summary, be sure to work through this checklist.
>
> ☐ 1. I have opened with the author, title, and/or thesis, topic, or purpose.
>
> ☐ 2. I have included only the thesis and major supporting details.
>
> ☐ 3. I have altered the author's sentence structure and wording.
>
> ☐ 4. I have not substituted synonyms.
>
> ☐ 5. I have preserved the original meaning.
>
> ☐ 6. I have used quotation marks around words that are part of the author's special phrasing.
>
> ☐ 7. I have not added meaning.
>
> ☐ 8. I have referred to the author and the essay in the present tense.
>
> ☐ 9. I have written a summary that is shorter than the original.
>
> ☐ 10. I have edited carefully to find and correct mistakes.
>
> ☐ 11. I have proofread carefully after copying or typing the summary into its final form.

A Sample Summary

The essay that follows, "How Bingeing Became the New College Sport," was written by Barrett Seaman. The main ideas and major supporting details have been underlined to mark them for inclusion in the summary that follows.

Read through the essay, paying particular attention to the underlined material. Then read the summary that follows the essay. Notes in the margin of the summary call your attention to important features.

How Bingeing Became the New College Sport

Barrett Seaman

In this 2005 *Time* magazine article, Barrett Seaman discusses the college practice of drinking large amounts of alcohol in a short period of time. He has also written *Binge: What Your College Student Won't Tell You* (2005). As you read this essay, think about the amount of drinking that occurs on your campus.

In the coming weeks, millions of students will begin their fall semester of college, with all the attendant rituals of campus life: freshman orientation, registering for classes, rushing by fraternities and sororities and, in a more recent nocturnal college tradition, "pregaming" in their rooms.   1

Pregaming is probably unfamiliar to people who went to college before the 1990s. But it is now a common practice among 18-, 19- and 20-year-old students who cannot legally buy or consume alcohol. It usually involves sitting in a dorm room or an off-campus apartment and drinking as much hard liquor as possible before heading out for the evening's parties. While reporting for my book *Binge,* I witnessed the hospitalization of several students for acute alcohol poisoning. Among them was a Hamilton College freshman who had consumed 22 shots of vodka while sitting in a dorm room with her friends. Such hospitalizations are routine on campuses across the nation. By the Thanksgiving break of the year I visited Harvard, the university's health center had admitted nearly 70 students for alcohol poisoning.   2

When students are hospitalized—or worse yet, die from alcohol poisoning, which happens about 300 times each year—college presidents tend to react by declaring their campuses dry or shutting down fraternity houses. But tighter enforcement of the minimum drinking age of 21 is not the solution. It's part of the problem.   3

Over the past 40 years, the U.S. has taken a confusing approach to the age-appropriateness of various rights, privileges and behaviors. It used to be that 21 was the age that legally defined adulthood. On the heels of the student revolution of the late '60s, however, came sweeping changes: the voting age   4

Source: Copyright ©2001 Time Inc. Reprinted with permission.

was reduced to 18; privacy laws were enacted that protected college students' academic, health and disciplinary records from outsiders, including parents; and the drinking age, which had varied from state to state, was lowered to 18.

5   Then, thanks in large measure to intense lobbying by Mothers Against Drunk Driving, Congress in 1984 effectively blackmailed states into hiking the minimum drinking age to 21 by passing a law that tied compliance to the distribution of federal-aid highway funds—an amount that will average $690 million per state this year. There is no doubt that the law, which achieved full 50-state compliance in 1988, saved lives, but it had the unintended consequence of creating a covert culture around alcohol as the young adult's forbidden fruit.

6   Drinking has been an aspect of college life since the first Western universities in the 14th century. My friends and I drank in college in the 1960s—sometimes a lot but not so much that we had to be hospitalized. Veteran college administrators cite a sea change in campus culture that began, not without coincidence, in the 1990s. It was marked by a shift from beer to hard liquor, consumed not in large social settings, since that is now illegal, but furtively and dangerously in students' residences.

7   In my reporting at colleges around the country, I did not meet any presidents or deans who felt that the 21-year age minimum helps their efforts to curb the abuse of alcohol on their campuses. Quite the opposite. They thought the law impeded their efforts since it takes away the ability to monitor and supervise drinking activity.

8   What would happen if the drinking age was rolled back to 18 or 19? Initially, there would be a surge in binge drinking as young adults savored their newfound freedom. But over time, I predict, U.S. college students would settle into the saner approach to alcohol I saw on the one campus I visited where the legal drinking age is 18: Montreal's McGill University, which enrolls about 2,000 American undergraduates a year. Many, when they first arrive, go overboard, exploiting their ability to drink legally. But by midterms, when McGill's demanding academic standards must be met, the vast majority have put drinking into its practical place among their priorities.

9   A culture like that is achievable at U.S. colleges if Congress can muster the fortitude to reverse a bad policy. If lawmakers want to reduce drunk driving, they should do what the Norwegians do: throw the book at offenders no matter what their age. Meanwhile, we should let the pregamers come out of their dorm rooms so that they can learn to handle alcohol like the adults we hope and expect them to be.

[1]The opening sentence includes the author, title, and thesis. Notice the present tense verb, *argues.*

[2]"The author" is used as transition. Note the present tense verb and restatement of the first important idea.

Summary of "How Bingeing Became the New College Sport"

[1]In "How Bingeing Became the New College Sport," Barrett Seaman argues that lowering the legal drinking age to 18 or 19 will reduce the amount of binge drinking that occurs on college campuses. [2]The author notes that currently 18-, 19-, and 20-year-old college students who are not old enough to drink legally engage in a practice called

[3]"pregaming," which [3]"involves sitting in a dorm room or an off-campus apartment and drinking as much hard liquor as possible before heading out for the evenings parties."

[4]Seaman, who researched college drinking for his book *Binge,* says that students are being hospitalized for alcohol poisoning because of their drinking habits. Some students even die. He goes on to say that colleges tend to respond by trying to enforce the legal drinking age law by making their campuses dry or by eliminating fraternity houses. However, Seaman maintains that this approach is [3]"part of the problem."

[5]Seaman gives the history of the drinking age. He says that after the late 1960s, the legal drinking age was lowered from 21 to 18, but in 1984 Congress tied federal highway funds to a 21-year-old drinking age. As a consequence, students began switching from beer drunk in public to hard liquor drunk secretly in dorms and apartments. The college presidents and deans that the author spoke to believe that the higher drinking age is part of the problem because it inhibits their [6]"ability to monitor and supervise drinking activity." If the drinking age were 18 or 19, Seaman believes that an initial increase in binge drinking would be followed by a [6]"saner approach to alcohol."

[3]Quotation marks appear around the author's exact words.

[4]The author's name and "he goes on to say" are used for transition; note the present tense and restatement of important ideas.

[5]This paragraph combines Seaman's points about the history of the drinking age with points about the solution to the problem. Notice the use of the author's name for transition and the present tense verbs.

[6]The quotation marks are used because the phrase is the author's distinctive style.

PRACTICE 28.1

Summarize paragraphs 6 and 7 of "Words That Wound" on page 501. Be sure to use the checklist on page 532 to guide your work.

WRITING ESSAY EXAMINATION ANSWERS

Essay examinations require you to write answers that are paragraph length or longer. Because these examinations are an important part of college, you should learn to deal with them effectively.

How to Take an Essay Examination

Remembering information is not enough when you are taking an essay examination. You must also present that information in a clear, well-written answer. The following steps can help you.

Step 1   Read the directions before doing anything. The directions may tell you how many questions to answer and how long your answers should be, like this:

Answer three of the five questions. Each of your answers should be at least a page.

Step 2   Read all the questions before you begin. Part of your brain can work on question 2 while you are answering question 1. Also, you may find clues to answers for later questions while you are working through the exam.

Step 3   Decide how to budget your time. If you must answer four questions in 60 minutes, then you know you can devote 15 minutes to each answer. However, pay attention to how many points each question is worth. If you must answer three questions in 60 minutes and one question is worth 50 points and the other two are worth 25 points, you should spend 30 minutes on the 50-point question and 15 minutes on each 25-point question.

Step 4   Check the question for direction words. Words like these direct the form your answer should take:

> **analyze**—Break something down into its parts and discuss each part.
>
> *Example:* Analyze the impact of U.S. isolationism after World War I.
>
> **classify**—Group things according to their characteristics.
>
> *Example:* Classify the most frequently occurring defense mechanisms.
>
> **compare**—Technically, this means "show the similarities," but often *compare* is used to mean "show the similarities *and* differences."
>
> *Example:* Compare the symbolism in the poetry of Maxine Kumin and Margaret Atwood.
>
> **contrast**—Show the differences.
>
> *Example:* Contrast the foreign policies of Presidents George W. Bush and Bill Clinton.
>
> **define**—Give the meaning of a term and include some information (often examples) to show you understand it.
>
> *Example:* Define manifest destiny.
>
> **describe**—Give the significant features or tell how something works.
>
> *Example:* Describe how plants convert carbon dioxide into oxygen.
>
> **discuss**—Mention all the important points about a topic.
>
> *Example:* Discuss the reasons for the creation of the League of Nations.
>
> **evaluate**—Give your view about the worth of something, being sure to support your opinions with detail.
>
> *Example:* Evaluate proficiency testing as a way to ensure that students learn basic skills.
>
> **explain**—Give the reasons for an occurrence.
>
> *Example:* Explain the main causes of the Great Depression.
>
> **illustrate**—Provide examples.

Example: Illustrate the use of intermittent positive reinforcement to control behavior.

show—Explain or demonstrate something.

Example: Show how hypnosis can improve the quality of daily life.

summarize—Briefly give the major points.

Example: Summarize Jackson's reasons for opposing the Bank of the United States.

support—Give reasons in favor of something.

Example: Support the plan to institute twelve-month school years in grades kindergarten through twelve.

Step 5   Plan your answer. Jot down the points you will cover (on the back of or in the margin of your test sheet), and then number the points in the order you will write them. This planning will help you write a well-organized answer. Also, if you list your points, you need not worry about forgetting something you intended to say. Organize simply—do not write introductions or conclusions; just give the information needed in the answer.

Step 6   Begin your answer with a sentence that reflects the question. For example, if the question is "Contrast the psychoanalytic views of Freud and Jung," you could begin with something like this: "The psychoanalytic views of Freud and Jung differ in several important ways."

Step 7   After writing your answer, revise and edit quickly. Pay special attention to clarity and completeness, but also look for serious mistakes in grammar and usage. Make changes directly on the original—you do not have time to recopy.

Test-Taking Strategies

The most important test-taking strategy is studying beforehand. Once you sit down to take your test, the following strategies can be helpful.

- If you do not understand the directions or a question, ask your instructor for clarification. You may not get help, but there is no harm in trying.

- Wear a watch to keep track of the time and know when to move on to the next question.

- Leave generous margins and write on every other line so you have space in case you must add something when you revise.

- Skip the questions you are unsure about and return to them after answering the ones you are more confident about. In the course of answering other questions, you may think of the answers to a question you skipped.

FAQ

Q: What if I run out of time before I've answered all the questions?

A: List the points you would include if you had more time. Although the answer is not in essay form, you may get partial credit.

- If you do not know an answer, guess. You may get partial credit.

- Do not write more than you are asked for. You will not get extra credit, and you are taking time away from answers that *will* give you credit.

- Never pad your answers with unrelated information to hide that you do not know the information requested. Your instructor will recognize the padding.

Two Answers to Study

To understand the traits of an effective essay examination answer, study the two answers that follow. They were written in response to this question:

Explain and illustrate the way language affects perception.

The first answer is acceptable, but the second is not. Study the marginal notes that call your attention to the traits of each answer.

acceptable answer:

The answer opens with words that reflect the question. Every sentence contributes accurate information to the answer. There is no padding and no unrelated information. Transitions help the answer flow well. There is no introduction or conclusion.

> Language affects perception because it determines what we know about the world and how we think. By emphasizing certain aspects of reality, language calls them to our attention; by deemphasizing other aspects, it causes us not to notice them. Thus, language structures our perception. For example, the Hopi Indians focus on the validity of information more than when actions occur, but English speakers are more interested in time than validity. This distinction is partly a result of the fact that Hopi verb conjugations indicate whether information is being reported directly, whether it is a belief, or whether it is a generalization. English verb conjugations, however, communicate when an event occurs.

The first two sentences stall. They contribute nothing, and they do not reflect the question. The third and fourth sentences begin to acknowledge the question, but they are wordy. Sentence 5 addresses the question directly, but it is the only one that does, so the answer is incomplete. Sentences 6 and 7 relate to the question, but they are unclear. The next sentence is repetitious, and the last two are padding.

unacceptable answer:

> [1]No one will deny that language is very important in many areas. [2]Language is so important that linguistics is a vital area of scholarship. [3]One thing that we know is that language is very important to perception. [4]In fact, it affects perception dramatically in many ways. [5]Most important is the fact that language affects our view of reality. [6]This can be seen by the way Hopi Indians conjugate verbs to show that validity is important. [7]For us, tense is important because our reality is related to time. [8]Everyone should understand that the perception of reality is based upon language. [9]We should, therefore, appreciate language far more than we do. [10]I know that I plan to take as many linguistics courses as I can, which should also help me learn more about reality.

PRACTICE 28.2

Answering the following essay questions will give you valuable practice and help you become more skilled.

1. Based on "They Shut My Grandmother's Room Door" (page 512). How does Andrew Lam say Americans respond to old age and death, and how *should* we respond? Do you think Americans can easily adopt his viewpoint? Why or why not?

2. Based on "How Bingeing Became the New College Sport" (page 533). Barrett Seaman makes a recommendation for solving the problem of binge drinking on campus. What is that recommendation and why does he think it will work? Do you agree with him? Explain why or why not.

3. Based on "Students in Shock" (page 490). Summarize the causes of shock among college students and what schools are doing to help students deal with that shock. Mention at least one other action schools can take to help students deal with shock.

SUCCEEDING IN COLLEGE

Prepare for Examinations

One way to prepare for an exam is to form a study group with some classmates. Each of you can develop two or three essay questions, and you can answer each other's questions. The person who wrote the question must determine whether all the necessary points were included in each answer.

Another way to prepare is to summarize parts of textbook chapters to be sure you understand the material. You can review your summaries as a study aid.

If you think you need to improve your test-taking skills, visit your campus study skills center to learn helpful strategies.

Write about It

Are you good at taking essay examinations? Explain why or why not.

Ten Tips for ESL Students

1. Be sure that all your sentences have both a subject and a complete verb.

    no: *Is happy* to help you find an apartment. [missing subject]

    yes: *Dimitri is happy* to help you find an apartment.

    no: The wind *blowing* at hurricane force. [part of the verb is missing]

    yes: The wind *is blowing* at hurricane force.

    no: Monica *been* in this country for three years. [part of the verb is missing]

    yes: Monica *has been* in this country for three years.

    Exception: Sentences that give a command or make a request do not always have stated subjects. Instead, the subject of such sentences is the unstated *you.*

    command: Leave that dog alone. [*You* leave that dog alone.]

    request: Please bring me that book. [*You* please bring me that book.]

2. Remember the *s* in third person singular verbs in the present tense.

    no: In the evenings, Juan *play* guitar in a band.

    yes: In the evenings, Juan *plays* guitar in a band.

    no: Ice *cover* all the major highways east of town.

    yes: Ice *covers* all the major highways east of town.

3. When a verb is made up of two words, do not add *s* or *es* to the second verb.

    no: My mother can *helps* me pay my tuition bill.

    yes: My mother can *help* me pay my tuition bill.

4. Use correct word order.

    a. Most often, the subject comes before the verb.

               V   S

    no: *Have been married* 25 years *my parents.*

               S   V

    yes: *My parents have been married* 25 years.

    Exception: When you ask a question, the main verb comes before the subject.

          V   S

    Was the chili too spicy?

    When a question has a helping verb and a main verb, place the subject after the helping verb:

         HV S MV

    Why *did you eat* your ice cream before your sandwich?

541

Exception: When sentences begin with *here is, here are, here was, here were, there is, there are, there was, there were,* the subject comes after the help-ing verb:

HV   S   MV

There *were five tornadoes sighted* in the area.

b. Refer to the following chart when you have questions about word order.

BASIC WORD ORDER

1. articles/demonstratives/possessives
2. adjectives of number
3. adjectives of judgment
4. adjectives of size or shape
5. adjectives of color
6. nouns used as modifiers
7. nouns/pronouns
8. helping verbs
9. main verbs
10. indirect object
11. direct object
12. adverbs of direction and place
13. adverbs of manner or means
14. adverbs of frequency
15. time expressions

EXAMPLES

article | adj. of number | adj. of size | adj. of color | noun as modifier | noun | main verb | adv. of frequency | time expression

The two large brown English terriers sleep daily in the afternoon.

possessive | adj. of judgment | noun | helping verb | helping verb | main verb | adv. of means (prepositional phrase) | adv. of frequency (prepositional phrase)

Sam's unusual play may be produced by the local theater group for three weekends in May.

(continued)

possessive
noun
main verb
indirect object
direct object
time expression

My aunt gave me this old bronze picture frame five years ago.

5. Use *a* or *an* with a singular count noun whose identity has not been made known.

> Note: A **count noun** refers to a person, place, item, idea, or emotion that can be counted; count nouns are words like these: city, muscle, sister, baseball.
> **no:** Maria is knitting *a* sweaters for her brothers.
> **yes:** Maria is knitting *sweaters* for her brothers. (*Sweaters* is plural.)
> **no:** Boris borrowed *a* luggage for his trip.
> **yes:** Boris borrowed *luggage* for his trip. (*Luggage* is not a count noun.)
> Note: Do not use *a* or *an* with plural nouns.
> **no:** The store is having a sale on *a* computers.
> **yes:** The store is having a sale on *computers.*

6. Use *the* with a singular count noun whose identity is known.

> Corrine's Ford is in the repair shop. *The* car needs a new fan belt. (The identity of the car has been established.)

7. Use *in, on,* and *at* correctly to show time and place.

   a. For seasons, months, and years without a specific date, use *in.*

   > *In* 1999, Stavros will graduate with two degrees.
   > I usually take my vacation *in* the winter.

   b. Use *on* for a specific day or date.

   > *On* the first of March, Joseph begins his new job.
   > This office will close *on* Friday.

   c. Use *in* for a period of the day.

   > My exercise class meets *in* the early evening.

   > Note: Sometimes *at* is used for a period of the day. Experience will show you when to use *in* and when to use *at.*

   > At midnight, Cinderella had to leave the ball.

   d. Use *at* for a specific location and *in* for a location surrounded by something else.

   > The dentist you should see is located *at* 3150 Fifth Avenue.
   > Gregory lived *in* Salzburg for a semester.

8. Use modals (helping verbs that indicate the manner or mode of an action) correctly. The following chart can help you with many of the modals.

MODALS

Modal	Indicates	Example
can	ability	Henri *can* speak three languages.
	informal request	*Can* you drive me to work?
could	request	*Could* I have a piece of your candy?
	possibility	We *could* leave later if you like.
may	request or grant	*May* I have an apple?
	permission	You *may* leave now.
might	possibility	It *might* rain tonight.
must	probability	Olin *must* be at school, for he is not here.
	need	You *must* submit an application by noon.
ought to	advisability	I *ought to* major in physical therapy.
	expectation	The play *ought to* begin at 8:00.
should	advisability	I *should* major in physical therapy.
	expectation	The play *should* begin at 8:00.
will	intention	I *will* begin eating more protein.
would	request	*Would* you answer the phone for me?
	preference	I *would* rather eat at home tonight.
be able to	ability	I *am able to* leave at noon.

Note: The following modals show past time.

could	ability	Charles *could* work harder than anyone.
could have	possibility	We *could have* gone if we wanted to.
might have	possibility	The team *might have* a chance at a championship.
must have	probability	The teacher *must have* been very angry at the class.
would	habitual	The team *would* always practice on Saturday morning.

9. Do not separate main clauses with a comma.

In some languages, two main clauses can correctly be separated with a comma. However, this is not the case in English, where main clauses must be separated with a period and capital letter or with a semicolon.

> **no:** The wind is getting stronger, I believe a storm is coming.
> **yes:** The wind is getting stronger. I believe a storm is coming.
> **yes:** The wind is getting stronger; I believe a storm is coming.

10. Do not use a pronoun to refer to a noun when that noun is already referred to by *who, whom, which,* or *that.*

> **no:** I gave the sales clerk my credit card, which I then forgot to get it back.

> **yes:** I gave the sales clerk my credit card, which I then forgot to get back.

Answers to Diagnostic Self-Assessments and Pretests

PAGE 203—DIAGNOSTIC SELF-ASSESSMENT FOR PART FOUR

1. *Subjects*   *Verbs*
   a. stores   have
   b. number   was increased
   c. Mateo   will be
   d. you   do know
   e. The union and management   have endorsed

2. a. S   c. C   e. S
   b. C   d. C

3. a. S   c. 2
   b. 1   d. 2

4. a. I   c. I
   b. C   d. I

5. No

6. a. Correct sentence: The instructor told the class to read Chapter 5 and to take careful notes.
   b. Correct sentence: Either I will get a part-time job, or I will apply for financial aid.

7. a. anything
   b. any

8. a. better sentence: Joanie asked Uri what chapters she should study for tomorrow's midterm exam.
   b. better sentence: I admire Conchetta because she can turn a negative situation into a positive one.

PAGE 206—IDENTIFYING SUBJECTS AND VERBS

   Subjects   *Verbs*
   1. mother   packed
   2. Tuition   is

3. Marcos	has eaten
4. Mother	returned, studied
5. people	do know
6. Joan, her brothers	bought
7. carton	is
8. Jacques	has been studying
9. keys	are
10. excuse	will be
11. (you)	answer
12. holidays; all of us	are; can relax, recover
13. students	are making
14. accidents	can be
15. my parents, I	will move, buy

PAGE 222—USING COORDINATION AND SUBORDINATION

1. S	5. S	9. C
2. C	6. S	10. C
3. S	7. C	
4. C	8. C	

PAGE 249—AVOIDING SENTENCE FRAGMENTS

1. F	5. F	9. F
2. F	6. F	10. F
3. F	7. F	
4. S	8. S	

PAGE 262—AVOIDING RUN-ON SENTENCES AND COMMA SPLICES

1. CS
2. RO
3. RO
4. C

5. RO
6. CS
7. C
8. C

9. RO
10. C

PAGE 272—WRITING SENTENCES WITH VARIETY AND PARALLELISM

1. a. no

   b. yes

   c. yes

   d. no

2. a. better sentence: The twins are energetic, talented, and personable.

   b. better sentence: Cal's blood test showed that both his cholesterol and triglyceride levels were high.

   c. better sentence: The new house is not only beautiful but energy efficient.

   d. better sentence: Either Hank will spend his savings on a trip to Europe, or he will use the money to buy a car.

PAGE 291—CHOOSING WORDS CAREFULLY

1. b
2. b
3. a

4. b
5. a

PAGE 307—DIAGNOSTIC SELF-ASSESSMENT FOR PART FIVE

1. a. no   f. no   k. no
   b. no   g. yes   l. no
   c. no   h. yes   m. no
   d. no   i. yes   n. no
   e. no   j. yes

2. a. yes   d. no   g. yes
   b. no   e. yes   h. yes
   c. no   f. yes   i. no

3. a. no   c. no   e. no
   b. yes   d. no   f. no

4. a. 2   b. yes   c. yes

5. a. yes   f. yes   k. yes
   b. 2   g. 1   l. 1
   c. yes   h. 1   m. yes
   d. yes   i. yes   n. 1
   e. 3   j. yes   o. yes

6. a. advice   b. their   c. argument

PAGE 311—USING VERBS CORRECTLY

A. 1. C   5. I   9. C
   2. I   6. I   10. I
   3. C   7. C
   4. I   8. I

B. 1. means   5.practices   9.work
    2. visits   6.decides   10.sleeps
    3. plan   7.are
    4. likes   8.wants

C. 1. C   3. TS   5. C
    2. C   4. TS

PAGE 345—USING PRONOUNS CORRECTLY

1. I   5. their   9. me
2. they   6. its   10. its
3. me   7. its
4. her   8. whom

PAGE 376—USING MODIFIERS CORRECTLY

1. no   5. no   9. yes
2. yes   6. no   10. no
3. no   7. yes
4. yes   8. no

PAGE 390—USING CAPITAL LETTERS AND PUNCTUATION CORRECTLY

A. 1. no   3. yes   5. no
    2. no   4. yes

B. 6. .   8. .   10. .
    7. !   9. ?

C. 11. no   15. no   19. no
12. no   16. yes   20. no
13. yes   17. yes
14. yes   18. no

D. 21. yes   23. yes   25. no
22. no   24. yes

E. 26. yes   28. yes   30. yes
27. no   29. yes

F. 31. no   34. yes   37. yes
32. yes   35. yes   38. yes
33. no   36. yes

PAGE 427—ELIMINATING PROBLEMS WITH FREQUENTLY CONFUSED WORDS AND SPELLING

1. no   5. yes   9. no
2. no   6. no   10. yes
3. yes   7. yes
4. yes   8. no

Credits

CREDITS

PHOTO CREDITS

Index